Issues of
JUSTICE

Issues of
JUSTICE

An Introduction to Law

MARK GIBNEY
Department of Political Science
Purdue University

Prentice Hall, Englewood Cliffs, New Jersey 07632

Library of Congress Cataloging-in-Publication Data

Gibney, Mark.
   Issues of justice : an introduction to law / Mark Gibney.
     p.   cm.
  ISBN 0-13-506262-4
   1. Law—United States—Cases. I. Title.
  KF385.A4G5 1990
  349.73—dc20
  [347.3]   89-8765
                                 CIP

Editorial/production supervision: Lynn Alden Kendall
Interior design: Karen Buck
Cover design: Wanda Lubelska Design
Manufacturing buyer: Peter Havens

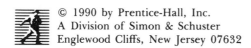 © 1990 by Prentice-Hall, Inc.
A Division of Simon & Schuster
Englewood Cliffs, New Jersey 07632

Printed in the United States of America
10 9 8 7 6 5 4 3 2 1

ISBN 0-13-506262-4

Prentice-Hall International (UK) Limited, *London*
Prentice-Hall of Australia Pty. Limited, *Sydney*
Prentice-Hall Canada Inc., *Toronto*
Prentice-Hall Hispanoamericana, S.A., *Mexico*
Prentice-Hall of India Private Limited, *New Delhi*
Prentice-Hall of Japan, Inc., *Tokyo*
Simon & Schuster Asia Pte. Ltd., *Singapore*
Editora Prentice-Hall do Brasil, Ltda., *Rio de Janeiro*

To my mother and father

CONTENTS

PREFACE

Education should be an exciting process, but all too often it is not. Where there should be fascination and exploration, there is, instead, recitation. Where there ought to be emotion and argument, students and professor alike encounter bored silence and listlessness. Finally, what passes for analysis is far too often someone simply repeating what others have said without questioning the validity of those beliefs.

This book is intended to provide students and educators with something different. One aim of the book is to study the relationship between law and justice. There is, however, an even larger goal, and that is to have students recognize and achieve a different way of looking at some of the most important issues facing us today and at those that will face subsequent generations. Obviously this is no small task to undertake, but one of the fundamental assumptions of this book is that academia is spending too much time focusing on the trivial or the peripheral at the expense of the essential. I am very confident in saying that this book will focus on large and, I dare say, important questions and issues.

There are a number of people I thank for their assistance with this book. Rich Pacelle of Indiana University, a former high school classmate, was very helpful with comments on an earlier draft. William Green of Morehead State University, a lawyer and political scientist, is really the person responsible for the tripartite division of this book. Penny Weiss in my own department provided me with a different way of looking at many issues addressed in this book. William McBride in the Philosophy Department at Purdue assisted me from that end. Terri Gregori was exceedingly helpful to me, not only with her research assistance but also through the contribution of an undergraduate's perspective. Terri would tell me what material from this book she thought worked in class and what did not, and why. I also thank Karen Horton, the senior editor at Prentice-Hall, for her great interest in and assistance with this project; Janice Murray for her copy editing skills; and Lynn Alden Kendall, the production editor.

As usual, the secretaries in Purdue's Political Science Department were exceedingly helpful with their prompt and cheerful work. In particular, I thank Beth Turner, whose interest and enthusiasm for this project not only made completion that much easier but at times even seemed to surpass my own.

I enjoy the luxury of receiving great support from my family for my work. As always, Rita has been understanding, loving, and patient. My final thanks go to my parents, to whom I dedicate this book. My mother was forever stressing to her children the virtue of compassion, and although it might not have appeared as if we were listening, we were. My father is a very kind person, a trait that is not always recognized and rewarded but is certainly appreciated by this beneficiary.

Issues of
JUSTICE

INTRODUCTION

THE CONCEPT OF JUSTICE

All of us use the term *justice*, but we often use it in a number of ways and with a variety of meanings. For example, members of the Supreme Court are referred to as justices, and there is some vague idea that this title is reflective of the pursuits of this body and other courts in this country, which may or may not be true. Of course, notions of justice are not applied only to our courts. When we say that something is "unfair" or "not right," we are also saying that the result is not just. What so often happens when we use such terms, however, is that we seldom spell out the rationale for our opinion that something is unjust. Instead, we conclude (or are given the *conclusion*) that some event, occurrence, or state of affairs is unjust, without also specifying the standard of justice we are employing.

What muddles our notions and use of the concept of justice is how often we equate, and at times confuse, it with other things. Two examples should suffice to explain this. The first involves the relationship between justice and the law. As noted earlier, we implicitly feel that our laws (and those interpreting and executing them) are seeking to achieve the ideal of justice. But even a cursory glance at the laws governing our society—right turns on red lights, for example—would show that there is not always an apparent connection between any notion of justice and the law. This is not to say that the law, generally, is not based on the idea or ideal of justice. We often consider the relationship between law and justice, however, only when the two are thought to be colliding. For example, those engaging in civil disobedience often claim that the law they are protesting or breaking is unfair, or unjust, or violative of their rights. In short, they are taking the position that the law does not meet the demands of justice. Can we (or do we) have laws that are unjust? What makes a particular law unjust? What should a judge who believes a law is unjust do? Should she apply the law anyway?

The second reason our notions of justice frequently are not clear is that morality and religious beliefs often influence what we claim to be just or not. For example, how do we explain society's prohibition against the use of certain drugs? Is such use somehow unjust (and if so, how)? Or are these laws based on certain visions of what is moral, and if something is considered immoral, is it therefore unjust? In short, all of us use the notion of justice, but by and large the term goes unexplored and unexplained. The purpose of this book is to provide students with an opportunity to take a more rigorous view of what justice is and what the demands of justice are. The point here is *not* to dictate to students what justice is and how and when it should be applied. Justice is a multifaceted concept, and there are competing visions of what justice entails. This is not to say, however, that any and every notion of what might pass as justice is a valid one. Instead, the aim of this book is to get away from the level of discourse, if we can call it that, where we simply label something as just or not or where we simply state that something or someone is violating our rights without offering any substantiation of this claim.

In order to ensure that students truly do wrestle with the concept of justice—in terms both of developing their own theories and of being able to defend these theories—the approach taken here is that of a casebook. Although law schools almost universally employ the casebook method of instruction, this approach has generally been ignored on the undergraduate level. As Thomas Hoban and Richard Brooks describe the difference: "A text presents historical or factual material in detail whereas a casebook forces the reader to come to grips with the principles underlying the decisions."[1]

What follows after this introduction are not essays on what justice is or excerpts from the writings of famous philosophers on what they conceive justice to be. Instead, students will be reading a series of legal cases that address various aspects of and raise questions concerning justice. These cases come from a variety of courts in this country—U.S. Supreme Court, federal courts, and state courts—and cover a wide area of the "law"—constitutional law, contract law, international law, and so on. The purpose is *not* to teach students what the law is, so the student expecting a mini-version of law school will generally be disappointed. Rather, the cases and the comments that follow them are intended to raise (rather than answer) various questions about justice. Again, the student should not think that because the book does not provide any definitive answers about what justice is and what its demands entail that, therefore, anything can be said to be just and the work of the reader is thereby diminished. To the contrary, the lack of definitive answers will force students to work that much harder to develop, define, and defend the standards of justice that they adopt.

Not just any justification or argument can be employed by the student. John Scanlan and O.T. Kent describe the demands of moral discourse this way: "To characterize a particular policy as 'unjust' is not merely to condemn it (that is, express a preference) but to do so for particular reasons. It is to make a claim that requires appropriate kinds of evidence for its justification."[2]

What I tell my students is that I am not particularly interested in their "mere" personal opinions. What students should strive for, instead, are well-reasoned and well-analyzed points of view that sufficiently consider both sides of an issue. Moreover, when taking a position, a student should be able to defend this position and detail to a critic where and why the critic has been misled. This is no easy thing to do, but this kind of discourse is infinitely more intelligible (and intelligent) than someone yelling that he is right and opponents are wrong or that something is just because that is the way things have always been.

Finally, students might soon find themselves using language that they have not used before. One word that might creep into their vocabularies is *ought*. Suffice it to say, however, that *ought* without strong substantiation and justification for the desired or proposed end is hollow indeed.

This book is divided into three main sections: Justice as Liberty, Justice as Equality, and Justice as Community. The discerning student will note that these divisions come from the Declaration of the Rights of Man and Citizen, which served as a rallying cry of sorts for the French Revolution. What these divisions also represent, however, are three different ways of looking at justice. We will now examine each concept in turn.

JUSTICE AS LIBERTY

American society has often been described as a Liberal democracy. It is a democracy (small *d*) because those who govern do so with the assent, and under the ultimate direction, of the people. It is Liberal (capital *L*) because the society is structured to allow each individual to pursue his or her own idea of the good life without unnecessary government control or interference. Much has been written about John Locke's influence on the structure of American government and society. In Locke's theory, government's function is simply to protect individuals from harming one another as they seek their own pursuits, usually the accumulation of property and wealth.[3] We do not have to go back to Locke to understand this strain in American society. Ronald Reagan often said that the government that governs least governs best. He also said on more than one occasion that government is not a solution to the problems affecting our society; it is the problem itself (or at least a large part of it).

How do such sentiments of government noninterference square with laws that tell us to wear motorcycle helmets for our own safety, or which drugs we can or cannot take, or when we can end our own lives, or what kinds of sexual practices we can engage in and with whom? Part I—Justice as Liberty—explores the relationship and the tension that exist in our society between the ideal of Liberalism and the reality that society does not give individuals complete liberty. In fact, in some cases just the opposite is true.

It is often said that we have become a society of rights, or at least proclaimed rights. Ronald Dworkin describes rights as "trumps" that can be used (or ought to be used) to overrule the mandates of those who oppose us, usually the government or some other bureaucratic institution.[4] "A right against the Government must be a right to do something even when the majority thinks it would be wrong to do it, and even when the majority would be worse off for having it done."[5] Some rights are legal rights, or rights protected by the law. Some philosophers claim that we have moral rights as well—rights that we possess but that might not (but ought to be) protected by the law.

There is much more agreement about what a right *is* than about what rights we possess or whether a particular right is a legal or a moral right. Whereas Part II will pay particular attention to what rights individuals might have in the economic realm, the focus of Part I is on one particular right: the right to privacy. Many of the most important issues of our age—euthanasia, abortion, AIDS and drug testing, drug use, and so on—involve, in one form or another, the notion of a right to privacy. Although such a right is so often (and so loosely) used today, it is of very recent origin. This purported right was not formally recognized by the U.S. Supreme Court until 1965 in *Griswold v. Connecticut*,[6] the first case discussed here. *Griswold* involved a challenge to a Connecticut statute that prohibited the sale of contraceptives, even to married couples. The Supreme Court struck down this state statute on the ground that it violated a married couple's right to privacy. Nowhere in the Constitution is there any explicit mention of such a right. Justice Douglas's majority opinion for the Court in *Griswold* holds that such a right comes from certain "penumbras" of specific provisions of the Constitution (the First, Third, Fourth, Fifth, and Ninth Amendments, to be specific).

We will explore many issues involving the notion of a right to privacy. The first is whether the Court was correct in establishing such a right and whether the reasoning that it employed was particularly persuasive in establishing that such a right existed. Did the framers intend there to be such a right, and if so, why did it take the Court so long to recognize such a right? If not, are we bound by the intentions of the framers, or should the Constitution be interpreted in light of modern times and values? We will also be examining how far the right to privacy should be extended. For example, does an individual's right to privacy mean that a school cannot tell a fifth grader how long he can wear his hair? If so, are there any limits to such a right? If not, what is to prevent the school from dictating dress and appearance?

Questions about the notion of a right to privacy will not be our only concern. In addition, many of the cases in this book raise important questions about the role that the judiciary should play in our system of government. Consider the role played by the Court in our second principal case, *Roe v. Wade.*[7] *Roe* extended the notion of a right to privacy so that a state could not prohibit women from having abortions during the first six months of pregnancy. In rendering its decision, the Court invalidated a number of state statutes that had proscribed abortion except to save the life of the mother. These statutes were passed by popularly elected legislative bodies. Was the Supreme Court invalidating the wishes of the people of those states and thereby playing an "antidemocratic" role?

Another issue raised throughout the book involves questions of judicial capacity. Consider the abortion example once again. The reader will note that Justice Blackmun's majority opinion in *Roe* divides pregnancy into trimesters, with "viability" the point at which a woman's right to privacy could be subsumed to the interests of the state (and when abortion could be prohibited). Viability here is based on medical technology as it existed in 1973, the year that *Roe* was decided. But as Justice O'Connor argues in her dissenting opinion in *Akron v. Akron Center for Reproductive Health,*[8] advances in medical technology threaten to make the technological basis for the *Roe* decision obsolete, particularly as viability moves toward the beginning of the pregnancy. O'Connor also claims that through the *Roe* approach, the Court essentially plays the role of a "science review board," a position, she maintains, it is ill-equipped to perform. What does such an argument mean for the notion of a right to privacy? What does this say about the competence of courts to decide difficult medical issues, not only in the abortion area but in other areas as well?

Another issue raised in Part I and addressed again at various parts of the book has already been mentioned: the extent to which the law reflects (or ought to reflect) moral values. For example, in *Bowers v. Hardwick,*[9] the Supreme Court upheld a Georgia sodomy statute, thereby refusing to recognize that homosexual acts between consenting adults are protected by an individual's right to privacy. One of the basic theses of the Court's opinion was that sodomy had long been considered immoral by society. This, of course, raises a number of interesting questions. One is whether historical approbation should have any bearing on how sodomy and homosexual behavior are treated today. Another is whether the moral values of a majority of the society (or even a vocal minority, as in the case of Prohibition) ought to be able to trump the moral values of those who do not share those same moral standards.

Justice Brandeis once remarked that there was a right "simply to be left alone." This view, however, is too simplistic. The focus of Part I is the extent to which individuals are given autonomy and the extent to which they are not. Unless we adopt the platform of the Libertarian party that individuals should have unfettered control over their own lives unless they harm others (and apparently few people adopt this position, or at least few vote for candidates from this party), difficult lines will have to be drawn in order to achieve justice. Part I explores what choices should be made and, more importantly, the basis for the choices that are adopted.

JUSTICE AS EQUALITY
In the previous section we discussed American Liberal democracy in terms of the pursuit of liberty. An essential part of this particular vision of Liberalism is the freedom to accumulate wealth and property. In fact, one of government's essential roles is to ensure this freedom and to protect the property accumulated. Louis Hartz explains the wholesale acceptance of Locke's theory in this country as an outgrowth of the considerable abundance of material goods available in the New World.[10]

Not all, however, accumulate equally. In "Federalist #10," James Madison maintains that the most common and durable source of faction is the "various and unequal distribution of property."[11] In his view, the *causes* of faction cannot be removed. Instead, this new experiment in government would have to attempt to control the *effects* of factions. As you know, what he and the other founders proposed was a large republic in which one faction would be counterbalanced by the existence and force of other factions.

Alexis de Tocqueville recognizes two strains of equality in American life.[12] In the first strain, equality is the much-sought-after ideal, even, in Tocqueville's view, to the point of creating and maintaining a society marked by a mere "middling standard." Tocqueville maintains that this obsessive focus on equality tends to magnify any existing inequalities. He also holds that people will never be able to establish an equality with which they will be contented.

The second strain, according to Tocqueville, is the equality of all in pursuing wealth and fortune (again, the Lockean influence). This freedom, however, has its price:

> It is odd to watch with what feverish ardor the Americans pursue prosperity and how they are ever tormented by the shadowy suspicion that they may not have chosen the shortest route to get it.
> Americans cleave to things of this world as if assured that they will never die, and yet are in such a rush to snatch any that come within their reach, as if expecting to stop living before they have relished them. They clutch everything but hold nothing fast, and so lose grip as they hurry after some new delight.[13]

What Tocqueville muses about, and fears for this experiment in democracy, is whether this focus on private goals will eventually come at the expense of the polity itself.

> When the taste for physical pleasures has grown more rapidly than either education or experience of free institutions, the time comes when men are carried away and lose control of themselves at sight of the new good things they are ready to snatch. Intent only on getting rich, they do not notice the

close connection between private fortunes and general prosperity. There is no need to drag their rights away from citizens of this type; they themselves voluntarily let them go. They find it a tiresome inconvenience to exercise political rights which distract them from industry. . . . Such folk think they are following the doctrine of self-interest, but they have a very crude idea thereof, and the better to guard their interests, they neglect the chief of them, that is, to remain their own masters.[14]

Robert Lane's landmark study of "Eastport" also offers insight into how Americans view the ideal of equality. Lane's respondents are blue-collar workers who actually fear equality. In their eyes, pure income equality would deprive individuals of their goals in life and the incentive to improve their positions. Lane also observes that these individuals are threatened by the notion of increased equality of opportunity because their world is already neatly ordered. There are individuals above them, who deserved to be there because of perceived efforts. Likewise, there are people below them, who also deserve to be there because of perceived laziness and apathy. Lane argues that the idea that there is insufficient equality of opportunity in American society would directly challenge the view these men have of the world and of their place in it. Thus, equality of opportunity is something that Americans fervently believe in, without directly facing the question of whether we do, in fact, have it.[15]

American society is marked by two views of equality. One is the ideal of equality, manifested in terms of the notion of equality of opportunity as well as notions such as political equality.[16] Another is the equality to pursue one's own version of the good life. Americans are seemingly not threatened by the inequalities that do exist because such inequalities can be rationalized on the basis that all have had an equal opportunity to achieve.[17] Is there a just distribution of societal goods in American society? The silence seems to indicate, "Yes."

There is, however, a strong possibility that most of us have never seriously considered whether the distribution of goods in our society is just or not. Lockean theory does not prompt this question. The authors of one of the most influential books of this decade, *Habits of the Heart: Individualism and Commitment in American Life*,[18] reach the conclusion that Americans are generally incapable of thinking in such terms:

> Our American traditions encourage us to think of justice as a matter of equal opportunities for every individual to pursue whatever he or she understands by happiness. Equal opportunities are guaranteed by fair laws and political procedures—laws and procedures applied in the same way to everyone. But this way of thinking about justice does not in itself contain a vision of what the distribution of goods in a society would end up looking like if individuals had an equal chance to pursue their interests. Thus, there could be great disparities in the income given to people in different occupations in a just society so long as everyone had an equal chance of getting a well-paid job. But if, as is now becoming painfully apparent, there are more qualified

applicants than openings for the interesting jobs, is equal opportunity enough to assure justice? What of the socially disadvantaged for whom a fair race is to no avail since they are left well short of the starting line?[19]

The authors continue:

> Even a self-styled radical such as Wayne Bauer [one of their respondents who worked for the Campaign for Economic Democracy] has a difficult time going beyond notions of procedural justice. He is outraged because in Santa Monica the political cards have been stacked against poor tenants in favor of wealthy landlords. He wants to liberate tenants from this unfair system, to give them the same opportunities as rich people to exercise their wills individually. But he becomes confused when asked what kind of society, with what kind of distribution of wealth, the tenants should try to create once they have achieved a fair chance. . . . To answer such questions, Wayne would have to do more than think about the fair procedures that should be created to give individuals the ability to exercise power over their own lives. He would need some sense of substantive goals, some way to think about distributive justice. But here his cultural resources fail him, as they do most of us.[20]

If it is true that most Americans have not developed a theory about what a just distribution of societal goods would look like, there is no short supply of such theories by political philosophers. Rather than going into a whole host of these theories, we will spend some time on the pathbreaking work of John Rawls, and then we will briefly examine the theories of Robert Nozick and David Miller.

Rawls maintains that much of what we consider to be just is simply what is in our own self-interest; it is not really justice in some universal sense of the word.[21] In order to arrive at justice, an individual must remove his or her own self-interest. It is interesting to note here that James Madison essentially holds the same view, but he forsees no way of removing self-interest, only the possibility of controlling or counterbalancing it. Rawls posits a thought experiment that actually attempts to remove self-interest.

Rawls creates a hypothetical situation that he calls the "original position." The original position is something all of us could enter at any time. People in the original position know nothing about themselves. They do not know if they are smart or stupid, old or young, strong or weak. They do not even know what society they are from. In the original position individuals are to agree upon the principles for the distribution of societal goods. Rawls argues that these principles would be just because they would not be based on mere self-interest. Instead, individuals would have to arrive at these principles without knowing how these principles would affect them.

To what would individuals in the original position agree? What would a just distribution of societal goods look like? Rawls maintains that individuals would tend to be careful because they would fear the possibility of severe negative consequences when they emerged from the original position and found out what kinds of talents they actually had. That is, individuals would seek to ensure that if they were, in fact, talentless, they would not also be destitute. But Rawls also maintains that individuals in the original position would not opt for an equal distribution of societal goods. Instead, individuals in the original position would select what he terms the "difference principle," which holds that social and economic inequalities would be arranged so that they were (1) reasonably expected to be to everyone's advantage and (2) attached to positions and offices open to all.[22]

The second part of the difference principle comprises the notion of equal opportunity, and this idea, in theory at least, is not particularly controversial, as we have seen. The first part of the difference principle, however, has been. According to Rawls, the just distribution of societal goods arrived at in the original position would allow inequalities among and between people but only when these inequalities would serve to benefit all in society. Rawls's theory of a just society is premised on something other than Lockean individualism; his "community" is one in which individuals within a given society share in each other's fate. Perhaps the most obvious manifestation of this idea is Rawls's perception of the talents individuals possess. He argues that most of the qualities that pass as talents—intelligence, strength, and so on—are really "morally arbitrary" because the individual has done nothing to achieve or acquire them. In Rawls's view, such talents should be shared with the society rather than being used for and by a particular individual.

Rawls's theory has been the center of controversy for nearly two decades. Some have argued that although justice cannot be equated with self-interest, under Rawls's scheme self-interest is removed to such an extent that individuals are not able to make any meaningful decisions. Others have suggested that individuals in the original position would establish some kind of safety net below which no individual would be allowed to fall. Another criticism, one to which we will return in our discussion in Part III, is that Rawls's scheme only considers the distribution of goods for a single society and does not extend its principles worldwide.

Perhaps the most direct criticism leveled against Rawls has been made by Robert Nozick.[23] Nozick maintains that we cannot determine *a priori* what a just distribution of income would look like. Instead, a just distribution of income would be determined by what the free market happened to bring. For example, Nozick posits a situation in which Wilt Chamberlain (for today's young, substitute Michael Jordan) signs a contract that pays him his usual salary plus twenty-five cents for each home-game ticket sold. Because Wilt is such a great basketball player, fans swarm into the arena, gladly having a part of their ticket price going to him, and at the end of the year Wilt ends up with a much-greater-than-average salary. Nozick asks whether this distribution of income is just and answers that it is, pointing out that individuals freely transferred their own money to Wilt Chamberlain for the pleasure of seeing him play. That he ends up with far more money than anyone else, Nozick argues, does not make the transaction or the end result unjust.

Although most of us in this society seem to implicitly accept that the free-market system will automatically bring a just distribution of societal income and wealth, there are several important counterarguments to this position. For one thing, consider the distribution of societal goods in a "free-market" country such as El Salvador. Ninety percent of the peasants in that country, who make up two-thirds of the population, have no land, whereas 2 percent of the people own 58 percent of the arable land. The average monthly income of the peasant families is $12, and four-fifths of the children are ill-nourished.[24] Is this just?

Another issue facing proponents of the position that the free-market system will necessarily be fair or equitable is how this position squares with the principle of equality of opportunity. To use a Third World example once again, wealth is often passed on from generation to generation, but so is poverty. The question of the propriety of advancing self-interest (and calling it justice) also needs to be addressed. For example, would the homeless defend the justness of the free-market system as much as would a CEO of a Fortune 500 corporation? Probably not. Would this mean that "mere" self-interest might dictate our views of the justness of the free-market system?

Philosopher David Miller offers another way of looking at distributive justice. He suggests that there are three different bases upon which to distribute societal goods: merit, desert, and need.[25] Distribution based on merit probably needs no introduction, presumably because the United States prides itself on being a meritocracy—that is, people are rewarded on the basis of their performances. (Is this true?) Distribution based on desert typically rewards those who exhibit some extraordinary effort. Distribution based on need usually entails providing someone with a social good because he is in want. Consider this situation. You are asked to select the winner of the Outstanding Senior Scholarship at your school. Should it go to student X, who has the highest grade-point average (although she is generally a lazy student who excels because of natural talent and the private tutors her parents have provided her); or to student Y, whose grades are not quite as high as X's but who works much harder in school; or to student Z, whose grades are slightly below X's and Y's but who has worked twenty-five hours per week and will not be able to afford college without the scholarship? It depends, does it not, on whether you base your decision on merit, desert, or need. What is your answer?

Although there is no shortage of theories of the just distribution of societal goods, there is very little evidence that individuals or policymakers in this country give these questions much thought. Again, the implicit but perhaps unexamined belief is that the free market will arrive at its own just result. The cases and notes in Part II do not directly challenge this view, but they do so indirectly. In Part I we examine the notion of a right to privacy. In many respects, the focus of Part II is whether individuals possess rights in the economic realm as well. Among other things, we examine whether there is a right to shelter, education (and what kind of education), welfare, and so on.

The courts have been hesitant to question the justness of the distribution of goods in American society. This hesitancy marks all of the branches of government as well.[26] The Lockean ideal establishes the government as the protector of what individuals accumulate, not the agency of redistribution.[27] Notwithstanding this dominant view of the role of government, there is some indication of judicial involvement in the distribution of societal goods. For example, welfare has historically been viewed as a charity to which the recipient possessed no property rights. But in *Goldberg v. Kelly*,[28] the U.S. Supreme Court ruled that welfare recipients did in fact have a property interest in these benefits, which could not be terminated without due process of law. There is a case in Part II in which a lower state court judge in Massachusetts attempted to rectify the homelessness problem in that state by ordering higher welfare payments. Is this a proper role for judges to play? On the other hand, how should judges respond to political indifference to public policy problems such as homelessness?

In addition to examining whether individuals can properly claim certain kinds of subsistence rights, Part II also raises the question of the extent to which the law perpetuates the relative power of various forces in our society and of the law's disparate effect on individuals in dissimilar situations. To use an example that may be familiar to you, should a judge in a landlord-tenant dispute consider as a factor that the lease was drafted by the landlord? What if there are onerous provisions in the lease? Should a judge enforce such provisions anyway, rationalizing that the tenant apparently agreed to such provisions as evidenced by his or her signature? Perhaps it is apt to close this section by quoting Anatole France's famous lines: "The law, in its majestic equality, forbids the rich as well as the poor to sleep under bridges, to beg in the streets, and to steal bread."

JUSTICE AS COMMUNITY

To a large extent Parts I and II revolve around the notion of rights. Part III—Justice as Community—focuses on the flip side, namely, the notion of duties to others. The first few sections of Part III look at different kinds of duties within a given society—duties of assistance to others, punishment as a duty to society, the duties of lawyers in our society—and the later chapters focus on whether our notions and principles of justice extend beyond our national borders and between generations.

It is in the American character to speak of rights and the protection and promotion of rights. It is far less evident that Americans feel the same way about having duties to others. Bellah et al. explain:

> Freedom is perhaps the most resonant, deeply held American value. In some ways, it defines the good in both personal and political life. Yet freedom

turns out to mean being left alone by others, not having other people's values, ideas, or styles of life forced upon one, being free of arbitrary authority in work, family, and political life. What it is that one might do with that freedom is much more difficult for Americans to define. And if the entire social world is made up of individuals, each endowed with the right to be free of others' demands, it becomes hard to forge bonds of attachment to, or cooperation with, other people, since such bonds would imply obligations that necessarily impinge on one's freedom.[29]

Some writers, such as Philip Slater, argue that we have paid a very steep price for this premium on individualism, that price being the loss of community and with that the loss of meaning in our individual lives.

Individualism finds its roots in the attempt to deny the reality of the importance of human interdependence. One of the major goals of technology in America is to "free" us from the necessity of relating to, submitting to, depending upon, or controlling other people. Unfortunately, the more we have succeeded in doing this the more we have felt disconnected, bored, lonely, unprotected, unnecessary, and unsafe.[30]

Is it true that our individualism has helped create a loss of community in this country? What exactly do we mean by community? Do we have duties to others in our own society, and if so, what kinds of duties? Do we have duties to individuals in other societies?

In order to undertake a more systematic analysis of the issues raised in Part III, we will spend some time on a hypothetical situation employed by Peter Singer.[31] Singer presents this hypothetical: a young child is drowning in a nearby pool, and others could save this child with little effort or little danger. Does this child have a right to be saved? If so, does anyone (or everyone) have a duty to save her, so that failure to do so will make this person morally blameworthy? Even if the child has no right to be saved, could we still posit a moral duty to offer assistance? If your position is that there is a moral duty to offer assistance, do you arrive at this conclusion based on a conception of community and all the rights and duties that are entailed therein, or is the conclusion based on something else?

Let us assume for the sake of argument that you conclude there is a moral duty to assist this child. Does this also mean that there ought to be a legal duty as well, so that failure to aid this child (or someone like her) will bring with it criminal penalties? The reader should note that such questions bring us back to the discussion raised in Part I, namely, the relationship between the law and morality.

To a large extent Part III forces us to address the no-longer-rhetorical question, Am I my brother's keeper? But who exactly is my brother (or sister) in this context? Is the child in the pond my sister in a figurative sense? To tease out some of the implications of these questions, let me continue with Singer's hypothetical. He argues that not only is there a moral duty to save the drowning child (no surprise there) but that individuals in other countries who are starving are very much like this small child. That is, starving individuals are in need, and our assistance could help save at least some of these lives. Thus, Singer concludes that foreign assistance is morally obligated.

Note that for Singer, national boundaries do not serve as moral boundaries. He also maintains that social organizations, such as family and community, have no role to play in determining what our moral duties to others happen to be. Even those who essentially share Singer's point of view are quite concerned about a problem of moral overload that they see inherent in his approach.[32]

If you are in agreement with Singer's argument thus far, let me add the final piece. Singer's philosophy is utilitarian in nature. What this means simply is that in determining the justness of some phenomenon, we balance the happiness from pursuing one course of action against another. Whatever gives the greatest amount of happiness will be the most just. In terms of individuals in Western societies and the question of foreign assistance, Singer maintains that those of us in the West must balance the happiness that our money would bring us in this society—cars, televisions, clothes, and so on—against the happiness that this money could bring when it is used to save a person's life. Singer concludes that there is a complete mismatch here: money spent on saving lives would bring infinitely more happiness (or utility) than our present expenditure does. He sees the balance as that between our mere "wants" and the "needs" of those on the edge of subsistence. He concludes that justness demands that individuals in the West provide considerably more foreign assistance than we do at present.

Singer is not the only political philosopher to posit a moral duty to assist individuals on the edge of subsistence in other societies. Both Brian Barry[33] and Charles Beitz[34] criticize John Rawls for not extending his difference principle worldwide. As noted earlier, Rawls's scheme only addresses the distribution of goods *within* a society, not *among* societies. This failure is particularly noteworthy, Barry and Beitz claim, because individuals in the original position will not know which society they are from (and thus which society they would return to after emerging from the original position). Barry concludes that individuals in the original position would most assuredly attempt to prevent the absolute destitution that living in a very poor country would bring. "Surely, viewing things from the 'original position' one would at all costs wish to avoid this kind of poverty if we turned out to live in a poor country even if this meant being less well off than otherwise if one turned out to live in North America or Western Europe."[35] Barry and Beitz also claim that a nation's natural resources—the oil beneath Saudi Arabia, for example—are "morally arbitrary," even more so than an individual's so-called talents. Thus, they conclude, such resources should belong to the entire world.[36]

As you might imagine, arguments that individuals in richer societies have a moral obligation to assist those in poorer nations have not gone unchallenged. Perhaps the most radical critique has been offered by Garrett Hardin.[37] His thesis is that our incomplete efforts to aid those who are now starving will ultimately only make matters worse. He maintains that those we save with our assistance will eventually have children of their own but without the ability to feed them. Thus, he argues, our assistance efforts today will only increase the likelihood of even greater destitution in the future. For Hardin, we can imagine our situation akin to being on a lifeboat in which there is a limited capacity to save those who are in need. Difficult decisions have to be made, but Hardin maintains that there is nothing morally wrong with saving ourselves rather than others.

Part III not only examines the question of duties to those within our own society and duties to those beyond our national borders; it also asks whether there are any duties that those in the present generation have to future generations. In this light, the student is asked to consider issues such as nuclear power not only as a technical problem but as an intergenerational issue of justice. An initial matter to consider, however, is whether we are even capable of thinking in terms of intergenerational justice. Christopher Lasch, one of the most influential commentators on the American psyche, maintains that American society no longer has any sense of continuity with the past and very little connection with the future.

> The perception of the world as a dangerous and forbidding place, though it originates in a realistic awareness of the insecurity of contemporary social life, receives reinforcement from the narcissistic projection of aggressive impulses outward. The belief that society has no future, while it rests on a certain realism about the dangers ahead, also incorporates a narcissistic inability to identify with posterity or to feel oneself part of a historical stream.[38]

As in Parts I and II, Part III raises questions of judicial involvement and judicial capacity. What we find often in this area (particularly regarding questions of justice beyond our borders) is a great deal of judicial deference to the political branches. Some of this deference is based on the perceived political nature of the question posed, some is based on the lack of judicial capacity to make certain determinations, and some is based on a perception of what the proper role of a court should be. One quintessential question for students to consider here, but really throughout the book, is whether those in the political branches will simply consider the political aspects of a question but miss certain issues of justice.

This is not to say that judges are necessarily any more concerned with achieving justice than the rest of us are. In his excellent study of the judiciary's role in perpetuating the institution of slavery in this country, Robert Cover writes, "The judicial conscience is an artful dodger and rightfully so. Before it will concede that a case is one that presents a moral dilemma, it will hide in the nooks and crannies of the professional ethics, run to the cave of role limits, seek the shelter of separation of powers."[39]

In closing this introduction we will consider how two leading legal philosophers answer the question of whether the judiciary is any better equipped to deal with issues of justice. Michael Perry argues for a vigorous judicial role in cases involving what he terms "human rights." Other analysts describe the role of the judiciary as that of a teacher in a national seminar, and Perry essentially adopts this position, claiming that politicians often miss the very essence of the questions they are considering.

> In twentieth-century America, there have been several such issues: for example, distributive justice and the role of government, freedom of political dissent, racism and sexism, the death penalty, human sexuality. Our electorally accountable policymaking institutions are not well suited to deal with such issues in a way that is faithful to the notion of moral evolution or, therefore, to our religious understanding of ourselves. Those institutions, when finally they confront such issues at all, tend simply to rely on established moral conventions and to refuse to see in such issues occasions for moral reevaluation and possible moral growth. This is not invariably the case, but sometimes, not infrequently it is.[40]

John Hart Ely takes the opposite position. He maintains that it is a myth that lawyers and judges are particularly adept at addressing these purportedly moral issues of our day:

> Now I know lawyers are a cocky lot: the fact that our profession brings us into contact with many disciplines often generates the delusion that we have mastered them all. But surely the claim here cannot be that lawyers and judges are the best imaginable people to tell good moral philosophy from bad: members of the clergy, novelists, maybe historians, to say nothing of professional moral philosophers, all seem more sensible candidates for this job. I suppose that this isn't the relevant comparison, though, and that all that has to be demonstrated is that of the institutions existing in our government, courts are the best equipped to make moral judgments, in particular that they are better suited to the task than legislatures.[41]

Ely argues, however, that the backgrounds and training of most judges are virtually identical to those of people now sitting in legislative bodies. Beyond this, an even greater obstacle to having judges and lawyers serve as interpreters of society's "fundamental values," Ely claims, is the simple fact that there is not one right method of moral philosophy. He asks, for example, if judges are supposed to vote according to their favorite moral philosopher: "We like Rawls, you like Nozick. We win, 6–3. Statute invalidated."[42]

So what role should the law and our courts play in the elusive struggle to formulate, to find, and to achieve justice? There is, of course, no right or ready answer to this and many other questions. The aim of this book is to expose students to various concepts of justice and have them wrestle with these concepts. Again, the reader is not told what is or is not just. That would be impossible to do, but in a sense that would also be unfair, or unjust, to the student even if it were possible. One of the overriding purposes of *Issues of Justice* is to have students begin to formulate their own concept of justice and, perhaps more importantly, be able to defend it. It should be apparent that most of the important issues of our day involve, to one degree or another, issues of justice. What standards of justice apply (or should apply) to these different issues, and have we met this standard?

NOTES

1. Thomas More Hoban and Richard Oliver Brooks, *Green Justice: The Environment and the Courts* (Boulder, Colo.: Westview Press, 1987), p. 12.

2. John Scanlan and O. T. Kent, "The Force of Moral Arguments for a Just Immigration Policy in a Hobbesian Universe," in Mark Gibney (ed.), *Open Borders? Closed Societies?: The Ethical and Political Issues* (Westport, Conn.: Greenwood Press, 1988), p. 82.

3. See, generally, John Locke, *The Second Treatise of Government*, edited by Thomas P. Reardon (Indianapolis: Bobbs-Merrill, 1952).

4. See, generally, Ronald Dworkin, *Taking Rights Seriously* (Cambridge, Mass.: Harvard University Press, 1978).

5. Ibid., p. 194.

6. 381 U.S. 479 (1965).

7. 410 U.S. 113 (1973).

8. 462 U.S. 416 (1983) (Justice O'Connor dissenting).

9. 478 U.S. 186 (1986).

10. Louis Hartz, *The Liberal Tradition in America* (New York: Harvest, 1955).

11. James Madison, Alexander Hamilton, and John Jay, *The Federalist*, edited by Jacob E. Cooke (Cleveland: Meridian Books, 1961), p. 59.

12. Alexis de Tocqueville, *Democracy in America*, edited by J. P. Mayer and Max Lerner (New York: Harper & Row, 1966).

13. Ibid., p. 508.

14. Ibid., p. 512.

15. Robert Lane, *Political Ideology: Why the American Common Man Believes What He Does* (New York: Free Press, 1962). For an excellent treatment of these issues, see Jennifer Hochschild, *What's Fair? American Beliefs About Distributive Justice* (Cambridge, Mass.: Harvard University Press, 1981).

16. For an excellent discussion of these different spheres of justice, see Michael Walzer, *Spheres of Justice: A Defense of Pluralism and Equality* (New York: Basic Books, 1983).

17. Consider a few examples of the inequalities that do exist. At the present time, the top fifth percentile receives 43 percent of the national income, whereas the lowest fifth receives 4.7 percent. U.S. Bureau of Census, *Money Income and Poverty Status of Families in the United States, 1985* (Washington, D.C.: GPO, 1986), p. 11.

There are even wider disparities in terms of wealth. The richest 10 percent of the families in this country own 70 percent of the total wealth. The poorest half of the American population—those at the median and below—own only 3.4 percent of the wealth. Adapted from data in Stephen J. Rose, *The American Profile Poster* (New York: Pantheon, 1986).

In terms of racial breakdowns, recent Census Bureau findings show a much greater disparity between the races in terms of wealth than income. Peter Kilborn, "U.S. Whites 10 Times Wealthier Than Blacks," *New York Times,* July 19, 1986, p. 1.

A comparison with other countries is also revealing. Lester Thurow writes:

> If you look at the earnings gap between the top and bottom 10 percent of the population, the West Germans work hard with 36 percent less inequality than we, and the Japanese work even harder with 50 percent less inequality. If income differentials encourage individual initiative, we should be full of initiative since among industrialized countries, only the French surpass us in terms of inequality.

Lester Thurow, *The Zero-Sum Society: Distribution and the Possibilities For Economic Change* (New York: Basic Books, 1980), p. 7.

18. Robert N. Bellah, William M. Sullivan, Richard Madsen, Ann Swidler, and Steven M. Tipton, *Habits of the Heart: Individualism and Commitment in American Life* (Berkeley: University of California Press, 1985).

19. Ibid., p. 25.

20. Ibid.

21. John Rawls, *A Theory of Justice* (Cambridge, Mass.: Harvard University Press, 1971).

22. Rawls also takes the position that the first principle agreed upon in the original position is that "each person is to have an equal right to the most extensive basic liberty compatible with a similar liberty for others." (p. 60) Although this principle is, by itself, not controversial, Rawls also argues that these principles are arranged in serial order, so that "a departure from the institutions of equal liberty required by the first principle cannot be justified by, or compensated for, by greater social and economic advantages." (p. 61) The point made by critics of Rawls is that individuals on the edge of subsistence would (gladly) trade off some liberty rights for food or shelter.

23. Robert Nozick, *Anarchy, State, and Utopia* (New York: Basic Books, 1974).

24. Penny Lernoux, *Cry of the People* (New York: Penguin Books, 1982), p. 62.

25. David Miller, *Social Justice* (Oxford: Clarendon Press, 1976).

26. Theodore Lowi describes our system of government as "interest group liberalism," under which policymakers attempt to avoid having to redistribute societal goods and instead, simply seek to distribute, the electoral rewards for pursuit of the latter being so much richer. Theodore Lowi, *The End of Liberalism: Ideology, Policy, and the Crisis of Public Authority* (New York: W. W. Norton, 1969).

27. Critics of this position might ask how we might explain the existence of the "welfare state" in this country. In fact, not only did the United States pursue such objectives much later than did other Western democracies, but the system that we have is much different in kind. Robert Kuttner explains:

> In a comparison of advanced welfare states, we find the United States at one extreme and the more social democratic nations of Northern Europe at the other. In the United States the term *welfare* is associated with wasteful aid for the (undeserving) poor. Opinion polls consistently show "welfare" as our least popular public program. The United States has a less universalistic model in two key respects. It spends less on social aid—about 12 percent of GNP com-

pared with over 20 percent in Northern Europe; but overall the spending levels are not the test of an effective welfare state. More important, poor relief in the American system is fragmented and isolated. The social benefits that do reach the poor in the United States are more heavily means tested— and America's version of means testing is more adversary, isolating, and punitive.

Robert Kuttner, *The Economic Illusion: False Choices Between Prosperity and Social Justice* (Boston: Houghton Mifflin, 1984), p. 238.

28. 397 U.S. 254 (1970).

29. Bellah et al., *Habits of the Heart*, p. 23.

30. Philip Slater, *The Pursuit of Loneliness: American Culture at the Breaking Point* (Boston: Beacon Press, 1970), p. 26.

31. Peter Singer, "Famine, Affluence, and Morality," *Philosophy and Public Affairs* 1:229–43 (1972).

32. See, generally, James Fishkin, *The Limits of Obligations* (New Haven, Conn.: Yale University Press, 1982); Susan James, "The Duty to Relieve Suffering," *Ethics* 93:4–21 (1982).

33. Brian Barry, *The Liberal Theory of Justice* (Oxford: Clarendon Press, 1973).

34. Charles Beitz, *Political Theory and International Relations* (Princeton, N.J.: Princeton University Press, 1979).

35. Barry, *The Liberal Theory of Justice*, p. 130.

36. The question of whether natural resources should be shared among the nations and individuals of the world has arisen in a real-world context. Debate has gone on now for several years concerning the exploitation of the minerals and resources beneath the floor of the world's oceans. The question yet to be resolved is whether those nations that have the technical capabilities to extract this enormous wealth should be able to do so (and keep it for their own purposes), or whether all of the nations of the world have some kind of claim, or right, to share in these proceeds. Adopting the first position would mean that the rich nations would become richer. On the other hand, if the rich nations had to share in the proceeds of their excavations, perhaps there would be less incentive to pursue these activities. A separate issue that generally has been ignored in this current debate is the duty, if any, to future generations.

37. Garrett Hardin, "Lifeboat Ethics: The Case Against Helping the Poor," in William Aiken and Hugh LaFollette (eds.), *World Hunger and Moral Obligation* (Englewood Cliffs, N.J.: Prentice-Hall, 1977), pp. 11–21.

38. Christopher Lasch, *The Culture of Narcissism: American Life in an Age of Diminishing Expectations* (New York: W. W. Norton, 1979), p. 102.

39. Robert Cover, *Justice Accused: Antislavery and the Judicial Process* (New Haven, Conn.: Yale University Press, 1975), p. 201.

40. Michael Perry, *The Constitution, the Courts, and Human Rights* (New Haven, Conn.: Yale University Press, 1982), p. 100.

41. John Hart Ely, *Democracy and Distrust: A Theory of Judicial Review* (Cambridge, Mass.: Harvard University Press, 1980), p. 56.

42. Ibid., p. 58.

1

REPRODUCTION AND ABORTION

In his dissenting opinion in *Griswold v. Connecticut,* Justice Black writes: "I get nowhere in this case by talk about a constitutional right to privacy as an emanation from one or more constitutional provisions. I like my privacy as well as the next one, but I am nevertheless compelled to admit that government has a right to invade it unless prohibited by some specific constitutional provision." Black does not think that the Constitution has a provision that prevents the state of Connecticut from proscribing contraceptives to married couples. To his way of thinking, there is nothing in the Constitution that protects a person's privacy or autonomy in general. In Black's view, although the idea of a right to privacy is attractive, there is no such "right" in the Constitution unless it can be found in the document itself or was intended by the framers. One of Black's major concerns is that the Court would use the due process clause of the Fourteenth Amendment to strike down legislation that it simply did not approve of, much as the Court had done during the Lochner era (discussed in Chapter 9).

As the reader knows, a majority of the Supreme Court disagreed with Justice Black's opinion and held in *Griswold* that individuals were protected at times by a constitutional "right to privacy." In *Roe v. Wade,* the Court extended this principle and held that a woman's right to privacy prevented a state from proscribing abortion.[1] The right to privacy, however, is not absolute. For example, in *Roe* the Court held that a woman's right to privacy diminished as the pregnancy progressed to the point at which viability occurred; then the state could proscribe abortion if it so chose. The Court has also held that the right to privacy is different for adolescents seeking abortions than it is for adults.[2] Finally, the Supreme Court has held that there is no constitutional "right" to an abortion, even a "medically necessary" abortion, at government expense.[3]

19

Is Justice Black correct in his assertion that there is no general right to privacy, or is Justice Douglas correct when he writes in the majority opinion in *Griswold*, "We deal with a right to privacy older than the Bill of Rights"? Rather than focusing solely on the answer to this question, we will use the question itself to examine some issues concerning the role that courts play in this country. Specifically, three issues will be addressed: how courts interpret the Constitution; the judiciary as a partner in our system of government; and the degree to which courts are capable of performing the roles that they have adopted.

Both *Griswold* and *Roe* involve questions of constitutional law. In fact, many of the cases in this book involve constitutional questions, but just as many do not. What does a court do when it interprets the Constitution? How does a court divine meaning from this two hundred-year-old document? There is common agreement by scholars in this area that the first place to look is to the language of the Constitution itself and to the intentions of the framers and/or those who drafted certain constitutional amendments. The "intentions" of state legislative bodies that voted in favor of particular constitutional amendments are also important to consider.[4]

Are courts restricted to this "original intent"? Some scholars argue that subsequent generations of jurists are indeed so limited. This school of thought is called interpretivism. Noninterpretivists, on the other hand, maintain that although original intent is certainly the starting point to any constitutional inquiry, it is not the only viable source. Scholars of this school maintain that the Constitution is a "living document" and that the framers intended the Constitution to be interpreted in the light of human development and changing social values.[5]

Even if we accept the noninterpretivist view, there is still the problem of discerning which societal values are "fundamental," and thus to be reflected in the interpretation of the Constitution, and which are not. Michael Perry is not as convinced (or concerned) that the judicial branch will necessarily supply the right answers, only that it will begin a productive societal dialogue.

> [A]nswers are morally correct *independently of what a majority of the American people comes to believe in the future.* My point is not that noninterpretive review is (or should be) aimed at predicting what tomorrow's majority might come to credit as progress, but that the dialectical relationship between noninterpretive review and the processes of electorally accountable policymaking leads to a far more self-critical morality, and likely, therefore, to a more mature political morality as well.[6]

The question of *how* the courts should interpret the Constitution ties into the second question: the proper role that the judiciary should play in our system of government. In "Federalist #78," Alexander Hamilton labels the judiciary the "least dangerous branch." Danger aside, it would be misleading to ignore the fact that the courts often have a very profound effect on our system of government and that they often play a vital role in determining who gets what, when, and how in our society. Is this a proper judicial function?

The issue of whether the framers of the Constitution intended the courts to have the power of judicial review has, for all intents and purposes, been settled. Most of the focus has moved instead to the question just considered—how the Constitution is to be interpreted and from what sources—as well as to the judicial restraint/judicial activism debate to which we will now turn.

Donald Horowitz is one of the staunchest opponents of what he and others describe as "judicial activism" or "judicial policymaking," and he describes a change in the methods and scope of the judicial branch in these terms:

> The last two decades have been a period of considerable expansion of judicial responsibility in the United States. Although the kinds of cases judges have long handled still occupy most of their time, the scope of judicial business has broadened. The result has been involvement of courts in decisions that would earlier have been thought unfit for adjudication. Judicial activity has extended to welfare administration, prison administration, and mental hospital administration, to education policy and employment policy, to road building and bridge building, to automotive safety standards, and to natural resource management.[7]

Proponents of judicial restraint[8] maintain that courts are ill-equipped to make public policy. They argue that the adjudication process is too narrow for policymaking because it asks whether one person has a right and someone else a duty. As a result, there is a possibility that judicial policymaking will be done on a basis of a small and skewed set of facts and circumstances. In contrast, legislative and bureaucratic settings ask these questions: What are the alternatives? What are the costs? And what is the optimal policy?

In response, proponents of judicial activism[9] claim that judges do not set out to be social architects but that courts have an essential role in protecting the rights of minorities from the wishes of majorities. This school of thought also maintains that the notion of judicial ignorance in this area is greatly overblown and that judges have ample opportunities to acquaint themselves with the facts and issues before them. Finally, this point of view maintains that judges cannot sit idly and watch legal transgressions, constitutional or otherwise, caused or perpetuated by the paralysis of the political branches.

Griswold and *Roe* provide an interesting study of the three themes discussed thus far: constitutional interpretation, judicial activism, and judicial capacity. In terms of the first, note the attempt in *Griswold* to discern from various provisions of the Bill of Rights whether there is a right to privacy. The majority agrees that there is such a right—somewhere—in the Constitution. In fact, there is a certain irony to Justice Douglas's majority opinion, which speaks about the right to privacy emanating from "penumbras" of particular constitutional provisions—the First, Third, Fourth, Fifth, and Ninth Amendments to be exact[10]—only to later conclude that the right to privacy involved in *Griswold* is extraconstitutional in the sense that it is "older than the Bill of Rights."

Justice Rehnquist's dissent in *Roe* is also an attempt at constitutional interpretation, in this case an effort to discern original intent (and have it prove dispositive of the issue). Rehnquist points out that in 1868 when the Fourteenth Amendment was ratified, an overwhelming number of states had laws proscribing abortion. Rehnquist concludes from this that the framers of the Fourteenth Amendment did not intend to overturn this state of affairs.

In subsequent chapters we will see other, perhaps better, examples of so-called judicial activism or judicial policymaking, but there is some evidence of this quality in *Roe*. That is, rather than simply striking down the challenged Texas statute on the ground that it was violative of the Constitution, as the more traditional use of judicial review would have dictated, the Court instead developed a very elaborate scheme marked by competing rights, diminishing interests, and so on.

In fact, it was this very feature of the *Roe* decision that was apparently so objectionable to Chief Justice Rehnquist in *Webster* v. *Reproductive Health Services*. While the nation waited for a clear statement on the constitutionality of abortion restrictions, the Court decided that the provisions in the Missouri statute under consideration did not violate the holding in *Roe*. The Court did, however, abandon the *Roe* framework. The Court is scheduled to hear three more abortion cases in its 1989 October term.

The *Baby M* scenario made national headlines a short time ago. As you will soon read, the Supreme Court of New Jersey held that surrogate mother contracts were null and void. In its discussion of the constitutional rights involved in the case, the court indicated the surrogate mother had a constitutional right to the companionship of her daughter (although it is by no means clear where that right came from and whether the U.S. Supreme Court would recognize such a "right"). But is there not a more fundamental right involved here: The right of a woman to have or not have a child for whatever reasons she so chooses?

The final case in this chapter, *Cook* v. *State*, involved an attempt to sterilize a young girl who was thought to be incapable of caring for a child. As an initial matter, are courts as well equipped as doctors, psychiatrists, and social workers to make such decisions? Why are courts involved here? Note that there already is ugly precedent in this area. In *Buck* v. *Bell*[12] the Supreme Court was squarely faced with this question. Carrie Buck was an eighteen-year-old patient in a state mental hospital. She was the daughter of a feebleminded mother of the same institution and the mother of an illegitimate child who was also thought to be feebleminded, but in fact was not. The question before the Court was whether the state could sterilize Carrie Buck. In an opinion by the great jurist Oliver Wendell Holmes, the Court allowed the sterilization, with Holmes reasoning (erroneously as it was later found out) that "three generations of imbeciles are enough." What safeguards should exist in sterilization cases? Were they followed in *Cook? Buck v. Bell?* Should fathers who are unable to care for their off-spring similarly be sterilized? Is there a fundamental right not to be sterilized?[13]

NOTES

1. A fascinating treatment of the implementation of the *Roe* decision has been provided by Charles Johnson and Bradley Canon, *Judicial Policies: Implementation and Impact* (Washington, D.C.: CQ Press, 1984). What they generally find is that although the number of abortions increased after 1973 (from 774,600 in 1973 to 1,588,600 in 1985), the Court's decision did not necessarily change the policy of many hospitals in this country. In fact, they estimate that in 80 percent of the country, no abortion facilities exist. Still, one in three pregnancies in the United States is terminated by an abortion. Harold Stanley and Richard Niemi, *Vital Statistics in American Politics* (Washington, D.C.: Congressional Quarterly Press, 1988), p. 31.

2. *Bellotti v. Baird*, 443 U.S. 622 (1979).

3. *Harris v. McRae*, 448 U.S. 297 (1980).

4. The problem with all of these "intentions," however, is that it becomes impossible to corral them all together and make sense of them. John Hart Ely writes:

> Now obviously there is no principled basis on which the intent of those voting to ratify can be counted less crucial in determining the "true meaning" of a constitutional provision than the intent of those in Congress who proposed it. That gets to include so many different people in so many different circumstances, however, that one cannot hope to gather a reliable picture of their intentions from any perusal of legislative history.

John Hart Ely, *Democracy and Distrust: A Theory of Judicial Review* (Cambridge, Mass.: Harvard University Press, 1980), p. 17.

5. Even a proponent of original intent, or interpretivism, such as John Hart Ely recognizes this fact: "For the constitutional document itself, the interpretivist's Bible, contains several provisions whose invitation to look beyond their four corners—whose invitation, if you will, to become at least to that extent a noninterpretivist—cannot be construed away. Ibid., p. 13.

6. Michael Perry, *The Constitution, the Courts and Human Rights: An Inquiry into the Legitimacy of Constitutional Policymaking by the Judiciary* (New Haven, Conn.: Yale University Press, 1982), p. 115.

7. Donald Horowitz, *The Courts and Social Policy* (Washington, D.C.: Brookings Institution, 1977), p. 4.

8. In addition to Horowitz, see J. Craig Youngblood and Parker C. Folse III, "Can Courts Govern? An Inquiry into Capacity and Purpose," in Richard A. Gambitta et al. (eds.), *Governing Through Courts* (Beverly Hills, Calif.: Sage, 1981), pp. 28–65.

9. See generally, Arthur S. Miller, "In Defense of Judicial Activism," in Stephen Halpern and Charles Lamb (eds.), *Supreme Court Activism and Restraint* (Lexington, Mass.: Lexington Books, 1983), pp. 167–199.

10. Justice Harlan concurs with the Court's judgment, but he finds the right to privacy bottomed squarely on the Fourteenth Amendment.

11. 274 U.S. 200 (1927).

12. In *Skinner v. Oklahoma*, 316 U.S. 535 (1942), the Court was faced with the question of the constitutionality of an Oklahoma statute that required sterilization for persons convicted of three or more felonies involving "moral turpitude." In 1926 Jack Skinner was convicted of stealing chickens and in 1929 and 1934 for robbery with firearms. Under state law these crimes involved moral turpitude, and the state began proceedings to order his sterilization. In an opinion by Justice Douglas, the Supreme Court struck down this statute. It is noteworthy that although the Court mentioned that the statute involved one of the "basic civil rights of man," it relied on the equal protection clause, not some notion of a right to privacy or the Eighth Amendment prohibition against cruel and unusual punishment, in overturning the statute.

Griswold v. Connecticut, 381 U.S. 479 (1965)

Justice Douglas delivered the opinion of the Court.

[A Connecticut statute makes it a crime to use contraceptives. Another statute makes it illegal to provide or assist another in using contraceptives. A married couple, their doctor, and the director of Planned Parenthood of Connecticut challenge their convictions under these statutes.]

. . . [W]e are met with a wide range of questions that implicate the Due Process Clause of the Fourteenth Amendment. Overtones of some arguments suggest that *Lochner v. New York* should be our guide. But we decline that invitation. We do not sit as a super-legislature to determine the wisdom, need, and propriety of laws that touch economic problems, business affairs, or social conditions. This law, however, operates directly on an intimate relation of husband and wife and their physician's role in one aspect of that relation.

The association of people is not mentioned in the Constitution nor in the Bill of Rights. The right to educate a child in a school of the parents' choice—whether public or private or parochial—is also not mentioned. Nor is the right to study any particular subject or any foreign language. Yet the First Amendment has been construed to include certain of those rights.

By *Pierce v. Society of Sisters*, the right to educate one's children as one chooses is made applicable to the States by the force of the First and Fourteenth Amendments. By *Meyer v. Nebraska*, the same dignity is given the right to study the German language in a private school. In other words, the State may not, consistently with the spirit of the First Amendment, contract the spectrum of available knowledge. The right of freedom of speech and press includes not only the right to utter or to print, but the right to distribute, the right to receive, the right to read and freedom of inquiry, freedom of thought, and freedom to teach, indeed the freedom of the entire university community. Without those peripheral rights the specific rights would be less secure. And so we reaffirm the principle of the *Pierce* and the *Meyer* cases.

In *NAACP v. Alabama,* we protected the "freedom to associate and privacy in one's associations," noting that freedom of association was a peripheral First Amendment right. . . .

. . . .

The foregoing cases suggest that specific guarantees in the Bill of Rights have penumbras, formed by emanations from those guarantees that help give them life and substance. Various guarantees create zones of privacy. The right of association contained in the penumbra of the First Amendment is one, as we have seen. The Third Amendment in its prohibition against the quartering of soldiers "in any house" in time of peace without the consent of the owner is another facet of that privacy. The Fourth Amendment explicitly affirms the "right of the people to be secure in their persons, houses, papers, and effects, against unreasonable searches and seizures." The Fifth Amendment in its Self-Incrimination Clause enables the citizen to create a zone of privacy which government may not force him to surrender to his detriment. The Ninth Amendment provides: "The enumeration in the Constitution, of certain rights, shall not be construed to deny or disparage others retained by the people."

. . . .

The present case concerns a relationship lying within the zone of privacy created by several fundamental constitutional guarantees. And it concerns a law which, in forbidding the use of contraceptives rather than regulating their manufacture or sale, seeks to achieve its goals by means having a maximum destructive impact upon that relationship. Would we allow the police to search the sacred precincts of marital bedrooms for telltale signs of the use of contraceptives? The very idea is repulsive to the notions of privacy surrounding the marriage relationship. . . .

We deal with a right of privacy older than the Bill of Rights—older than our political parties, older than our school system. Marriage is a coming together for better or for worse, hopefully enduring, and intimate to the degree of being sacred. It is an association that promotes a way of life, not causes; a harmony in living, not political faiths; a bilateral loyalty, not commercial or social projects. Yet it is an association for as noble a purpose as any involved in our prior decisions.

Reversed.

Justice Goldberg, whom the Chief Justice and Justice Brennan join, concurring.

I agree with the Court that Connecticut's birth-control law unconstitutionally intrudes upon the right of marital privacy, and I join in its opinion and judgment. Although I have not accepted the view that "due process" as used in the Fourteenth Amendment incorporates all of the first eight Amendments, I do agree that the concept of liberty protects those personal rights that are fundamental, and is not confined to the specific terms of the Bill of Rights. My conclusion that the concept of liberty is not so restricted and that it embraces the right of marital privacy though that right is not mentioned explicitly in the Constitution is supported both by numerous decisions of this Court, referred to in the Court's opinion, and by the language and history of the Ninth Amendment. In reaching the conclusion that the right of marital privacy is protected, as being within the protected penumbra of specific guarantees of the Bill of Rights, the Court refers to the Ninth Amendment, I add these words to emphasize the relevance of that Amendment to the Court's holding.

The Court stated many years ago that the Due Process Clause protects those liberties that are "so rooted in the traditions and conscience of our people as to be ranked as fundamental." In *Gitlow v. New York,* 268 U.S. 652, 666, the Court said:

For present purposes we may and do assume that freedom of speech and of the press—which are protected by the First Amendment from abridgment by Congress—are among the *fundamental* personal rights and "liberties" protected by the due process clause of the Fourteenth Amendment from impairment by the States. (Emphasis added.)

And, in *Meyer v. Nebraska*, 262 U.S. 390, 399, the Court, referring to the Fourteenth Amendment, stated:

While this Court has not attempted to define with exactness the liberty thus guaranteed, the term has received much consideration and some of the included things have been definitely stated. Without doubt, it denotes not merely freedom from bodily restraint but also [for example,] the right . . . to marry, establish a home and bring up children.

This Court, in a series of decisions, has held that the Fourteenth Amendment absorbs and applies to the States those specifics of the first eight amendments which express fundamental personal rights. The language and history of the Ninth Amendment reveal that the Framers of the Constitution believed that there are additional fundamental rights, protected from governmental infringement, which exist alongside those fundamental rights specifically mentioned in the first eight constitutional amendments.

The Ninth Amendment reads, "The enumeration in the Constitution, of certain rights, shall not be construed to deny or disparage others retained by the people." The Amendment is almost entirely the work of James Madison. It was introduced in Congress by him and passed the House and Senate with little or no debate and virtually no change in language. It was proffered to quiet expressed fears that a bill of specifically enumerated rights could not be sufficiently broad to cover all essential rights and that the specific mention of certain rights would be interpreted as a denial that others were protected.

. . . .

While this Court has had little occasion to interpret the Ninth Amendment, "[i]t cannot be presumed that any clause in the Constitution is intended to be without effect." *Marbury v. Madison.* In interpreting the Constitution, real effect should be given to all the words it uses. The Ninth Amendment to the Constitution may be regarded by some as a recent discovery and may be forgotten by others, but since 1791 it has been a basic part of the Constitution which we are sworn to uphold. To hold that a right so basic and fundamental and so deep-rooted in our society as the right of privacy in marriage may be infringed because that right is not guaranteed in so many words by the first eight amendments to the Constitution is to ignore the Ninth Amendment and to give it no effect whatsoever. Moreover, a judicial construction that this fundamental right is not protected by the Constitution because it is not mentioned in explicit terms by one of the first eight amendments or elsewhere in the Constitution would violate the Ninth Amendment, which specifically states that "[the] enumeration in the Constitution, of certain rights, shall not be *construed* to deny or disparage others retained by the people." (Emphasis added.)

A dissenting opinion suggests that my interpretation of the Ninth Amendment somehow "[broadens] the powers of this Court." With all due respect, I believe that it misses the import of what I am saying. . . . The Ninth Amendment simply shows the intent of the Constitution's authors that other fundamental personal rights should not be denied such protection or disparaged in any other way simply because they are not specifically listed in the first eight constitutional amendments. I do not see how this broadens the authority of the Court; rather it serves to support what this Court has been doing in protecting fundamental rights.

. . . .

In determining which rights are fundamental, judges are not left at large to decide cases in light of their personal and private notions. Rather, they must look to the "traditions and [collective] conscience of our people" to determine whether a principle is so rooted [there] . . . as to be ranked as fundamental. The inquiry is whether a right involved is of such a character that it cannot be denied without violating those fundamental principles of liberty and justice which lie at the base of all our civil and political institutions. . . .

. . . .

The Connecticut statutes here involved deal with a particularly important and sensitive area of privacy—that of the marital relation and the marital home. . . .

Although the Constitution does not speak in so many words of the right of privacy in marriage, I cannot believe that it offers these fundamental rights no protection. The fact that no particular provision of the Constitution explicitly forbids the State from disrupting the traditional relation of the family—a relation as old and as fundamental as our entire civilization—surely does not show that the Government was meant to have the power to do so. Rather, as the Ninth Amendment expressly recognizes, there are fundamental personal rights such as this one, which are protected from abridgment by the Government though not specifically mentioned in the Constitution.

. . . .

The logic of the dissents would sanction federal or state legislation that seems to me even more plainly unconstitutional than the statute before us. Surely the Government, absent a showing of a compelling subordinating state interest, could not decree that all husbands and wives must be sterilized after two children have been born to them. Yet by their reasoning such an invasion of marital privacy would not be subject to constitutional challenge because, while it might be "silly," no provision of the Constitution specifically prevents the Government from curtailing the marital right to bear children and raise a family. While it may shock some of my Brethren that the Court today holds that the Constitution protects the right of marital pri-

vacy, in my view it is far more shocking to believe that the personal liberty guaranteed by the Constitution does not include protection against such totalitarian limitation of family size, which is at complete variance with our constitutional concepts. Yet, if upon a showing of a slender basis of rationality, a law outlawing voluntary birth control by married persons is valid, then, by the same reasoning, a law requiring compulsory birth control also would seem to be valid. In my view, however, both types of law would unjustifiably intrude upon rights of marital privacy which are constitutionally protected.

Justice Black, with whom Justice Stewart joins, dissenting.

I agree with my Brother Stewart's dissenting opinion. And like him I do not to any extent whatever base my view that this Connecticut law is constitutional on a belief that the law is wise or that its policy is a good one. In order that there may be no room at all to doubt why I vote as I do, I feel constrained to add that the law is every bit as offensive to me as it is to my Brethren of the majority and my Brothers Harlan, White and Goldberg who, reciting reasons why it is offensive to them, hold it unconstitutional. There is no single one of the graphic and eloquent strictures and criticisms fired at the policy of this Connecticut law either by the Court's opinion or by those of my concurring Brethren to which I cannot subscribe—except their conclusion that the evil qualities they see in the law make it unconstitutional.

. . . .

The Court talks about a constitutional "right of privacy" as though there is some constitutional provision or provisions forbidding any law ever to be passed which might abridge the "privacy" of individuals. But there is not. There are, of course, guarantees in certain specific constitutional provisions which are designed in part to protect privacy at certain times and places with respect to certain activities. Such, for example, is the Fourth Amendment's guarantee against "unreasonable searches and seizures." But I think it belittles that Amendment to talk about it as though it protects nothing but "privacy." To treat it that way is to give it a niggardly interpretation, not the kind of liberal reading I think any Bill of Rights provision should be given. The average man would very likely not have his feelings soothed any more by having his property seized openly than by having it seized privately and by stealth. He simply wants his property left alone. And a person can be just as much, if not more, irritated, annoyed and injured by an unceremonious public arrest by a policeman as he is by a seizure in the privacy of his office or home.

One of the most effective ways of diluting or expanding a constitutionally guaranteed right is to substitute for the crucial word or words of a constitutional guarantee another word or words, more or less flexible and more or less restricted in meaning. This fact is well illustrated by the use of the term "right of privacy" as a comprehensive substitute for the Fourth Amendment's guarantee against "unreasonable searches and seizures." "Privacy" is a broad, abstract and ambiguous concept which can easily be shrunken in meaning but which can also, on the other hand, easily be interpreted as a constitutional ban against many things other than searches and seizures. . . . For these reasons I get nowhere in this case by talk about a constitutional "right of privacy" as an emanation from one or more constitutional provisions. I like my privacy as well as the next one, but I am nevertheless compelled to admit that government has a right to invade it unless prohibited by some specific constitutional provision. For these reasons I cannot agree with the Court's judgment and the reasons it gives for holding this Connecticut law unconstitutional.

. . . .

While I completely subscribe to the holding of *Marbury v. Madison,* and sub-

sequent cases, that our Court has constitutional power to strike down statutes, state or federal, that violate commands of the Federal Constitution, I do not believe that we are granted power by the Due Process Clause or any other constitutional provision or provisions to measure constitutionality by our belief that legislation is arbitrary, capricious or unreasonable, or accomplishes no justifiable purpose, or is offensive to our own notions of "civilized standards of conduct." Such an appraisal of the wisdom of legislation is an attribute of the power to make laws, not of the power to interpret them. The use by federal courts of such a formula or doctrine or what not to veto federal or state laws simply takes away from Congress and States the power to make laws based on their own judgment of fairness and wisdom and transfers that power to this Court for ultimate determination—a power which was specifically denied to federal courts by the convention that framed the Constitution.

. . . .

My Brother Goldberg has adopted the recent discovery that the Ninth Amendment as well as the Due Process Clause can be used by this Court as authority to strike down all state legislation which this Court thinks violates "fundamental principles of liberty and justice," or is contrary to the "traditions and [collective] conscience of our people." He also states, without proof satisfactory to me, that in making decisions on this basis judges will not consider "their personal and private notions." One may ask how they can avoid considering them. Our Court certainly has no machinery with which to take a Gallup Poll. And the scientific miracles of this age have not yet produced a gadget which the Court can use to determine what traditions are rooted in the "[collective] conscience of our people." Moreover, one would certainly have to look far beyond the language of the Ninth Amendment to find that the Framers vested in this Court any such awesome veto powers over lawmaking, either by the States or by the Congress. Nor does anything in the history of the Amendment offer any support for such a shocking doctrine. . . . That Amendment was passed, not to broaden the powers of this Court or any other department of "the General Government," but, as every student of history knows, to assure the people that the Constitution in all its provisions was intended to limit the Federal Government to the powers granted expressly or by necessary implication. If any broad, unlimited power to hold laws unconstitutional because they offend what this Court conceives to be the "[collective] conscience of our people" is vested in this Court by the Ninth Amendment, the Fourteenth Amendment, or any other provision of the Constitution, it was not given by the Framers, but rather has been bestowed on the Court by the Court. This fact is perhaps responsible for the peculiar phenomenon that for a period of a century and a half no serious suggestion was ever made that the Ninth Amendment, enacted to protect state powers against federal invasion, could be used as a weapon of federal power to prevent state legislatures from passing laws they consider appropriate to govern local affairs. Use of any such broad, unbounded judicial authority would make of this Court's members a day-to-day constitutional convention.

· ·

I realize that many good and able men have eloquently spoken and written, sometimes in rhapsodical strains, about the duty of this Court to keep the Constitution in tune with the times. The idea is that the Constitution must be changed from time to time and that this Court is charged with a duty to make those changes. For myself, I must with all deference reject that philosophy. The Constitution makers knew the need for change and provided for it. Amendments suggested by the people's elected representatives can be submitted to the people or their selected agents for ratification. That method of change was good for our Fathers, and being somewhat old-

fashioned I must add it is good enough for me. And so, I cannot rely on the Due Process Clause or the Ninth Amendment or any mysterious and uncertain natural law concept as a reason for striking down this state law.

Justice Stewart, whom Justice Black joins, dissenting.

Since 1879 Connecticut has had on its books a law which forbids the use of contraceptives by anyone. I think this is an uncommonly silly law. As a practical matter, the law is obviously unenforceable, except in the oblique context of the present case. As a philosophical matter, I believe the use of contraceptives in the relationship of marriage should be left to personal and private choice, based upon each individual's moral, ethical, and religious beliefs. As a matter of social policy, I think professional counsel about methods of birth control should be available to all, so that each individual's choice can be meaningfully made. But we are not asked in this case to say whether we think this law is unwise, or even asinine. We are asked to hold that it violates the United States Constitution. And that I cannot do.

In the course of its opinion the Court refers to no less than six Amendments to the Constitution: the First, the Third, the Fourth, the Fifth, the Ninth, and the Fourteenth. . . .

· ·

What provision of the Constitution, then, does make this state law invalid? The Court says it is the right of privacy "created by several fundamental constitutional guarantees." With all deference, I can find no such general right of privacy in the Bill of Rights, in any other part of the Constitution, or in any case ever before decided by this Court.

At the oral argument in this case we were told that the Connecticut law does not "conform to current community standards." But it is not the function of this

Court to decide cases on the basis of community standards. We are here to decide cases agreeably to the Constitution and laws of the United States. It is the essence of judicial duty to subordinate our own personal views, our own ideas of what legislation is wise and what is not. If, as I should surely hope, the law before us does not reflect the standards of the people of Connecticut, the people of Connecticut can freely exercise their true Ninth and Tenth Amendment rights to persuade their elected representatives to repeal it. That is the constitutional way to take this law off the books.

COMMENTS

1. You will see the notion of a right to privacy again and again. How would you define it? How convincing is the Supreme Court's enunciation of this principle in *Griswold?* Which opinion is the most convincing? Why? Do the multiple opinions (the right to privacy is in the Constitution—somewhere) detract from the principle of the right to privacy?

2. Note that although a large part of Justice Douglas's opinion is premised on the sanctity of the marital bedroom, this particular grounding for the right to privacy was soon removed in later cases. See *Eisenstadt v. Baird,* 405 U.S. 438 (1972), which struck down a similar law when challenged by an unmarried person.

3. How far should the right to privacy be extended? In *Kelly v. Johnson,* 425 U.S. 238 (1976), the Supreme Court rejected such an argument by a police officer who was fighting a department hair regulation. The Court based its opinion on the need for uniformity in the police ranks. In contrast to this, however, in *Breese v. Smith,* 501 P. 2d 159 (1972), the Supreme Court of Alaska refused to uphold the suspension of a junior high student for violating the school's hair length code. The court held that although an individual had no absolute right to wear his/her hair any length (why not?), the state needed a "compelling" interest in order to interfere with the individual's interest in preserving his/her self-autonomy.

Roe v. Wade, 410 U.S. 113 (1973)

Justice Blackmun delivered the opinion of the Court.

The Texas statutes that concern us here make it a crime to "procure an abortion," or to attempt one, except with respect to "an abortion procured or attempted by medical advice for the purpose of saving the life of the mother." Similar statutes are in existence in a majority of the States.

. . . .

The principal thrust of appellant's attack on the Texas statutes is that they improperly invade a right, said to be possessed by the pregnant woman, to choose to terminate her pregnancy. Appellant would dis-

cover this right in the concept of personal "liberty" embodied in the Fourteenth Amendment's Due Process Clause; or in personal, marital, familial, and sexual privacy said to be protected by the Bill of Rights or its penumbras; or among those rights reserved to the people by the Ninth Amendment.

. . . .

The Constitution does not explicitly mention any right of privacy. In a line of decisions, however, the Court has recognized that a right of personal privacy, or a guarantee of certain areas or zones of privacy, does exist under the Constitution. In varying contexts, the Court or individual Justices have, indeed, found at least the roots of that right in the First Amendment, *Stanley v. Georgia*, 394 U.S. 557 (1969); in the Fourth and Fifth Amendments, *Terry v. Ohio*, 392 U.S. 1 (1968); in the penumbras of the Bill of Rights, *Griswold v. Connecticut;* in the Ninth Amendment, id., at 486 (Goldberg, J., concurring); or in the concept of liberty guaranteed by the first section of the Fourteenth Amendment. These decisions make it clear that only personal rights that can be deemed "fundamental" or "implicit in the concept of ordered liberty," *Palko v. Connecticut*, 302 U.S. 319 (1937), are included in this guarantee of personal privacy. They also make it clear that the right has some extension to activities relating to marriage, procreation, contraception, family relationships, child rearing and education.

This right of privacy, whether it be founded in the Fourteenth Amendment's concept of personal liberty and restrictions upon state action, as we feel it is, or, as the District Court determined, in the Ninth Amendment's reservation of rights to the people, is broad enough to encompass a woman's decision whether or not to terminate her pregnancy. The detriment that the State would impose upon the pregnant woman by denying this choice altogether is apparent. Specific and direct harm medically diagnosable even in early pregnancy may be involved. Maternity, or additional offspring, may force upon the woman a distressful life and future. Psychological harm may be imminent. Mental and physical health may be taxed by child care. There is also the distress, for all concerned, associated with the unwanted child, and there is the problem of bringing a child into a family already unable, psychologically and otherwise, to care for it. In other cases, as in this one, the additional difficulties and continuing stigma of unwed motherhood may be involved. All these are factors the woman and her responsible physician necessarily will consider in consultation.

On the basis of elements such as these, appellant and some amici argue that the woman's right is absolute and that she is entitled to terminate her pregnancy at whatever time, in whatever way, and for whatever reason she alone chooses. With this we do not agree. Appellant's arguments that Texas either has no valid interest at all in regulating the abortion decision, or no interest strong enough to support any limitation upon the woman's sole determination, is unpersuasive. The Court's decisions recognizing a right of privacy also acknowledge that some state regulation in areas protected by that right is appropriate. . . . A state may properly assert important interests in safeguarding health, in maintaining medical standards, and in protecting potential life. At some point in pregnancy, these respective interests become sufficiently compelling to sustain regulation of the factors that govern the abortion decision. The privacy right involved, therefore, cannot be said to be absolute. In fact, it is not clear to us that the claim asserted by some amici that one has an unlimited right to do with one's body as one pleases bears a close relationship to the right of privacy previously articulated in the Court's decisions. The Court has refused to recognize an unlimited right of this kind in the past.

We, therefore, conclude that the right of personal privacy includes the abortion decision, but that this right is not unqualified and must be considered against important state interests in regulation.

. . . .

Where certain "fundamental rights" are involved, the Court has held that regulation limiting these rights may be justified only by a "compelling state interest," and that legislative enactments must be narrowly drawn to express only the legitimate state interests at stake.

. . . .

Texas urges that . . . life begins at conception and is present throughout pregnancy, and that, therefore, the State has a compelling interest in protecting that life from and after conception. We need not resolve the difficult question of when life begins. When those trained in the respective disciplines of medicine, philosophy, and theology are unable to arrive at any consensus, the judiciary, at this point in the development of man's knowledge, is not in a position to speculate as to the answer.

[The Court concludes that the point where the state's interest in the life of the unborn fetus may supercede the woman's right to privacy is at viability—the point where the fetus is potentially able to live outside the mother's womb, albeit with aid. This occurs at approximately 7 months, but can occur as early as 24 weeks.]

. . . .

. . . [W]e do not agree that, by adopting one theory of life, Texas may override the rights of the pregnant woman that are at stake. We repeat, however, that the State does have an important and legitimate interest in preserving and protecting the health of the pregnant woman, whether she be a resident of the State or a non-resident who seeks medical consultation and treatment there, and that it has still another important and legitimate interest in protecting the potentiality of human life. These interests are separate and distinct. Each grows in substantiality as the woman approaches term and, at a point during pregnancy, each becomes "compelling."

With respect to the State's important and legitimate interest in the health of the mother, the "compelling" point, in the light of present medical knowledge, is at approximately the end of the first trimester. This is so because of the now-established medical fact, that until the end of the first trimester mortality in abortion may be less than mortality in normal childbirth. It follows that, from and after this point, a State may regulate the abortion procedure to the extent that the regulation reasonably relates to the preservation and protection of maternal health. Examples of permissible state regulation in this area are requirements as to the qualifications of the person who is to perform the abortion; as

to the licensure of that person; as to the facility in which the procedure is to be performed, that is, whether it must be a hospital or may be a clinic or some other place of less-than-hospital status; as to the licensing of the facility; and the like.

This means, on the other hand, that, for the period of pregnancy prior to this "compelling" point, the attending physician, in consultation with his patient, is free to determine, without regulation by the State, that, in his medical judgment, the patient's pregnancy should be terminated. If that decision is reached, the judgment may be effectuated by an abortion free of interference by the State.

With respect to the State's important and legitimate interest in potential life, the "compelling" point is at viability. This is so because the fetus then presumably has the capability of meaningful life outside the mother's womb. State regulation protective of fetal life after viability thus has both logical and biological justifications. If the State is interested in protecting fetal life after viability, it may go so far as to proscribe abortion during that period, except when it is necessary to preserve the life or health of the mother.

. . . .

Justice White, with whom Justice Rehnquist joins, dissenting.

At the heart of the controversy in these cases are those recurring pregnancies that pose no danger whatsoever to the life or health of the mother but are, nevertheless, unwanted for any one or more of a variety of reasons—convenience, family planning, economics, dislike of children, the embarrassment of illegitimacy, etc. The common claim before us is that for any one of such reasons, or for no reason at all, and without asserting or claiming any threat to life or health, any woman is entitled to an abortion at her request if she is able to find a medical advisor willing to undertake the procedure.

The Court for the most part sustains this position: During the period prior to the time the fetus becomes viable, the Constitution of the United States values the convenience, whim, or caprice of the putative mother more than the life or potential life of the fetus; the Constitution therefore guarantees the right to an abortion as against any state law or policy seeking to protect the fetus from an abortion not prompted by more compelling reasons of the mother.

With all due respect, I dissent. I find nothing in the language or history of the Constitution to support the Court's judgment. The Court simply fashions and announces a new constitutional right for pregnant mothers and, with scarcely any reason or authority for its action, invests that right with sufficient substance to override most existing state abortion statutes. The upshot is that the people and the legislatures of the 50 States are constitutionally disentitled to weigh the relative importance of the continued existence and development of the fetus, on the one hand, against a spectrum of possible impacts on the mother, on the other hand. As an exercise of raw judicial power, the Court perhaps has authority to do what it does today; but in my view its judgment is an improvident and extravagant exercise of the power of judicial review that the Constitution extends to this Court.

The Court apparently values the convenience of the pregnant mother more than the continued existence and development of the life or potential life that she carries. Whether or not I might agree with that marshaling of values, I can in no event join the Court's judgment because I find no constitutional warrant for imposing such an order of priorities on the people and legislatures of the States. In a sensitive area such as this, involving as it does issues over which reasonable men may easily and heatedly differ, I cannot accept the Court's exercise of its clear power of choice by interposing a constitutional barrier to state efforts to protect human life and by investing mother and doctors with the constitutionally protected right to exterminate it. This issue, for the most part, should be left with the people and to the political processes the people have devised to govern their affairs.

Justice Rehnquist dissenting.

. . . .

The fact that a majority of the States reflecting, after all, the majority sentiment in those States, have had restrictions on abortions for at least a century is a strong indication, it seems to me, that the asserted right to an abortion is not "so rooted in the traditions and conscience of our people as to be ranked as fundamental." . . .

To reach its result the Court necessarily has had to find within the scope of the Fourteenth Amendment a right that was apparently completely unknown to the drafters of the Amendment. . . . By the time of the adoption of the Fourteenth Amendment in 1868, there were at least 36 laws enacted by state or territorial legislatures limiting abortion. While many States have amended or updated their laws, 21 of the laws on the books in 1868 remain in effect today. . . .

There apparently was no question concerning the validity of this provision or of any of the other state statutes when the Fourteenth Amendment was adopted. The only conclusion possible from this history is that the drafters did not intend to have the Fourteenth Amendment withdraw from the States the power to legislate with respect to this matter.

Webster v. Reproductive Health Services (1989 Lexis 3290)

Chief Justice Rehnquist delivered the plurality opinion of the Court.

[The Court examined several provisions of a Missouri statute that regulated the procurement of an abortion as follows: (1) the statute set forth "findings" that "the life of each human being begins at conception," and that "unborn children have protectable interests in life, health, and well-being"; (2) it prohibited the use of public employees and facilities to perform or assist abortions not necessary to save the mother's life; and (3) it specified that a physician, prior to performing an abortion on any woman whom he has reason to believe is 20 or more weeks pregnant, must ascertain whether the fetus is "viable" by performing "such medical examinations and tests as are necessary to make a finding of [the fetus's] gestational age, weight, and lung maturity."]

This appeal concerns the constitutionality of a Missouri statute regulating the performance of abortions. The United States Court of Appeals for the Eighth Circuit struck down several provisions of the statute on the ground that they violated the Court's decision in *Roe v. Wade,* and cases following it. We noted probable jurisdiction, and now reverse.

. . . .

[The Court first addressed the constitutionality of the "findings" by the Missouri legislature that "the life of each human begins at conception." The Court held that these findings did not, by themselves, regulate abortion, and that *Roe* "implies no limitation on the authority of a State to make a value judgment favoring childbirth over abortion" (quoting *Maher v. Roe*). The Court then addressed the statute's

provisions that prohibited abortions from being performed in any "public facility," or to be performed by a "public employee," except to save the life of the mother.]

As we said earlier this Term in *DeShaney v. Winnebago County Dept. of Social Services,* "Our cases have recognized that the Due Process Clauses generally confer no affirmative right to governmental aid, even where such aid may be necessary to secure life, liberty, or property interests of which the government itself may not deprive the individual." In *Maher v. Roe,* the Court upheld a Connecticut welfare regulation under which Medicaid recipients received payments for medical services related to childbirth, but not for nontherapeutic abortions. . . .

. . . .

More recently, in *Harris v. McRae,* the Court upheld the most restrictive version of the Hyde Amendment which withheld from States federal funds under the Medicaid program to reimburse the costs of abortions "except where the life of the mother would be endangered if the fetus were carried to term." . . .

The Court of Appeals distinguished these cases on the ground that "to prevent access to a public facility does more than demonstrate a political choice in favor of childbirth; it clearly narrows and in some cases forecloses the availability of abortion to women." . . .

We think that this analysis is much like that we rejected in *Maher* . . . and *McRae.* As in those cases, the State's decision here to use public facilities and staff to encourage childbirth over abortion places no government obstacle in the path of a woman who chooses to terminate her pregnancy.

Just as Congress' refusal to fund abortions in *McRae* left "an indigent woman with at least the same range of choice in deciding whether to obtain a medically necessary abortion as she would have had if Congress had chosen to subsidize no health care costs at all," Missouri's refusal to allow public employees to perform abortions in public hospitals leaves a pregnant woman with the same choices as if the State had chosen not to operate any public hospitals at all.

[The Court then addressed that part of the Missouri statute that required doctors to conduct certain viability tests when performing an abortion on a woman whom "he has reason to believe is carrying an unborn child of twenty or more weeks gestation age." The Court held that this provision was simply a "presumption of viability at 20 weeks," which the physician had to rebut. The Court then went on to hold that the constitutional uncertainty of statutory provisions such as that mandating viability-testing was the result of the "rigid trimester analysis" enunciated by *Roe*, which, at last, necessitated an abandonment of the *Roe* framework.]

In the first place, the rigid *Roe* framework is hardly consistent with the notion of a Constitution cast in general terms, as ours is, and usually speaking in general principles, as ours does. The key elements of the *Roe* framework—trimesters and viability—are not found in the text of the Constitution or in any place else one would expect to find a constitutional principle. Since the bounds of the inquiry are essentially indeterminate, the result has been a web of legal rules that have become increasingly intricate, resembling a code of regulations rather than a body of constitutional doctrine. . . .

In the second place, we do not see why the State's interest in protecting potential human life should come into existence only at the point of viability, and that there should therefore be a rigid line allowing state regulation after viability but prohibiting it before viability. . . .

The tests that [the Missouri statute] requires the physician to perform are designed to determine viability. The State here has chosen viability as the point at which its interest in potential life must be safeguarded. . . .

The dissent takes us to task for our failure to join in a "great issues" debate as to whether the Constitution includes an "unenumerated" general right to privacy as recognized in cases such as *Griswold v. Connecticut* and *Roe*. But *Griswold*, unlike *Roe*, did not purport to adopt a whole framework, complete with detailed rules and distinctions, to govern the cases in which the asserted liberty interest would apply. As such, it was far different from the opinion, if not the holding, of *Roe v. Wade*, which sought to establish a constitutional framework for judging state regulation of abortion during the entire term of pregnancy. . . . The Missouri testing requirement here is reasonably designed to ensure that abortions are not performed where the fetus is viable—an end which all concede is legitimate—and that is sufficient to sustain its constitutionality.

The dissent also accuses us . . . of cowardice and illegitimacy in dealing with "the most politically divisive domestic legal issue of our time." . . . The dissent's suggestion that legislative bodies, in a Nation where more than half of our population is women, will treat the decision today as an invitation to enact abortion regulation reminiscent of the dark ages not only misreads our views but does scant justice to those who serve in such bodies and the people who elect them.

Both appellants and the United States as Amicus Curiae have urged that we overrule our decision in *Roe v. Wade*. The facts of the present case, however, differ from those at issue in *Roe*. Here, Missouri has determined that viability is the point at which its interest in potential human life must be safeguarded. In *Roe*, on the other hand, the Texas statute criminalized the performance of all abortions, except when the mother's life was at stake. This case therefore affords us no occasion to revisit the holding of *Roe*, which was that the Texas statute unconstitutionally infringed the right to an abortion derived from the Due Process Clause, and we leave it undisturbed. To the extent indicated in our opinion, we would modify and narrow *Roe* and succeeding cases.

Justice Scalia concurring.

The outcome of today's case will doubtless be heralded as a triumph of judicial statesmanship. It is not that, unless it is statesmanlike needlessly to prolong this Court's self-awarded sovereignty over a field where it has little proper business since the answers to most of the cruel questions posed are political and not juridical—a sovereignty which therefore quite properly, but to the great damage of the Court, makes it the object of the sort of organized pressure that political institutions in a democracy ought to receive.

. . . .

Given the Court's newly contracted abstemiousness, what will it take, one must wonder, to permit us to reach the fundamental question? The result of our vote today is that we will not reconsider that prior opinion [*Roe v. Wade*] even if most of the Justices think it is wrong, unless we have before us a statute that in fact contradicts it—and even then . . . only minor problematical aspects of *Roe* will be reconsidered, unless one expects State legislatures to adopt provisions whose compliance with *Roe* cannot even be argued with a straight face. It thus appears that the mansion of constitutionalized abortion-law, constructed overnight in *Roe v. Wade*, must be disassembled door-jamb by door-jamb, and never entirely brought down, no matter how wrong it may be.

Justice Blackmun, with whom Justice Brennan and Justice Marshall join, concurring in part and dissenting in part.

Today, *Roe v. Wade*, and the fundamental constitutional right of women to decide whether to terminate a pregnancy, survive but are not secure. Although the Court extricates itself from this case without making a single, even incremental, change in the law of abortion, the plurality and Justice Scalia would overrule *Roe* (the first silently, the other explicitly) and would return to the States virtually unfettered authority to control the quintessentially intimate, personal, and life-directing decision whether to carry a fetus to term. . . . Never in my memory has a plurality announced a judgment of this Court that so foments disregard for the law and for our standing decisions. Nor in my memory has a plurality gone about its business in such a deceptive fashion. . . . With feigned restraint, the plurality announces that its analysis leaves *Roe* "undisturbed" albeit "modified and narrowed." But this disclaimer is totally meaningless. The plurality opinion is filled with winks, and nods, and knowing glances to those who would do away with *Roe* explicitly, but turns a stone face to anyone in search of what the plurality conceives as the scope of a woman's right under the Due Process Clause to terminate a pregnancy free from the coercive and brooding influence of the State. The simple truth is that *Roe* would not survive the plurality's analysis, and the plurality provides no substitute for *Roe*'s protective umbrella.

I fear for the future. I fear for the liberty and equality of millions of women who have lived and come of age in the 16 years since Roe was decided. I fear for the integrity of, and public esteem for, this Court.

[Justice Blackmun then addressed Missouri's statutory provision that prohibits abortions in "public facilities." Blackmun notes that "public facility" is defined so broadly as to include any private hospital that is on land leased from the state. Blackmun then addressed the issue of viability-testing and argued that the plurality misconstrued the Missouri statute so as to cause an unnecessary conflict with the analysis in *Roe,* and a pretext for abandoning the trimester approach in that case.]

The plurality opinion is far more remarkable for the arguments that it does not advance than for those that it does. The plurality does not even mention, much less join, the true jurisprudential debate underlying this case: whether the Constitution includes an "unenumerated" general right to privacy as recognized in many of our decisions, most notably *Griswold v. Connecticut* and *Roe,* and, more specifically, whether and to what extent the right to privacy extends to matters of childbearing and family life, including abortion. . . .

But rather than arguing that the text of the Constitution makes no mention of the right to privacy, the plurality complains that the critical elements of the *Roe* framework—trimesters and viability—do not appear in the Constitution and are, therefore, somehow inconsistent with a Constitution cast in general terms. . . .

. . . The trimester framework simply defines and limits the right to privacy in the abortion context to accommodate, not destroy, a State's legitimate interest in protecting the health of pregnant women and in preserving potential human life. Fashioning such accommodations between individual rights and the legitimate interests of the government, establishing benchmarks and standards with which to evaluate the competing claims of individuals and government, lies at the very heart of constitutional adjudication. To the extent that the trimester framework is useful in this enterprise, it is not only consistent with constitutional interpretation, but necessary to the wise and just exercise of this Court's paramount authority to define the scope of constitutional rights. . . .

For my own part, I remain convinced, as six other Members of this Court 16 years ago were convinced, that the *Roe* framework, and the viability standard in particular, fairly, sensibly, and effectively functions to safeguard the constitutional liberties of pregnant women while recognizing and

accommodating the State's interest in potential life. The viability line reflects the biological facts and truths of fetal development; it marks that threshold moment prior to which a fetus cannot survive separate from the woman and cannot reasonably and objectively be regarded as a subject of rights and interests distinct from, or paramount to, those of the pregnant woman. . . .

. . . .

The plurality pretends that *Roe* survives, explaining that the facts of this case differ from those in *Roe:* here, Missouri has chosen to assert its interest in potential life only at the point of viability, whereas, in *Roe,* Texas had asserted that interest from the point of conception, criminalizing all abortions, except where the life of the mother was at stake. This, of course, is a distinction without a difference. The plurality repudiates every principle for which *Roe* stands. . . . If the Constitution permits a State to enact any statute that reasonably furthers its interest in potential life, and if that interest arises as of conception, why would the Texas statute fail to pass muster? One suspects that the plurality agrees. . . .

. . . .

Thus, "not with a bang, but a whimper," the plurality discards a landmark case of the last generation, and casts into darkness the hopes and visions of every woman in the country who had come to believe that the Constitution guaranteed her the right to exercise some control over her unique ability to bear children. . . . The plurality would clear the way once again for government to force upon women the physical labor and specific and direct medical and psychological harms that may accompany carrying a fetus to term. The plurality would clear the way again for the State to conscript a woman's body and to force upon her a "distressful life and future."

The result, as we know from experience, see Cates & Rocket, "Illegal Abortion in the United States: 1972–1974," 8 *Family*

Planning Perspectives 86, 92 (1976), would be that every year hundreds of thousands of women, in desperation, would defy the law, and place their health and safety in the unclean and unsympathetic hands of back-alley abortionists, or they would attempt to perform abortions upon themselves, with disastrous results. Every year, many women, especially poor and minority women, would die or suffer debilitating physical trauma, all in the name of enforced morality or religious dictates or lack of compassion as it may be.

· ·

For today, at least, the law of abortion stands undisturbed. For today, the women of this Nation still retain the liberty to control their destinies. But the signs are evident and very ominous, and a chill wind blows.

COMMENTS

1. Assume a state now adopts a statute that prohibits abortions one week after conception, claiming that this is where it will begin to assert its "compelling" interest in protecting potential life. Is this constitutional?

2. Is Justice Blackmun correct in asserting that the majority completely ignores the principle of the right to privacy?

3. Consider the following statistics: in the United States, 23 percent of all babies are born out of wedlock; one in six teenage girls gets pregnant at least once before marriage; half of all welfare payments go to women who gave birth as teenagers; and half of all children in foster care were born out of wedlock. Jacqueline Plumez, "Abortion's Grim Alternatives," *New York Times,* November 18, 1987, p. 27.

In re: Baby M, 537 A. 2d 1227 (1988)

Chief Justice Wilentz delivered the opinion of the Court.

[William and Elizabeth Stern were unsuccessful in having a child. Mrs. Stern was afflicted with multiple sclerosis, and there was some real concern that if she had a child, it would be born deformed. Efforts to adopt were unsuccessful due to a shortage of infants. At that point William Stern and Mary Beth Whitehead entered into a surrogacy contract under which Mrs. Whitehead agreed to become impregnated by Mr. Stern, by artificial means. In exchange, Mrs. Whitehead would be paid $10,000 and agreed to divest herself of any rights as natural mother to the child. After the child—Baby M—was born, Mary Beth Whitehead had a change of heart and attempted to keep the baby. The present action involves the validity of the surrogacy contract.]

We invalidate the surrogacy contract because it conflicts with the law and public policy of this State. While we recognize the depth of the yearning of infertile couples to have their own children, we find the payment of money to a "surrogate" mother illegal, perhaps criminal, and potentially degrading to women. Although in this case we grant custody to the natural father, the evidence having clearly proved such custody to be in the best interests of the infant, we void both the termination of the surrogate mother's parental rights and the adoption of the child by the wife/stepparent. We thus restore the "surrogate" as the mother of the child. . . .

We find no offense to our present laws where a woman voluntarily and without payment agrees to act as a "surrogate" mother, provided that she is not subject to a binding agreement to surrender her child. Moreover, our holding today does not preclude the Legislature from altering the current statutory scheme, within constitutional limits, so as to permit surrogacy contracts. Under current law, however, the surrogacy agreement before us is illegal and invalid.

. . . .

We [conclude] that this surrogacy contract is invalid. Our conclusion has two bases: direct conflict with existing statutes and conflict with the public policies of this State, as expressed in its statutory and decisional law.

One of the surrogacy contract's basic purposes, to achieve the adoption of a child through private placement, though permitted in New Jersey is very much disfavored. Its use of money for this purpose—and we have no doubt whatsoever that the money is being paid to obtain an adoption and not, as the Sterns argue, for the personal services of Mary Beth Whitehead—is illegal and perhaps criminal. N.J.S.A. 9:3–54. In addition to the inducement of money, there is the coercion of contract: the natural mother's irrevocable agreement, prior to birth, even prior to conception, to surrender the child to the adoptive couple. Such an agreement is totally unenforceable in private placement adoption. Even where the adoption is through an approved agency, the formal agreement to surrender occurs only after birth and then, by regulation, only after the birth mother has been counseled. Integral to these invalid provisions of the surrogacy contract is the related agreement, equally invalid, on the part of the natural mother to cooperate with, and not to contest, proceedings to terminate her parental rights, as well as her contractual concession, in aid of the adoption, that the child's best interests would be served by awarding custody to the natural father and his wife—all of this before she has even conceived, and, in some cases, before she has the slightest idea of what the natural father and adoptive mother are like. . . .

The surrogacy contract's invalidity, resulting from its direct conflict with the above statutory provisions, is further underlined when its goals and means are measured against New Jersey's public policy. The contract's basic premise, that the natural parents can decide in advance of birth which one is to have custody of the child, bears no relationship to the settled law that the child's best interests shall determine custody. . . .

. . . .

The surrogacy contract creates, it is based upon, principles that are directly contrary to the objectives of our laws. It guarantees the separation of a child from its mother; it looks to adoption regardless of suitability; it totally ignores the child; it takes the child from the mother regardless of her wishes and her maternal fitness; and it does all of this, it accomplishes all of its goals, through the use of money.

Beyond that is the potential degradation of some women that may result from this arrangement. In many cases, of course, surrogacy may bring satisfaction, not only to the infertile couple, but to the surrogate mother herself. The fact, however, that many women may not perceive surrogacy negatively but rather see it as an opportunity does not diminish its potential for devastation to other women.

In sum, the harmful consequences of this surrogacy arrangement appear to us all too palpable. In New Jersey the surrogate mother's agreement to sell her child is void. Its irrevocability infects the entire contract, as does the money that purports to buy it.

COMMENTS

1. The court goes out of its way to state that surrogate mother situations without money are not illegal but that those involving the transfer of cash and goods are. Why the distinction?

2. If a woman's right to privacy allows her *not* to have a child for whatever reasons, why should not this same right allow a woman to *have* a child for whatever reasons she chooses?

3. Who won and who lost in this case? The Sterns end up with primary custody of the baby.

Mary Beth Whitehead has her parental rights restored, but she loses custody of the baby and loses $10,000 as well.

4. Feminists have come out on both sides of this case. Some feminists claim that the court's decision violates a woman's right to do as she pleases with her own body with regard to procreation matters. Other feminists claim that surrogate motherhood perpetuates a situation in which women play a subservient role in a male-dominated society. Are these positions as mutually exclusive as they might seem?

5. During the hearings, Mary Beth Whitehead was subject to a lot of scrutiny and criticism, including an expert witness who testified that she had Baby M play with the "wrong" toys. To what extent did the public depiction of the people involved have any bearing on whom you thought should get custody? For example, both William and Elizabeth Stern had doctoral degrees, and their combined income was close to $100,000. Mary Beth Whitehead, on the other hand, was a high school dropout

who married at sixteen and who, at one time, worked as a topless dancer. The standard the court applied in making its custody decision was what was in the "best interest" of the young child. Is there any question here what would be in the best interest of the child? Does the Sterns' higher social class contribute to "best interest"? If so, what are the implications for poorer people and their children?

6. How fair was the contract between the Sterns and Mary Beth Whitehead? Under its terms, Mary Beth Whitehead was not to smoke, drink, or take drugs during the course of the pregnancy. She was also to assume all medical risks—including death. The contract also stipulated that she was to submit to amniocentesis (which she underwent) and/or abortion upon demand by the Sterns. There was to be no compensation if, after trying, Ms. Whitehead failed to conceive, and $1,000 if she miscarried or gave birth to a stillborn. Phyllis Chesler, *Sacred Bond: The Legacy of Baby M* (New York: Vintage Books, 1988), pp. 3–4.

Cook v. State, 495 P. 2d 768 (1972)

Judge Foley delivered the opinion of the Court.

[An Oregon statute authorizes sterilization if in the opinion of the Board of Social Protection, the condition of the examinee is such that procreation would produce a child who would become neglected or dependent as a result of the parent's inability by reason of mental illness or mental retardation to provide adequate medical care and that there is no probability that the condition of the examinee will improve to such an extent to avoid this.]

. . . .

Plaintiff is a 17-year-old girl with a history of severe emotional disturbance. At age 13 she was declared a ward of the

court and was taken out of her home under circumstances which indicate that she had been physically and sexually abused by her family for some period of time. During the last four years she has been placed in two foster homes, juvenile detention home, F. W. Dammasch State Hospital and Hillcrest School of Oregon. The longest period in any one place was one and one-half years at Dammasch. Her behavior has vacilated between periods of stability that lasted up to three months and aggressive hostility expressed in verbal or physical threats towards others, self-inflicted injury, and running away. A petition was filed with the Board of Social Protection after appellant engaged in a series of indiscriminate and impulsive sexual involvements while she was in the hospital.

A psychiatrist who specializes in child guidance has followed plaintiff's care since she became a ward of the court. His uncontradicted testimony was that she would never be able to provide the parental guidance and judgment which a child requires even though she might be able to master the skills necessary to take physical care of herself and a child. He based this conclusion on the girl's lack of emotional control, her consistent low scores in areas of judgment on psychological tests, and the likelihood that she would abuse a child. He said the prognosis is poor because the presence of brain damage makes her condition inherently unstable despite continuous medication. . . .

· ·

In *Buck v. Bell*, 274 U.S. 200 (1927), the United States Supreme Court upheld a Virginia sterilization law. Sterilization was considered beneficial to the patient and to society because it allowed people to be discharged from state institutions, to return to the community, and to become self-supporting. The only other case involving sterilization laws to come before the United States Supreme Court was *Skinner v. Oklahoma*, 316 U.S. 535 (1942). The purpose of the Oklahoma law was to prevent criminal traits from being inherited by ordering the sterilization of those who had been thrice-convicted of various specified felonies. The law was held unconstitutional as a violation of equal protection because there was no rational basis for distinguishing those felonies which would result in sterilization (one of petitioner's convictions was for chicken stealing) from other felonies which were exempt (embezzlement, for example). The premise that state sterilization laws are constitutional when validly drawn was not disturbed.

· ·

The state's concern for the welfare of its citizenry extends to future generations and when there is overwhelming evidence, as there is here, that a potential parent will be unable to provide a proper environment for a child because of his own mental illness or mental retardation, the state has sufficient interest to order sterilization.

COMMENTS

1. One of the arguments made by the Right to Life movement in its attempt to have abortion proscribed is that adoption is always an option. Could a similar rationale be employed here as well? That is, rather than violating Ms. Cook's right to privacy by ordering sterilization, the state always has the option of removing her offspring when it can be shown that she is not able to care for them.

2. One of the rather odd features of the Cook case was how the court approvingly cited the U.S. Supreme Court's decision in *Buck v. Bell*. As noted in the introductory material to this chapter, the medical authorities in *Buck* made at least one major error: concluding that Carrie Buck's first child was an imbecile.

3. As far as I can discern, all sterilization cases of the kind examined in the *Cook* case involve women. Should men who cannot "adequately care" for their offspring be sterilized as well?

4. In the spring of 1988, an eighteen-year-old woman, Debra Ann Forster, was ordered to remain on birth control for the rest of her child-bearing years because she had abandoned her two infant sons in a sweltering apartment. Was this sentence less intrusive than that ordered in the *Cook* case? More intrusive (particularly with constant court monitoring)?

5. Medical authorities now estimate that approximately 375,000 newborns a year are prenatally exposed to illegal drugs, frequently cocaine in the form of crack. Prosecutors have begun to file criminal charges against mothers whose babies have been harmed by drug use. Do you agree that criminal charges should be brought? Would you also press charges against women who use alcohol and tobacco during pregnancy?

2

LIFE AND DEATH

The first chapter examined the right to privacy in regard to reproduction and abortion. The rest of the chapters in Part I focus on whether this right goes beyond this particular area. The present chapter examines the right to privacy in the context of euthanasia and of a right to treatment for babies born with serious birth defects. Then we will be looking at a case in which two rights apparently collide head on—one individual's right to privacy with someone else's right to subsistence or life.

Matter of Quinlan is our first principal case. The entire scenario of this case caused quite a national stir a number of years ago. Karen Ann Quinlan was a young woman who went into a coma after ingesting a vast quantity of drugs and alcohol. For many years she remained in this vegetative state, and in the opinion of her doctors she would remain so until she died of natural causes. In the present action her father petitioned the court to be appointed her guardian and to be allowed to remove her respirator; the idea being that this action by itself would be enough to halt her life and allow her to die a peaceful and dignified death.

Aside from the question of euthanasia quite generally, there are a number of interesting issues raised by this case. The first is the applicability of the right to privacy to a situation such as this. On one level we might argue that the right to privacy would indeed be germane, and arguably controlling, to the very question of whether to continue one's life. But the right to privacy does not necessarily protect activities just because they are in their nature quite private. As we will see in the next chapter, the Supreme Court has said that the right to privacy only arises in the area of "family, marriage or procreation." The *Quinlan* case does not involve this area. Is the right to privacy restricted to this realm? If not, should it be?

Another question raised by this case is whether one person can claim the protection of the right to privacy for another person. In this case Mr.

Quinlan wanted to remove his daughter's respirator based on *her* right to privacy, the court finding that he was without such a right in the present case. How can we say that someone's privacy interest is being violated when she is not even aware of this fact?

There is a related question of intentions. At the trial court hearing evidence was presented that Ms. Quinlan had made some remarks several years earlier expressing a general belief in euthanasia. Should such remarks carry much weight? In the present case, the Supreme Court of New Jersey did not think it had to rely on such remarks in order to arrive at its conclusion. Should it have? What if there had been the opposite kind of evidence—some remarks by Karen as an adolescent against euthanasia? Would this settle the matter the other way?

There was no apparent conflict within the Quinlan family. But what if there had been? For example, suppose that while Karen's father wanted to remove her respirator, her mother felt the other way, perhaps on religious grounds or because she thought the doctors might be wrong. What happens in this kind of situation? Is it simply a race to see who first becomes the guardian? Do we fashion a rule that in the case of any disagreement the status quo remains? What role do the so-called experts play here? Note that Karen originally had a lawyer as her guardian, but the guardian refused to pursue actions to remove her respirator. Who would better represent the interests of Ms. Quinlan? A lawyer? Her parents? A judge?

Rosewell Gilbert's case offers more than a bit of a contrast to the Quinlan situation. The case drew national media attention, and a television docudrama starring Robert Young further dramatized Gilbert's situation. Rosewell's wife suffered from Alzheimer's disease. He testified that she begged him to rid her of her misery, which he did by shooting and killing her. By way of defense at his murder trial, Rosewell Gilbert tried to argue that his actions were not murderous, that he ended his wife's life to spare her further suffering; their daughter supported her father's actions. Nevertheless, this elderly man is now in prison for the killing of his wife. To ask the question in its essential form: is Gilbert's case any different from Quinlan's?

I have found that when these cases are compared in class, students generally see only Mr. Quinlan's actions as justifiable. The usual rationale given is that Quinlan followed "legal procedure," whereas Gilbert did not. Should this really matter? Does this mean that an individual has a right to privacy only when a court so decrees, only when we can get the court's imprimatur? Does this mean also that we will necessarily punish those who, on their own, exercise someone else's right to privacy without court supervision? If so, what does this really say about the right to privacy? Indeed, what do judges know about what constitutes a "meaningful life"? Rosewell Gilbert knew much more about his wife, her suffering, and her intentions than any outsiders would, did he not?

Could it be argued that what really distinguishes the two cases is the method of death? Certainly the Gilbert situation appears quite gruesome, whereas the Quinlan situation does not. If so, does that mean that Mr. Quinlan should be charged with murder if instead of removing his daughter's respirator, as the court allowed, he simply took out a gun and shot her? Why would the method of ending life matter, or would it?

The second principal case, *Procanik by Procanik v. Cillo,* was a suit brought on behalf of a seriously deformed infant for "wrongful life." Can there be such a thing as a wrongful life? Wrongful in whose eyes? The comments following this case raise a number of issues involving babies born with birth defects. One is the "Baby Doe" situation, where a baby is born with severe birth defects; the name comes from the situation in Indiana several years ago. Do such children have a right to medical treatment, or do their parents have a right to refuse such treatment and allow the baby to die? If they have a right to treatment, at whatever cost and no matter how long the baby will ultimately end up living? Also, what do you premise this right on? Is it simply the right to privacy, or is there some kind of right to life more generally? If you do not think that a deformed infant has a right to any and all life-saving medical treatment, who is to decide what kind of medical attention is given: the parents? Doctors? Hospital ethics committees? Legislators? Judges?

A somewhat related situation occurs when a baby or young child has certain medical problems, but the parents claim that their religion (and, quite often, the religion of the child) prohibits the treatment sought by the medical staff. Here we seem to have a number of "rights" in apparent conflict. One right is that of the parents to raise their children as they choose. A related right is freedom of religion, which is expressly protected by the First Amendment. But the child arguably has a right to adequate medical treatment. When faced with this question, most courts have overridden the parents' wishes and ordered medical treatment.[1] Nevertheless, nearly every state has statutory provisions that protect Christian Science parents and others who use an organized form of spiritual healing from child abuse charges when they fail to seek medical treatment for their children.[2]

The final case in this chapter, *Head v. Colloton,* seems to represent another clash of rights. Head desperately needed to receive a bone marrow transplant—he would die without one—but the hospital refused to divulge the name of a would-be donor or take special measures to talk to "Mrs. X" and apprise her of Head's condition. Most of us would agree that our identities should not be made known to others unless we so choose. But should this right to privacy, if we can call it that, be overridden when someone's life is in danger and we may be able to save this person? Did Head have a right to know this name? A "right to life"? Any rights?

NOTES

1. See, for example, *Jehovah's Witnesses v. King County Hosp.,* 278 F. Supp. 488 (D.D.C. 1967) (children may be declared wards of court to obtain lifesaving blood transfusions for which parents refuse consent based on religious convictions); *Wal-*

lace v. Labrenz, 104 N.E. 2d 769 (1952) (a lifesaving transfusion was ordered for a child despite parental objection based on religious beliefs); *In re: Clark,* 185 N.E. 2d 128 (1962) (court upheld order for emergency blood transfusion for three-year-old burn victim).

2. Tamar Lewin, "When It's One Absolute Right Against Another," *New York Times,* May 29, 1988, p. E18. There has been a case in Florida, however, where a jury convicted a couple of third-degree murder and child abuse in the death of their seven-year-old daughter, ruling that the parents should not have deprived her of medical care because of their religious beliefs. "Religion Is Rejected as Murder Defense," *New York Times,* April 20, 1989, p. 12.

Matter of Quinlan, 355 A. 2d 647 (1976)

Chief Justice Hughes delivered the opinion of the Court.

[On the evening of April 15, 1975, Karen Ann Quinlan lapsed into a coma after ingesting a very large quantity of drugs and alcohol. She has remained in a "chronic and persistent vegetative state" since that time, and the diagnosis of the medical authorities is that she will never be restored to a cognitive and sapient life. The question before the Supreme Court of New Jersey is whether Ms. Quinlan's father should be appointed her legal guardian, and whether he should be able to pull the plug of her respirator. Mr. Quinlan maintains that he can do so under the notion of a right to privacy.]

. . . .

It is the issue of the constitutional right of privacy that has given us most concern, in the exceptional circumstances of this case. Here a loving parent, qua parent and raising the rights of his incompetent and profoundly damaged daughter, probably irreversibly doomed to no more than a biologically vegetative remnant of life, is before the court. He seeks authorization to abandon specialized technological procedures which can only maintain for a time a body having no potential for resumption or continuance of other than a "vegetative" existence.

We have no doubt, in these unhappy circumstances, that if Karen were herself miraculously lucid for an interval (not altering the existing prognosis of the condition to which she would soon return) and perceptive of her irreversible condition, she could effectively decide upon discontinuance of the life-support apparatus, even if it meant the prospect of natural death. . . .

We have no hesitancy in deciding . . . that no external compelling interest of the State could compel Karen to endure the unendurable, only to vegetate a few measurable months with no realistic possibility of returning to any semblance of cognitive or sapient life. We perceive no thread of logic distinguishing between such a choice on Karen's part and a similar choice which, under the evidence in this case, could be made by a competent patient terminally ill, riddled by cancer and suffering great pain; such a patient would not be resuscitated or put on a respirator and a fortiori would not be kept against his will on a respirator.

Although the Constitution does not explicitly mention a right of privacy, Supreme Court decisions have recognized that a right of personal privacy exists and that certain areas of privacy are guaranteed under the Constitution. The Court has interdicted judicial intrusion into many aspects of personal decision, sometimes basing this restraint upon the conception of a limitation of judicial interest and responsibility, such as with regard to contraception and its relationship to family life and decision. *Griswold v. Connecticut,* 381 U.S. 479 (1965).

The Court in *Griswold* found the unwritten constitutional right of privacy to exist in the penumbra of specific guarantees of the Bill of Rights "formed by emanations from those guarantees that help give them life and substance." Presumably this right is broad enough to encompass a patient's decision to decline medical treatment under certain circumstances, in much the same way as it is broad enough to encompass a woman's decision to terminate pregnancy under certain conditions. *Roe v. Wade,* 410 U.S. 113 (1973).

. . . .

The claimed interests of the State in this case are essentially the preservation and sanctity of human life and defense of the right of the physician to administer medical treatment according to his best judgment. In this case the doctors say that removing Karen from the respirator will conflict with their professional judgment. The plaintiff answers that Karen's present treatment serves only a maintenance function; that the respirator cannot cure or improve her condition but at best can only prolong her inevitable slow deterioration and death; and that the interests of the patient, as seen by her surrogate, the guardian, must be evaluated by the court as predominant, even in the face of an opinion contra by the present attending physicians. Plaintiff's distinction is significant. The nature of Karen's care and the realistic chances of her recovery are quite unlike those of the patients discussed in many of the cases where treatments were ordered. In many of those cases the medical procedure required (usually a transfusion) constituted a minimal bodily invasion and the chances of recovery and return to functioning life were very good. We think that the State's interest contra weakens and the individual's right to privacy grows as the degree of bodily invasion increases and the prognosis dims. Ultimately there comes a point at which the individual's rights overcome the State interest. It is for that reason that we believe Karen's choice, if she were competent to make it, would be vindicated by the law. Her prognosis is extremely poor— she will never resume cognitive life. And the bodily invasion is very great—she requires 24 hour intensive nursing care, antibiotics, the assistance of a respirator, a catheter and feeding tube.

Our affirmation of Karen's independent right of choice, however, would ordinarily be based upon her competency to assert it. The sad truth, however, is that she is grossly incompetent and we cannot discern her supposed choice based on the testimony of her previous conversations with friends, where such testimony is without sufficient probative weight. Nevertheless we have concluded that Karen's right of privacy may be asserted on her behalf by her guardian under the peculiar circumstances here present.

If a putative decision by Karen to permit this non-cognitive, vegetative existence to terminate by natural forces is regarded as a valuable incident of her right of privacy, as we believe it to be, then it should not be discarded solely on the basis that her condition prevents her conscious exercise of the choice. The only practical way to prevent destruction of the right is to permit the guardian and family of Karen to render their best judgment . . . as to whether she would exercise it in these circumstances. If their conclusion is in the affirmative this decision should be accepted by a society the overwhelming majority of whose members would, we think, in similar circumstances, exercise such a choice in the same way for themselves or for those closest to them. It is for this reason that we determine that Karen's right of privacy may be asserted in her behalf, in this respect, by her guardian and family under the particular circumstances presented by this record.

COMMENTS

1. One of the most ironic features of the *Quinlan* case was that after Mr. Quinlan obtained permission to remove his daughter's respirator, she did not die as the medical authorities had predicted. In fact, she continued to live in a comatose state for several more years. Should her father have taken (or been allowed to take) more active steps to end her existence?

2. Do you agree with the court's determination that the right to privacy extends to the decision whether to terminate one's own life? What if the individual wants to end her own life—say she is a professional violinist who has suddenly lost both of her arms—but friends and family unanimously disagree?

3. A few years ago there was a case in Connecticut in which a young woman was four and one-half months pregnant but had been in a coma for three months. The question before the court was whether a guardian could procure an abortion. The medical authorities concluded that there was a 90 percent chance that the baby would be born healthy. What factors would you have considered in making such a determination? Would an abortion violate this woman's right to privacy? Or would *not* procuring an abortion violate her right to privacy?

Procanik by Procanik v. Cillo, 478 A. 2d 755 (1984)

Judge Pollock delivered the opinion of the Court.

[Infant plaintiff, Peter Procanik, alleges that defendant doctors failed to diagnose that his mother, Rosemary, had contracted German measles in the first trimester of pregnancy. As a result of this disease, Procanik was born with congenital rubella syndrome. Procanik claims that this negligence on the part of the doctors deprived his parents of the choice of terminating the pregnancy. He seeks special damages for extraordinary medical expenses incurred because of this medical condition (which are granted by the court), and general damages for a "wrongful life."]

. . . .

The terms "wrongful birth" and "wrongful life" are but shorthand phrases that describe the causes of action of parents and children when negligent medical treatment deprives parents of the option to terminate a pregnancy to avoid the birth of a defective child. In the present context, "wrongful life" refers to a cause of action brought by or on behalf of a defective child who claims that but for the defendant doctor's negligent advice to or treatment of its parents, the child would not have been born. "Wrongful birth" applies to the cause of action of parents who claim that the negligent advice or treatment deprived them of the choice of avoiding conception or, as here, of terminating the pregnancy.

Both causes of action are distinguishable from the situation where negligent injury to a fetus causes an otherwise normal child to be born in an impaired condition. In the present case, the plaintiffs do not allege that the negligence of the defendant doctors caused the congenital rubella syndrome from which the infant plaintiff suffers. Neither do plaintiffs claim that the infant ever had a chance to be a normal child. The essence of the infant's claim is that the defendant doctors wrongfully deprived his mother of information that would have prevented his birth.

. . . .

The crux of the problem is that there is no rational way to measure non-existence or to compare non-existence with the pain and suffering of his impaired existence. Whatever theoretical appeal one might find in recognizing a claim for pain and suffering is outweighed by the essentially irrational and unpredictable nature of that claim. Although damages in a personal injury action need not be calculated with mathematical precision, they require at their base some modicum of rationality.

Underlying our conclusion is an evaluation of the capability of the judicial system, often proceeding in these cases through trial by jury, to appraise such a claim. Also at work is an appraisal of the role of tort law in compensating injured parties, involving as that role does, not only reason, but also fairness, predictability, and even deterrence of future wrongful acts. In brief, the ultimate decision is a policy choice summoning the most sensitive and careful judgment.

From that perspective it is simply too speculative to permit an infant plaintiff to recover for emotional distress attendant on birth defects when that plaintiff claims he would be better off if he had not been born. Such a claim would stir the passions of jurors about the nature and value of life, the fear of non-existence, and about abortion. That mix is more than the judicial system can digest. We believe that the interests of fairness and justice are better served through more predictably measured damages—the cost of the extraordinary medical expenses necessitated by the infant plaintiff's handicaps. Damages so measured are not subject to the same wild swings as a claim for pain and suffering and will carry a sufficient sting to deter future acts of medical malpractice.

Judge Handler concurring in part and dissenting in part.

. . . .

. . . I am firmly convinced that we should recognize a cause of action on behalf of the afflicted child with a full and fair measure of damages that adequately encompasses the enormity of the wrong. . . .

The Court posits as the only basis for permitting a recovery on behalf of the infant the preference of nonlife over life. This is a self-created hypothesis. The Court professes a lack of competence to deal with this dilemma, denying the infant's cause of action. I do not think it right, however, to deny damages to the afflicted child because we are confounded by the complexities of comparing existence with nonexistence. We have dealt with this intractable conundrum in other settings. In human affairs persons sometimes are driven to this ultimate, awesome choice. However, the Court itself need not express a preference of life over nonlife but only to understand that individuals in necessitous situations have the right to make that choice. We should acknowledge, therefore, that in determining whether the afflicted infant has a cause of action for wrongful life, the Court is neither compelled nor asked to assume a Hamlet role. We should recognize that the wrongful deprivation of the individual choice either to bear or to not bear a handicapped child is a tort—to the infant as well as the parents—and embark upon the important task of defining the infant's damages.

. . . .

This Court has recognized that an individual may in certain circumstances have the right to make a decision that favors nonexistence over existence. The Court, it is to be emphasized, can recognize that individual right without itself expressing a preference. There is a right of personal autonomy and self-determination with respect to an individual's control of his or her own body and destiny. This can implicate the fundamental choice of life itself. In some situations, the Court has accepted the substituted judgment of a surrogate, guardian or family as the only means of preserving the right of personal choice or self-determination on the part of an individual otherwise unable to exercise that right. Some people may be helpless or incompetent and devoid of the means to express their will on matters concerning their own care, including survival. This does not mean, however, that they lack a right of individual autonomy that involves personal choice and self-determination. When the right exists but the ability or will to exercise it does not, courts will struggle to find a way to effectuate that right. *In re: Quinlan,* 70 N.J. 10.

. . . .

In vindicating this individual right, the court does not arrogate to itself the individual's choice. Rather, it allows the individual's guardian or surrogate to make that choice, recognizing not only the legitimacy of a personal right to opt for nonexistence, but also the necessity of protecting that choice in order to preserve a basic right of personal autonomy and self-determination. We should, therefore, acknowledge in this case that individuals may lawfully determine in a necessitous or exigent setting that nonlife may reasonably be preferred over life. If we accept that premise—as we must, encompassing as it does both a fundamental personal right and, frequently, the best interests of the individual—then we ought to conclude that damages flow from the deprivation of this right and that the infant plaintiff should be reasonably compensated.

Judge Schreiber, dissenting in part.

I join in substantially all of Justice Pollock's sensitive opinion concerning the infant's claim of general damages for wrongful life. However, I cannot agree that the defendant doctors must pay the infant the costs of medical and other health-care expenses that were not incurred as a result of any breach of duty owed by the doctors to the infant.

The majority recognizes, as do I, that the child's wrongful life action for general damages is fundamentally flawed. The bedrock for that conclusion is that man does not know whether nonlife would have been preferable to an impaired life. As Chief Justice Weintraub so eloquently framed the issue:

With respect to the claim advanced on behalf of the infant, I agree with the majority that it cannot be maintained. Ultimately, the infant's complaint is that he would be better off not to have been born. Man, who knows nothing of death or nothingness, cannot possibly know whether that is so.

We must remember that the choice is not between being born with health or being born without it; it is not claimed the defendants failed to do something to prevent or reduce the ravages of rubella. Rather the choice is between a worldly existence and none at all. Implicit, beyond this claim against a physician for faulty advice, is the proposition that a pregnant woman who, duly informed, does not seek an abortion, and all who urge her to see the pregnancy through, are guilty of wrongful injury to the fetus, and indeed that every day in which the infant is sustained after birth is a day of wrong. To recognize a right not to be born is to enter an area in which no one could find his way. [*Fleitman v. Cosgrove,* 49 N.J. 22, 63, 227 A.2d 689 1967 (Weintraub, C.J., dissenting in part).]

Once one acknowledges, as the majority has, that the child has no cause of action for general damages stemming from wrongful life, it is unfair and unjust to charge the doctors with the infant's medical expenses. The position that the child may recover special damages despite the failure of his underlying theory of wrongful life violates the moral code underlying our system of justice from which the fundamental principles of tort law are derived.

An essential element of negligence law is that the defendant's conduct must proximately cause the plaintiff's damages. Most significant is the fact here that the defendant doctors did not injure the child. The doctors did not cause or fail to do something to prevent the multiple birth defects. Yet the damages with which the doctors are being charged are the costs of the medical expenses necessitated by those birth defects. . . .

. . . .

. . . It would be unwise—and, what is more, unjust—to permit the plaintiff to recover damages from persons who caused him no injury. I cannot concur in such a result.

COMMENTS

1. There are three different opinions here. Judge Pollock would allow the deformed child to recover medical expenses but not damages for an impaired childhood. Judge Handler would allow recovery for medical expenses as well as for an impaired childhood. Finally, in dissent, Judge Schreiber would not allow any recovery. Which decision do you agree with most, and why?

2. One of the issues that has recently been raised involves the life of the severely deformed newborn. Do seriously deformed newborns have a right to treatment? In all cases? (Would you say the same about seriously deformed or sick adults?) If there is no absolute right to treatment in all cases, who should decide whether treatment be made available? Parents? Doctors? Judges? Legislators? What standards should be applied?

3. Other ethical questions have been raised about children born with severe birth defects. In 1987, Brenda Winner discovered that the fetus she was carrying had anencephaly, meaning that it lacked most of the brain's cerebral cortex, a condition that is always fatal. Rather than aborting the child, Mrs. Winner decided to give birth so that the baby's organs could be donated to other infants. One of the questions raised was whether doctors would/should have to wait until the baby was brain dead before transplanting organs (anencephalic infants are not brain dead because their brain stems are intact, and they can breathe on their own during their short lives). How should the hospital's "ethics" committee or a court of law decide, and on what basis? To what extent should those near death be "used" to save those who are living?

4. Another ethical issue arises. A lot of the medical procedures we have been discussing are quite expensive; at the same time, large numbers of people cannot afford any kind of medical treatment. Are doctors and hospitals doing anything "wrong" by tending to those who can pay for these expensive medical services while at the same time often ignoring those who cannot pay? We will be addressing such issues in Part II.

5. Finally, there is an issue of justice among generations. Daniel Callahan points out that medical care is increasingly being consumed by the elderly. In the early 1960s, less than 15 percent of the federal health budget went to those over the age of 65. By 1985, that figure had grown to 28 percent (p. 21). Moreover, in Callahan's view, "a disproportionately large portion of health-care expenditures goes for the care of the elderly dying" (p. 21). He suggests adoption of a national medical policy that would withhold medical care from elderly people with no prospects of recovery. Daniel Callahan, *Setting Limits: Medical Care in an Aging Society* (New York: Touchstone, 1987).

Head v. Colloton, 331 N.W. 2d 870 (1983)

Judge McCormick.

This appeal presents a question concerning the right of access of a member of the general public to a hospital's record of the identity of a potential bone marrow donor. . . .

. . . .

Plaintiff William Head is a leukemia victim who is currently undergoing chemotherapy in a Texas clinic. His illness is in relapse, and the prognosis is grim.

The University of Iowa Hospitals and Clinics include a bone marrow transplant unit. That unit maintains a bone marrow transplant registry, listing persons whose blood has been tissue-typed by the hospital. The tissue typing reveals blood antigen characteristics which must be known for determining whether a donor's bone marrow will be a suitable match-up for the bone marrow of a donee. A bone marrow transplant consists of removing bone marrow from a healthy person and infusing it into the body of a patient in the hope it will generate healthy white blood cells. The procedure is experimental between unrelated persons.

Late in 1982, plaintiff phoned the transplant unit and, through a series of conversations with a staff member, learned that the hospital's registry included the name of a woman who might, upon further testing, prove to be a suitable donor to him. Only one in approximately 6,000 persons would have blood with the necessary antigen characteristics.

The tissue typing of the woman, referred to in the record as "Mrs. X," had not been done for reasons of her own health but to determine her suitability as a blood platelet donor to a member of her family who was ill. The hospital subsequently placed her name in its platelet donor registry. Then, when it later established an experimental program involving bone marrow transplants between unrelated persons, the hospital, without Mrs. X's knowledge or consent, placed her name in the bone marrow transplant registry. When the hospital established the new program, its institutional review board approved a procedure for contacting persons listed on the registry to determine whether they would act as donors. The procedure involved sending a letter informing the person of the program, its nature and goals, and inviting the person's participation in it. If the letter was not answered, a staff member was authorized to telephone the person and ask a series of general questions designed to determine whether the person would volunteer as a donor.

After plaintiff's contact with the bone marrow unit, the unit staff on December 31, 1982, sent Mrs. X the general letter informing her about the program and encouraging her to participate in it. When no response to the letter was received, a staff member telephoned Mrs. X on January 10, 1983, and asked her the series of questions. In responding to those questions, Mrs. X said she was not interested in being a bone marrow donor. When asked if she might ever be interested in being a donor, she said, "Well, if it was for family, yes. Otherwise, no." Despite plaintiff's subsequent request that the hospital make a specific inquiry of Mrs. X in plaintiff's behalf or to disclose her identity to him so he could contact her, the hospital refused to contact her or to disclose her identity to plaintiff. He then brought the present action.

. . . .

This case involves application of the provisions of chapter 68A, Iowa's public records statute. . . . Section 68A.2 provides for public access to all public records "unless some other provision of the Code expressly limits such right or requires such records to be kept confidential."

Defendants contend that the registry is required to be kept confidential pursuant to section 68A.7(2). In material part, section 68A.7 provides:

The following public records shall be kept confidential, unless otherwise ordered by a court, by the lawful custodian of the records, or by another person duly authorized to release information:

2. Hospital records and medical records of the condition, diagnosis, care, or treatment of a patient or former patient, including outpatient.

. . . .

The critical issue is whether Mrs. X was a hospital patient for purposes of section 68A.7(2) when she submitted to tissue typing as a potential platelet donor. . . .

The evidence shows the hospital believed Mrs. X became a patient when she submitted to tissue typing. Dr. Roger Gingrich, director of the hospital's bone marrow transplant program, testified she was a patient. He said: "I would regard any person who interfaces themselves with the medical profession and out of that interaction there's biologic information obtained about the . . . person, in fact to be a patient, to [have] established a doctor-patient relationship." Dr. James Armitage, former director of the unit, testified to the same effect. . . .

. . . .

Perhaps even more importantly the doctors' testimony is consistent with the reality of the situation. When a person submits to a hospital procedure, the hospital's duty should not depend on whether the procedure is for that person's benefit or the potential benefit of someone else. . . . In addition, just as with patients generally, a potential donor has a valuable right of privacy.

An individual's interest in avoiding disclosure of personal matters is constitutionally based. This right is also recognized at common law. A valuable part of the right of privacy is the right to avoid publicity concerning private facts. This right can be as important to a potential donor as to a person in ill health. . . .

. . . .

We conclude that the hospital record of Mrs. X is the hospital record of the "condition, diagnosis, care or treatment of a patient, or former patient" within the meaning of section 68A.7(2). Therefore the record is confidential.

Plaintiff contends this does not necessarily decide the case. He points to the provision in the first paragraph of section 68A.7 that provides for confidentiality "unless otherwise ordered by a court." He argues that this provision gives a court discretion to breach confidentiality otherwise required under the statute. We do not read the provision in that way nor do we understand that the trial court did so. To do so would undermine the careful legislative delineation of statutory exemptions. We hold, instead, that the power of a court is limited to ordering disclosure of otherwise confidential records only when a statute or rule outside of chapter 68A gives a party a specific right of access superior to that of the public generally.

. . . If public access is available at all under chapter 68A, it is a right of general public access. The statute does not permit the singling out of one member of the public for special access on special terms.

We have carefully considered all of plaintiff's contentions and arguments, whether expressly addressed in this opinion or not, and find they are without merit.

COMMENTS

1. Did this case miss the ethical question by simply focusing on the legal question?
2. Did this case simply take the right to privacy (Mrs. X's) to its logical (illogical) conclusion?

3. If you were William Head, what would you do following this decision? What would you be justified in doing?

4. Did William Head have any rights or are you attributing rights to him because you do not like the results?

5. Did not the court implicitly rely on a "slippery slope" rationale? That is, if we command an individual to save the life of another, this principle would ultimately know no bounds. (It is called slippery slope because once you begin the process, there is no logical stopping place.)

6. Medical authorities have told me that a bone marrow transplant is not just a minor inconvenience. What if Head had needed something as "simple" as a pint of Mrs. X's blood? Same result?

3

SEXUALITY

One of the more famous lines from Justice Douglas's majority opinion in *Griswold* is this one: "Would we allow the police to search the secret precincts of marital bedrooms for telltale signs of the use of contraceptives?" Douglas then writes, "The very idea is repulsive to the notions of privacy surrounding the marriage relationship."

The first of the two cases in this chapter, *Bowers v. Hardwick*, certainly did not involve a marital relationship, but it did involve the sexual activities—albeit homosexual—of two consenting adults behind bedroom doors. There are several noteworthy features to this opinion. The first is how Justice White, in the Court's majority opinion, restricts the right to privacy to matters concerning "family, marriage or procreation" and thus renders the right inapplicable to a situation of homosexual relations. Should the right to privacy be so limited to these areas? Why or why not?

Another noteworthy feature of Justice White's opinion is how it phrases the question before the Court: "Respondent would have us announce . . . a fundamental right to engage in homosexual sodomy." Although in legal terminology Hardwick was in fact asking for this, was he not *really* asking for something much different and arguably much less threatening to the majority population: the right to be left alone and allowed to engage in sexual practices with other consenting adults.

Another interesting point raised by the *Hardwick* case is whether it matters (or should matter) if the homosexual activities occurred in a public place, as opposed to a person's own home. The Court's opinion suggests that this fact would have had no bearing on the outcome of the case, but should it have? Hardwick unsuccessfully attempted to have his situation likened to that in *Stanley v. Georgia*.[1] In *Stanley*, the Court overturned a conviction for possession of obscene material when possession occurred in the accused's home. The Court stated that "if the First Amendment means anything, it means that a State has no business telling a man, sitting alone in his house, what books he may read or what films he may watch." The Court in *Hardwick* disagreed that *Stanley* was the controlling case, arguing that the result in *Stanley* was firmly grounded on the First Amendment. Is *Stanley* really so different? After *Hardwick*, does the privacy of a person's home make any kind of difference or offer any kind of protection? Can we expect no more privacy in our own homes than we would in the streets or in public places?

The *Hardwick* case also raises, once again, the question of the relationship between law and morals. Justice White does not think that the fact that antisodomy laws are premised on moral grounds offers any problem.

> Even if the conduct at issue here is not a fundamental right, respondent [Hardwick] asserts that there must be a rational basis for the law and that there is none in this case other than the presumed belief of a majority of the electorate in Georgia that homosexual sodomy is immoral and unacceptable. This is said to be an inadequate rationale to support the law. The law, however, is constantly based on notions of morality, and if all laws representing essentially moral choices are to be invalidated . . . the courts will be very busy indeed.

It is interesting to contrast the American view of the relationship between law and morality in the context of laws against homosexuality with the British experience. In 1957 the Wolfenden Committee Report was issued in Great Britain. Among its recommendations were decriminalization of prostitution but heavier penalties against streetwalkers because of their loitering and because solicitation was an affront to public order and decency.[2] The report also recommended the decriminalization of homosexual behavior. The committee reasoned that there was no evidence supporting the view that homosexuality was a cause of the "demoralization and decay of civilization." Instead, the committee viewed homosexuality as properly within the realm of morals *rather than* in the realm of the legal system. After several years of struggle, the British Parliament eventually adopted both of these recommendations.

A related point is the relevance of historical perspectives regarding homosexuality. For example, in his concurring opinion in *Hardwick*, Chief Justice Burger makes much of the fact that homosexual sodomy was a capital offense in ancient Rome and that the great jurist Blackstone described such activities as "the infamous crime against nature."[3] Justice White relies on history of a more recent vintage, pointing out that sodomy was forbidden by the law in all of the thirteen original colonies, that when the Fourteenth Amendment was passed in 1868 all but five of the thirty-seven states had criminal sodomy laws, and that at the time *Hardwick* was decided, twenty-four states continued to provide criminal penalties for sodomy. How relevant is all this? Actually, if we want to rely on history, does not history, or at least the clear historical trend, work against the majority? After all, fully half of the states no longer had sodomy statutes by the time *Bowers* was decided. Is not the Court going against a liberalization in this area?

A final point that the *Hardwick* decision raises is the effect such a decision will have on public attitudes toward homosexuals. Of course, this is particularly pertinent given the national concern with AIDS and the fact that homosexuals are in a "high risk" group. Will a decision such as *Hardwick* be taken by the public and by government officials as an implicit license granted by the Supreme Court to discriminate against homosexuals? Will *Hardwick* drive homosexuals back into "the closet"? *Should* the sexual practices of homosexuals (or homosexuals themselves) be back in the closet because of a moral revulsion that the majority might feel? Finally, might the decision perpetuate certain ill-founded fears about AIDS, how the disease is contracted, and how we should treat those in a high risk group?

Some of these issues are also taken up in the second case in this chapter, *Rowland v. Mad River School District,* and in the comments following the case. The case involved a schoolteacher who was fired from her job. She alleged that the firing was a result of the fact that she was a lesbian. The school board denied this. Address the larger issue: is there anything wrong with homosexuals teaching in our public school system?

NOTES

1. 394 U.S. 537 (1986).
2. For an account of the Wolfenden Committee Report, see Gilbert Geis, *Not the Law's Business: An Examination of Homosexuality, Abortion, Prostitution, Narcotics and Gambling in the United States* (New York: Schocken Books, 1979).
3. I am reminded of Winston Churchill's purported depiction of the "traditions" of the Royal Navy: "What are they? Rum, sodomy, and the lash."

Bowers v. Hardwick, 478 U.S. 186 (1986)

Justice White delivered the opinion of the Court.

In August 1982, respondent was charged with violating the Georgia statute criminalizing sodomy[1] by committing that act with

[1] Ga. Code Ann. Sec. 16–6–2 (1984) provides, in pertinent part, as follows:

(a) A person commits the offense of sodomy when he performs or submits to any sexual act involving the sex organs of one person and the mouth or anus

another adult male in the bedroom of respondent's home. . . .

· ·

This case does not require a judgment on whether laws against sodomy between consenting adults in general, or between homosexuals in particular, are wise or de-

of another. . . .

(b) A person convicted of the offense of sodomy shall be punished by imprisonment for not less than one nor more than 20 years.

sirable. It raises no question about the right or propriety of state legislative decisions to repeal their laws that criminalize homosexual sodomy, or of state court decisions invalidating those laws on state constitutional grounds. The issue presented is whether the Federal Constitution confers a fundamental right upon homosexuals to engage in sodomy and hence invalidates the laws of the many States that still make such conduct illegal and have done so for a very long time. The case also calls for some judgment about the limits of the Court's role in carrying out its constitutional mandate.

We first register our disagreement with the Court of Appeals and with respondent that the Court's prior cases have construed the Constitution to confer a right of privacy that extends to homosexual sodomy and for all intents and purposes have decided this case. The reach of this line of cases was sketched in *Carey v. Population Services International,* 431 U.S. 678 (1977), and were described as dealing with child rearing and education; with family relationships; with procreation; with marriage; with contraception; and with abortion.

. . . We think it evident that none of the rights announced in those cases bears any resemblance to the claimed constitutional right of homosexuals to engage in acts of sodomy that is asserted in this case. No connection between family, marriage, or procreation on the one hand and homosexual activity on the other has been demonstrated, either by the Court of Appeals or by respondent. Moreover, any claim that these cases nevertheless stand for the proposition that any kind of private sexual conduct between consenting adults is constitutionally insulated from state proscription is unsupportable. . . .

Precedent aside, however, respondent would have us announce, as the Court of Appeals did, a fundamental right to engage in homosexual sodomy. This we are quite unwilling to do. . . .

Striving to assure itself and the public that announcing rights not readily identi-

fiable in the Constitution's text involves much more than the imposition of the Justices' own choice of values on the States and the Federal Government, the Court has sought to identify the nature of the rights qualifying for heightened judicial protection. In *Palko v. Connecticut,* 302 U.S. 319 (1937), it was said that this category includes those fundamental liberties that are "implicit in the concept of ordered liberty," such that "neither liberty nor justice would exist if [they] were sacrificed." A different description of fundamental liberties appeared in *Moore v. East Cleveland,* 431 U.S. 503 (1977), where they are characterized as those liberties that are "deeply rooted in this Nation's history and tradition."

It is obvious to us that neither of these formulations would extend a fundamental right to homosexuals to engage in acts of consensual sodomy. Proscriptions against that conduct have ancient roots. Sodomy was a criminal offense at common law and was forbidden by the laws of the original thirteen States when they ratified the Bill of Rights. In 1868, when the Fourteenth Amendment was ratified, all but 5 of the 37 States in the Union had criminal sodomy laws. In fact, until 1961, all States outlawed sodomy, and today, 24 States and the District of Columbia continue to provide criminal penalties for sodomy performed in private and between consenting adults. Against this background, to claim that a right to engage in such conduct is "deeply rooted in this Nation's history and tradition" or "implicit in the concept of ordered liberty" is, at best, facetious.

Nor are we inclined to take a more expansive view of our authority to discover new fundamental rights imbedded in the Due Process Clause. The Court is most vulnerable and comes nearest to illegitimacy when it deals with judge-made constitutional law having little or no cognizable roots in the language or design of the Constitution. That this is so was painfully demonstrated by the face-off between the Executive and the Court in the 1930's, which resulted in the repudiation of much of the substantive gloss that the Court had placed on the Due Process Clause of the Fifth and Fourteenth Amendments. There should be, therefore, great resistance to expand the substantive reach of those Clauses, particularly if it requires redefining the category of rights deemed to be fundamental. Otherwise, the Judiciary necessarily takes to itself further authority to govern the country without express constitutional authority. The claimed right pressed on us today falls far short of overcoming this resistance.

Respondent, however, asserts that the result should be different where the homosexual conduct occurs in the privacy of the home. He relies on *Stanley v. Georgia*, 394 U.S. 557 (1969), where the Court held that the First Amendment prevents conviction for possessing and reading obscene material in the privacy of his home: "If the First Amendment means anything, it means that a State has no business telling a man, sitting alone in his house, what books he may read or what films he may watch."

Stanley did protect conduct that would not have been protected outside the home, and it partially prevented the enforcement of state obscenity laws; but the decision was firmly grounded in the First Amendment. The right pressed upon us here has no similar support in the text of the Constitution, and it does not qualify for recognition under the prevailing principles for construing the Fourteenth Amendment. Its limits are also difficult to discern. Plainly enough, otherwise illegal conduct is not always immunized whenever it occurs in the home. Victimless crimes, such as the possession and use of illegal drugs, do not escape the law where they are committed at home. *Stanley* itself recognized that its holding offered no protection for the possession in the home of drugs, firearms, or stolen goods. And if respondent's submission is limited to the voluntary sexual conduct between consenting adults, it would

be difficult, except by fiat, to limit the claimed right to homosexual conduct while leaving exposed to prosecution adultery, incest, and other sexual crimes even though they are committed in the home. We are unwilling to start down that road.

Even if the conduct at issue here is not a fundamental right, respondent asserts that there must be a rational basis for the law and that there is none in this case other than the presumed belief of a majority of the electorate in Georgia that homosexual sodomy is immoral and unacceptable. This is said to be an inadequate rationale to support the law. The law, however, is constantly based on notions of morality, and if all laws representing essentially moral choices are to be invalidated under the Due Process Clause, the courts will be very busy indeed. Even respondent makes no such claim, but insists that majority sentiments about the morality of homosexuality should be declared inadequate. We do not agree, and are unpersuaded that the sodomy laws of some 25 States should be invalidated on this basis.

Chief Justice Burger concurring.

I join the Court's opinion, but I write separately to underscore my view that in constitutional terms there is no such thing as a fundamental right to commit homosexual sodomy.

As the Court notes, the proscriptions against sodomy have very "ancient roots." Decisions of individuals relating to homosexual conduct have been subject to state intervention throughout the history of Western Civilization. Condemnation of those practices is firmly rooted in Judeao-Christian moral and ethical standards. Homosexual sodomy was a capital crime under Roman law. During the English Reformation when powers of the ecclesiastical courts were transferred to the King's Courts, the first English statute criminalizing sodomy was passed. Blackstone described "the infamous crime against nature" as an offense of "deeper malignity" than rape, an heinous act "the very mention of which is a disgrace to human nature," and "a crime not fit to be named." *Blackstone's Commentaries*, 215. The common law of England, including its prohibition of sodomy, became the received law of Georgia and the other Colonies. In 1816 the Georgia Legislature passed the statute at issue here, and that statute has been continuously in force in one form or another since that time. To hold that the act of homosexual sodomy is somehow protected as a fundamental right would be to cast aside millennia of moral teaching.

Justice Blackmun, with whom Justice Brennan, Justice Marshall, and Justice Stevens join, dissenting.

This case is no more about "a fundamental right to engage in homosexual sodomy," as the Court purports to declare, than *Stanley v. Georgia* was about a fundamental right to watch obscene movies. Rather, this case is about "the most comprehensive of rights and the right most valued by civilized men," namely, "the right to be let alone." *Olmstead v. United States*, 277 U.S. 438, 478 (1928) (Brandeis, J., dissenting).

The statute at issue, Ga. Code Ann. Sec. 16–6–2, denies individuals the right to decide for themselves whether to engage in particular forms of private, consensual sexual activity. The Court concludes that Sec. 16–6–2 is valid essentially because "the laws of . . . many States . . . still make such conduct illegal and have done so for a very long time." But the fact that the moral judgments expressed by statutes like Sec. 16–6–2 may be "natural and familiar . . . ought not to conclude our judgment upon the question whether statutes embodying them conflict with the Constitution of the United States." Like Justice Holmes, I believe that "[i]t is revolting to have no better reason for a rule of law than that it was laid down in the time of

Henry IV. It is still more revolting if the grounds upon which it was laid down have vanished long since, and the rule simply persists from blind imitation of the past." Holmes, "The Path of the Law," 10 *Harv. L. Rev.* 457, 469 (1897). I believe we must analyze respondent's claim in the light of the values that underlie the constitutional right to privacy. If that right means anything, it means that, before Georgia can prosecute its citizens for making choices about the most intimate aspects of their lives, it must do more than assert that the choice they have made is an "abominable crime not fit to be named among Christians."

. . . .

Our cases long have recognized that the Constitution embodies a promise that a certain private sphere of individual liberty will be kept largely beyond the reach of government. In construing the right to privacy, the Court has proceeded along two somewhat distinct, albeit complementary, lines. First, it has recognized a privacy interest with reference to certain decisions that are properly for the individual to make, e.g., *Roe v. Wade*. Second, it has recognized a privacy interest with reference to certain places without regard for the particular activities in which the individuals who occupy them are engaged. The case before us implicates both the decisional and the spatial aspects of the right to privacy.

The Court concludes today that none of our prior cases dealing with various decisions that individuals are entitled to make free of governmental interference "bears any resemblance to the claimed constitutional right of homosexuals to engage in acts of sodomy that is asserted in this case." While it is true that these cases may be characterized by their connection to protection of the family, the Court's conclusion that they extend no further than this boundary ignores the warning in *Moore v. East Cleveland*, against "clos[ing] our eyes to the basic reasons why certain rights associated with the family have been accorded shelter under the Fourteenth Amendment's Due Process Clause." We protect those rights not because they contribute, in some direct and material way, to the general public welfare, but because they form so central a part of an individual's life. "[T]he concept of privacy embodies the 'moral fact that a person belongs to himself and not others nor to society as a whole.' "

And so we protect the decision whether to marry precisely because marriage "is an association that promotes a way of life, not causes; a harmony in living, not political faiths; a bilateral loyalty, not commercial or social projects." *Griswold v. Connecticut*, 381 U.S., at 486. We protect the decision whether to have a child because parenthood alters so dramatically an individual's self-definition, not because of demographic considerations or the Bible's command to be fruitful and multiply. And we protect the family because it contributes so powerfully to the happiness of individuals, not because of a preference of stereotypical households. . . .

Only the most willful blindness could obscure the fact that sexual intimacy is "a sensitive, key relationship of human existence, central to family life, community welfare, and the development of human personality." The fact that individuals define themselves in a significant way through their intimate sexual relationships with others suggests, in a Nation as diverse as ours, that there may be many "right" ways of conducting those relationships, and that much of the richness of a relationship will come from the freedom an individual has to choose the form and nature of these intensely personal bonds.

. . . .

The behavior for which Hardwick faces prosecution occurred in his own home, a place to which the Fourth Amendment attaches special significance. The Court's treatment of this aspect of the case is symp

tomatic of its overall refusal to consider the broad principles that have informed our treatment of privacy in specific cases. Just as the right to privacy is more than the mere aggregation of a number of entitlements to engage in specific behavior, so too, protecting the physical integrity of the home is more than merely a means of protecting specific activities that often take place there. . . . Indeed, the right of an individual to conduct intimate relationships in the intimacy of his or her own home seems to me to be the heart of the Constitution's protection of privacy.

COMMENTS

1. In *Stanley v. Georgia*, the Supreme Court overturned a conviction for possession of obscene materials found in Stanley's home. The Court held that an individual's privacy interest and the interest in receiving information superceded the interest the government has in protecting citizens from obscene material. Why is it that a person can do certain illegal things in the privacy of his home, (possess obscene material) but not do other things?

2. In *Bowers*, the Court was deeply split on the relevance of historical views of homosexuality. Which side has a better-reasoned view?

3. Justice White's majority opinion unabashedly accepts the premise that laws against homosexual behavior are premised on certain moral views. In Great Britain homosexuality between consenting adults was *decriminalized* for these same exact reasons. How do you explain these contrary results?

4. Note that the majority opinion limits the right to privacy to situations involving "family, marriage or procreation." Should the right to privacy be so limited? If yes, would this mean that the *Quinlan* case was wrongly decided by the Supreme Court of New Jersey?

5. The majority only considered whether the Georgia statute applied to homosexual behavior. In portions of the dissent that have been omitted here, the argument was made that the statute was aimed at prohibiting sodomy among heterosexuals as well. If the Court had been

faced with this situation, how should it have decided the matter?

6. In dicta, Justice White held that statutes proscribing adultery were not violative of the Constitution. Do you agree with the position that criminal penalties could be applied against someone who has committed adultery? Where is the right to privacy in all this?

Rowland v. Mad River School District, 730 F. 2d 444 (1984)

Circuit Judge Edwards dissenting.

Respectfully, I dissent.

[Rowland worked as a high school vocational guidance counselor with a one-year contract. A short time after she began this position, Rowland notified her secretary and then administrators and teachers of the school that she was bisexual. These school officials suggested that she resign. When Rowland refused, the school suspended her with pay for the remainder of the school year. Rowland obtained a temporary injunction against this action, and she was then reassigned to a position with no student contact. At the end of the school year Rowland's contract was not renewed. The trial court held that this was an unlawful discharge, but the circuit court reversed, holding that it was not clear from the trial court's holding that Rowland was fired for her sexual preferences, rather than for professional incompetence. Included below are portions of the dissenting opinion from Circuit Judge Edwards.]

This school teacher has been deprived of her job solely because she let it be known to some colleagues and, through them, to her administrative superiors that her sexual preference was for another woman. . . .

This record presents a clearcut issue as to whether a citizen's mere statement of a homosexual preference may be punished by job loss by the joint decision of a school superintendent, a public school principal, and the school board, as a matter of institutional policy. I find no language in the Constitution of the United States which excludes citizens who are bisexual or homosexual from its protection, and particularly of the protection of the First and Fourteenth Amendments thereto. The Constitution protects all citizens of the United States; no language therein excludes the homosexual minority. Like all citizens, homosexuals are protected in these great rights, certainly to the extent of being homosexual and stating their sexual preference in a factual manner where there is no invasion of any other person's rights.

While the Supreme Court of the United States has not, to this date, decided this specific issue, it has also decided no case to the contrary of the view expressed above.

. . . .

. . . I perceive no reason to deny plaintiff her rights under the equal protection clause of [the Fourteenth] amendment. Assume for a moment that all the same facts applicable to this case were before us in a case where the first disclosure to the secretary had been by a teacher whose appearance was consistent with majority race status, but who revealed she had a black parent. If community protests in this rural southwest Ohio county had convinced the principal and school board to non-renew that teacher, would there be any doubt about whether or not this was "policy" and a case for a federal constitutional remedy. I find no logical equal protection distinction between these two minority discrimination situations, both of which evoke deeply felt prejudices and fears on the part of many people. . . .

. . . .

THE REALITY OF THIS CASE
My colleague's opinion seems to me to treat this case, sub silentio, as if it involved only a single person and a sick one at that—in short, that plaintiff's admission of homosexual status was sufficient in itself to justify her termination. To the contrary, this record does not disclose that she is subject to mental illness; nor is she alone.

Careful studies of homosexuality have now established two facts of which the courts should be aware and should take judicial notice. The first is that homosexuality is not a mental disease, like insanity or a psychopathic personality. The second is the extent of homosexuality in the United States.

In 1979, the Surgeon General issued a memorandum as follows:

The public Health Service policy regarding the physical and mental examination of aliens has been revised. According to this revision homosexuality per se will no longer be considered a "mental disease or defect." [T]he change will reflect current and generally accepted canons of medical practice with respect to homosexuality.

While this statement directly related to exclusion from the United States of aliens seeking admission either as visitors or permanent residents, . . . the Surgeon General's memorandum is nonetheless an authoritative statement of modern medical opinion concerning homosexuality.

In dealing with this type of case, this court (and others) should be aware and take judicial notice of the monumental works concerning the incidence of homosexuality in males and females in the United States. The following sentences represent cumulative summaries of Kinsey's authoritative works on homosexual incidence in males and females:

. . . .

[T]he accumulative incidences of overt contact to the point of orgasm among the females had reached 13 per cent; among the males they had reached 37 per cent.

Kinsey et al., *Sexual Behavior in the Human Female*, 474–75 (1953).

Perhaps the quickest summary of Kinsey's work is found in Marmor, *Homosexual Behavior: A Modern Reappraisal* (1980):

The Kinsey reports represent the most thorough and extensive surveys done to date. A number of smaller studies have been made in Europe, and all are in approximate agreement with the Kinsey findings [cites omitted]. On the basis of these various studies it is fair to conclude, conservatively, that the incidence of more or less exclusively homosexual behavior in Western culture ranges from 5 to 10 percent for adult males and from 3 to 5 percent for adult females. If bisexual behavior is included, the incidence may well be twice these figures. It is clear, therefore, that the propensity for homosexual reactivity is a widespread one even in societies such as ours which strongly discourage it.

On the facts and circumstances presented here, I would affirm the jury's verdict and the judgment entered by the Magistrate and the District Judge.

COMMENTS
1. The majority opinion and the dissent vigorously disagree on whether Rowland was fired for her sexual preferences. Assume for the sake of argument that she was. Would that have been a justifiable decision? In another words, should someone's sexual preference have a bearing on whether she is fit to teach children? If you think so, how far would you extend that principle? (More importantly, *why* would you extend it?) College professors? College presidents? Auto mechanics? Postal workers? Sales clerks?

2. For those who believe that homosexuals should not be schoolteachers, what kind of

"proof" of these sexual preferences would you need? Would rumor and innuendo be enough?

3. In *Webster v. Doe,* 100 L.Ed. 2d 632 (1988), the Supreme Court was faced with the issue whether a homosexual who was fired from the CIA for his sexual preferences could challenge his dismissal through judicial means or whether statutory provisions precluded judicial review. The pertinent federal law was section 102(c) of the National Security Act of 1947, which provides that "the Director of Central Intelligence may, in his discretion, terminate the employment of any officer or employee of the Agency whenever he shall deem such termination necessary or advisable in the interests of the United States."

The Court held that "nothing in 102(c) persuades us that Congress meant to preclude consideration of colorable constitutional claims arising out of the actions of the Director." This result does not necessarily mean that the firing in question would ultimately be found to be unlawful, just that it was not beyond judicial scrutiny.

4. Should homosexual couples be allowed to adopt children or act as foster parents?

4

SEARCH AND SEIZURE: DRUGS AND AIDS

One chapter in a book such as this cannot possibly hope to cover even a small part of Fourth Amendment—search and seizure—law. What the reader will instead find in this chapter are cases that avoid most of the minutia of law in this area but still raise some of the most interesting and vital questions of the day.

The first principle case, *New Jersey v. T.L.O.*, has a background that I suppose all of you will be familiar with in one form or another: smoking in the high school lavatory. As you might have guessed, the perpetrators were caught. It is here that the search and the possible constitutional violation occur.

What constitutional rights do students have? In *Tinker v. Des Moines School District,*[1] the Supreme Court held that "it can hardly be argued that either students or teachers shed their constitutional rights . . . at the schoolhouse gate." Subsequent decisions, however, called into serious question whether the Constitution offers much protection to school age children.[2] You might also ask how far the Constitution *should* protect these students, but remember you do so having already graduated from this school setting. Would Vice Principal Choplick's search in *T.L.O.* be reasonable on a college campus? Why or why not?

The second principal case, *State v. Deskins*, involved the legality of roadblocks to catch drunk drivers. Undoubtedly, the public policy goal is a good one. Do the means, however, violate the Constitution? Note that in this opinion the judge provides a number of criteria for determining whether a particular roadblock would be lawful. Although the listing here is quite impressive and extensive, does it ultimately provide all that much guidance? Moreover, does it help to obscure the more essential question that the case raises: whether individuals enjoy a right to privacy when driving their automobiles that can only be contravened when the state can demonstrate there is reason to believe that this driver is intoxicated?

For those who believe that roadblocks are in fact constitutional, how far would you be willing to take this principle? For example, would you allow a breathalyzer to be given to every driver who is stopped? Would you allow the police to take urine samples to test for drug use? On the other hand, for those who believe that roadblocks per se violate the Constitution, are you thereby taking the position that we must, for all intents and purposes, wait for tragedy before "something" is done to curb drunk driving in this country? Do we give up certain "rights" when we take to the public highways? If so, which ones, and why?

The issue of drug testing is raised in *National Treasury Employees Union v. von Raab*. Most conversations I have had with students regarding drug testing have left me baffled. For example, the vast majority of my students believe in testing college athletes "for their own safety." When asked if those who participate in school-sponsored intramural sports should also be tested (that is, my students), for "their own safety," of course, the overwhelming response is a negative one. What kind of distinction are students attempting to make here, and is it a valid one? The high schools in Indiana not only test high school athletes but cheerleaders as well. Why cheerleaders? What about members of the marching band?

In terms of the workplace, I have found students to take the position that an employer has a right to know whether his/her employees are using drugs, even if the job does not involve any likelihood of danger (college professor, for example). If this is the case, I have argued to them, then I have a right to know if my students are using drugs, and on one occasion I ordered the students in one class to each bring in a urine sample after the weekend. No student complied. In fact, they argued that because I was an employee of the university and they were not, they had the right to know if *I* used drugs. As a result, they ordered *me* to bring in a urine sample. Needless to say, there was a decided stalemate on this issue.

I have often heard it said that the only people against drug testing are those who have "something to hide." This may or may not be true, but certainly constitutional principles should not be lowered to the level of gamesmanship. Would the person who gives this simplistic response to the question of drug testing allow the police to search his/her home at any time and for any reason? Certainly not. Does this mean that this person is "hiding something"? Of course not.

One of the great uncertainties in this area is whether Fourth Amendment prohibitions, and the right to privacy generally, ought to apply when we are talking about screening workers when there is no attempt to take recourse in criminal prosecution for those who test positive. But we could argue, however, that the loss of a job, or a job prospect, is as "serious" to an individual as the prospect of criminal prosecution.

If employers do in fact have a right to know about their employees, how far does this line of reasoning extend? Drug testing on the job might not tell the employer whether you have used drugs in the past or during the weekend (the traces no longer show) or whether you have committed criminal violations and so on. Should an employer know these things about someone she is entrusting with a job? *Long Beach City Emp. v. City of Long Beach* involved the use of polygraphs at the workplace. Is this simply a logical extension of drug tests?

The final case in this chapter, *School Board of Nassau County v. Arline*, has been labeled the AIDS case, although factually it had nothing to do with AIDS. The case involved the question whether a person afflicted with tuberculosis, a contagious disease, could be considered "handicapped" under a federal law that prohibits a federally funded state program from discriminating against handicapped persons. Although the case addressed the rights of those afflicted with tuberculosis (and, presumably, those with AIDS), do those who fear contracting the disease, even if their fears are founded on completely erroneous information, have any rights not to come into contact with afflicted persons? Justice Brennan writes, "Few aspects of a handicap give rise to the same level of public fear and misapprehension as contagiousness." Yet, should not the Court be sensitive to this public fear and attempt to quell the misapprehension? Or is this exactly what the Court is doing in this case?

NOTES

1. 393 U.S. 503 (1969).

2. For example, in *Hazelwood School District v. Kuhlmeier*, 98 L.Ed. 2d 592 (1988), the Court allowed a high school principal to censor the school newspaper. In *Goss v. Lopez*, 419 U.S. 565 (1975), the Court mandated a due process hearing for a student who was to be suspended from school, although the extent of the process due was not great. This was underscored two years later in *Ingraham v. Wright*, 430 U.S. 651 (1977), where the Supreme Court held that a student was not protected by substantive or procedural constitutional rights when school authorities were inflicting corporal punishment on the student.

New Jersey v. T.L.O., 469 U.S. 325 (1985)

Justice White delivered the opinion of the Court.

. . . .

On March 7, 1980, a teacher at Piscataway High School in Middlesex County, N.J., discovered two girls smoking in a lavatory. One of the two girls was the respondent T.L.O., who at that time was a 14-year-old high school freshman. Because smoking in the lavatory was a violation of a school rule, the teacher took the two girls to the Principal's office, where they met with Assistant Vice Principal Theodore Choplick. In response to questioning by Mr. Choplick, T.L.O.'s companion admitted that she had violated the rule. T.L.O., however, denied that she had been smoking in the lavatory and claimed that she did not smoke at all. Mr. Choplick asked T.L.O to come into his private office and demanded to see her purse. Opening the purse, he found a pack of cigarettes, which he removed from the purse and held before T.L.O. as he accused her of having lied to him. As he reached into the purse for the cigarettes, Mr. Choplick also noticed a package of cigarette rolling papers. In his experience, possession of rolling papers by high school students was closely associated with the use of marihuana. Suspecting that a closer examination of the purse might yield further evidence of drug use, Mr. Choplick proceeded to search the purse thoroughly. The search revealed a small amount of marihuana, a pipe, a number of empty plastic bags, a substantial quantity of money in one-dollar bills, an index card that appeared to be a list of students who owed T.L.O. money, and two letters that implicated T.L.O. in marihuana dealing.

[T.L.O. was arrested. She challenges this arrest on the grounds that the search violated the Fourth Amendment.]

. . . .

We have recognized that even a limited search of the person is a substantial invasion of privacy. *Terry v. Ohio*, 392 U.S. 1 (1968). We have also recognized that searches of closed items of personal luggage are intrusions on protected privacy interests, for the Fourth Amendment provides protection to the owner of every container that conceals its contents from plain view. A search of a child's person or of a closed purse or other bag carried on her person, no less than a similar search carried out on an adult, is undoubtedly a severe violation of subjective expectations of privacy.

. . . .

Against the child's interest in privacy must be set the substantial interest of teachers and administrators in maintaining discipline in the classroom and on school grounds. Maintaining order in the classroom has never been easy, but in recent years, school disorder has often taken particularly ugly forms: drug use and violent crime in the schools have become major social problems. Even in schools that have been spared the most severe disciplinary problems, the preservation of order and a proper educational environment requires close supervision of schoolchildren, as well as the enforcement of rules against conduct that would be perfectly permissible if undertaken by an adult. . . .

How, then, should we strike the balance between the schoolchild's legitimate expectations of privacy and the school's equally legitimate need to maintain an environment in which learning can take place? It is evident that the school setting requires some easing of the restrictions to which searches by public authorities are ordinarily subject. . . .

. . . .

We join the majority of courts that have examined this issue in concluding that the accommodation of the privacy interests of schoolchildren with the substantial need of teachers and administrators for freedom to maintain order in the schools does not require strict adherence to the requirement that searches be based on probable cause to believe that the subject of the search has violated or is violating the law. Rather, the legality of a search of a student should depend simply on the reasonableness, under all the circumstances, of the search. Determining the reasonableness of any search involves a twofold inquiry: first, one must consider "whether the . . . action was justified at its inception." *Terry v. Ohio.* Second, one must determine whether the search as actually conducted "was reasonably related in scope to the circumstances which justified the interference in the first place." Under ordinary circumstances, a search of a student by a teacher or other school official will be "justified at its inception" when there are reasonable grounds for suspecting that the search will turn up evidence that the student has violated or is violating either the law or the rules of the school. Such a search will be permissible in its scope when the measures adopted are reasonably related to the objectives of the search and not excessively intrusive in light of the age and sex of the student and the nature of the infraction.

[The Court then concluded that Vice Principal Choplick's initial search was reasonable because there was reason to believe that T.L.O. was smoking in the bathroom, and that a purse might contain evidence of that fact—cigarettes. The extent of the search was also found to be reasonable, because after finding rolling papers, Choplick had reason to believe that T.L.O. had marijuana in her possession.]

Justice Stevens, with whom Justice Marshall joins, and with whom Justice Brennan joins as to Part I, concurring in part and dissenting in part.

. . . .

. . . The majority holds that "a search of a student by a teacher or other school official will be 'justified at its inception' when there are reasonable grounds for suspecting that the search will turn up evidence that the student has violated or is violating either the law or the rules of the school." This standard will permit teachers and school administrators to search students when they suspect that the search will reveal evidence of even the most trivial school regulation or precatory guideline for student behavior. The Court's standard for deciding whether a search is justified "at its inception" treats all violations of the rules of the school as though they were fungible. For the Court, a search for curlers and sunglasses in order to enforce the school dress code is apparently just as important as a search for evidence of heroin addiction or violent gang activity.

. . . .

The logic of distinguishing between minor and serious offenses in evaluating the reasonableness of school searches is almost too clear for argument. In order to justify the serious intrusion on the persons and privacy of young people that New Jersey asks this Court to approve, the State must identify some real, immediate and serious consequences. While school administrators have entirely legitimate reasons for adopting school regulations and guidelines for student behavior, the authorization of searches to enforce them displays a shocking lack of all sense of proportion.

. . . .

. . . Like the New Jersey Supreme Court, I would view this case differently if the Assistant Vice Principal had reason to believe T.L.O.'s purse contained evidence of criminal activity, or of an activity that would seriously disrupt school discipline. There was, however, absolutely no basis for any such assumption—not even a "hunch."

In this case, Mr. Choplick overreacted to what appeared to be nothing more than a minor infraction—a rule prohibiting smoking in the bathroom of the freshmen's and sophomores' building. It is, of course, true that he actually found evidence of serious wrongdoing by T.L.O., but no one claims that the prior search may be justified by his unexpected discovery. As far as the smoking infraction is concerned, the search for cigarettes merely tended to corroborate a teacher's eyewitness account of T.L.O.'s violation of a minor regulation designed to channel student smoking behavior into designated locations. Because this conduct was neither unlawful nor significantly disruptive of school order or the educational process, the invasion of privacy associated with the forcible opening of T.L.O.'s purse was entirely unjustified at its inception.

. . . .

The schoolroom is the first opportunity most citizens have to experience the power of government. Through it passes every citizen and public official, from schoolteachers to policemen and prison guards. The values they learn there, they take with them in life. One of our most cherished ideals is the one contained in the Fourth

Amendment: that the government may not intrude on the personal privacy of its citizens without a warrant or compelling circumstance. The Court's decision today is a curious moral for the Nation's youth.

COMMENTS

1. The facts of this case should be familiar enough. I also venture to say that the response by Vice Principal Choplick is what we have come to expect, and have experienced ourselves, from school administrators. But I continually tell my students who tell their own "war stories" that just because something is standard practice in their hometown, or at their old high school, this does not mean it is ultimately legal.

2. What would constitute "reasonable suspicion"? For example, would school authorities have "reasonable suspicion" to search the locker of a student with a reputation for drug use (like the character played by Sean Penn in the movie *Fast Times at Ridgemont High*) when that student has very red eyes? Is late for school? Repeatedly asks to be excused to go to the bathroom?

3. The present case involved searches of high school students. You would agree (I am sure) that the same principle would not apply on the college level. Why the difference?

4. What about other kinds of searches? Because of the level of violence at some high schools, there have been efforts to have pat down searches and/or metal detector searches of all students. Could *T.L.O.* be extended this far? *Should* it be extended this far?

5. What about events in the school parking lot? Should the reasonable suspicion standard apply here as well? Just to school authorities? Or law enforcement authorities, too?

6. Is the *T.L.O.* case a search and seizure case or a right to privacy case? Does not your answer to this question largely determine whether you approve or disapprove of the result?

State v. Deskins, 673 P. 2d 1174 (1983)

Justice Holmes delivered the opinion of the Court.

[Defendant Rick Deskins was stopped at a roadblock at 1:20 A.M. at an intersection in Topeka, Kansas. All vehicles traveling in a north-south direction were stopped and the driver's license checked. An officer testified that he could smell a strong odor of alcohol from Deskins, and that his eyes were "bloodshot and watery." The police officer requested that Deskins step out of his car and take a sobriety and coordination test, which Deskins did in a manner unsatisfactory to the officer. Deskins was then arrested for driving while intoxicated, which he is now challenging. The trial court found this to be an unlawful search and seizure.]

. . . .

There can be no doubt that the stopping of a motorist for the sole purpose of checking for a valid driver's license, let alone to seek evidence of the commission of a crime such as DUI, constitutes a "seizure" under the Fourth Amendment.

. . . .

. . . In *Delaware v. Prouse*, 440 U.S. 648 (1979), the Court stated:

The Fourth and Fourteenth Amendments are implicated in this case because stopping an automobile and detaining its occupants constitute a "seizure" within the meaning of those Amendments, even though the purpose of the stop is limited and the resulting detention quite brief. 440 U.S. at 653.

[The Court then went on to hold:]

Accordingly, we hold that except in those situations in which there is at least articulable and reasonable suspicion that a motorist is unlicensed or that an automobile is not registered, or that either the vehicle or an occupant is otherwise subject to seizure for violation of law, stopping an automobile and detaining the driver in order to check his driver's license and the registration of the automobile are unreasonable under the Fourth Amendment. This holding does not preclude the State of Delaware or other States from developing methods for spot checks that involve less intrusion or that do not involve the unconstrained exercise of discretion. Questioning of all oncoming traffic at road-block-type stops is one possible alternative. We hold only that persons in automobiles on public roadways may not for that reason alone have their travel and privacy interfered with at the unbridled discretion of police officers. p. 663.

. . . .

. . . The essence of the Fourth Amendment prohibition is to "safeguard the privacy and security of individuals against arbitrary invasions by governmental officials" by imposing a standard of reasonableness upon the exercise of those officials' discretion. The governing principle of the amendment is that except in certain carefully defined classes of cases, a search of private property without proper consent is unreasonable unless it has been authorized by a valid search warrant. Whether a warrantless search and seizure falls within these limited exceptions is determined by balancing the degree of legitimate governmental interests against the resulting intrusion of the particular law enforcement practice on individuals' Fourth Amendment rights. . . .

In applying the balancing test of the degree of governmental or public interest against the degree of intrusion upon the individual's constitutionally protected rights, the courts have developed a three factor test or analysis. . . .

[A] weighing of the gravity of the public concerns served by the seizure, the degree to which the seizure advances the public interest, and the severity of the interference with individual liberty. *Brown v. Texas*, 443 U.S. at 50–51.

Numerous conditions and factors must be considered in determining whether a DUI roadblock meets the balancing test in favor of the state. Among the factors which should be considered are: (1) the degree of discretion, if any, left to the officer in the field; (2) the location designated for the roadblock; (3) the time and duration of the roadblock; (4) standards set by superior officers; (5) advance notice to the public at large; (6) advance warning to the individual approaching motorist; (7) maintenance of safety conditions; (8) degree of fear or anxiety generated by the mode of operation; (9) average length of time each motorist is detained; (10) physical factors surrounding the location, type and method of operation; (11) the availability of less intrusive methods for combating the problem; (12) the degree of effectiveness of the procedure; and (13) any other relevant circumstances which might bear upon the test. Not all of the factors need to be favorable to the state but all which are applicable to a given roadblock should be considered. Some, of course, such as unbridled discretion of the officer in the field, would run afoul of *Prouse* regardless of other favorable factors.

When the test enunciated in the cases and the foregoing factors are taken into consideration and applied to the DUI roadblock in question, does it pass constitutional muster? We think it does. The roadblock in question was a joint effort of the highway patrol, Shawnee County sheriff's officer and Topeka police department. Thirty-five to forty officers were briefed ahead of time by supervisory personnel of the Topeka police department. The officers were specifically advised to check for driver's license violations and signs of drunk driving. The roadblock was established in a well-lighted area of a four-lane highway. Several police cars were utilized, with a car with its red lights flashing located at each of the four corners of the roadblock. The time of detention was minimal, unless violations were noted, and sufficient officers were present to assure minimum intrusion, time-wise. All vehicles going in either direction were stopped and subjected to the license check. The officers in the field had no discretion to pick and choose who would or would not be stopped. The officers were in uniform and readily recognizable as being police officers. The location was selected by supervisory personnel and not the officers in the field.

The Topeka DUI roadblock did not involve the unbridled discretion of the officer in the field which was held oppressive and subject to abuse in *Prouse*. When we consider the enormity of the injury and damage caused by the drinking driver and the vital interest of every citizen in being protected as far as possible upon the streets and roadways, we find that the public interest in a properly conducted DUI roadblock containing appropriate safeguards outweighs the individual's right to be free from unfettered intrusion upon his Fourth Amendment rights. . . .

Justice Prager dissenting.

. . . .

As I see it, the basic issue is this: Does the public interest in a DUI roadblock of the type established in this case outweigh the individual's right to be free from intrusion on his or her right of privacy? The majority opinion correctly states that the burden of proof rests upon the State to prove the validity of the roadblock.

As to the public interest involved, no one can seriously contest the grave concern over the public peril created by drunk drivers. It is safe to say that official efforts to discover and deter drunk drivers are, and should remain, a high priority. . . .

The most pressing question before us is the degree to which this roadblock checkpoint actually promoted the public interest in deterring drunk drivers. . . .

Generally drunk drivers, through their behavior behind the wheel, manifest their presence to even lay observers. They can easily be discerned by law enforcement officers skilled in identifying the signals indicating a driver is operating the vehicle under the influence of alcohol or drugs. In this case, the trial court specifically found that there are alternative less intrusive means available to officers to identify drunk drivers, and police officials need not go to the degree of stopping all traffic at a roadblock. The record in this case shows that the roadblock was in effect for a period of four hours from 10:00 P.M. to 2:00 A.M. The officer testified that during that period, between 2,000 and 3,000 motor vehicles were stopped at the roadblock. A total of 74 violations were discovered at the checkpoint, only 15 of which were for driving while intoxicated. During this period of time 35 police officers were on duty, which for the four-hour period involved a total of 140 man hours. Although it does not specifically appear in the record before us, it was not unreasonable for the trial court to assume that the same or greater productivity in arresting drunk drivers could have been achieved by distributing the 35 officers at various places throughout the city for the sole purpose of observing erratic driving and stopping and checking drunk drivers. In my judgment, the trial court correctly concluded that the State failed in its burden of proof in establishing that the roadblock/checkpoint promoted the public interest in light of available less drastic alternative measures which could have been used by the officers to combat the problem, without setting up a roadblock and stopping between 2,000 and 3,000 motorists.

COMMENTS

1. The majority opinion enunciates a number of standards to be applied to discern whether a particular roadblock is reasonable. Although the list of factors certainly is comprehensive, do they really provide all that much guidance?

2. Would it be constitutional for all those stopped at a roadblock to be given a quick breathalyzer test? An argument in favor of this proposition might contend that there is a much greater infringement on individual liberty from being stopped than from blowing into an instrument.

National Treasury Employees Union v. Von Raab, 103, L. Ed. 2d 685 (1989)

Justice Kennedy delivered the opinion of the Court.

The United States Customs Service, a bureau of the Department of Treasury, is the federal agency responsible for processing persons, carriers, cargo, and mail into the United States, collecting revenue from imports, and enforcing customs and related laws. An important responsibility of the Service is the interdiction and seizure of contraband, including illegal drugs. In 1987 alone, Customs agents seized drugs with a retail value of nearly 9 billion dollars. In the routine discharge of their duties, many customs employers have direct contact with those who traffic in drugs for profit. Drug import operations, often directed by sophisticated criminal syndicates, may be affected by violence or its threats. As a necessary response, many Customs operatives carry and use firearms in connection with their official duties.

. . . .

In May 1986, the Commissioner announced implementation of [a] drug testing program. Drug tests were made a condition of placement or employment for positions that meet one or more . . . criteria. The first is direct involvement in drug interdiction or enforcement of related laws. . . . The second criterion is a requirement that the incumbent carry firearms, as the Commissioner concluded that "public safety demands that employees who carry deadly arms and are prepared to make instant life or death decisions be drug free. . . .

. . . .

Customs employees who test positive for drugs and who can offer no satisfactory explanation are subject to dismissal from the Service. Test results may not, however, be turned over to any other agency, including criminal prosecutors, without the employee's written consent.

In *Skinner v. Railway Labor Executives' Assn.*, decided today, we hold that federal regulations requiring employees of private railroads to produce urine samples for chemical testing implicate the Fourth Amendment, as those tests invade reasonable expectations of privacy. . . . [I]n view of our holding in *Railway Labor Executives'* that urine tests are searches, it follows that the Customs Service's drug testing program must meet the reasonable requirement of the Fourth Amendment.

. . . As we note in *Railway Labor Executives'*, our cases establish that where a Fourth Amendment intrusion serves special governmental needs, beyond the normal need for law enforcement, it is necessary to balance the individual's privacy expectations against the Government's interest to determine whether it is impractical to require . . . some level of individualized suspicion in the particular context.

. . . .

The Customs Service is our Nation's first line of defense against one of the greatest problems affecting the health and welfare of our population. . . .

Many of the Service's employees are often exposed to . . . criminal elements and to the controlled substances they seek to smuggle into the country. The physical safety of these employees may be threatened, and many may be tempted not only by bribes from the traffickers with whom they deal, but also by their own access to vast sources of valuable contraband seized and controlled by the Service. The Commissioner indicated . . . that Customs officers have been shot, stabbed, run over, dragged by automobiles, and assaulted with blunt objects while performing their duties. At least nine officers have died in the line of duty since 1974. He also noted that Customs officers have been the targets of bribery by drug smugglers on numerous occasions, and several have been removed from the Service for accepting bribes and other integrity violations. . . .

It is readily apparent that the Government has a compelling interest in ensuring that front-line interdiction personnel are physically fit, and have unimpeachable integrity and judgment. . . . A drug user's indifference to the Service's basic mission or, even worse, his active complicity with the malefactors, can facilitate importation of sizable drug shipments or block apprehension of dangerous criminals. The public interest demands effective measures to bar drug users from positions directly involving the interdiction of illegal drugs.

The public interest likewise demands effective measures to prevent the promotion of drug users to positions that require the incumbent to carry a firearm, even if the incumbent is not engaged directly in the interdiction of drugs. Customs employees who may use deadly force plainly discharge duties fraught with such risks of injury to others that even a momentary lapse of attention can have disastrous consequences. We agree with the Government that the public should not bear the risk that employees who may suffer from impaired perception and judgment will be promoted to

positions where they may need to employ deadly force. . . .

Against these valid public interests we must weigh the interference with individual liberty that results from requiring these classes of employees to undergo a urine test. The interference with individual privacy that results from the collection of a urine sample for subsequent chemical analysis could be substantial in some circumstances. . . .

We think Customs employees who are directly involved in the interdiction of illegal drugs or who are required to carry firearms in the line of duty . . . have a diminished expectation of privacy in respect to the intrusions occasioned by a urine test. Unlike most private citizens or government employees in general, employees involved in drug interdiction reasonably should expect effective inquiry into their fitness and probity. Much the same is true of employees who are required to carry firearms. Because successful performance of their duties depends uniquely on their judgment and dexterity, these employees cannot reasonably expect to keep from the Service personal information that bears directly on their fitness. While reasonable tests designed to elicit this information doubtless infringe some privacy expectations, we do not believe these expectations outweigh the Government's compelling interests in safety and in the integrity of the borders.

. . . .

Without disparaging the importance of the governmental interests that support the suspicionless searches of these employees, petitioners nevertheless contend that the Service's drug testing program is unreasonable in two particulars. First petitioners argue that the program is unjustified because it is not based on a belief that testing will reveal any drug use by covered employees. In pressing this argument, petitioners point out that the Service's testing scheme was not implemented in response to any perceived drug problem among Customs employees, and that the program actually has not led to the discovery of a significant number of drug users. Counsel for petitioners informed us at oral argument that no more than 5 employees out of 3,600 have tested positive for drugs. Second, petitioners contend that the Service's scheme is not a sufficiently productive mechanism to justify its intrusion upon Fourth Amendment interests because illegal drug users can avoid detection with ease by temporary abstinence or by surreptitious adulteration of their urine specimens. These contentions are unpersuasive.

Petitioner's first contention evinces an unduly narrow view of the context in which the Service's testing program was implemented. Petitioners do not dispute, nor can there be doubt, that drug abuse is one of the most serious problems confronting our society today. There is little reason to believe that American workplaces are immune from their pervasive social problem. . . . Detecting drug impairment on the part of employees can be a difficult task, especially where, as here, it is not feasible to subject employees and their work-product to the kind of day-to-day scrutiny that is the norm in more traditional office environments. . . .

The mere circumstance that all but a few of the employees tested are entirely innocent of wrongdoing does not impugn the program's validity. . . . The Service's program is designed to prevent the promotion of drug users to sensitive positions as much as it is designed to detect those employees who use drugs. Where, as here, the possible harm against which the Government seeks to guard is substantial, the need to prevent its occurrence furnishes an ample justification for reasonable searches calculated to advance the Government's goal.

. . . .

We think petitioners' second argument—that the Service's testing program is ineffective because employees may attempt to deceive the test by a brief ab-

stention before the test date, or by adultering their urine specimens—overstates the case. As the Court of Appeals noted, addicts may be unable to abstain even for a limited period of time, or may be unaware of the "fade-away effect" of certain drugs. . . .

. . . .

We hold that the suspicionless testing of employees who apply for promotion to positions directly involving the interdiction of illegal drugs, or to positions which require the incumbent to carry a firearm, is reasonable. The Government's compelling interests in preventing the promotion of drug users to positions where they might endanger the integrity of our Nation's borders or the life of the citizenry outweigh the privacy interests of those who seek promotion to these positions, who enjoy a diminished expectation of privacy by virtue of the special, and obvious, physical and ethical demands of those positions. . . .

Justice Scalia, with whom Justice Stevens joins, dissenting.

. . . .

Until today this Court had upheld a bodily search separate from arrest and without individualized suspicion of wrongdoing only with respect to prison inmates, relying upon the uniquely dangerous nature of that environment. See *Bell v. Wolfish*, 441 U.S. 520 (1979). Today, in *Skinner*, we allow a less intrusive bodily search of railroad employees involved in train accidents. I joined the Court's opinion there because the demonstrated frequency of drug and alcohol use by the targeted class of employees, and the demonstrated connection between such use and grave harm, rendered the search a reasonable means of protecting society. I decline to join the Court's opinion in the present case because neither frequency of use nor connection to harm is demonstrated or even likely. In my view, the Customs Service rules are a kind of immolation of privacy and human dignity in symbolic opposition to drug use.

. . . .

The Court's opinion in the present case . . . will be searched in vain for real evidence of a real problem that will be solved by urine testing of Customs Service employees. Instead, there are assurances that "the Customs Service is our Nation's first line of defense against one of the greatest problems affecting the health and welfare of our population"; that "many of the Service's employees are often exposed to [drug smugglers] and to the controlled substances they seek to smuggle into the country"; that "Customs officers have been the targets of bribery by drug smugglers on numerous occasions, and several have been removed from the Service for accepting bribes and other integrity violations"; . . . that the "national interest in self protection could be irreparably damaged if those charged with safeguarding it were, because of their own drug use, unsympathetic to their mission of interdicting narcotics. . . ." To paraphrase Churchill, all this contains much that is obviously true, and much that is relevant; unfortunately, what is obviously true is not relevant, and what is relevant is not obviously true. The only pertinent points, it seems to me, are supported by nothing but speculation, and not very plausible speculation at that. It is not apparent to me that a Customs Service employee who uses drugs is significantly more likely to be bribed by a drug smuggler, any more than a Customs Service employee who wears diamonds is significantly more likely to be bribed by a diamond smuggler. . . .

What is absent from the Government's justifications—notably absent, revealingly absent, and as far as I am concerned dispositively absent—is the recitation of even a single instance in which any of the speculated horribles actually occurred: an instance, that is, in which the cause of bribetaking, or of poor aim, or of unsympathetic law enforcement . . . was drug use. Although the Court points out that several employees have in the past been removed from the Service for accepting bribes and other integrity violations, and that at least

nine officers have died in the line of duty since 1974, there is no indication whatever that these incidents were related to drug use by Service employees. . . .

. . . I do not believe for a minute that the driving force behind these drug-testing rules was any of the feeble justifications put forward by counsel here and accepted by the Court. The only plausible explanation, in my view, is what the Commissioner himself offered in the concluding sentence of his memorandum to Customs Service employees announcing the program: "Implementation of the drug screening program would set an important example in our country's struggle with this most serious threat to our national health and security." Or as respondent's brief to this Court asserted: "if a law enforcement agency and its employees do not take the law seriously, neither will the public on which the agency's effectiveness depends." What better way to show the Government is serious about its "war on drugs" than to subject its employees on the front line of that war to this invasion of their privacy and affront to their dignity? To be sure, there is only a slight chance that it will prevent some serious public harm resulting from Service employee drug use—most important of all—it will demonstrate the determination of the Government to eliminate this scourge of our society! I think it obvious that this justification is unacceptable; that the impairment of individual liberties cannot be the means of making a point; that symbolism, even symbolism for so worthy a cause as the abolition of unlawful drugs, cannot validate an otherwise unreasonable search.

. . . Experience should teach us to be most on our guard to protect liberty when the Government's purposes are beneficent. Men born to freedom are naturally alert to repel invasion of their liberty by evil-minded rulers. The greatest dangers to liberty lurk in insidious encroachment by men of zeal, well-meaning but without understanding. Those who lose because of the lack of understanding that begot the present exercise in symbolism are not just the Customs Service employees, whose dignity is thus offended, but all of us—who suffer a coarsening of our national manners that ultimately give the Fourth Amendment its content, and who become subject to the administration of federal officials whose respect for our privacy can hardly be greater than the small respect they have been taught to have for their own.

COMMENTS

1. In the majority opinion, Justice Kennedy suggested that Customs Service employees had a diminished expectation of privacy. Do you think this is necessarily true? Would not the lawsuit against the drug-testing program indicate the opposite?

2. Reference is made in *National Treasury Employees Union* to a companion case, *Skinner v. Railway Labor Executives' Association*. In *Railway Labor Executives' Association*, the Court upheld Federal Railroad Administration regulations that required drug and alcohol testing of railroad employees who operated a train that was involved in an accident.

3. After *National Treasury*, is it clear what government employees can now be tested for drugs? What about employees in the private sphere?

4. Do employers have a right to know whether their employees have used drugs? What else do they have a right to know about their employees?

Long Beach City Emp. v. City of Long Beach, 227 Cal. Rptr. 90 (1986)

Justice Broussard delivered the opinion of the Court.

· ·

Long Beach City Employees Association (hereinafter CEA) brings this lawsuit on behalf of a group of public employees who assert that orders by defendant City of Long Beach (hereinafter City) to submit to polygraph examinations violate their rights of privacy. CEA sues to enjoin such examinations in the future.

[$218 was found missing from municipal vending machines. An investigation was conducted, and certain city employees interrogated, but there was not enough evidence to arrest anyone. The city then ordered all those with keys to these machines to submit to polygraph examination.]

· ·

If there is a quintessential zone of human privacy, it is the mind. Our ability to exclude others from our mental processes is intrinsic to the human personality. . . .

A polygraph examination is specifically designed to overcome this privacy by compelling communication of "thoughts, sentiments, and emotions" which the examinee may have chosen not to communicate. The standard polygraph test is far more intrusive than a series of questions related directly to the employee's job performance or knowledge of the crimes under investigation. When an employee first arrives for an examination, he or she is typically seated in a reception area for several minutes where, unbeknownst to the employee, observation has already begun. During this period the employee's behavior is observed to evaluate his or her attitude toward the examination, whether hostile or cooperative. This evaluation becomes part of the guilt determination.

A pretest interview is then administered by the polygraph examiner to determine whether there are "any emotional or psychological factors which would adversely affect the reliability of test results." The type of questions that must be asked to make this determination are highly personal and are unrelated to the employee's official duties. . . .

In the instant case, the following questions appeared on the pretest interview transcript of a Bureau employee: "Ever been arrested for any reason? . . . Any history of heart trouble or epilepsy? . . . Under the care of a doctor now for any reason? . . . Ever been treated by or consulted a psychiatrist for any reason? . . . Have you ever experimented with any type of drugs—reds, whites, LSD, heroin, or cocaine? . . . Have you ever smoked marijuana in your life? . . . When was the last time?"

Physical instruments are then attached to the examinee's body: "The subject is seated in a chair specially constructed to permit the attachment of the various measuring devices: the pneumograph tube is tied to his chest, the blood-pressure cuff is wrapped round his upper arm, and a set of electrodes is attached to his hands. The subject looks straight ahead. The examiner is seated to his side behind a desk containing a set of controls which the subject cannot see. These instruments begin a continuous graphic recording when the examination commences."

The test questions that are then administered include a "control question" calculated to cause the subject to lie. The purpose is to provide the examiner with a recorded example of deception that can be used to judge the subject's answers to other questions. . . .

A typical control question is, "Did you ever steal anything?" If the answer given is "no," the examiner is then directed to question the subject concerning attempted thefts and thefts committed during childhood. It has been stated that "[t]he polygraph technique forces an individual to incriminate himself and confess to past actions which are not pertinent to the current investigation. He must dredge up his past so he can approach the polygraph machine with an untroubled soul. The polygraph operator and his supervisors then decide whether to refer derogatory information to other agencies or officials." Where polygraph testing is used as a preemployment screening device, "fishing expeditions" and shockingly intrusive questions have been reported.

The intrusiveness of polygraph questions on private matters is exacerbated by three factors that make the process fundamentally different from verbal interrogation. First, the polygraph merely records general emotional arousal. It cannot distinguish anxiety or indignation from guilt. Thus, repressed beliefs, guilt feelings and fantasized events—not just actual events—can be discovered by a polygraph. Second, an employee who is asked an embarrassing personal question may be reluctant to refuse to answer it for fear of appearing dishonest. The coercive circumstances of a polygraph test thus compel employees to divulge private information for fear of losing their jobs. Finally, even if an employee chooses not to verbally answer a question on a personal matter, the polygraph will record his or her psychological response in any event. Intrusion occurs because the polygraph device continuously records the monitored physiological functions. Consequently, an examinee cannot prevent a response to a test question even by remaining silent.

The City contends that privacy concerns are not implicated by the polygraph examinations at issue here because the questions asked of its employees related directly and narrowly to performance of their official duties. The City is correct that a public employee may be required—on pain of dismissal—to answer questions specifically, directly, and narrowly relating to the performance of his official duties. We cannot agree, however, that all of the questions asked of employees here can be so characterized. If the City had demanded only that its employees answer questions pertaining directly to performance of their duties upon pain of dismissal, without using the intrusive intermediary of polygraph testing, this case would be entirely different. . . .

· ·

We conclude that the Bureau's orders to its employees to submit to polygraph examinations as a condition of their employment intruded upon the employees' constitutionally protected zone of individual privacy and also violated their right to equal protection under the law.

COMMENTS

1. I would assume that many students think that drug testing of employees is perfectly legal.

Is not a polygraph test simply an extension of this principle? Do employers have a right to find out what kind of person you *really* are? Should employers be able to find out if you have engaged in criminal activity?

2. In 1988 Congress passed legislation that bans the use of most lie detector tests by private-sector employers. Only companies providing security services for specified purposes and those manufacturing and distributing controlled drugs are exempted from the ban. Polygraph tests are also allowed in connection with an ongoing criminal investigation if the employer has a reasonable suspicion that one of her workers was involved in a crime that caused economic harm to the company. Any such examination would have to be conducted under strict conditions, with no questions about personal beliefs and sexual behavior.

In all cases, these test results cannot be the sole basis for the firing or demotion of the individual. Finally, federal, state, and local units of government are exempt from the ban, as are consultants to national security agencies. Is this legislation unduly infringing on an employer's right to know?

School Board of Nassau County v. Arline, 480 U.S. 273 (1987)

Justice Brennan delivered the opinion of the Court.

[In 1957 Gene Arline was hospitalized for tuberculosis. For the next twenty years the disease was in remission. However, in 1977 and in 1979 a culture revealed that tuberculosis was active in her system again. The Nassau County school system terminated Arline's job as an elementary school teacher because of tuberculosis. Arline challenged this discharge.]

Section 504 of the Rehabilitation Act of 1973, prohibits a federally funded state

program from discriminating against a handicapped individual solely by reason of his or her handicap. This case presents the questions whether a person afflicted with tuberculosis, a contagious disease, may be considered a "handicapped individual" within the meaning of Sec. 504 of the Act, and, if so, whether such an individual is "otherwise qualified" to teach elementary school.

· ·

Section 504 of the Rehabilitation Act reads in pertinent part:

No otherwise qualified handicapped individual in the United States . . . shall, solely by reason of his handicap, be excluded from participation in, be denied the benefits of, or be subjected to discrimination under any program or activity receiving Federal financial assistance.

In 1974 Congress expanded the definition of "handicapped individual" for use in Sec. 504 to read as follows:

[A]ny person who (i) has a physical or mental impairment which substantially limits one or more of such person's major life activities, (ii) has a record of such an impairment, or (iii) is regarded as having such an impairment.

The amended definition reflected Congress' concern with protecting the handicapped against discrimination stemming not only from simple prejudice, but from "archaic attitudes and laws" and from "the fact that the American people are simply unfamiliar with and insensitive to the difficulties confront[ing] individuals with handicaps." S. Rep. No. 93–1297, p. 50 (1974). To combat the effects of erroneous but nevertheless prevalent perceptions about the handicapped, Congress expanded the definition of "handicapped individual" so as to preclude discrimination against "[a] person who has a record of, or is regarded as having, an impairment [but who] may at present have no actual incapacity at all."

. . . .

Petitioners concede that a contagious disease may constitute a handicapping condition to the extent that it leaves a person with "diminished physical or mental capabilities," and concede that Arline's hospitalization for tuberculosis in 1957 demonstrates that she has a record of physical impairment. Petitioners maintain, however, Arline's record of impairment is irrelevant in this case, since the School Board dismissed Arline not because of her diminished physical capabilities, but because of the threat that her relapses of tuberculosis posed to the health of others.

We do not agree with petitioners that, in defining a handicapped individual under

Sec. 504, the contagious effects of a disease can be meaningfully distinguished from the disease's physical effects on a claimant in a case such as this. Arline's contagiousness and her physical impairment each resulted from the same underlying condition, tuberculosis. It would be unfair to allow an employer to seize upon the distinction between the effects of a disease on others and the effects of a disease on a patient and use that distinction to justify discriminatory treatment.[1]

Nothing in the legislative history of Sec. 504 suggests that Congress intended such a result. That history demonstrates that Congress was as concerned about the effect of an impairment on others as it was about its effect on the individual. Congress extended coverage to those individuals who are simply "regarded as having" a physical or mental impairment. The Senate Report provides as an example of a person who would be covered under this subsection "a person with some kind of visible physical impairment which in fact does not substantially limit that person's functioning." Such an impairment might not diminish a person's physical or mental capabilities, but could nevertheless substantially limit that person's ability to work as a result of the negative reactions of others to the impairment.

---

[1] The United States argues that it is possible for a person to be simply a carrier of a disease, that is, to be capable of spreading a disease without having a "physical impairment" or suffering from any other symptoms associated with the disease. The United States contends that this is true in the case of some carriers of the Acquired Immune Deficiency Syndrome (AIDS) virus. From this premise the United States concludes that discrimination solely on the basis of contagiousness is never discrimination on the basis of a handicap. The argument is misplaced in this case, because the handicap here, tuberculosis, gave rise both to a physical impairment and to contagiousness. This case does not present, and we therefore do not reach, the questions whether a carrier of a contagious disease such as AIDS could be considered to have a physical impairment, or whether such a person could be considered, solely on the basis of contagiousness, a handicapped person as defined by the Act.

Allowing discrimination based on the contagious effects of a physical impairment would be inconsistent with the basic purpose of Sec. 504, which is to ensure that handicapped individuals are not denied jobs or other benefits because of the prejudiced attitudes or the ignorance of others. By amending the definition of "handicapped individual" to include not only those who are actually physically impaired, but also those who are regarded as impaired and who, as a result, are substantially limited in a major life activity, Congress acknowledged that society's accumulated myths and fears about disability and disease are as handicapping as are the physical limitations that flow from actual impairment. Few aspects of a handicap give rise to the same level of public fear and misapprehension as contagiousness. Even those who suffer or have recovered from such noninfectious diseases as epilepsy or cancer have faced discrimination based on the irrational fear that they might be contagious. The Act is carefully structured to replace such reflexive reactions to actual or perceived handicaps with actions based on reasoned and medically sound judgments: the definition of "handicapped individual" is broad, but only those individuals who are both handicapped and otherwise qualified are eligible for relief. The fact that some persons who have contagious diseases may pose a serious health threat to others under certain circumstances does not justify excluding from the coverage of the Act all persons with actual or perceived contagious diseases. Such exclusion would mean that those accused of being contagious would never have the opportunity to have their condition evaluated in light of medical evidence and a determination made as to whether they were "otherwise qualified." Rather, they would be vulnerable to discrimination on the basis of mythology—precisely the type of injury Congress sought to prevent. We conclude that the fact that a person with a record of a physical impairment is also contagious does not suffice to remove that person from coverage under Sec. 504.

COMMENTS

1. Despite Justice Brennan's assertion that AIDS was not the issue in this case, *Arline* was labeled the AIDS case when it was decided. Simply stated, should people with AIDS be able to maintain their jobs? Go to school?

2. Let us turn to testing of another kind: AIDS testing. Recently there have been proposals to automatically test individuals applying for marriage licenses as well as immigrants (why immigrants?) and prison inmates. In fact, there has even been discussion about mandatory testing for all people. Would you mandate testing, and if so, for whom?

3. Much of this discussion of AIDS testing may be meaningless because it appears as if many individuals are being tested without their knowledge or consent. "AIDS Testing Without Consent Reported," *New York Times*, January 9, 1988, p. 7.

4. An interesting ethical question has been raised by the New York state policy of providing needles to drug addicts, the rationale being that this would help prevent the spread of AIDS among intravenous drug user population. Should the state be doing this?

5. A survey taken in early 1988 showed a number of public misperceptions about AIDS ("Survey Finds Wide AIDS Ignorance," *New York Times*, January 30, 1988, p. 7). In particular, a large portion of the public believed that AIDS could be spread by casual contact. In Kokomo, Indiana, parents boycotted classes to prevent AIDS-infected Ryan White from attending classes. Should a court of law be sensitive to public opinion in determining whether schools should admit AIDS victims, even if such opinion is based on misperception? What is a proper role for courts to play here?

6. One of the concerns expressed by civil libertarians is that those with AIDS should have their confidentiality protected in order to prevent discrimination. I assume all are in agreement with confidentiality in theory. What should the state do, however, when it has some reason to believe that certain afflicted individuals are continuing to have sexual relations with others? Among the questions to consider are these: should the government attempt to monitor the sexual practices of those with AIDS? Does the

government have an affirmative duty to warn the sexual partners of those with AIDS about this condition, or should the state wait until it has some solid evidence that the AIDS victim has not done this? Where does the right to privacy fit in here?

7. Marc Christian, Rock Hudson's former lover, was awarded $21.75 million in damages by a jury in a suit for emotional distress. The basis for the suit by Christian was that Hudson had not disclosed to him that he, Hudson, was afflicted with AIDS. Hudson died in 1986, and thus far Christian has not tested positive for the AIDS virus. Is this award justified?

5

VICTIMLESS CRIMES

This last chapter in Part I examines the appropriateness and wisdom of laws prohibiting what have been termed "victimless crimes"—crimes that purportedly harm only the individual committing the unlawful act (if they do in fact cause any harm at all). Is it any of the law's business if someone likes to gamble, for example, or if another finds it desirable to sell her body for sexual favors, or another enjoys getting high on drugs?[1] As noted, American Liberalism is based on the notion of each individual pursuing her own version of the good, unless and until she threatens to harm others. This sentiment was best expressed by John Stuart Mill in his famous essay *On Liberty*. "The only purpose for which power can rightfully be exercised over any member of a civilised community against his will is to prevent harm to others."

Despite these sentiments, does the government have a duty to protect us from our own folly? If so, how does this duty arise, and what if we do not want such protection? If there is such a duty, does it apply to every folly, or just some, and how do we reasonably draw a line here? Where does the right to privacy fit into all of this, or is talk of a right to privacy misplaced in this context?

One of the first questions to ask is whether victimless crimes actually do harm anyone. Consider the issue in the first case, *Ravin v. State,* a case involving the constitutionality of a law proscribing possession of marijuana. Are drugs necessarily harmful to individuals? In this day and age of "Just Say NO," and "crack" in our inner cities, we might be hard pressed to say that drugs do not harm the individual who takes them.[2] A majority of the Supreme Court of Alaska, however, concluded that the evidence of harm from marijuana was inconclusive enough to prohibit its use and possession in the privacy of a person's home. In that vein, could the same be said for other drugs as well?

Assuming for the sake of argument that we agree that drugs necessarily harm the individual, and again assuming that the law has a duty to protect the individual from harm that she might bring upon herself, why is it that the law protects only against certain kinds of self-inflicted harms but not others? In Part II we will be examining a cigarette smoking liability case, but the question posed at this time is that if the government is so certain that cigarette smoking is harmful to our health, as warning labels on cigarettes strongly indicate, why does it not prohibit the cultivation of tobacco and its use? The same kind of question might be asked, and should be asked, of alcohol. This drug has caused far more damage to American society than illegal drugs have. Why do we not prohibit the sale and use of alcohol? The answer might be that we have tried and failed. Does this mean, however, that we only prohibit what we might be able to prohibit (drugs), but we ignore those things that cause harm that we cannot prohibit (alcohol) or do not have the political will to do so (tobacco)? How else can we explain the kinds of distinctions that American society has apparently made here?

State v. Mueller involved another so-called victimless crime: prostitution. Note the unique defense presented by the accused in this case, namely, that her activities were protected by the right to privacy. Is she really so far off the mark? Apparently the Supreme Court of Hawaii did not think so, nor did the state legislature, although both felt compelled to maintain the status quo. Return to the issue of harm and whether prostitution is a victimless crime or not. Is this not simply sex between two consenting adults, albeit for a fee? Is it any different from the *Bowers* situation, with probably even *less* public moral approbation (under the surface at least)? But can we really describe prostitution as a "victimless crime" when studies find that most prostitutes were abused as children and that many prostitutes have been raped at some point in their lives?[3] On the other hand, is it not possible to separate the prostitute from the act of prostitution?

One of the charges made against the criminal prohibitions in victimless crimes is that they are simply a means by which the state enforces private morality. Consider gambling. How do we explain laws against gambling? Who is the victim? Is it the foolhardy individual? Perhaps, but individuals throw good money away all the time in this consumer-crazy society, and no one wants to legislate against this kind of thing. Some have made the argument that gambling aids organized crime, and for that reason it ought to be prohibited. Would not the fight against organized crime be much more successful if all forms of gambling were *legalized*? In addition, is there not more than a touch of hypocrisy in the legalization of *some* forms of gambling—lotteries for example—but in the prohibition of other forms? What does this say about the state's role in protecting the individual from harming herself?

The last case in this chapter, *Rutherford v. U.S.*, involved a "miracle" drug from a few years ago—laetrile. There were many who believed that laetrile was a cure for cancer. The U.S. government, however, disagreed with this conclusion, and it refused to allow laetrile to be sold or imported into the United States. As a result, some U.S. citizens traveled to other countries, usually Mexico, to obtain the drug. Glen Rutherford decided to fight the prohibition in the courtroom. Although this particular decision (later overturned) concerned itself with the effectiveness of laetrile (and, again, the question of judicial capacity should be raised), is this not really a right to privacy case? If desperate individuals are able to *end* their own lives, as they were in *Quinlan*, why should individuals not be able to attempt to *save* their own lives by whatever means that they want to? What interests does the state have here? Are there state interests aside from the possibility of physical harm to the individual? Do they outweigh an individual's right to privacy or, if not that, an individual's right to life or subsistence?

NOTES

1. For an extensive discussion of many of the issues raised in this chapter, see Gilbert Geis, *Not the Law's Business: An Examination of Homosexuality, Abortion, Prostitution, Narcotics, and Gambling in the United States* (New York: Schocken Books, 1979).

2. For an argument that drugs do not cause nearly the harm that they are reported to cause, see David A. J. Richards, *Sex, Drugs, Death, and the Law: An Essay on Human Rights and Overcriminalization* (Totowa, N. J.: Rowman and Littlefield, 1982).

3. See Nancy Erbe, "Prostitutes: Victims of Men's Exploitation and Abuse," *Law and Inequality* 2:609–28 (1984). At one point Erbe writes, "In studies of prostitutes' childhood abuse, inside and outside of prostitutes' families, 72.2% of the prostitutes interviewed reported having bad sexual experiences forced upon them; 84.7% of these experiences occurred when the women were 15 or younger; 49.5% reported that men had raped them; and 16.7% were raped more than once." At p. 614, note 36.

Ravin v. State, 537 P. 2d 499 (1975)

Chief Justice Rabinowitz delivered the opinion of the Court.

[Defendant Ravin was arrested for possession of marijuana.]

. . . .

Here Ravin raises two basic claims: first, that there is no legitimate state interest in prohibiting possession of marijuana by adults for personal use, in view of the right to privacy; and secondly, that the statutory classification of marijuana as a dangerous drug, while use of alcohol and tobacco is not prohibited, denies him due process and equal protection of law.

. . . .

The home . . . carries with it associations and meanings which make it particularly important as the situs of privacy. Privacy in the home is a fundamental right, under both the federal and Alaska constitutions. We do not mean by this that a person may do anything at any time as long as the activity takes place within a person's home. There are two important limitations on this facet of the right to privacy. First, we agree with the Supreme Court of the United States, which has strictly limited the *Stanley* guarantee to possession for purely private, noncommercial use in the home. And secondly, we think this right must yield when it interferes in a serious manner with the health, safety, rights and privileges of others or with the public welfare. No one has an absolute right to do things in the privacy of his own home which will affect himself or others adversely. Indeed, one aspect of a private matter is that it is private, that is, that it does not adversely affect persons beyond the actor, and hence is none of their business. When a matter does affect the public, directly or indirectly, it loses its wholly private character, and can be made to yield when an appropriate public need is demonstrated.

Thus, we conclude that citizens of the State of Alaska have a basic right to privacy in their homes under Alaska's constitution. This right to privacy would encompass the possession and ingestion of substances such as marijuana in a purely personal, noncommercial context in the home unless the State can meet its substantial burden and show that proscription of possession of marijuana in the home is supportable by achievement of a legitimate state interest.

This leads us to the second facet of our inquiry, namely, whether the State has demonstrated sufficient justification for the prohibition of possession of marijuana in general in the interest of public welfare; and further, whether the State has met the greater burden of showing a close and substantial relationship between the public welfare and control of ingestion or possession of marijuana in the home for personal use.

The evidence which was presented at the hearing before the district court consisted primarily of several expert witnesses familiar with various medical and social aspects of marijuana use. . . .

Marijuana is the common term for dried leaves or stalk of the plant *Cannabis sativa L.* The primary psychoactive ingredient in the plant is delta-9-tetrahydrocannabinol (THC). Most marijuana available in the United States has a THC content of less than one percent. Other cannabis derivatives with a higher THC content, such as hashish, are available in the United States although much less common than is marijuana.

According to figures published by the National Commission on Marihuana and Drug Abuse in 1973, an estimated 26 million Americans have used marijuana at least once. The incidence generally cuts across social and economic classes, though use is greatest among young persons (55% of 18–21 year-olds have used it). . . .

. . . .

The short-term physiological effects are relatively undisputed. An immediate slight increase in the pulse, decrease in salivation, and a slight reddening of the eyes are usually noted. There is also impairment of psychomotor control. These effects generally end within two to three hours of the end of smoking.

Long-term physiological effects raise more controversy among the experts. The National Commission on Marihuana and Drug Abuse reported that among users "no significant physical, biochemical, or mental abnormalities could be attributed solely to their marijuana smoking." Certain researchers have pointed to possible deleterious effects on the body's immune defenses, on the chromosomal structures of users, and on testosterone levels in the body. The methodology of certain of these studies has been extensively criticized by other qualified medical scientists, however. These studies cannot be ignored. It should be noted that most of the damage suggested by these studies comes in the context of intensive use of concentrated forms of THC. It appears that the use of marijuana, as it is presently used in the United States today, does not constitute a public health problem of any significant dimensions. It is, for instance, far more innocuous in terms of physiological and social damage than alcohol or tobacco. But the studies suggesting dangers in intensive cannabis use do raise valid doubts which cannot be dismissed or discounted.

. . . .

The National Commission rejected the notion that marijuana is physically addicting. It also rejected the notion that marijuana as used in the United States today presents a significant risk of causing psychological dependency in the user. Rather, the experimental or intermittent user develops little or no psychological dependence. Lengthy use on a regular basis does present a risk of such dependence and of subsequent heavier use, and strong psychological dependence is characteristic of heavy users in other countries. This pattern of use is rare in the United States today, however.

. . . .

. . . [I]mplicit in the State's catalogue of possible dangers of marijuana use is the assumption that the State has the authority to protect the individual from his own folly, that is, that the State can control activities which present no harm to anyone except those enjoying them. Although some courts have found the "public interest" to be broad enough to justify protecting the individual against himself, most have found inherent limitations on the police power of the State. . . .

. . . .

The state cannot impose its own notions of morality, propriety, or fashion on in-

dividuals when the public has no legitimate interest in the affairs of those individuals. The right of the individual to do as he pleases is not absolute, of course: it can be made to yield when it begins to infringe on the rights and welfare of others.

. . . .

Thus we conclude that no adequate justification for the state's intrusion into the citizen's right to privacy by its prohibition of possession of marijuana by an adult for personal consumption in the home has been shown. The privacy of the individual's home cannot be breached absent a persuasive showing of a close and substantial relationship of the intrusion to a legitimate governmental interest. Here, mere scientific doubts will not suffice. The state must demonstrate a need based on proof that the public health or welfare will in fact suffer if the controls are not applied.

COMMENTS

1. As you might guess, *Ravin* is an anomaly in American law. Do you agree or disagree with its result? With its reasoning? Note that the court took the position that doubts about the safety of marijuana should not be allowed to interfere with an individual's right to privacy. Many claim, however, that medical evidence presents more than doubts about marijuana use. For example, see Curtis L. Janeczek, *Marijuana: Time for a Closer Look* (Columbus, Ohio: Healthstar, 1980).

2. How would a member of the Alaska Supreme Court know so much about marijuana and its effects?

3. At one point in his opinion Judge Rabinowitz writes: "The State cannot impose its own notions of morality, propriety, or fashion on individuals when the public has no legitimate interest in the affairs of those individuals. The right of the individual to do as he pleases is not absolute, of course; it can be made to yield when it begins to infringe on the rights and welfare of others."

What do you make of this argument? In his opinion Judge Rabinowitz makes reference to laws on the mandatory use of motorcycle helmets. Are such restrictions to protect the general public? Are not such laws, instead, to protect the foolhardy individual who drives without one? Should the law protect an individual from his/her own foolishness?

4. Are you convinced that marijuana is as innocuous as the Alaska Supreme Court thinks it is? Do you think Judge Rabinowitz could/should make the same argument for cocaine? LSD? Heroin?

5. How is it that people can smoke cigarettes and drink alcohol, but they cannot use drugs such as cocaine? Does this dichotomy reflect strange (and conflicting) societal values?

6. The state of Massachusetts now has a law that prohibits firefighters and police personnel from smoking, period, whether on or off the job. The state's policy is based on the increased insurance risks and costs that smoking causes, for which the state previously had to pay. Is this fair? Is this an invasion of an individual's right to privacy?

7. Finally, I am sure that all of you are aware of the heated battle going on in various places between cigarette smokers and nonsmokers. Both claim to be protected by a right. Is this a perversion of the idea of having a right, or do both groups really have a right (and if so, what is it)?

State v. Mueller, 671 P. 2d 1351 (1983)

Judge Nakamura delivered the opinion of the Court.

The defendant was charged in the District Court of the First Circuit that she "did engage in, or agree to engage in, sexual conduct with another person, in return for a fee, in violation of Section 712-1200 of the Hawaii Revised Statutes." She moved to dismiss the charge, asserting a "constitutional right to privacy for activities that were conducted in the privacy of her own home." At the hearing on the motion the parties entered into a stipulation of facts, agreeing that the activity in question took place in Lauren Mueller's apartment, the participants were willing adults, and there were "no signs of advertising" anywhere in the apartment building.

The defendant's argument to the court was that the activity's private setting and the absence of public solicitation set her case apart "from every other prostitution case." And she maintained a decision to engage in sex with "a voluntary adult companion" was "well within her constitutional right to privacy." The district court, however, found her argument unpersuasive, ruled the State had a "compelling interest in controlling prostitution in private residences as well as on the streets," and denied the motion.

. . . .

The United States Constitution contains "no express provisions guaranteeing to persons the right to carry on their lives protected from the 'vicissitudes of the political process' by a zone of privacy or a right of personhood." L. Tribe, *American Constitutional Law* 893 (1978). But in *Griswold v. Connecticut*, 381 U.S. 479 (1965), the Supreme Court found "that specific guarantees in the Bill of Rights have penumbras, formed by emanations from those guarantees that help give them life and substance," 381 U.S. at 484, and concluded "[v]arious guarantees create zones of privacy." Id. The marriage relationship, it held, was one "lying within the zone of privacy created by several fundamental constitutional guarantees." 381 U.S. at 485.

And the Connecticut statute forbidding the use of contraceptives was struck down as being "repulsive to the notions of privacy surrounding the . . . relationship." 381 U.S. at 486.

Thus the privacy accorded constitutional protection by *Griswold* inhered in the marital relationship. But when the Court subsequently invalidated a Massachusetts law regulating the distribution of contraceptives in *Eisenstadt v. Baird*, 405 U.S. 438 (1972), it recognized that this right also existed apart from marriage. For, as the Court explained, "[i]f the right of privacy means anything, it is the right of the *individual*, married or single, to be free from unwarranted governmental intrusions into matters so fundamentally affecting a person as the decision whether to bear or beget a child." 405 U.S. at 453 (emphasis in original).

. . . .

The Court has also spoken very clearly in another area of intimate decision. The issue in *Stanley v. Georgia*, 394 U.S. 557 (1969), was whether "the Georgia obscenity statute, insofar as it punishes mere private possession of obscene matter, violates the First Amendment, as made applicable to the States by the Fourteenth Amendment." Id. at 559. The appellant's thesis was characterized as "asserting the right to read or observe what he pleases—the right to satisfy his intellectual and emotional needs in the privacy of his own home." Id. at 565. Though it acknowledged "the States retain broad power to regulate obscenity," the Court nevertheless held that the "power simply does not extend to mere possession by the individual in the privacy of his own home." Id. at 568.

. . . .

Since the guaranteed freedom from intrusion extends to sexual activity among unmarried adult couples as *Eisenstadt v. Baird* suggests and to autoeroticism in the home as *Stanley v. Georgia* implies, we would have to agree there is room for argument

that the right encompasses any decision to engage in sex at home with another willing adult. Moreover, as the defendant reminds us, the commentary on HRS Sec. 712-1200 evidences that the drafters of the Penal Code found the usual reasons advanced for suppressing prostitution "are not convincing."[1] Still, every enactment of the legislature is presumptively constitutional, and a party challenging the statute has the burden of showing unconstitutionality beyond a reasonable doubt. The defendant has not met this burden, for she has not demonstrated in a convincing manner that a decision to engage in prostitution has been recognized as a fundamental right.

. . . .

The defendant has directed us to nothing suggesting a decision to engage in sex for hire at home should be considered basic to ordered liberty. Our review of Supreme Court case law in the relevant area leaves us with a distinct impression to the contrary, for we perceive no inclination on

---

[1] The commentary on the penal code provision at issue reads in part as follows:

History has proven that prostitution is not going to be abolished either by penal legislation nor the imposition of criminal sanctions through the vigorous enforcement of such legislation. Yet the trend of modern thought on prostitution in this country is that "public policy" demands that the criminal law go on record against prostitution. Defining this "public policy" is a difficult task. Perhaps it more correctly ought to be considered and termed "public demand"—a widespread community attitude which the penal law must take into account regardless of the questionable rationales upon which it is based.

A number of reasons have been advanced for the suppression of prostitution, the most often repeated of which are: "the prevention of disease, the protection of innocent girls from exploitation, and the danger that more sinister activities may be financed by the gains from prostitution." These reasons are not convincing. Venereal disease is not prevented by laws attempting to suppress prostitution. If exploitation were a significant factor, the offense could be dealt with solely in terms of coercion. Legalizing prostitution would decrease the prostitute's dependence upon and connection with the criminal underworld and might decrease the danger that "organized crime" might be financed in part by criminally controlled prostitution.

the part of the Court to exalt sexual freedom per se or to promote an anomic society. . . .

The drafters of the Hawaii Penal Code justified the enactment of HRS Sec. 712–1200 on "the need for public order." We would not dispute that it was reasonable for the legislature to act on that basis. A large segment of society undoubtedly regards prostitution as immoral and degrading, and the self-destructive or debilitating nature of the practice, at least for the prostitute, is often given as a reason for outlawing it. We could not deem these views irrational.

COMMENTS

1. Mueller attempted to argue that she was having sex in the privacy of her own home (albeit for a fee). We might also add that apparently no one was physically harmed (and perhaps even the opposite might be concluded). Should her conviction have been overturned?

2. Are we agreed that prostitution will not disappear? Is Mueller's claim so different from Ravin's? What would you say to the argument that diseases such as AIDS or venereal disease could be much better controlled by the legalization and regulation of prostitution?

3. What explains the existence of laws against prostitution? Is it moral disapproval? What if other people have a different sense of morality? Do they have to conform to the morality of the majority? Is prostitution, by definition, the exploitation of women (or mainly of women), and are laws against it for the protection of those who are being exploited? Is this a role the law ought to play?

4. One of the cliches used to describe America's ill-fated attempt to prohibit liquor is that "you can't legislate morality." We have seen, however, that to a certain extent we can and we have. Does the prevalence of prostitution and drug use, to cite these two examples, show that perhaps we cannot (and should not) legislate in these particular areas? Will there be an increase in disrespect for the law generally when certain laws such as prostitution and drug use are so widely violated?

5. As noted in the introductory material to this chapter, some argue that prostitution is not a victimless crime because prostitutes are often a victim in some larger sense—whether at the hands of abusive pimps or childhood sexual abusers. What do you make of this argument?

6. Another so-called victimless crime is gambling. How do states that have lotteries justify the laws they have against other forms of gambling? According to a New Jersey commission on gambling, between 1974 and 1987, gambling in the United States (usually in the form of state lotteries) increased by 950 percent. This study also found that 36 percent of residents earning less than $10,000 spent one-fifth or more of their household income on the state lottery. (Alf Siewers, "States, Individuals Getting Hooked on Lawful Gambling," *Christian Science Monitor*, November 4, 1988, p. 1.)

Rutherford v. United States, 399 F. Supp. 1208 (1975)

District Judge Bohanon.

[Rutherford seeks an injunction ordering the Federal Drug Administration (FDA), a branch of the Department of Health, Education and Welfare (HEW), to allow shipments of laetrile into the United States. Thus far the FDA has not approved use of this drug.]
. . . .

Plaintiff Glen L. Rutherford testified that he became ill with cancer in the summer and fall of 1971 and that he was examined by local medical doctors who concluded that he was suffering from cancer. . . .

. . . .

The plaintiff Glen L. Rutherford testified that he was tremendously upset and concerned about the prospects of surgery and the results thereof and that he went to Centro Medico Del Mar in Tijuana, Mexico, for examination and treatment. . . . He stated that at Centro Medico Del Mar he was treated with Vitamin B17 or laetrile for a period of weeks and that through this treatment his condition was cured; that he has returned to his home and has been working at all times since, averaging 10 to 12 hours per day. Mr. Rutherford stated that he has no ill effect of the cancer. However, he feels that without continued use of laetrile . . . he faces the prospect of escalation of the lethal cancer cells and thus is seeking relief in this Court for the privilege of buying laetrile for his own use and not for sale or barter to others.

. . . .

The Court is compelled to find from the testimony and the exhibits that plaintiff Glen L. Rutherford was in late 1971 suffering from invasive adenocarcinoma and that by the use of laetrile, B17 or amygdalin (all being the same drug) his condition was cured, as there is no evidence to the contrary.

The Court finds that plaintiff's Exhibit 2 is a letter from Mr. Rutherford's supplier of B17 or laetrile stating plaintiff's last order of laetrile was seized. It states that the carrier is in jail facing a $10,000 fine and five years in prison for his efforts to furnish Mr. Rutherford his 1975 supply of laetrile. The writer says that the clinic cannot be responsible and that therefore there will be no more mail orders of laetrile in the future.

The Court finds that the plaintiff Rutherford is not free to have shipped to him, nor is he free to directly purchase and bring back to the United States from Mexico quantities of laetrile for preventative treatment of his cancer. To do so would violate the law and would subject him to criminal prosecution.

. . . .

The Court finds from the record, testimony and exhibits that laetrile is not lethal in any sense of the word. It is not harmful to the human body and when used in proper amounts under proper control and supervision can effect relief from cancer disease to the satisfaction of many who are privileged to use the same.

The Court further finds from the record that the plaintiff Rutherford herein and those similarly situated have been denied this right of choice in using B17 or laetrile without just cause on the part of the Secretary of HEW and its agency FDA.

The Court finds . . . that for the plaintiff Rutherford and those similarly situated to be denied the freedom of choice for treatment by laetrile to alleviate or cure their cancer, was and is a deprivation of life, liberty or property without due process of law guaranteed by the Fifth Amendment to the Constitution of the United States.

. . . .

From all the facts and circumstances in this case the Court concludes that proper equitable injunctive relief should be granted and a proper Order will accordingly be filed.

COMMENTS

1. In his opinion, Judge Bohanon concludes that laetrile is not "a toxic harmful substance," a position that has been disputed by medical authorities and that raises an interesting question of a judge's capability of making such determinations.

2. Another question raised by this case that deserves more attention is this: to what extent should the state be able to say a man (or woman) dying of some disease that he cannot take a certain drug in order to attempt to save his life? The same issue faces us today with the AIDS epidemic. Until recently, the government

refused to allow AIDS victims in the United States to import unapproved medicine. Philip M. Boffey, "F.D.A. Will Allow AIDS Patients to Import Unapproved Medicines," *New York Times* July 25, 1988, p. 1. Should there be *any* restrictions on an AIDS victim's ability to use whatever drug he may be able to get his hands on? What are the arguments *for* some limitations?

3. The *Rutherford* case has an interesting history. The decision you have read was appealed and upheld by the Court of Appeals for the Tenth Circuit. This court held that terms in the act such as "safety" and "effectiveness"

had no reasonable application to terminally ill cancer patients. 582 F. 2d 1234, 1236 (1978). In an opinion by Justice Marshall, the Supreme Court, 442 U.S. 544 (1979), overturned this decision, holding that there was nothing in the language of the Food, Drug, and Cosmetic Act that suggests Congress intended protection only for persons suffering from curable diseases.

4. Go back to the question raised in the introductory material for this chapter. Why is it that people have been allowed to "kill" themselves *(Quinlan)* but not "save" themselves *(Rutherford)*?

6

EQUAL OPPORTUNITY
AND POLITICAL EQUALITY

Apparently, few individuals in this country give much thought to the fairness or justness of the distribution of goods. Put in other terms, graduating seniors are not particularly concerned whether the salaries for jobs they are seeking are just. Instead, like the rest of us, they are far more concerned with getting the best job, which often translates into the best-paying job. Whether it is just that an executive for Exxon makes considerably more money than a schoolteacher or gas station attendant is simply not an issue, nor is it a way of thinking about the world that we feel comfortable doing.

This lack of thought derives from our society's firm belief in the notion of equality of opportunity. It is not coincidental that all Americans can recite the humble background of Abraham Lincoln or that Horatio Alger continues to hold a special attraction. The universally accepted ideal is that through hard work, perseverance, talent, and perhaps a little luck, we can all achieve our goals in life. This is not to say that we all start equal. Obviously we do not. Certain individuals come from wealthy families, and some children and their parents are homeless. The dominant vision, however, is that notwithstanding these differences in where we start, the race is essentially open to all.

Our educational system lies at the very heart of this notion of equality of opportunity. The first principal case in this chapter, *San Antonio Independent School Dist. v. Rodriguez,* directly challenged the notion that the American educational system is *the* avenue through which we pursue, and achieve, equality of opportunity. The case involved a challenge to the method by which Texas financed public education. Like most other states, the financing scheme in Texas was based largely on local property taxes. As a result, some school districts spent considerably more money on educating their young than other school districts did.

The plaintiffs in the case were a group of Mexican-American parents whose children were in the Edgewood school district of San Antonio. The assessed property values in Edgewood were $5,960 per pupil, whereas in Alamo, the richest area in San Antonio, the tax base was more than $49,000 per pupil. Although the residents of Edgewood taxed themselves at a rate of $1.05 per $100 of assessed value (compared with the $.85 the residents of Alamo taxed themselves), because of the vast differences in property values, per pupil expenditures were $356 in Edgewood and $594 in Alamo.

The claim made by the plaintiffs was that this state scheme violated the equal protection clause of the Fourteenth Amendment. The key question in the case, however, was what level of judicial review the Court should be employing. Put in other terms, how closely should the judiciary examine the method of funding public education? The Mexican-American parents challenging the statutory scheme argued that the Supreme Court should employ the "strict scrutiny" standard. As its name suggests, this standard provides a very searching analysis of what a legislature or the executive branch has done; very few enactments are able to withstand such scrutiny. In order to pass constitutional muster under this standard, the state must show a "compelling" interest and that it is pursuing these goals by the best means possible.

When is it appropriate for a court to subject the actions of a coordinate branch of government to such a difficult level of review? The answer given by the Supreme Court was that the strict scrutiny standard applies when either a "fundamental right" is involved *or* when a "suspect class" is afforded disparate treatment. If neither situation obtains, the Court has held that the appropriate level of review is "rational basis," which is a very mild review. In contrast to the strict scrutiny standard, very few legislative or executive actions are struck down when the judiciary provides this level of review.

But what is a fundamental right, and what constitutes a suspect class? The answers here are by no means certain. It is clear that voting is a fundamental right,[1] but education is not; in fact, in his majority opinion in *Rodriguez*, Justice Powell claims there is no right to an education. In terms of the other category of cases that would invoke the strict scrutiny standard by the Court, blacks or religious minorities would constitute prototypes of a suspect class.[2] We term them *suspect* because of their minority status and the history or likelihood of persecution at the hands of the dominant majority. At one time aliens were considered by the Supreme Court to be a suspect class,[3] but since that time the Court has retreated from this position.[4] Women almost achieved the distinction of being considered a suspect class, but the proponents of this position were never able to achieve a majority of the Court.[5] The question posed for the Court was whether the "poor" constitute a "suspect class."

Although there is common acceptance of the Court's two-tier level of review—strict scrutiny and rational basis—there has also been some dissatisfaction with it. Justice Marshall's dissenting opinion in *Rodriguez* is an indication of this. Marshall suggests that the Court should abandon the two-tier level of review and instead employ a level of review that is a "sliding scale" depending on the constitutional significance of the interests affected and the invidiousness of the particular classification. Although Justice Marshall's proposal has apparently not found any other adherents, we might also ask whether the Court has in fact applied this level of review without stating what it has done. For example, we could argue that this is exactly what the Court has done in the second principal case, *Plyler v. Doe*.

Plyler involved a lawsuit brought by a group of undocumented children of Mexican origin who challenged the constitutionality of a Texas statute that denied free public education to undocumented school age children. As Justice Brennan's majority opinion points out, *Plyler* must be read against the background of our porous national borders in Texas and in other southwestern states. Before passage of the Simpson/Rodino bill in 1986, there were, according to estimates, between 3 and 12 million illegal aliens in the United States. Until Simpson/Rodino, there was no federal statute that prohibited the hiring of illegal aliens (this was termed the "Texas Proviso"). In addition to employer sanctions, Simpson/Rodino also provided amnesty to undocumented aliens who have lived in the United States since 1982.

At issue in *Plyler* was whether children of undocumented aliens could be denied an education. Once again, the Court initially had to determine what level of judicial review to apply. In *Rodriguez*, the Court had already held that there was no constitutional right to equal expenditures for educational purposes; but the issue in *Plyler* was whether children could totally be denied an education. Another claim put forward by the representatives of these children was that they constituted a suspect class. The contention was that as a group undocumented aliens are kept out of the political processes of this country, and the stories of the ill-treatment suffered by these individuals at the hands of immigration officials and private employers are legion.[6] On the other hand, it could also be argued that these children, more particularly their parents, were uninvited guests to the United States, notwithstanding the benefits their presence accrued to certain U.S. employers and American consumers. Should the courts offer these people special protection? You might not be surprised by the Supreme Court's answer to that question, but you probably will be by the Court's result in this case.

The last principal case in this chapter looks at political equality. As you know, political equality has long been recognized more in theory than in practice, as evidenced by the fact that women only received the vote well into this century and virtually all blacks in the South were disenfranchised until a little more than two decades ago. Although we have now achieved a certain kind of political equality, *First National Bank of Boston v. Bellotti* raised questions concerning a different kind of political equality—namely, whether those with money now dominate the electoral arena. Some have called this the Golden Rule: those who have the gold, rule.

Does money make a difference in the electoral arena? Politicians certainly seem to think that it does. Elizabeth Drew comments this way on the consequences of the rapidly increasing costs involved in Congressional campaigns:

> A candidate for office doesn't set out to spend a half million or a million dollars for the sheer joy of it; he does it because he fears the consequences of not doing it. And unless he is independently wealthy he has to raise that money—or be more vulnerable to defeat. It is not accidental that the number of independently wealthy people entering politics is rising. And the quest for money has distended and distorted the political system to the point where it bears little resemblance to what it was supposed to be.[7]

Bellotti involved the constitutionality of a Massachusetts statute that prohibited certain expenditures by banks and business corporations for the purpose of influencing the vote on referendum proposals. Your analysis of the *Bellotti* case might hinge largely on whether you accept the majority's view that this statutory scheme would infringe on the First Amendment rights of corporations or on whether you accept Justice White's position in dissent that the restriction in question was to protect the First Amendment rights of those without the resources and political power of banks and corporations.

The *Bellotti* case raises a number of noteworthy questions concerning political equality and the workings of democracy in our country. I noted in the introduction Madison's view that the most common and durable source of faction is the "various and unequal distribution of property." But you will also recall that Madison is of the opinion that factions can not be eradicated; therefore, a system of government must be established in which faction counterbalances faction. Theodore Lowi has been a sharp critic of this view of government.[8] In Lowi's view, interests are not always organized and therefore not represented in the political arena. Thus, the very premise upon which "interest group Liberalism" is founded is faulty. In terms of money in the electoral arena in particular, the empirical evidence shows quite clearly that resources are by no means evenly distributed.[9] Whether resources *should* be more equal or whether measures such as that unsuccessfully attempted in Massachusetts are appropriate are different questions.

NOTES

1. *Harper v. Virginia Board of Elections*, 383 U.S. 663 (1966).
2. The basis for this higher level of review comes from the famous footnote 4 in Justice Stone's opinion in *United States v. Carolene Products Co.* 304 U.S. 144 (1938).
3. *Graham v. Richardson* 403 U.S. 365 (1971).

4. For example, see *Foley v. Connelie,* 435 U.S. 291 (1978) (Court upheld a New York law that barred employment of aliens as state troopers); *Ambach v. Norwick,* 441 U.S. 68 (1979) (Court upheld a state law refusing to employ as elementary and secondary school teachers aliens who were eligible for citizenship but who refused to seek naturalization).

5. In *Frontiero v. Richardson,* 411 U.S. 677 (1973), four members of the Court maintained the position that women are a suspect class. Justice Brennan's plurality opinion explains:

> It is true, of course, that the position of women in America has improved markedly in recent decades. Nevertheless, it can hardly be doubted that, in part because of the high visibility of the sex characteristic, women still face pervasive, although at times more subtle, discrimination in our education institutions, in the job market and, perhaps most conspicuously, in the political arena. Moreover, since sex, like race and national origin, is an immutable characteristic, the imposition of special disabilities upon the members of a particular sex because of their sex would seem to violate "the basic concept of our system that legal burdens should bear some relationship to individual responsibility." . . . And what differentiates sex from such nonsuspect statuses as intelligence or physical disability, and aligns it with the recognized suspect criteria, is that the sex characteristic frequently bears no relation to ability to perform or contribute to society. As a result, statutory distinctions between the sexes often have the effect of invidiously relegating the entire class of females to inferior legal status without regard to the actual capabilities of its individual members.

6. See, for example, John Crewsdon, *The Tarnished Door: The New Immigrants and the Transformation of America* (New York: Times Books, 1983).

7. Elizabeth Drew, *Politics and Money: The New Road to Corruption* (New York: Macmillan, 1983), p. 94.

8. Theodore Lowi, *The End of Liberalism: Ideology, Policy, and the Crisis of Public Authority* (New York: W. W. Norton, 1969).

9. For example, Larry Sabato has shown how incumbents have a commanding edge over their challengers in terms of PAC contributions. See Larry Sabato, *PAC Power: Inside the World of Political Action Committees* (New York: W. W. Norton, 1985).

San Antonio School District v. Rodriguez, 411 U.S. 1 (1973)

Justice Powell delivered the opinion of the Court.

[This is a suit by Mexican-American parents whose children attend Edgewood school district schools, claiming that the method by which Texas finances public education, relying principally on local property taxes for revenue, violates the Fourteenth Amendment. The assessed property in Edgewood is $5,960 per pupil, compared with an assessed value per pupil of over $49,000 in the Alamo school district. Per pupil expenditures in Edgewood were $356 per pupil and $594 in Alamo. The parents claim that the proper level of judicial review in testing the constitutionality of this financing scheme is the "strict scrutiny" standard because the plaintiffs constitute a "suspect class," and/or that education is a "fundamental right." The district court found for the parents.]

. . . .

The wealth discrimination discovered by the District Court in this case is quite unlike any of the forms of wealth discrimination heretofore reviewed by this Court. Rather than focusing on the unique features of the alleged discrimination, the courts in these cases have virtually assumed their findings of a suspect classification through a simplistic process of analysis: since, under the traditional systems of financing public schools, some poorer people receive less expensive educations than other more affluent people, these systems discriminate on the basis of wealth. This approach largely ignores the hard threshold questions, including whether it makes a difference for purposes of consideration under the Constitution that the class of disadvantaged "poor" cannot be identified or defined in customary equal protection terms, and whether the relative—rather than absolute—nature of the asserted deprivation is of significant consequence. Before a State's laws and the justifications for the classifications they create are subjected to strict judicial scrutiny, we think these threshold considerations must be analyzed more closely than they were in the court below.

. . . .

. . . Even a cursory examination demonstrates that neither of the two distinguishing characteristics of wealth classifications can be found here. First, in support of their charge that the system discriminates against the "poor," appellees have made no effort to demonstrate that it operates to the peculiar disadvantage of any class fairly definable as indigent, or as composed of persons whose incomes are beneath any designated poverty level. Indeed, there is reason to believe that the poorest families are not necessarily clustered in the poorest property districts. . . .

Second, neither appellees nor the District Court addressed the fact that . . . lack of personal resources has not occasioned an absolute deprivation of the desired benefit. The argument here is not that the children in districts having relatively low assessable property values are receiving no public education; rather, it is that they are receiving a poorer quality education than that available to children in districts having more assessable wealth. Apart from the unsettled and disputed question whether the quality of education may be determined by the amount of money expended for it, a sufficient answer to appellees' argument is that, at least where wealth is involved, the Equal Protection Clause does not require absolute equality or precisely equal advantages. Nor, indeed, in view of the infinite variables affecting the educational process, can any system assure equal quality of education except in the most relative sense. . . .

However described, it is clear that appellees' suit asks this Court to extend its most exacting scrutiny to review a system that allegedly discriminates against a large, diverse, and amorphous class, unified only by the common factor of residence in districts that happen to have less taxable wealth than other districts. The system of alleged discrimination and the class it defines have none of the traditional indicia of suspectness: the class is not saddled with such disabilities, or subjected to such a history or purposeful unequal treatment, or relegated to such a position of political powerlessness as to command extraordinary protection from the majoritarian political process.

We thus conclude that the Texas system does not operate to the peculiar disadvantage of any suspect class. But in recognition of the fact that this Court has never heretofore held that wealth discrimination alone provides an adequate basis for involving strict scrutiny, appellees have not relied solely on this contention. They also assert that the State's system impermissibly interferes with the exercise of a "fundamental" right and that accordingly the prior decisions of this Court require the application of the strict standard of judicial review.

In *Brown v. Board of Education,* a unanimous Court recognized that "education is perhaps the most important function of state and local governments." . . . Nothing this Court holds today in any way detracts from our historic dedication to public education. We are in complete agreement with the conclusion of the three-judge panel below that "the grave significance of education both to the individual and to our society" cannot be doubted. But the importance of a service performed by the State does not determine whether it must be regarded as fundamental for purposes of examination under the Equal Protection Clause. . . .

. . . .

. . . It is not the province of this Court to create substantive constitutional rights in the name of guaranteeing equal protection of the laws. Thus, the key to discovering whether education is "fundamental" is not to be found in comparisons of the relative societal significance of education as opposed to subsistence or housing. Nor is it to be found by weighing whether education is as important as the right to travel. Rather, the answer lies in assessing whether there is a right to education explicitly or implicitly guaranteed by the Constitution.

. . . .

Education, of course, is not among the rights afforded explicit protection under our Federal Constitution. Nor do we find any basis for saying it is implicitly so protected. As we have said, the undisputed importance of education will not alone cause this Court to depart from the usual standard for reviewing a State's social and economic legislation. It is appellees' conten-

tion, however, that education is distinguishable from other services and benefits provided by the State because it bears a peculiarly close relationship to other rights and liberties accorded protection under the Constitution. Specifically, they insist that education is itself a fundamental personal right because it is essential to the effective exercise of First Amendment freedoms and to intelligent utilization of the right to vote. In asserting a nexus between speech and education, appellees urge that the right to speak is meaningless unless the speaker is capable of articulating his thoughts intelligently and persuasively. The "marketplace of ideas" is an empty forum for those lacking basic communicative tools. Likewise, they argue that the corollary right to receive information becomes little more than a hollow privilege when the recipient has not been taught to read, assimilate, and utilize available knowledge.

. . . .

We need not dispute any of the propositions. The Court has long afforded zealous protection against unjustifiable governmental interference with the individual's rights to speak and to vote. Yet we have never presumed to possess either the ability or the authority to guarantee to the citizenry the most effective speech or the most informed electoral choice. That these may be desirable goals of a system of freedom of expression and of a representative form of government is not to be doubted. These are indeed goals to be pursued by a people whose thought and beliefs are freed from governmental interference. But they are not values to be implemented by judicial intrusion into otherwise legitimate state activities.

Even if it were conceded that some identifiable quantum of education is a constitutionally protected prerequisite to the meaningful exercise of either right, we have no indication that the present levels of educational expenditure in Texas provide an education that falls short. Whatever merit appellees' argument might have if a

State's financing system occasioned an absolute denial of educational opportunities to any of its children, that argument provides no basis for finding an interference with fundamental rights where only relative differences in spending levels are involved and where—as is true in the present case—no charge fairly could be made that the system fails to provide each child with an opportunity to acquire the basic minimal skills necessary for the enjoyment of the rights of speech and of full participation in the political process.

Furthermore, the logical limitations on appellees' nexus theory are difficult to perceive. How, for instance, is education to be distinguished from the significant personal interests in the basics of decent food and shelter? Empirical examination might well buttress an assumption that the ill-fed, ill-clothed, and the ill-housed are among the most ineffective participants in the political process, and that they derive the least enjoyment from the benefits of the First Amendment. . . .

. . . .

In sum, to the extent that the Texas system of school financing results in unequal expenditures between children who happen to reside in different districts, we cannot say that such disparities are the product of a system that is so irrational as to be invidiously discriminatory. Texas has acknowledged its shortcomings and has persistently endeavored—not without some success—to ameliorate the differences in levels of expenditures without sacrificing the benefits of local participation. The Texas plan is not the result of hurried, ill-conceived legislation. It certainly is not the product of purposeful discrimination against any group or class. On the contrary, it is rooted in decades of experience in Texas and elsewhere, and in major part is the product of responsible studies by qualified people. . . . One also must remember that the system here challenged is not peculiar to Texas or to any other State. In its essential characteristics, the Texas plan

for financing public education reflects what many educators for a half century have thought was an enlightened approach to a problem for which there is no perfect solution. We are unwilling to assume for ourselves a level of wisdom superior to that of legislators, scholars, and educational authorities in 50 States, especially where the alternatives proposed are only recently conceived and not here yet tested. The constitutional standard under the Equal Protection Clause is whether the challenged state action rationally furthers a legitimate state purpose or interest. We hold that the Texas plan abundantly satisfies this standard.

Mr. Justice Marshall, with whom Mr. Justice Douglas concurs, dissenting.

. . . .

The appellants do not deny the disparities in educational funding caused by variations in taxable district property wealth. They do contend, however, that whatever the differences in per-pupil spending among Texas districts, there are no discriminatory consequences for the children of the disadvantaged districts. They recognize that what is at stake in this case in the quality of the public education provided Texas children in the districts in which they live. But appellants reject the suggestion that the quality of education in any particular district is determined by money—beyond some minimal level of funding which they believe to be assured every Texas district by the Minimum Foundation School Program. In their view, there is simply no denial of equal educational opportunity to any Texas school children as a result of the widely varying per-pupil spending power provided districts under the current financing scheme.

In my view, though, even an unadorned restatement of this contention is sufficient to reveal its absurdity. Authorities concerned with educational quality no doubt disagree as to the significance of variations in per-pupil spending. Indeed, conflicting expert testimony was presented to the District Court in this case concerning the effect of spending variations on educational achievement. We sit, however, not to resolve disputes over educational theory but to enforce our Constitution. It is an inescapable fact that if one district has more funds available per pupil than another district, the former will have greater choice in educational planning than will the latter. In this regard, I believe the question of discrimination in educational quality must be deemed to be an objective one that looks to what the State provides its children, not to what the children are able to do with what they receive. That a child forced to attend an underfunded school with poorer physical facilities, less experienced teachers, larger classes, and a narrower range of courses than a school with substantially more funds—and thus with greater choice in educational planning—may nevertheless excel is to the credit of the child, not the State. Indeed, who can ever measure for such a child the opportunities lost and the talents wasted for want of a broader, more enriched education? Discrimination in the opportunity to learn that is afforded a child must be our standard.

. . . .

This Court has repeatedly held that state discrimination which either adversely affects a "fundamental interest," or is based on a distinction of a suspect character, must be carefully scrutinized to ensure that the scheme is necessary to promote a substantial, legitimate state interest. The majority today concludes, however, that the Texas scheme is not subject to such a strict standard of review under the Equal Protection clause. Instead, in its view, the Texas scheme must be tested by nothing more than that lenient standard of rationality which we have traditionally applied to discriminatory state action in the context of economic and commercial matters. By doing so the Court avoids the telling task of searching for a substantial state interest

which the Texas financing scheme, with its variations in taxable district property wealth, is necessary to further. I cannot accept such an emasculation of the Equal Protection Clause in the context of this case.

To begin, I must once more voice my disagreement with the Court's rigidified approach to equal protection analysis. The Court apparently seeks to establish today that equal protection cases fall into one of two neat categories which dictate the appropriate standard of review—strict scrutiny or mere rationality. But this Court's decisions in the field of equal protection defy such easy categorization. A principled reading of what this Court has done reveals that it has applied a spectrum of standards in reviewing discrimination allegedly violative of the Equal Protection Clause. This spectrum clearly comprehends variations in the degree of care with which the Court will scrutinize particular classifications, depending, I believe, on the constitutional and societal importance of the interest adversely affected and the recognized invidiousness of the basis upon which the particular classification is drawn. . . .

. . . .

. . . It is true that this Court has never deemed the provision of free public education to be required by the Constitution. Indeed, it has on occasion suggested that state-supported education is a privilege bestowed by a State on its citizens. Nevertheless, the fundamental importance of education is amply indicated by the prior decisions of this Court, by the unique status accorded public education by our society, and by the close relationship between education and some of our most basic constitutional values.

. . . .

. . . Appellees do not now seek the best education Texas might provide. They do seek, however, an end to state discrimination resulting from the unequal distribution of taxable district property wealth that directly impairs the ability of some districts to provide the same educational opportunity that other districts can provide with the same or even substantially less tax effort. The issue is, in other words, one of discrimination that affects the quality of the education which Texas has chosen to provide its children; and, the precise question here is what importance should attach to education for purposes of equal protection analysis of that discrimination. As this Court held in *Brown v. Board of Education,* the opportunity of education, "where the state has undertaken to provide it, is a right which must be made available to all on equal terms." . . .

The Court seeks solace for its action today in the possibility of legislative reform. The Court's suggestions of legislative redress and experimentation will doubtless be of great comfort to the schoolchildren of Texas' disadvantaged districts, but considering the vested interests of wealthy school districts in the preservation of the status quo, they are worth little more. The possibility of legislative action is, in all events, no answer to this Court's duty under the Constitution to eliminate unjustified state discrimination. In this case we have been presented with an instance of such discrimination, in a particularly invidious form, against an individual interest of large constitutional and practical importance. To support the demonstrated discrimination in the provision of educational opportunity the State has offered a justification which, on analysis, takes on at best an ephemeral character. Thus, I believe that the wide disparities in taxable district property wealth inherent in the local property tax element of the Texas financing scheme render that scheme violative of the Equal Protection Clause.

COMMENTS

1. Is the holding in this case strong evidence that American society only pays lip service to the notion of equality of opportunity?

2. As Justice Powell's majority opinion points out, the empirical evidence is apparently unclear in establishing whether increased expenditures improve the quality of education that children receive. But parents and politicians certainly act as if it does matter. For example, do you think that the parents in the Alamo school district would have wanted to send their children to the Edgewood school district?

3. What would John Rawls's scheme of justice dictate in this area? Recall that Rawls maintains that a just decision is one in which individual self-interest is removed so that the person does not simply arrive at a decision that is convenient (but not necessarily just). One means of achieving this state of affairs might be to assign school placements on a random basis each year, so that parents are not sure which school district their children will attend. It seems likely—does it not?—that if such a procedure were adopted, there would be far fewer disparities in the level of school expenditures from school district to school district.

4. Justice Powell uses a number of arguments in support of the constitutionality of this financing scheme. Among them is his position that these schoolchildren were receiving at least an "adequate" education. How can he, or any other judge, make such a determination (for that matter, how does a legislator make such determinations)? Could he say this if the gap in per pupil expenditures were even wider? For example, if Edgewood were able to spend only $156 per pupil but Alamo ten times that? Even if you agree with the Court's holding, at what point do per pupil expenditures violate the Constitution? At what point do they violate the principle of equal opportunity? Are these necessarily the same points?

5. Which district is more interested in providing its children with a good education? Note that the residents of the Edgewood District are taxing themselves at a much higher rate than are the residents of Alamo, but the vast disparity in assessed property between the two districts accounts for the differences in spending.

6. If you agree with the dissenting opinion that education expenses in Texas should be made more equal, does that mean that the next step dictated by the Constitution is that educational expenditure differences among states must also be eliminated?

Plyler v. Doe, 457 U.S. 202 (1982)

Justice Brennan delivered the opinion of the Court.

In May 1975, the Texas Legislature revised its education laws to withhold from local school districts any state funds for the education of children who were not "legally admitted" into the United States. The 1975 revision also authorized local school districts to deny enrollment in their public schools to children not "legally admitted" to the country. These cases involve constitutional challenges to those provisions. [Sec. 21.031]

. . . .

The Fourteenth Amendment provides that "[n]o State shall . . . deprive any person of life, liberty, or property, without due process of law; nor deny to any person within its jurisdiction the equal protection of the laws." Appellants argue at the outset that undocumented aliens, because of their immigration status, are not "persons within the jurisdiction" of the State of Texas, and that they therefore have no right to the equal protection of Texas law. We reject this argument. Whatever his status under the immigration laws, an alien is surely a "person" in any ordinary sense of that term. Aliens, even aliens whose presence in this country is unlawful, have long been recognized as "persons" guaranteed due process of law by the Fifth and Fourteenth Amendments. . . .

Our conclusion that the illegal aliens who are plaintiffs in these cases may claim the benefit of the Fourteenth Amendment's guarantee of equal protection only begins the inquiry. The more difficult question is whether the Equal Protection Clause has been violated by the refusal of the State of Texas to reimburse local school boards for the education of children who cannot demonstrate that their presence within the

United States is lawful, or by the imposition by those school boards of the burden of tuition on those children. It is to this question that we now turn.

The Equal Protection Clause directs that "all persons similarly circumstanced shall be treated alike." But so, too, "[t]he Constitution does not require things which are different in fact or opinion to be treated in law as though they were the same." The initial discretion to determine what is "different" and what is "the same" resides in the legislatures of the States. A legislature must have substantial latitude to establish classifications that roughly approximate the nature of the problem perceived, that accommodate competing concerns both public and private, and that account for limitations on the practical ability of the State to remedy every ill. In applying the Equal Protection Clause to most forms of state action, we thus seek only the assurance that the classification at issue bears some fair relationship to a legitimate public purpose.

But we would not be faithful to our obligations under the Fourteenth Amendment if we applied so deferential a standard to every classification. The Equal Protection Clause was intended as a restriction on state legislative action inconsistent with elemental constitutional premises. Thus we have treated as presumptively invidious those classifications that disadvantage a "suspect class," or that impinge upon the exercise of a "fundamental right." With respect to such classifications, it is appropriate to enforce the mandate of equal protection by requiring the State to demonstrate that its classification has been precisely tailored to serve a compelling governmental interest. . . .

Sheer incapability or lax enforcement of the laws barring entry into this country, coupled with the failure to establish an effective bar to the employment of undocumented aliens, has resulted in the creation of a substantial "shadow population" of illegal migrants—numbering in the millions—within our borders. This situation raises the specter of a permanent caste of undocumented resident aliens, encouraged by some to remain here as a source of cheap labor, but nevertheless denied the benefits that our society makes available to citizens and lawful residents. The existence of such an underclass presents most difficult problems for a Nation that prides itself on adherence to principles of equality under law.

The children who are plaintiffs in these cases are special members of this underclass. Persuasive arguments support the view that a State may withhold its beneficence from those whose very presence within the United States is the product of their own unlawful conduct. These arguments do not apply with the same force to classifications imposing disabilities on the minor children of such illegal entrants. At the least, those who elect to enter our territory by stealth and in violation of our law should be prepared to bear the consequences, including, but not limited to, deportation. But the children of those illegal entrants are not comparably situated. Their parents have the ability to conform their conduct to societal norms, and presumably the ability to remove themselves from the State's jurisdiction; but the children who are plaintiffs in these cases can affect neither their parents' conduct nor their own status. Even if the State found it expedient to control the conduct of adults by acting against their children, legislation directing the onus of a parent's misconduct against his children does not comport with fundamental conceptions of justice.

. . . .

Public education is not a "right" granted to individuals by the Constitution. *San Antonio Independent School Dist. vs. Rodriguez.* But neither is it merely some governmental "benefit" indistinguishable from other forms of social welfare legislation. Both the importance of education in maintaining our basic institutions, and the lasting impact of its deprivation on the life of the child, mark the distinction. The American people have always regarded education and the acquisition of knowledge as matters of supreme importance. We have recognized the public schools as a most vital civic institution for the preservation of a democratic system of government, and as the primary vehicle for transmitting the values on which our society rests. . . . In addition, education provides the basic tools by which individuals might lead economically productive lives to the benefit of us all. In sum, education has a fundamental role in maintaining the fabric of our society. We cannot ignore the significant social costs borne by our Nation when select groups are denied the means to absorb the values and skills upon which our social order rests.

. . . .

These well-settled principles allow us to determine the proper level of deference to be afforded Sec. 21.031. Undocumented aliens cannot be treated as a suspect class because their presence in this country in violation of federal law is not a "constitutional irrelevancy." Nor is education a fundamental right; a State need not justify by compelling necessity every variation in the manner in which education is provided to its population. But more is involved in these cases than the abstract question whether Sec. 21.031 discriminates against a suspect class, or whether education is a fundamental right. Section 21.031 imposes a lifetime hardship on a discrete class of children not accountable for their disabling status. The stigma of illiteracy will mark them for the rest of their lives. By denying these children a basic education, we deny them the ability to live within the structure of our civic institutions, and foreclose any realistic possibility that they will contribute in even the smallest way to the progress of our Nation. In determining the rationality of Sec. 21.031, we may appropriately take into account its costs to the Nation and to the innocent children who are its victims. In light of these countervailing costs, the discrimination contained in Sec. 21.031 can hardly be considered rational unless it furthers some substantial goal of the State. . . .

[The Court then found that the state's interest in the preservation of its limited resources for the education of its own citizens was insufficient in light of the negative consequences in denying an education to those children. In arriving at this conclusion the Court held that the purported state interest in preventing illegal aliens from entering the state was not well addressed by the current restriction on education. In addition, the Court argued that there was no evidence that the exclusion of these children would necessarily improve the quality of education in the state. Finally, to the state's argument that undocumented children are less likely to remain in the state in the future than other children, the Court responded by arguing that this was mere speculation, and that a state could not deny an education to a child based on the mere possibility that the child would not remain in the state as an adult.]

. . . .

If the State is to deny a discrete group of innocent children the free public education that it offers to other children residing within its borders, that denial must be justified by a showing that it furthers some substantial state interest. No such showing was made here. Accordingly, the judgment of the Court of Appeals in each of these cases is affirmed.

Chief Justice Burger, with whom Justice White, Justice Rehnquist, and Justice O'Connor join, dissenting.

. . . .

The Court's holding today manifests the justly criticized judicial tendency to attempt speedy and wholesale formulation of "rem-

edies" for the failures—or simply the laggard pace—of the political processes of our system of government. The Court employs, and in my view abuses, the Fourteenth Amendment in an effort to become an omnipotent and omniscient problem solver. That the motives for doing so are noble and compassionate does not alter the fact that the Court distorts our constitutional function to make amends for the defaults of others.

. . . .

The Court acknowledges that, except in those cases when state classifications disadvantage a "suspect class" or impinge upon a "fundamental right," the Equal Protection Clause permits a State "substantial latitude" in distinguishing between different groups of persons. Moreover, the Court expressly—and correctly—rejects any suggestion that illegal aliens are a suspect class, or that education is a fundamental right. Yet by patching together bits and pieces of what might be termed quasi-suspect-class and quasi-fundamental-rights analysis, the Court spins out a theory custom-tailored to the facts of these cases.

. . . .

The Court first suggests that these illegal alien children, although not a suspect class, are entitled to special solicitude under the Equal Protection Clause because they lack "control" over or "responsibility" for their unlawful entry into this country. Similarly, the Court appears to take the position that Sec. 21.031 is presumptively "irrational" because it has the effect of imposing "penalties" on "innocent" children. However, the Equal Protection Clause does not preclude legislators from classifying among persons on the basis of factors and characteristics over which individuals may be said to lack "control." Indeed, in some circumstances persons generally, and children in particular, may have little control over or responsibility for such things as their ill health, need for public assistance, or place of residence. Yet a state legislature is not barred from considering, for example, relevant differences between the mentally healthy and the mentally ill, or between the residents of different counties, simply because these may be factors unrelated to individual choice or to any "wrongdoing." The Equal Protection Clause protects against arbitrary and irrational classifications, and against invidious discrimination stemming from prejudice and hostility; it is not an all-encompassing "equalizer" designed to eradicate every distinction for which persons are not "responsible."

. . . .

The second strand of the Court's analysis rests on the premise that, although public education is not a constitutionally guaranteed right, neither is it merely some governmental benefit indistinguishable from other forms of social welfare legislation. Whatever meaning or relevance this opaque observation might have in some other context, it simply has no bearing on the issues at hand. Indeed, it is never made clear what the Court's opinion means on this score.

The importance of education is beyond dispute. Yet we have held repeatedly that the importance of a governmental service does not elevate it to the status of a "fundamental right" for purposes of equal protection analysis. In *San Antonio Independent School Dist.*, Justice Powell, speaking for the Court, expressly rejected the proposition that state laws dealing with public education are subject to special scrutiny under the Equal Protection Clause. Moreover, the Court points to no meaningful way to distinguish between education and other governmental benefits in this context. Is the Court suggesting that education is more "fundamental" than food, shelter, or medical care?

. . . .

Once it is conceded—as the Court does—that illegal aliens are not a suspect class, and that education is not a fundamental right, our inquiry should focus on and be limited to whether the legislative

classification at issue bears a rational relationship to a legitimate state purpose.

The State contends primarily that Sec. 21.031 serves to prevent undue depletion of its limited revenues available for education, and to preserve the fiscal integrity of the State's school-financing system against an ever-increasing flood of illegal aliens—aliens over whose entry or continued presence it has no control. Of course such fiscal concerns alone could not justify discrimination against a suspect class or an arbitrary and irrational denial of benefits to a particular group of persons. Yet I assume no Member of this Court would argue that prudent conservation of finite state revenues is per se an illegitimate goal. . . .

Without laboring what will undoubtedly seem obvious to many, it simply is not "irrational" for a state to conclude that it does not have the same responsibility to provide benefits for persons whose very presence in the state and this country is illegal as it does to provide for persons lawfully present. By definition, illegal aliens have no right whatever to be here, and the state may reasonably, and constitutionally, elect not to provide them with governmental services at the expense of those who are lawfully in the State. . . .

It is significant that the Federal Government has seen fit to exclude illegal aliens from numerous social welfare programs, such as the food stamp program, the old-age assistance, aid to families with dependent children, aid to the blind, aid to the permanently and totally disabled, and supplemental security income programs, the Medicare hospital insurance benefits program, and the Medicaid hospital insurance benefits for the aged and disabled program. Although these exclusions do not conclusively demonstrate the constitutionality of the State's use of the same classification for comparable purposes, at the very least they tend to support the rationality of excluding illegal alien residents of a State from such programs so as to preserve the State's finite revenues for the benefit of lawful residents.

. . . .

Denying a free education to illegal alien children is not a choice I would make were I a legislator. Apart from compassionate considerations, the long-range costs of excluding any children from the public schools may well outweigh the costs of educating them. But that is not the issue; the fact that there are sound policy arguments against the Texas Legislature's choice does not render that choice an unconstitutional one.

The Constitution does not provide a cure for every social ill, nor does it vest judges with a mandate to try to remedy every social problem. Moreover, when this Court rushes in to remedy what it perceives to be the failings of the political processes, it deprives those processes of an opportunity to function. When the political institutions are not forced to exercise constitutionally allocated powers and responsibilities, those powers, like muscles not used, tend to atrophy. Today's cases, I regret to say, present yet another example of unwarranted judicial action which in the long run tends to contribute to the weakening of our political processes.

COMMENTS

1. Given the Supreme Court's decision in *Rodriguez*, *Plyler* comes as somewhat of a surprise, does it not? Was the Court here more concerned with what the lack of education would mean for the well-being of those individuals who would be denied an education or for the well-being of the U.S. community in having a pool of illiterates?

2. As noted at the beginning of this chapter, the Simpson/Rodino bill has finally made it a federal offense to hire illegal aliens. Thus, it can no longer be argued that this nation has looked the other way in terms of the presence of illegal aliens in this country. Does this mean that *Plyler* should now be overturned?

3. Note that the expense of educating these children will not fall directly on the federal government and particularly not on the Supreme Court of the United States. Is it fair that the Court would burden the citizens of the state of Texas with this kind of duty in order to meet the so-called rights of these children?

First National Bank of Boston v. Bellotti, 435 U.S. 765 (1978)

Mr. Justice Powell delivered the opinion of the Court.

[This case is a challenge to a Massachusetts statute which prevents banks and business corporations from making campaign contributions "for the purpose of influencing or affecting the vote on any question submitted to the voters, other than one materially affecting any of the property, business or assets of the corporation." The statute further specified that "no question submitted to the voters solely concerning the taxation of the income, property or transactions of individuals shall be deemed materially to affect the property, business or assets of the corporation."]

. . . .

The court below framed the principal question in this case as whether and to what extent corporations have First Amendment rights. We believe that the court posed the wrong question. The Constitution often protects interests broader than those of the party seeking their vindication. The First Amendment, in particular, serves significant societal interests. The proper question therefore is not whether corporations "have" First Amendment rights and, if so, whether they are coextensive with those of natural persons. Instead, the question must be whether Sec. 8 abridges expression that the First Amendment was meant to protect. We hold that it does.

. . . .

Section 8 permits a corporation to communicate to the public its views on certain referendum subjects—those materially affecting its business—but not others. It also singles out one kind of ballot question—individual taxation—as a subject about which corporations may never make their ideas public. The legislature has drawn the line between permissible and impermissible speech according to whether there is a sufficient nexus, as defined by the legislature, between the issue presented to the voters and the business interests of the speaker.

In the realm of protected speech, the legislature is constitutionally disqualified from dictating the subjects about which persons may speak and the speakers who may address a public issue. If a legislature may direct business corporations to "stick to business," it also may limit other corporations—religious, charitable, or civic—to their respective "business" when addressing the public. Such power in government to channel the expression of views is unacceptable under the First Amendment. Especially where, as here, the legislature's suppression of speech suggests an attempt to give one side of a debatable public question an advantage in expressing its views to the people, the First Amendment is plainly offended. Yet the State contends that its action is necessitated by governmental interests of the highest order. We next consider these asserted interests.

. . . .

Appellee advances a number of arguments in support of his view that these interests are endangered by corporate participation in discussion of a referendum issue. They hinge upon the assumption that such participation would exert an undue influence on the outcome of a referendum vote, and—in the end—destroy the confidence of the people in the democratic process and the integrity of government. According to appellee, corporations are wealthy and powerful and their views may drown out other points of view. If appellee's arguments were supported by record or legislative findings that corporate advocacy threatened imminently to undermine democratic processes, thereby denigrating rather than serving First Amendment interests, these arguments would merit our consideration. But there has been no showing that the relative voice of corporations has been overwhelming or even significant in influencing referenda in Massachusetts, or that there has been any threat to the confidence of the citizenry in government.

Nor are appellee's arguments inherently persuasive or supported by the precedents of this Court. Referenda are held on issues, not candidates for public office. The risk of corruption perceived in cases involving candidate elections simply is not present in a popular vote on a public issue. To be sure, corporate advertising may influence the outcome of the vote; this would be its purpose. But the fact that advocacy may persuade the electorate is hardly a reason to suppress it: The Constitution protects expression which is eloquent no less than that which is unconvincing. . . . Moreover, the people in our democracy are entrusted with the responsibility for judging and evaluating the relative merits of conflicting arguments. They may consider, in making their judgment, the source and credibility of the advocate. . . .

Mr. Justice White, with whom Justice Brennan and Justice Marshall join, dissenting.

There is now little doubt that corporate communications come within the scope of the First Amendment. This, however, is merely the starting point of analysis, because an examination of the First Amendment values that corporate expression furthers and the threat to the functioning of a free society it is capable of posing reveals that it is not fungible with communications emanating from individuals and is subject to restrictions which individual expression is not. Indeed, what some have considered to be the principal function of the First Amendment, the use of communication as a means of self-expression, self-realization, and self-fulfillment, is not at all furthered by corporate speech. It is clear that the communications of profit-making corporations are not an integral part of the development of ideas, of mental exploration and of the affirmation of self. They do not represent a manifestation of individual freedom or choice. Undoubtedly, there are some corporations formed for the express purpose of advancing certain ideological causes shared by all their members, or, as in the case of the press, of disseminating information and ideas. Under such circumstances, association in a corporate form may be viewed as merely a means of achieving effective self-expression. But this is hardly the case generally with corporations operated for the purpose of making profits. Shareholders in such entities do not share a common set of political or social views, and they certainly have not invested their money for the purpose of advancing political or social causes or in an enterprise engaged in the business of disseminating news and opinion. . . .

. . . .

The governmental interest in regulating corporate political communications, especially those relating to electoral matters, also raises considerations which differ significantly from those governing the regulation of individual speech. Corporations are artificial entities created by law for the purpose of furthering certain economic goals. In order to facilitate the achievement of such ends, special rules relating to such matters as limited liability, perpetual life, and the accumulation, distribution, and taxation of assets are normally applied to them. States have provided corporations with such attributes in order to increase their economic viability and thus strengthen the economy generally. It has long been recognized, however, that the special status of corporations has placed them in a position to control vast amounts of economic power which may, if not regulated, dominate not only the economy but also the very heart of our democracy, the electoral process. . . . The State need not permit its own creation to consume it. Massachusetts could permissibly conclude that not to impose limits upon the political activities of corporations would have placed it in a position of departing from neutrality and indirectly assisting the propagation of corporate views because of the advantages its laws give to the corporate acquisition of funds to finance such activities. Such expenditures may be viewed as seriously threatening the role of the First Amendment as a guarantor of a free marketplace of ideas. Ordinarily, the expenditure of funds to promote political causes may be assumed to bear some relation to the fervency with which they are held. Corporate political expression, however, is not only divorced from the convictions of individual corporate shareholders, but also, because of the ease with which corporations are permitted to accumulate capital, bears no relation to the conviction with which the ideas expressed are held by the communicator.

The Court's opinion appears to recognize at least the possibility that fear of corporate domination of the electoral process would justify restrictions upon corporate expenditures and contributions in connection with referenda but brushes this interest aside by asserting that "there has been no showing that the relative voice of corporations has been overwhelming or even significant in influencing referenda in

Massachusetts," and by suggesting that the statute in issue represents an attempt to give an unfair advantage to those who hold views in opposition to positions which would otherwise be financed by corporations. It fails even to allude to the fact, however, that Massachusetts' most recent experience with unrestrained corporate expenditures in connection with ballot questions establishes precisely the contrary. In 1972, a proposed amendment to the Massachusetts Constitution which would have authorized the imposition of a graduated income tax on both individuals and corporations was put to the voters. The Committee for Jobs and Government Economy, an organized political committee, raised and expended approximately $120,000 to oppose the proposed amendment, the bulk of it raised through large corporate contributions. Three of the present appellant corporations each contributed $3,000 to this committee. In contrast, the Coalition for Tax Reform, Inc., the only political committee organized to support the 1972 amendment, was able to raise and expend only approximately $7,000. Perhaps these figures reflect the Court's view of the appropriate role which corporations should play in the Massachusetts electoral process, but it nowhere explains why it is entitled to substitute its judgment for that of Massachusetts and other States, as well as the United States, which have acted to correct or prevent similar domination of the electoral process by corporate wealth.

COMMENTS

1. Although there is no certainty that money assures electoral success, there is a very strong correlation between winning and outspending your opponent. Moreover, politicians certainly *act* as if outspending their rivals matters a great deal. Can we still speak of having political equality even when there are vastly different sums of money spent on campaigns and candidates?

2. What is "wrong," if anything, with allowing individuals to sell their votes to the highest bidder? Do you not have a right to do what you please with your rights?

7

WELFARE

Americans are generally ambivalent about welfare and the poor population. If we are speaking theoretically about the "truly needy" or the "deserving poor," then there is near universal agreement that those who are in this population deserve our assistance and aid. One of the leading writers in this area, former Reagan administration counsel Martin Anderson, summarizes a number of studies in this area this way: "The public favors help for people who cannot help themselves, but not for those who can. Americans apparently feel government could both increase aid to the truly poor *and* cut overall welfare spending—if welfare program administrators would get rid of dishonest welfare recipients. This seems to be what they have in mind when they think of welfare 'reform.' "[1] The problem that arises, however, is in determining who is truly needy and which part of the poor population is deserving of our assistance.

There are a number of misperceptions concerning poverty and welfare use that must be addressed at the outset.[2] The first is the notion that poverty affects someone else, not people like you and me. Although this is statistically correct, it might surprise you to find out that during a ten-year period, one in four people in this country will experience poverty in at least one year in ten. Moreover, many of those who do experience poverty are "typical" American citizens, who have become victims of some unpleasant situation in life, often divorce.

Welfare is often viewed as a program for blacks, particularly young black women. In fact, in any given year there are more whites than blacks receiving welfare, usually on the order of 58 to 42 percent. Blacks, however, are much more likely to be poor for longer periods of time than whites are. There is also a common perception that those who are on welfare undoubtedly come from welfare families themselves and that their offspring, too, will be welfare recipients. But one of the most noteworthy aspects of welfare is how much mobility there is in and among the welfare population. Duncan and his associates find that during a ten-year period, between one-third and one-half of those who were poor one year were *not* poor the next. Moreover, among women who have left the homes of parents who received welfare income, most are not likely to be receiving welfare themselves.

Another common view is that very few individuals on welfare work, and concomitant with this view is another: that if welfare recipients did in fact work, they would not need the public dole. The Income Dynamic Study at the University of Michigan finds instead that

> the typical able-bodied, non-elderly male household head living below the poverty line worked 85 percent of normal full-time work hours, and increasing work hours to 100 percent would have lifted very few out of poverty. Female household heads in poverty, on the other hand, did work many fewer hours than their nonpoor counterparts. However, their wage rates were so low that even large increases in work hours would not have pulled many of them above the poverty line.[3]

If you want to test this position, figure out what a full-time worker being paid minimum wage makes a year. Multiply forty hours per week by $3.35 an hour. (Note that it is quite likely that the minimum wage will soon increase to $4 an hour.) This total comes to $134 per week, multiplied by fifty-two weeks a year (an unlikely proposition, by the way), for a yearly salary of less than $7,000. At the present time the poverty line for a family of four is more than $11,000. What we find is that our full-time worker at minimum wage garners a salary considerably lower than the poverty level. In 1988, 31 percent of the black population fell below the poverty line compared with 11 percent of the white population.

Another fact of some interest is the marked increase in the number of female-headed families in this country. In 1968, 27 percent of the black households and 9 percent of the white households in the United States were headed by a female. Twenty years later, more than 25 percent of the white households and fully 44 percent of the black households were headed by women. Families headed by women quite often translate into households beneath the poverty line and often for long periods of time.

There is also the view that the U.S. government spends considerable sums of money on welfare.[4] Consider 1981 as an example. In that year the federal government spent $497.4 billion on nondefense items. Of this amount, interest payments, which generally benefit the rich and federal retirees, amounted to $82.5 billion of this total. Payments to individuals amounted to $316.6 billion. Of this amount, $60 billion went to Medicare and Medicaid. Sixty-five percent of the former and more than 50 percent of the latter went to people older than sixty-five. Various retirement expenditures (Social Security, Federal Employee, Railroad Retirement, and so on) came to $256 billion. Moreover, most of these monies went to people who were not poor. In fact, the funds directly assigned to the income security of those at the bottom of the society amounted to a little less than $43 billion. What this also suggests is that the federal government could completely eliminate any and all welfare programs and still not come close to balancing the federal budget.

A final point to be made concerns how much individual welfare recipients receive. There is little doubt that some, perhaps many, of those who receive welfare cheat the system, although studies have also shown the opposite: that many of those eligible for welfare never receive it.[5] What has to be recognized, however, is that the sums of money received from welfare will make very few rich. Because there are no national guidelines, welfare payments vary dramatically from state to state. Nevertheless, let me use welfare payments in Indiana as an example of benefit amounts. The maximum that a mother with two children can receive in Indiana at the present time is $288 per month in AFDC and $236 in food stamps. This amount comes out to $524 per month (calculating food stamps at their face value), or $6,288 per year. Out of this amount the family has to pay for shelter, transportation, clothes, food, utilities, and so on. In addition, AFDC recipients receive Medicaid, which essentially provides free medical services. Note two things. The first is that the benefits received are rather minimal by any standard. The second relates to the first. Although welfare benefits are not generous, there is not a very large gap between what a full-time worker making minimum wage receives and what a welfare mother receives using Indiana's benefit level.

The discussion thus far of poverty and welfare use should not be interpreted as a sanctification of either poverty or those receiving welfare. There are, however, some common misperceptions in this area that seem to perpetuate themselves. In fairness, some theorists do maintain that welfare is counterproductive and is responsible for many of the social ills affecting the poor population. This is the thesis of a very powerful book by Charles Murray entitled *Losing Ground.*[6]

Murray argues that the enormous increase in social welfare expenditures during the past two decades has done very little to eradicate poverty and quite likely has exacerbated the problem.[7] His thesis is that the welfare state, as we now know it, offers strong disincentives for people to work and to marry. This is particularly true because welfare benefits are often comparable to pay at minimum wage and because a live-in boyfriend's wages are not counted as part of a woman's assets for welfare purposes. In light of this, Murray offers this policy prescriptive: the dismantling of the entire social welfare system in the United States.

Congress enacted major welfare reform in 1988. Among the major provisions enacted into federal law was the general requirement that those receiving welfare benefits work for those benefits. This was accompanied by a push to promote job training for welfare recipients, the rationale being that large numbers of the welfare population did not possess adequate job skills. Finally, Congress attempted to eliminate the disincentive not to marry by allowing married couples to receive welfare.

As a general rule the judicial branch has not concerned itself with the structures and policies of the welfare system in this country. A rare exception has already been noted—*Kelly v. Goldberg*[8]—in which the Supreme Court decided that welfare benefits constituted a property right that could not be terminated without some form of due process of law. But *Goldberg* involved a procedural question. In terms of substantive issues, particularly benefit levels, courts generally have been quite leery of entering into this fray. The first two cases in this chapter are evidence of this judicial hesitancy. *Dandridge v. Williams* involved a statutory and constitutional challenge to a Maryland regulation that set a maximum amount of AFDC that a family could receive, regardless of family size or the computed standard of need. *Lyng v. International Union et al.* was a challenge to a Department of Agriculture regulation that prohibited a family from receiving food stamps when a member of that household was on strike. A question raised by both of these cases, and that was raised earlier in *Plyler,* is whether "innocent" children are paying for the "sins" of their parents.

Massachusetts Coalition for the Homeless v. Dukakis, a decision by a lower court in Massachusetts, is included in this volume because it offered a rare judicial challenge to the welfare policies of a state. Are Judge Grabau's orders proper? Or are these kinds of decisions better left to the political branches of government? What will happen if judges do not force the issue as Judge Grabau did in this particular case? In short, what should a judge do in the face of human suffering *and* legislative inertia?

The last case in this chapter, *State v. Moe,* occurred during the Great Depression, and the issue before the court was whether an individual could claim "necessity" as a defense in a criminal action for stealing. The issue is still with us today, particularly with the teeming homeless population that exists in this country. Simply stated, if you were a judge, would you punish a homeless person who had broken into an abandoned building, say, or stolen a loaf of bread?

NOTES

1. Martin Anderson, *Welfare* (Stanford, Calif.: Hoover Institution Press, 1978), p. 63.

2. The research for this information comes from a panel study at the Institute for Social Research at the University of Michigan and can be found in Greg Duncan et al., *Years of Poverty, Years of Plenty: The Changing Economic Fortunes of Workers and Families* (Ann Arbor, Mich.: Institute for Social Research, 1984).

3. Ibid., p. 53.

4. This example comes from Michael Harrington, *The New American Poverty* (New York: Penguin Books, 1985), p. 89.

5. Martin Tolchin, "Many Rejected for Welfare Aid over Paperwork," *New York Times,* October 29, 1988, p. 1.

6. Charles Murray, *Losing Ground: American Social Policy, 1950–1980* (New York: Basic Books, 1984).

7. Murray writes: "In 1968, as Lyndon Johnson left office 13 percent of the Americans were poor, using the official definition. Over the next twelve years, our expenditures on social welfare quadrupled. And, in 1980, the percentage of poor Americans was—13 percent." Ibid., p. 8.

8. 397 U.S. 254 (1970).

Dandridge v. Williams, 397 U.S. 471 (1970)

Justice Stewart delivered the opinion of the Court.

This case involves the validity of a method used by Maryland, in the administration of an aspect of its public welfare program, to reconcile the demands of its needy citizens with the finite resources available to meet those demands. . . .

The operation of the Maryland welfare system is not complex. . . . It computes the standard of need for each eligible family based on the number of children in the family and the circumstances under which the family lives. In general, the standard of need increases with each additional person in the household, but the increments become proportionately smaller. The regulation here in issue imposes upon the grant that any single family may receive an upper limit of $250 per month in certain counties and Baltimore City, and of $240 per month elsewhere in the State. The appellees all have large families. . . . The appellees urged in the District Court that the maximum grant limitation operates to discriminate against them merely because of the size of their families, in violation of the Equal Protection Clause of the Fourteenth Amendment. . . .

. . . .

. . . Maryland says that its maximum grant regulation is wholly free of any invidiously discriminatory purpose or effect, and that the regulation is rationally supportable on at least four entirely valid grounds. The regulation can be clearly justified, Maryland argues, in terms of legitimate state interests in encouraging gainful employment, in maintaining an equitable balance in economic status as between welfare families and those supported by a wage-earner, in providing incentives for family planning, and in allocating available public funds in such a way as fully to meet the needs of the largest possible number of families. . . .

In the area of economics and social welfare, a State does not violate the Equal Protection Clause merely because the classifications made by its laws are imperfect. If the classification has some "reasonable basis," it does not offend the Constitution simply because the classification is not made with mathematical nicety or because in practice it results in some inequality. The problems of government are practical ones and may justify, if they do not require, rough accommodations—illogical, it may be, and unscientific. A statutory discrimination will not be set aside if any state of facts reasonably may be conceived to justify it.

To be sure, the cases cited [omitted], and many others enunciating this fundamental standard under the Equal Protection Clause, have in the main involved state regulation of business or industry. The administration of public welfare assistance, by contrast, involves the most basic economic needs of impoverished human beings. We recognize the dramatically real factual difference between the cited cases and this one, but we can find no basis for applying a different constitutional standard. . . .

Under this long-established meaning of the Equal Protection Clause, it is clear that the Maryland maximum grant regulation is constitutionally valid. We need not explore all the reasons that the State advances in justification of the regulation. It is enough that a solid foundation for the regulation can be found in the State's legitimate interest in encouraging employment and in avoiding discrimination between welfare families and the families of the working poor. . . .

· ·

We do not decide today that the Maryland regulation is wise, that it best fulfills the relevant social and economic objectives that Maryland might ideally espouse, or that a more just and humane system could not be devised. Conflicting claims of morality and intelligence are raised by opponents and proponents of almost every measure, certainly including the one before us. But the intractable economic, social, and even philosophical problems presented by public welfare assistance programs are not the business of this Court. The Constitution may impose certain procedural safeguards upon systems of welfare administration, *Goldberg v. Kelly*, 397 U.S. 254 (1970). But the Constitution does not empower this Court to second-guess state officials charged with the difficult responsibility of allocating limited public welfare funds among the myriad of potential recipients.

Justice Marshall, whom Justice Brennan joins, dissenting.

Under the so-called "traditional test," a classification is said to be permissible under the Equal Protection Clause unless it is "without any reasonable basis." On the other hand, if the classification affects a "fundamental right," then the state interest in perpetuating the classification must be "compelling" in order to be sustained.

This case simply defies easy characterization in terms of one or the other of these "tests." The cases relied on by the Court, in which a "mere rationality" test was actually used, e.g., *Williamson v. Lee Optical Co.*, 348 U.S. 483 (1955), are most accurately described as involving the application of equal protection reasoning to the regulation of business interests. The extremes to which the Court has gone in dreaming up rational bases for state regulation in that area may in many instances be ascribed to a healthy revulsion from the Court's earlier excesses in using the Constitution to protect interests that have more than enough power to protect themselves in the legislative halls. This case, involving the literally vital interests of a powerless minority—poor families without breadwinners—is far removed from the area of business regulation, as the Court concedes. Why then is the standard used in those cases imposed here? We are told no more than that this case falls in "the area of economics and social welfare," with the implication that from there the answer is obvious.

In my view, equal protection analysis of this case is not appreciably advanced by the a priori definition of a "right," fundamental or otherwise. Rather, concentration must be placed upon the character of the classification in question, the relative importance to individuals in the class discriminated against of the governmental benefits that they do not receive, and the asserted state interests in support of the classification. . . .

It is the individual interests here at stake that, as the Court concedes, most clearly distinguish this case from the "business regulation" equal protection cases. AFDC support to needy dependent children provides the stuff that sustains those children's lives: food, clothing, shelter. . . .

· ·

Maryland has urged that the maximum grant regulation serves to maintain a rough equality between wage earning families and

AFDC families, thereby increasing the political support for—or perhaps reducing the opposition to—the AFDC program. . . .

. . . .

Vital to the employment-incentive basis found by the Court to sustain the regulation is, of course, the supposition that an appreciable number of AFDC recipients are in fact employable. For it is perfectly obvious that limitations upon assistance cannot reasonably operate as a work incentive with regard to those who cannot work or who cannot be expected to work. In this connection, Maryland candidly notes that "only a very small percentage of the total universe of welfare recipients are employable." The State, however, urges us to ignore the "total universe" and to concentrate attention instead upon the heads of AFDC families. Yet the very purpose of the AFDC program since its inception has been to provide assistance for dependent children. The State's position is thus that the State may deprive certain needy children of assistance to which they would otherwise be entitled in order to provide an arguable work incentive for their parents. But the State may not wield its economic whip in this fashion when the effect is to cause a deprivation to needy dependent children in order to correct an arguable fault of their parents.

Even if the invitation of the State to focus upon the heads of AFDC families is accepted, the minimum rationality of the maximum grant regulation is hard to discern. The District Court found that of Maryland's more than 32,000 AFDC families, only about 116 could be classified as having employable members, and, of these, the number to which the maximum grant regulation was applicable is not disclosed by the record. The State objects that this figure includes only families in which the father is unemployed and fails to take account of families in which an employable mother is the head of the household. At the same time, however, the State itself

has recognized that the vast proportion of these mothers are in fact unemployable because they are mentally or physically incapacitated, because they have no marketable skills, or, most prominently, because the best interests of the children dictate that the mother remain in the home. Thus, it is clear, although the record does not disclose precise figures, that the total number of "employable" mothers is but a fraction of the total number of AFDC mothers. Furthermore, the record is silent as to what proportion of large families subject to the maximum have "employable" mothers. Indeed, one must assume that the presence of the mother in the home can be less easily dispensed with in the case of large families, particularly where small children are involved and alternative provisions for their care are accordingly more difficult to arrange. . . .

. . . .

In the final analysis, Maryland has set up an AFDC program structured to calculate and pay the minimum standard of need to dependent children. Having set up that program, however, the State denies some of those needy children the minimum subsistence standard of living, and it does so on the wholly arbitrary basis that they happen to be members of large families. . . .

COMMENTS

1. Note that one of the arguments employed by the Court in *Plyler* in mandating that undocumented school age children be admitted to public schools was that these children should not pay for the misdeeds of their parents. Why does this same argument not apply here? Is it not true that children will have no control over how many other children their parents have? Are not children in large families paying for the "sins" of their folks?

2. For those of you who think that *Dandridge* was wrongly decided, how far are you willing to extend the principle of the dissent? The argument about "innocent" children is a compelling one. Yet would you let it dictate welfare

policy? For example, do you think that a state should be prohibited from ever withdrawing or reducing welfare benefits (in order to protect the innocent child), even if it can be shown that the parent has defrauded the state?

3. What if a state does not have *any* means of public assistance—could some poor person claim that he (and others like him) has a right to some form of public assistance?

Lyng v. International Union et al., 99 L. Ed. 2d 380 (1988)

Justice White delivered the opinion of the Court.

A 1981 amendment to the Food Stamp Act, Sec. 109, states that no household shall become eligible to participate in the food stamp program during the time that any member of the household is on strike or shall increase the allotment of food stamps that it was receiving already because the income of the striking member has decreased. We must decide whether this provision is valid under the First and the Fifth Amendments.

. . . .

Because the statute challenged here has no substantial impact on any fundamental interest and does not "affect with particularity any protected class," we confine our consideration to whether the statutory classification "is rationally related to a legitimate governmental interest." We have stressed that this standard of review is typically quite deferential; legislative classifications are "presumed to be valid," largely for the reason that the drawing of lines that create distinctions is peculiarly a legislative task and an unavoidable one.

The Government submits that this statute serves three objectives. Most obvious . . . is to cut federal expenditures. Second, the limited funds available were to be used when the need was likely to be greatest, an approach which Congress thought did not justify food stamps for strikers. Third was the concern that the food stamp program was being used to provide one-sided support for labor strikes; the Senate Report indicated that the amendment was intended to remove the basis for that perception and criticism.

We have little trouble in concluding that Sec. 109 is rationally related to the legitimate governmental objective of avoiding undue favoritism to one side or the other in private labor disputes. The Senate Report declared: "Public policy demands an end to the food stamp subsidization of all strikers who become eligible for the program solely through the temporary loss of income during a strike. Union strike funds should be responsible for providing support and benefits to strikers during labor-management disputes." It was no part of the purposes of the Food Stamp Act to establish a program that would serve as a weapon in labor disputes; the Act was passed to alleviate hunger and malnutrition and to strengthen the agricultural economy. The Senate Report stated that "allowing strikers to be eligible for food stamps has damaged the program's public integrity" and thus endangers these other goals served by the program. Congress acted in response to these problems.

It would be difficult to deny that this statute works at least some discrimination against strikers and their households. For the duration of the strike, those households cannot increase their allotment of food stamps even though the loss of income occasioned by the strike may well be enough to qualify them for food stamps or to increase their allotment if the fact of the strike itself were ignored. Yet Congress was in a difficult position when it sought to address the problems it had identified. Because a striking individual faces an immediate and often total drop in income during a strike, a single controversy pitting an employer against its employees can lead to a large number of claims for food stamps for as long as the controversy endures. It is the disbursement of food stamps in response to such a controversy that constitutes the source of the concern, and of the dangers to the program, that Congress believed it was important to remedy. We are not free in this instance to reject Congress' views about what constitutes wise economic or social policy.

. . . .

In view of the foregoing, we need not determine whether either of the other two proffered justifications for Sec. 109 would alone suffice. But it is relevant to note that protecting the fiscal integrity of government programs, and of the Government as a whole, is a legitimate concern of the State. This does not mean that Congress can pursue the objective of saving money by discriminating against individuals or groups. But our review of distinctions that Congress draws in order to make allocations from a finite pool of resources must be deferential, for the discretion about how best to spend money to improve the general welfare is lodged in Congress rather than the courts. . . .

Appellees contend and the District Court held that the legislative classification is irrational because of the "critical" fact that it "impermissibly strikes at the striker through his family." This, however, is nothing more than a description of how the food stamp program operates as a general matter. Whenever an individual takes any action that hampers his or her ability

to meet the program's eligibility requirements, such as quitting a job or failing to comply with the work-registration requirements, the entire household suffers accordingly. We have never questioned the constitutionality of the entire Act on this basis. . . . Reversed.

Justice Marshall, with whom Justice Brennan and Justice Blackmun join, dissenting.

The Secretary asserts that the striker amendment is rationally related to three legitimate governmental goals. First, the Secretary points out that denying food stamps to households containing a striker will reduce federal expenditures. Second, the Secretary contends that the striker amendment channels limited public funds to the most needy. Finally, the Secretary maintains that the striker amendment fosters governmental neutrality in private labor disputes. Although the asserted goals are legitimate, it is difficult to discern a rational relationship between them and the striker amendment. The arguments of the Secretary and the Court seeking to establish such a relationship are fraught with pervasive inconsistencies.

The Secretary's argument that the striker amendment will save money proves far too much. According to the Secretary's reasoning, the exclusion of any unpopular group from a public benefit program would survive rational basis scrutiny, because exclusion always would result in a decrease in governmental expenditures. Although it is true, as the Court observes, that preserving the fiscal integrity of the government is a legitimate concern of the state, this Court . . . has noted that a concern for the preservation of resources standing alone can hardly justify the classification used in allocating those resources. . . .

Perhaps recognizing this necessity, the Secretary defends the singling out of strikers and their households as rationally related to the goal of channeling resources to those persons most "genuinely in need." As a threshold matter, however, households denied food stamps because of the presence of a striker are as "needy" in terms of financial resources as households that qualify for food stamps: the former are denied food stamps despite the fact that they meet the financial eligibility requirements of even after strike-fund payments are counted as household income. This point has particular poignancy for the infants and children of a striking worker. Their need for nourishment is in no logical way diminished by the striker's action. The denial to these children of what is often the only buffer between them and malnourishment and disease cannot be justified as a targeting of the most needy: they are the most needy. The record below bears witness to this point in a heartbreaking fashion.

The Secretary argues, however, that the striker amendment is related to need at least in the sense of willingness to work, if not in the strict sense of financial eligibility. Because the Food Stamp Act generally excludes persons unwilling to work—and their households—the Secretary argues that it is consistent to exclude strikers and their households as well, on the ground that strikers remain "unwilling to work," at least at the struck business, for the duration of the strike. In the Secretary's eyes, a striker is akin to an unemployed worker who day after day refuses to accept available work. One flaw in this argument is its false factual premise. It is simply not true, as the Secretary argues, that a striker always has a job that "remains available to him." Many strikes result in the complete cessation of a business's operations, so that the decision of an individual striker to return to work would be unavailing. Moreover, many of the businesses that continue to operate during a strike hire permanent replacements for the striking workers. In this situation as well, a striker no longer has the option of returning to work. In fact, the record in this case reveals that a number of appellees were denied food stamps even though they had been permanently replaced by their employers.

But even if it were true that strikers always can return to their jobs, the Secretary's "willingness to work" rationale falls apart in light of the glaring disparity between the treatment of strikers and the treatment of those who are unwilling to work for other reasons. People who voluntarily quit their jobs are not disqualified from receiving food stamps if, after notice and a hearing, they can demonstrate that they quit with "good cause." Moreover, even if the state agency determines that the quit was without good cause, the voluntary quitter is disqualified only for a period of 90 days, and the quitter's household is disqualified only if the quitter was the "head of household." In contrast, a striker is given no opportunity to demonstrate that the strike was for "good cause," even though strikers frequently allege that unfair labor practices by their employer precipitated the strike. In addition, strikers and their entire households, no matter how minimal the striker's contribution to the household's income may have been, are disqualified for the duration of the strike, even if the striker is permanently replaced or business operations temporarily cease.

. . . .

Unable to explain completely the striker amendment by the "willingness to work" rationale, the Secretary relies most heavily on yet a third rationale: the promotion of governmental neutrality in labor disputes. . . .

. . . .

The "neutrality" argument reflects a profoundly inaccurate view of the relationship of the modern federal government to the various parties to a labor dispute. Both individuals and businesses are connected to the government by a complex web of supports and incentives. On the one hand, individuals may be eligible to receive a wide variety of health, education, and welfare-related benefits. On the other hand, businesses may be eligible to receive a myriad of tax subsidies through deductions, depreciation, and credits or direct subsidies in the form of government loans through the Small Business Administration (SBA). Businesses also may receive lucrative government contracts and invoke the protections of the Bankruptcy Act against their creditors. None of these governmental subsidies to businesses is made contingent on the businesses' abstention from labor disputes, even if a labor dispute is the direct cause of the claim to a subsidy. For example, a small business in need of financial support because of labor troubles may seek a loan from the SBA. And a business that claims a net operating loss as a result of a strike or a lockout presumably may carry the loss back three years and forward five years in order to maximize its tax advantage. In addition, it appears that businesses may be eligible for special tax credits for hiring replacement workers during a strike under the Targeted Jobs Tax Credit program. When viewed against the network of governmental support of both labor and management, the withdrawal of the single support of food stamps—a support critical to the continued life and health of an individual worker and his or her family— cannot be seen as a "neutral" act. Altering the backdrop of governmental support in this one-sided and devastating way amounts to a penalty on strikers, not neutrality.

. . . .

I agree with the Court that "[i]t was no part of the purposes of the Food Stamp Act to establish a program that would serve as a weapon in labor disputes." The striker amendment under consideration today, however, seems to have precisely that purpose—one admittedly irreconcilable with the legitimate goals of the food stamp program. No other purpose can adequately explain the especially harsh treatment reserved for strikers and their families by the 1981 enactment. Because I conclude that the striker amendment cannot survive even rational basis scrutiny, I would affirm the District Court's invalidation of the amendment. I dissent.

COMMENTS

1. Are you convinced that the government purpose behind the change in the food stamp program in 1981, the first year of the Reagan administration, was simply to be "neutral" in management-labor disputes?

2. The same issue we have seen before of children paying for the sins of their parents comes up again in *Lyng.* Does the Court offer a consistent answer?

3. Should the principle in *Lyng* be extended to other areas of social welfare as well? For example, should the family of a striking worker also be denied welfare benefits even if otherwise eligible?

Massachusetts Coalition for the Homeless v. Dukakis, Superior Court Civil Action No. 80109

Judge Grabau.

This action was brought by the plaintiffs to force an increase in A.F.D.C. benefits, which they believe the Department of Public Welfare is statutorily obliged to pay

pursuant to G.L. c. 118, Sec. 2. The part of the statute which the plaintiffs claim is being violated requires that "the aid furnished shall be sufficient to enable such parent to bring up such child or children properly in his or her own home, and shall be in an amount to be determined in accordance with budgetary standards of the department." In support of their contention, the plaintiffs have entered into the record hundreds of pages of affidavits attesting to the fact that there are a large number of citizens of the Commonwealth who are financially unable to raise their children in their own homes and, as a result, are currently living in emergency shelters or under even less habitable conditions.

. . . .

In analyzing the adequacy of A.F.D.C. benefits, this court relied primarily on information provided by the Department of Public Welfare. It is important to note, however, that the plaintiffs in this case claim that most of the statistical data provided by the DPW underrepresents the true scope of the problems A.F.D.C. recipients encounter in trying to survive in the Commonwealth.

With this in mind, the living conditions of those currently receiving A.F.D.C. benefits can be evaluated. One of the best summaries comes from the Department of Public Welfare itself, which stated in its *Budget Narrative* for FY 1987 at 96:

Most A.F.D.C. families do not have an adequate income to compete successfully for housing in the tight private housing market. Currently, the median rent of housing units in Boston of $530 is above the entire $432 monthly grant for an A.F.D.C. family of 3. As a result, families devote a disproportionate share of their income to housing, scrimping on other necessities such as food and clothing. Currently, A.F.D.C. recipients spend 70% of their A.F.D.C. grant on fuel and housing, leaving the remaining 30% to cover all other expenditures. Often this level of housing expenditures cannot be maintained and families become homeless.

It is difficult to know how many A.F.D.C. families are currently homeless, but again the Department of Public Welfare's 1987 *Budget Narrative* is instructive:

The 1985 *Massachusetts Report on Homelessness* from the Executive Office of Human Services

estimated that there are 8,000 to 10,000 homeless persons statewide. Figures from the 1985 Boston Emergency Shelter Commission's *Plan for Boston's Homeless,* however, indicate that there are 9,800 homeless men, women and children in Boston alone. There is ample evidence that homelessness is increasing. . . . Historically, the homeless population consisted largely of "street people." . . . However, the 1985 EOHS *Report of Homelessness* indicates that families now constitute a substantial proportion of the Massachusetts homeless population. These families, typically a mother and her children, make up a portion of the homeless population that is continuing to grow rapidly. . . . Homeless families are frequently recipients of A.F.D.C.

The psychological effects of homelessness were summed up in the affidavit of Dr. Mathew P. Dumont:

The fear of losing one's home, of being "on the streets," as expressed by many of my patients, is not merely the threat of exposure to the elements. . . . What gives the experience its particular horror, particularly among mothers of young children, is a whole ecology of stressful realities. At some deep and central level of our emotional lives we all carry a sense of dread that we will someday be alone and abandoned in the world, like atoms in the void. The heartrending cry of a child momentarily lost in a downtown crowd is the expression of that dread. And, later in the essence of the fear of death is the same sense of isolation, of being cut off, alone in the universe. . . . The existence of a "home," an address, a place where someone we know can always be found, where we belong, is the only source of solace for that universal dread. Every homeless mother and child carries within them empty space where the solace can be found in the rest of us. It affects the ways they will deal with the subsequent experience, giving the anxieties that most of us carry with us a whole new dimension of depth.

The plaintiffs claim in their affidavits that the current level of A.F.D.C. benefits combined with food stamps is 40% below the federal poverty line. The defendants claim that the combined benefits are about 18% below the federal poverty line. This court notes that in 1973 A.F.D.C. benefits were 15% *greater* than the federal poverty line. Significantly, this court recognizes that in his deposition, Mathew W. Fishman, Assistant Commissioner for Budget Control at the Department of Public Welfare, admitted that the 1987 budget request of the Governor, *"would not meet their* [people for whom A.F.D.C. is the only income] *minimum subsistence needs."* This court neither has the duty nor the expertise to say what dollar amount would enable "[a] parent to bring up such a child or children properly in his or her own home," but based on the affidavits of the plaintiffs and the admissions of the defendants themselves, this court can say, as a matter of law, that the current level is inadequate to conform to the statutory mandate of G.L. c. 118, Sec. 1.

· ·

VII. *RULINGS AND ORDERS*

· ·

(6) This Court declares as a matter of law that the current level of A.F.D.C. benefits fails to meet the mandate of G.L. c. 118, Sec. 2, which states that "the aid furnished shall be sufficient to enable such parent to bring up such child or children properly in his or her own home."

· ·

(8) This court orders Charles M. Atkins, as he is the commissioner of the Department of Public Welfare, to formulate a revised standard of assistance that complies with the statutory mandate of G.L. c. 118, Sec. 2 and c. 18, Sec. 2 (B)(g), and that is sufficient to enable A.F.D.C. recipients to bring up their children properly in their homes.

COMMENTS

1. Is Judge Grabau's order an appropriate one for the judicial branch? Or is this a shining example of an activist judge, attempting to cure one of society's ills, taking it upon himself to order the state to do something it might not be capable of doing?

2. Is there a fundamental right to shelter? The U.S. Supreme Court has suggested that there is not. In dicta in *Lindsey v. Normet*, 405 U.S. 56, 74 (1972), the Court held: "We do not denigrate the importance of decent, safe and sanitary housing. But the Constitution does not provide judicial remedies for every social and economic ill. We are unable to perceive in that document any constitutional guarantee of access to dwellings of a particular quality or any recognition of the right of a tenant to occupy the real property of his landlord beyond the term of his lease without payment of rent."

3. The subtlety of the ethical dilemma raised in the principal case was highlighted in a case in Denver in 1988. Dorothy King, the operator of a shelter for abused women and children, led a group of squatters who broke into and occupied HUD-owned property that had been foreclosed and lay vacant. (HUD is steward to more than forty-seven thousand vacant and foreclosed homes nationally, but fewer than 500 are used to shelter the homeless.) Not all in the community agreed with such self-help actions. The strongest reaction to the squatters came from former residents of these houses: "I get foreclosed on, and now you're going to give my house to some homeless person?" How would you respond?

State v. Moe, 24 P. 2d 638 (1933)

Justice Blake delivered the opinion of the Court.

In the afternoon of September 3, 1932, a large number of unemployed people, among whom were the appellants, gathered together and marched to the Red Cross commissary in the city of Anacortes. Their purpose was to make a demonstration in support of a demand for a greater allowance of flour than had theretofore been made by the relief committee. Not finding the chairman of the committee at the commissary, they dispatched a messenger for him. On being informed that the chairman could not leave his place of business, they then marched to his office. . . .

The chairman advised them that it was impossible to comply with the demand, whereupon someone asked if that was final. Being informed that it was, several persons in the crowd said, in substance: "Very well, we'll get it." Up to this point the assemblage had been peaceable and lawful.

The crowd then left the chairman's office, and a large number of them (variously estimated from forty to seventy-five) proceeded to the Skaggs store, which they entered. Many of them helped themselves to groceries, which they took away without paying for them. . . .

. . . .

Appellants offered to prove the conditions of poverty and want among the unemployed of Anacortes and Skagit county on and prior to September 3d. This proof was offered for the purpose of showing a motive and justification for the raid on the Skaggs store and to show that the raid was spontaneous and not premeditated.

Economic necessity has never been accepted as a defense to a criminal charge. The reason is that, were it ever countenanced, it would leave to the individual the right to take the law into his own hands. In larceny cases economic necessity is frequently invoked in mitigation of punishment, but has never been recognized as a defense. Nor is it available as a defense to the charge of riot. The fact that a riot is spontaneous makes it nonetheless premeditated. Premeditation may, and frequently does, arise on the instant. A lawful assembly may turn into a riotous one in a moment of time over trivial incident or substantial provocation. When it does, those participating are guilty of riot, and neither the cause of the riot nor their reason for participation in it can be interposed as a defense. The causes, great or small, are available to the participants only in mitigation of punishment. The court did not err in rejecting the offer of proof.

COMMENTS

1. One of the greatest novels ever written, Victor Hugo's *Les Misérables*, has as its genesis a comparable situation to the *Moe* case. Are you so sure that if you were in Moe's place (or that of Jean Valjean, for those of you who have read the book), you would not have done the same thing? Does this mean, however, that you would not still be morally and legally blameworthy?

2. Note that the decisions in this chapter do not really begin to consider whether the distribution of societal goods is just. For example, the *Moe* case was decided during the nadir of the Great Depression. Should that matter? Can a court arrive at a just decision without considering the question of the distribution of goods in our society at the time? Are courts equipped to do this?

3. What *is* a just distribution of societal goods? Would it be what John Rawls posits—economic inequalities, but only when they serve the purpose of those least well off? Does the United States at the present time have a just distribution of societal goods? Robert Nozick argues that we cannot determine the justness of societal

goods from the *outcome*, only from the *process* of achieving that outcome. In his view, if the ultimate distribution of income and wealth (no matter what it looks like) is the result of freely chosen transactions, then they are, by definition, just. Do you think the process can be separated from the outcome?

4. One of the more striking phenomenon of the past few years is the growing gap in income between rich and poor. Between 1979 and 1986 the average income of the wealthiest one-fifth of Americans *grew* from $70,260 to $76,300, while among the poorest one-fifth average income *fell* from $8,761 to $8,033 (in constant dollars). Put in other terms, for every $9.50 in income gained at the top, $1 was lost among the poorest among us. See Frank Levy, "A Growing Gap Between Rich and Poor," *New York Times*, May 1, 1988. Section III, p. 3. Does this mean that American society is becoming more unjust, or simply that the rich are getting richer and the poor are getting poorer?

5. An interesting point emerges from a comparison in income disparities between the United States and other Western industrialized nations. For example, Japan has an income gap only half as large as that in the United States. Does this make Japanese society more just than our own? Does it at least say that there may not necessarily be a trade-off between economic strength and income inequality?

6. In a country such as Brazil, the top 10 percent of the population receives more than 50 percent of the national income, whereas the bottom 40 percent receive 7 percent. Is this just?

8

AFFIRMATIVE ACTION OR REVERSE DISCRIMINATION?

One of the most controversial policy prescriptives in this country is affirmative action. To opponents of such programs, affirmative action is "reverse discrimination"; now white males suffer because of the color of their skin or their gender. To proponents of affirmative action, such programs are needed to redress centuries of the worst forms of discrimination as well as the residue that remains from such practices.

The Supreme Court certainly has not steered a steady course here. In *Regents of University of California v. Bakke,* our first principal case, the Court struck down a special admissions program at the University of California–Davis medical school, holding that racial quotas were violative of the Constitution. In terms of the level of judicial review, Justice Powell in his majority opinion holds that the "strict scrutiny" standard applies because the school is making classifications solely according to race. "Racial and ethnic distinctions of any sort are inherently suspect and thus call for the most exacting judicial scrutiny."

Justice Brennan disagrees with the Court's level of review in this case. He argues that it is vital to distinguish between racial classifications that discriminate *against* racial minorities and those that seek to *remedy* past and present discrimination. "[U]nlike discrimination against minorities, the use of racial preferences for remedial purposes does not inflict a pervasive injury upon individual whites in the sense that wherever they go or whatever they do, there is a significant likelihood that they will be treated as second-class citizens because of their color."

Brennan argues that the strict scrutiny standard should not apply because no fundamental right is involved here, nor can we consider whites as a group to be a suspect class. Brennan, however, is also of the mind that the rational basis standard is not appropriate in these kinds of situations either. In his view, racial classifications "designed to further remedial purposes must serve important governmental objectives and must be substantially related to achievement of those objectives."

Although the *Bakke* decision had the effect of striking down racial quotas, the Court did not rule out the possibility of using race as *a* factor when making admission decisions. In fact, Justice Powell praises the admission program at Harvard University in which an individual's race, but also his background, geographical region, and so on are considered in the admission decision.

Cases decided subsequent to *Bakke*, however, indicated that affirmative action programs, in both the public and private sector, would generally pass constitutional muster. In *United Steelworkers v. Weber*,[1] the Court held that a "voluntary" affirmative action program did not violate Title VII of the 1964 Civil Rights Act. In this case, union and management had collectively bargained for an affirmative action program that reserved for black employees 50 percent of the openings in a plant craft-training program until the percentage of the black craftworkers reflected the percentage of blacks in the local labor force. Applying standards that have often been used in subsequent affirmative action decisions, the Court justified such a remedial program this way:

> We need not today define in detail the line of demarcation between permissible and impermissible affirmative action plans. It suffices to hold that the challenged plan falls on the permissible side of the line. It does not unnecessarily trammel the interests of the white employees. It does not require the discharge of white workers and their replacement with new black hires. Nor does it create an absolute bar to the advancement of white employees; half of those trained will be white. Moreover, it is a temporary measure not to maintain racial balance, but simply to eliminate a manifest racial imbalance. Preferential selection of craft trainees at the plant will end as soon as the percentage of black skilled craft workers approximates the percentage of blacks in the local labor force.

The apparent move by the Supreme Court to uphold affirmative action programs was further evidenced by its decision in *Fullilove v. Klutznick*.[2] In this case the Court upheld a requirement in a congressional spending program that mandated that 10 percent of the federal funds granted for local public works projects be used by state or local grantees to procure services or supplies from businesses owned and controlled by statutorily defined minority groups.[3] Although the 10 percent set-aside looks very much like a quota, the Court justified the racial classification as a remedial measure taken by a coordinate branch of government.[4]

The second principal case in this chapter, *Wygant v. Jackson Board of Education*, involved a situation in which the Court has not been willing to uphold affirmative action programs—namely when such programs have the effect of interfering with the principle of seniority at the workplace. In *Wygant,* a collectively bargained contract provided that in the case of lay-offs, the percentage of minority teachers was not to be reduced. The Court overturned this provision by holding that a distinction should be made between affirmative action plans for *hiring* workers and for protecting workers from *job displacement.* "Denial of future employment opportunity is not as intrusive as loss of an existing job."

One of the arguments against affirmative action programs is that individuals are paying for the discriminatory practices of past generations. Although this statement underestimates the amount of discrimination that still exists, the generational features of affirmative action programs are too often ignored. In particular, those who have benefited from racial or gender discrimination are not necessarily long gone from this world, nor are they often singled out to make restitution. In fact, the opposite is often true. The *Wygant* decision raised such questions of intergenerational justice, but a 1987 Supreme Court decision, *U.S. v. Paradise,* highlighted this point even better.[5]

The factual background to the *Paradise* case was important to the argument made, and thus some time will be spent recounting it. In 1972, federal district court judge Johnson ruled that for almost four decades the Alabama Department of Public Safety had systematically excluded blacks from employment as state troopers. In response to this finding, Johnson imposed a hiring quota.[6] Although some black state troopers were subsequently hired at entry-level positions, by 1979 no blacks had attained the upper ranks in the department. At that time, the district court approved a partial consent decree under which the department agreed to implement a plan to promote blacks. But by 1981 no black troopers had yet been promoted. In late 1983 Judge Johnson's frustrations were evident from language in this, his latest, order: "[O]n February 10, 1984, less than two months from today, twelve years will have passed since this court condemned the racially discriminatory policies and practices of the Alabama Department of Public Safety. Nevertheless, the effects of those policies and practices remain pervasive and conspicuous at all ranks above the entry level position.[7] The court then ordered a remedy whereby at least 50 percent of the promotions were to be awarded to black troopers, if qualified black candidates were available. The Supreme Court upheld this order in the *Paradise* case.

The simple question raised is this. Are those individuals who have benefited the most from racial discrimination—whites who did not have to compete with blacks for state trooper jobs—the same individuals who will be making restitution? Clearly not. Consider white troopers in different cohort groups. The whites who benefited most from racial discrimination were those working in the department during the four decades of discrimination that Judge Johnson originally described. This group did not have to compete with blacks for jobs because blacks were systematically excluded from employment. Making *this group* a part of any restitution policy is problematic, however, simply because of the passage of time. In a sense, the continual stalling by the department probably (and unfortunately) protected this group from being a part of a restitution plan.

Whites who worked for the department before 1972 were not the only group to benefit from racial discrimination. Those whites who worked for the department from 1972 to 1984 only had to compete with blacks for entry-level positions and thus benefited from racial discrimination, although of a slightly different kind. Presumably some members of this cohort will have retired, but we might also imagine that many of these whites are now ensconced in positions of authority in the department. Will this group be seriously affected by the particular affirmative action order requiring that 50 percent of those promoted beyond the trooper level be blacks? This appears quite unlikely.

What is noteworthy about this entire situation is that the group that has benefited the *least* from racial discrimination (and perhaps did not benefit at all)—the present generation of white troopers currently in entry-level positions and those seeking their first promotion—will be the group most affected by the court's order, whereas those who have greatly benefited from "pervasive" racial discrimination—whites already in positions of power—will generally be unaffected by such orders and perhaps not at all. Has justice been achieved here?

The final case in this chapter, *Johnson v. Transportation Agency, Santa Clara County,* examined a male-female affirmative action program. Are such programs justifiable (or not justifiable, depending on your position) for the same reasons advanced for racial affirmative action programs? Note from the facts in *Johnson* that we seem to have a classic case of women working in "female" jobs and men doing "man's work." *Johnson* is an affirmative action case, and it will be examined as such, but the factual situation calls into mind another policy prescriptive: comparable worth.

The rationale behind comparable worth is that women are herded into positions already dominated by females and that they often perform jobs that are comparable to what many men do, but they receive far less pay. For example, at the present time the average female, white, full-time worker in this country earns only 56 percent of what the average male, white, full-time worker earns, and the gap is larger than it was several years ago.[8] Moreover, the mean earnings of female college graduates are lower than the mean earnings of white men with an eighth grade education. Comparable worth does not attempt to change "male" and "female" jobs as much as it attempts to have females paid for the education and skills that they possess, and presumably that they bring to *their* jobs, just as men bring their skills to their jobs, which presumably is reflected in the wages *they* earn.

In his strong dissent in *Johnson,* Justice Scalia argues that the existence of "male" and "female" jobs is not the result of discrimination but of deeply entrenched socialization patterns. If this is true, should more efforts be made to pay women what they are worth, or does the free market already do that?

NOTES

1. 443 U.S. 193 (1979).
2. 448 U.S. 448 (1980).
3. The roster of "minority groups" listed by Congress was quite unique, and it caused some concern to members of the Court. The classification defined minorities as "Negroes, Spanish-speaking, Orientals, Indians, Eskimos and Aleuts." As Justice Stevens points out, "Even if we assume that each of the six racial subclasses has suffered its own special injury at some time in our history, surely it does not necessarily follow that each of those subclasses suffered harm of identical magnitude."
4. The Court has rejected a similar effort by a local community in *City of Richmond v. J. A. Croson Co.* 102 L. Ed. 2d 854 (1989). The city of Richmond, Virginia, adopted a plan requiring prime contractors awarded city construction contracts to subcontract at least 30 percent of the dollar amount of each contract to one or more Minority Business Enterprises (MBEs). Prior to this plan, only 0.67 percent of the city's public construction expenditures over the previous five years had gone to MBEs. The population of Richmond is evenly split between blacks and whites. The Supreme Court struck down the affirmative action program, holding that these statistical disparities did not offer proof of actual racial discrimination.
5. 480 U.S. 149 (1987).
6. *NAACP v. Allen*, 340 F. Supp. 703 (MD Ala. 1972).
7. *Paradise v. Prescott*, 585 F. Supp. 72, 74 (MD Ala. 1983).
8. See, generally, Michael Evan Gold, *A Dialogue on Comparable Worth* (Ithaca, N.Y.: Cornell University Press, 1983).

Regents of the University of California v. Bakke, 438 U.S. 265 (1978)

Justice Powell delivered the opinion of the Court.

[Alan Bakke, a white male, was twice denied admission to the University of California-Davis medical school. Bakke challenges the constitutionality of the special admissions program at the school under which 16 of the 100 admission slots are set aside for minority admissions. Both times that he applied, applicants were admitted under the special admissions program with Grade Point Averages, MCAT scores, and personal interview scores significantly lower than Bakke's.]

. . . .

Petitioner does not deny that decisions based on race or ethnic origin by faculties and administrations of state universities are reviewable under the Fourteenth Amendment. For his part, respondent does not argue that all racial or ethnic classifications are per se invalid. The parties do disagree as to the level of judicial scrutiny to be applied to the special admissions program.

Petitioner argues that the court below erred in applying strict scrutiny, as this inexact term has been applied in our cases. That level of review, petitioner asserts, should be reserved for classifications that disadvantage "discrete and insular minorities." See *United States v. Carolene Products Co.*, 304 U.S. 144, 152 n 4, (1938). Respondent, on the other hand, contends that the California court correctly rejected the notion that the degree of judicial scrutiny accorded a particular racial or ethnic classification hinges upon membership in a discrete and insular minority and duly recognized that the "rights established [by the Fourteenth Amendment] are personal rights."

En route to this crucial battle over the scope of judicial review, the parties fight a sharp preliminary action over the proper characterization of the special admissions program. Petitioner prefers to view it as establishing a "goal" of minority representation in the Medical School. Respondent, echoing the courts below, labels it a racial quota.

This semantic distinction is beside the point; the special admissions program is undeniably a classification based on race and ethnic background. To the extent that there existed a pool of at least minimally qualified minority applicants to fill the 16 special admissions seats, white applicants could compete only for 84 seats in the entering class, rather than the 100 open to minority applicants. Whether this limitation is described as a quota or a goal, it is a line drawn on the basis of race and ethnic status.

The guarantees of the Fourteenth Amendment extend to all persons. Its language is explicit: "No State shall . . . deny to any person within its jurisdiction the equal protection of the laws." It is settled beyond question that the "rights created by the first section of the Fourteenth Amendment are, by its terms, guaranteed to the individual. The rights established are personal rights. The guarantee of equal protection cannot mean one thing when applied to one individual and something else when applied to a person of another color. If both are not accorded the same protection, then it is not equal.

. . . .

Petitioner urges us to adopt for the first time a more restrictive view of the Equal Protection Clause and hold that discrimination against members of the white "majority" cannot be suspect if its purpose can be characterized as "benign." The clock of our liberties, however, cannot be turned back to 1868. *Brown v. Board of Education*, at 492. It is far too late to argue that the guarantee of equal protection to all persons permits the recognition of special wards entitled to a degree of protection greater than that accorded others. "The Fourteenth Amendment is not directed solely against discrimination due to a 'two-class theory'—that is, based upon differences between 'white' and Negro."

Once the artificial line of a "two-class theory" of the Fourteenth Amendment is put aside, the difficulties entailed in varying the level of judicial review according to a perceived "preferred" status of a particular racial or ethnic minority are intractable. The concepts of "majority" and "minority" necessarily reflect temporary arrangements and political judgments. As observed above, the white "majority" itself is composed of various minority groups, most of which can lay claim to a history of prior discrimination at the hands of the State and private individuals. Not all of these groups can receive preferential treatment and corresponding judicial tolerance of distinctions drawn in terms of race and nationality, for then the only "majority" left would be a new minority of white Anglo-Saxon Protestants. There is no principled basis for deciding which groups would merit "heightened judicial solicitude" and which would not. Courts would be asked to evaluate the extent of the prejudice and consequent harm suffered by various minority groups. Those whose societal injury is thought to exceed some arbitrary level of tolerability then would be entitled to preferential classifications at the expense of individuals belonging to other groups. Those classifications would be free from exacting judicial scrutiny. As these preferences began to have their desired effect, and the consequences of past discrimination were undone, new judicial rankings would be necessary. The kind of variable sociological and political analysis necessary to produce such rankings simply does not lie within the judicial competence—even if they otherwise were politically feasible and socially desirable.

Moreover, there are serious problems of justice connected with the idea of preference itself. First, it may not always be clear that a so-called preference is in fact benign. Courts may be asked to validate burdens imposed upon individual members of a particular group in order to advance the group's general interest. Nothing in the Constitution supports the notion that individuals may be asked to suffer otherwise impermissible burdens in order to enhance the societal standing of their ethnic groups. Second, preferential programs may only reinforce common stereotypes holding that certain groups are unable to achieve success without special protection based on a factor having no relationship to individual worth. Third, there is a measure of inequity in forcing innocent persons in respondent's position to bear the burden of redressing grievances not of their making.

By hitching the meaning of the Equal Protection Clause to these transitory considerations, we would be holding, as a constitutional principle, that judicial scrutiny of classifications touching on racial and ethnic background may vary with the ebb and flow of political forces. Disparate constitutional tolerance of such classifications well may serve to exacerbate racial and ethnic antagonisms rather than alleviate them. Also, the mutability of a constitutional principle, based upon shifting political and social judgments, undermines the chances for consistent application of the Constitution from one generation to the

next, a critical feature of its coherent interpretation. In expounding the Constitution, the Court's role is to discern "principles sufficiently absolute to give them roots throughout the community and continuity over significant periods of time, and to lift them above the level of the pragmatic political judgments of a particular time and place."

. . . .

It may be assumed that the reservation of a specified number of seats in each class for individuals from the preferred ethnic groups would contribute to the attainment of considerable ethnic diversity in the student body. But petitioner's argument that this is the only effective means of serving the interest of diversity is seriously flawed. In a most fundamental sense the argument misconceives the nature of the state interest that would justify consideration of race or ethnic background. It is not an interest in simple ethnic diversity, in which a specified percentage of the student body is in effect guaranteed to be members of selected ethnic groups, with the remaining percentage an undifferentiated aggregation of students. The diversity that furthers a compelling state interest encompasses a far broader array of qualifications and characteristics of which racial or ethnic origin is but a single though important element. Petitioner's special admission program, focused solely on ethnic diversity, would hinder rather than further attainment of genuine diversity.

Nor would the state interest in genuine diversity be served by expanding petitioner's two-track system into a multitrack program with a prescribed number of seats set aside for each identifiable category of applicants. Indeed, it is inconceivable that a university would thus pursue the logic of petitioner's two-track program to the illogical end of insulating each category of applicants with certain desired qualifications from competition with all other applicants.

The experience of other university admissions programs, which take race into account in achieving the educational diversity valued by the First Amendment, demonstrates that the assignment of a fixed number of places to a minority group is not a necessary means toward the end. An illuminating example is found in the Harvard College program. . . .

In such an admissions program, race or ethnic background may be deemed a "plus" in a particular applicant's file, yet it does not insulate the individual from comparison with all other candidates for the available seats. The file of a particular black applicant may be examined for his potential contribution to diversity without the factor of race being decisive when compared, for example, with that of an applicant identified as an Italian-American if the latter is thought to exhibit qualities more likely to promote beneficial educational pluralism. Such qualities could include exceptional personal talents, unique work or service experience, leadership potential, maturity, demonstrated compassion, a history of overcoming disadvantage, ability to communicate with the poor, or other qualifications deemed important. In short, an admissions program operated in this way is flexible enough to consider all pertinent elements of diversity in light of the particular qualifications of each applicant, and to place them on the same footing for consideration, although not necessarily according them the same weight. Indeed, that weight attributed to a particular quality may vary from year to year depending upon the "mix" both of the student body and the applicants for the incoming class.

This kind of program treats each applicant as an individual in the admissions process. The applicant who loses out on the last available seat to another candidate receiving a "plus" on the basis of ethnic background will not have been foreclosed from all consideration for that seat simply because he was not the right color or had the wrong surname. It would mean only that his combined qualifications, which may have included similar nonobjective factors, did not outweigh those of the other applicant. His qualifications would have been weighed fairly and competitively, and he would have no basis to complain of unequal treatment under the Fourteenth Amendment.

It has been suggested that an admissions program which considers race only as one factor is simply a subtle and more sophisticated—but no less effective—means of according racial preference than the Davis program. A facial intent to discriminate, however, is evident in petitioner's preference program and not denied in this case. No such facial infirmity exists in an admissions program where race or ethnic background is simply one element—to be weighed fairly against other elements—in the selection process. . . .

In summary, it is evident that the Davis special admissions program involves the use of an explicit racial classification never before countenanced by this Court. It tells applicants who are not Negro, Asian, or Chicano that they are totally excluded from a specific percentage of the seats in an entering class. No matter how strong their qualifications, quantitative and extracurricular, including their own potential for contribution to educational diversity, they are never afforded the chance to compete with applicants from the preferred groups for the special admissions seats. At the same time, the preferred applicants have the opportunity to compete for every seat in the class.

The fatal flaw in petitioner's preferential program is its disregard of individual rights as guaranteed by the Fourteenth Amendment. Such rights are not absolute. But when a State's distribution of benefits or imposition of burdens hinges on ancestry or the color of a person's skin or ancestry, that individual is entitled to a demonstration that the challenged classification is necessary to promote a substantial state interest. Petitioner has failed to carry this burden. . . .

In enjoining petitioner from ever considering the race of any applicant, however, the courts below failed to recognize that the State has a substantial interest that legitimately may be served by a properly devised admissions program involving the competitive consideration of race and ethnic origin. For this reason, so much of the California court's judgment as enjoins petitioner from any consideration of the race of any applicant must be reversed.

Opinion of Justice Brennan, Justice White, Justice Marshall, and Justice Blackmun, concurring in the judgment in part and dissenting in part.

. . . .

Our Nation was founded on the principle that "all men are created equal." Yet candor requires acknowledgment that the framers of our Constitution, to forge the 13 Colonies into one Nation, openly compromised this principle of equality with its antithesis: slavery. The consequences of this compromise are well known and have aptly been called our "American Dilemma." Still, it is well to recount how recent the time has been, if it has yet come, when the promise of our principles has flowered into the actuality of equal opportunity for all regardless of race or color.

The Fourteenth Amendment, the embodiment in the Constitution of our abiding belief in human equality, has been the law of our land for only slightly more than half its 200 years. And for half of that half, the Equal Protection Clause of the Amendment was largely moribund so that, as late as 1927, Mr. Justice Holmes could sum up the importance of that Clause by remarking that it was the "last resort of constitutional argument." Worse than desuetude, the Clause was early turned against those whom it was intended to set free, condemning them to a "separate but equal" status before the law, a status always separate but seldom equal. Not until 1954— only 24 years ago—was this odious doctrine interred by our decision in *Brown v. Board of Education,* and its progeny, which proclaimed that separate schools and public facilities of all sorts were inherently une-

qual and forbidden under our Constitution. Even then inequality was not eliminated with "all deliberate speed." In 1968 and again in 1971, for example, we were forced to remind school boards of their obligation to eliminate racial discrimination root and branch. And a glance at our docket and at dockets of lower courts will show that even today officially sanctioned discrimination is not a thing of the past.

Against this background, claims that law must be "colorblind" or that the datum of race is no longer relevant to public policy must be seen as aspiration rather than as description of reality. This is not to denigrate aspiration; for reality rebukes us that race has too often been used by those who would stigmatize and oppress minorities. Yet we cannot let color blindness become myopia which makes the reality that many "created equal" have been treated within our lifetimes as inferior both by the law and by their fellow citizens.

. . . .

Respondent argues that racial classifications are always suspect and, consequently, that this Court should weigh the importance of the objectives served by Davis' special admissions program to see if they are compelling. In addition, he asserts that this Court must inquire whether, in its judgment, there are alternatives to racial classifications which would suit Davis' purposes. Petitioner, on the other hand, states that our proper role is simply to accept petitioner's determination that the racial classifications used by its program are reasonably related to what it tells us are its benign purposes. We reject petitioner's view, but, because our prior cases are in many respects inapposite to that before us now, we find it necessary to define with precision the meaning of that inexact term, "strict scrutiny."

Unquestionably we have held that a government practice or statute which restricts "fundamental rights" or which contains "suspect classifications" is to be subjected to "strict scrutiny" and can be justified only if it furthers a compelling government purpose and, even then, only if no less restrictive alternative is available. But no fundamental right is involved here. Nor do whites as a class have any of the "traditional indicia of suspectness: the class is not saddled with such disabilities, or subjected to such a history or purposeful unequal treatment, or relegated to such a position of political powerlessness as to command extraordinary protection from the majoritarian political process."

. . . .

On the other hand, the fact that this case does not fit neatly into our prior analytic framework for race cases does not mean that it should be analyzed by applying the very loose rational-basis standard of review that is the very least that is always applied in equal protection cases. The mere recitation of a benign, compensatory purpose is not an automatic shield which protects against any inquiry into the actual purposes underlying a statutory scheme. Instead, a number of considerations—developed in gender-discrimination cases but which carry even more force when applied to racial classifications—lead us to conclude that racial classifications designed to further remedial purposes must serve important governmental objectives and must be substantially related to achievement of those objectives.

. . . .

Davis' articulated purpose of remedying the effects of past societal discrimination is, under our cases, sufficiently important to justify the use of race-conscious admissions programs where there is a sound basis for concluding that minority underrepresentation is substantial and chronic, and that the handicap of past discrimination is impeding access of minorities to the Medical School.

. . . .

Certainly, on the basis of the undisputed factual submissions before this Court, Davis had a sound basis for believing that the problem of underrepresentation of minor-

ities was substantial and chronic and that the problem was attributable to handicaps imposed on minority applicants by past and present racial discrimination. Until at least 1973, the practice of medicine in this country was, in fact, if not in law, largely the prerogative of whites. In 1950, for example, while Negroes constituted 10% of the total population, Negro physicians constituted only 2.2% of the total number of physicians. The overwhelming majority of these, moreover, were educated in two predominantly Negro medical schools, Howard and Meharry. By 1970, the gap between the proportion of Negroes in medicine and their proportion in the population had widened: The number of Negroes employed in medicine remained frozen at 2.2% while the Negro population had increased to 11.1%. The number of Negro admittees to predominantly white medical schools, moreover, had declined in absolute numbers during the year 1955 to 1964.

Moreover, Davis had very good reason to believe that the national pattern of underrepresentation of minorities in medicine would be perpetuated if it retained a single admissions standard. For example, the entering classes in 1968 and 1969, the years in which such a standard was used, included only 1 Chicano and 2 Negroes out of the 50 admittees for each year. Nor is there any relief from this pattern of underrepresentation in the statistics for the regular admissions program in later years.

Davis clearly could conclude that the serious and persistent underrepresentation of minorities in medicine depicted by these statistics is the result of handicaps under which minority applicants labor as a consequence of a background of deliberate, purposeful discrimination against minorities in education and in society generally, as well as in the medical profession. . . .

. . . .

The second prong of our test—whether the Davis program stigmatizes any discrete group or individual and whether race is reasonably used in light of the program's objectives—is clearly satisfied by the Davis program.

It is not even claimed that Davis' program in any way operates to stigmatize or single out any discrete and insular, or even any identifiable, nonminority group. Nor will harm comparable to that imposed upon racial minorities by exclusion or separation on grounds of race be the likely result of the program. It does not, for example, establish an exclusive preserve for minority students apart from and exclusive of whites. Rather, its purpose is to overcome the effects of segregation by bringing the races together. True, whites are excluded from participation in the special admissions program, but this fact only operates to reduce the number of whites to be admitted in the regular admissions program in order to permit admission of a reasonable percentage—less than their proportion of the California population—of otherwise underrepresented qualified minority applicants.

Nor was Bakke in any sense stamped as inferior by the Medical School's rejection of him. Indeed, it is conceded by all that he satisfied those criteria regarded by the school as generally relevant to academic performance better than most of the minority members who were admitted. Moreover, there is absolutely no basis for concluding that Bakke's rejection as a result of Davis' use of racial preference will affect him throughout his life in the same way as the segregation of the Negro school children in *Brown I* would have affected them. Unlike discrimination against racial minorities, the use of racial preferences for remedial purposes does not inflict a pervasive injury upon individual whites in the sense that wherever they go or whatever they do there is a significant likelihood that they will be treated as second-class citizens because of their color. This distinction does not mean that the exclusion of a white resulting from the preferential use of race is not sufficiently serious to require justification; but it does mean that the injury

inflicted by such a policy is not distinguishable from disadvantages caused by a wide range of government actions, none of which has ever been thought impermissible for that reason alone.

In addition, there is simply no evidence that the Davis program discriminates intentionally or unintentionally against any minority group which it purports to benefit. The program does not establish a quota in the invidious sense of a ceiling on the number of minority applicants to be admitted. Nor can the program reasonably be regarded as stigmatizing the program's beneficiaries or their race as inferior. The Davis program does not simply advance less qualified applicants; rather, it compensates applicants, who it is uncontested are fully qualified to study medicine, for educational disadvantages which it was reasonable to conclude were a product of state-fostered discrimination. Once admitted, these students must satisfy the same degree requirements as regularly admitted students; they are taught by the same faculty in the same classes; and their performance is evaluated by the same standards by which regularly admitted students are judged. Under these circumstances, their performance and degrees must be regarded equally with the regularly admitted students with whom they compete for standing. Since minority graduates cannot justifiably be regarded as less well qualified than nonminority graduates by virtue of the special admissions program, there is not reasonable basis to conclude that minority graduates at schools using such programs would be stigmatized as inferior by the existence of such programs.

. . . .

Accordingly, we would reverse the judgment of the Supreme Court of California holding the Medical School's special admissions program unconstitutional and directing respondent's admission, as well as that portion of the judgment enjoining the Medical School from according any consideration to race in the admissions process.

Justice Marshall.

I agree with the judgment of the Court only insofar as it permits a university to consider the race of an applicant in making admissions decisions. I do not agree that petitioner's admissions program violates the Constitution. For it must be remembered that, during most of the past 200 years, the Constitution as interpreted by this Court did not prohibit the most ingenious and pervasive forms of discrimination against the Negro. Now, when a State acts to remedy the effects of that legacy of discrimination, I cannot believe that this same Constitution stands as a barrier.

. . . .

The position of the Negro today in America is the tragic but inevitable consequence of centuries of unequal treatment. Measured by any benchmark of comfort or achievement, meaningful equality remains a distant dream for the Negro.

A Negro child today has a life expectancy which is shorter by more than five years than that of a white child. The Negro child's mother is over three times more likely to die of complications in childbirth, and the infant mortality rate for Negroes is nearly twice that for whites. The median income of the Negro family is only 60% that of the median of a white family, and the percentage of Negroes who live in families with incomes below the poverty line is nearly four times greater than that of whites.

When the Negro child reaches working age, he finds that America offers him significantly less than it offers his white counterpart. For Negro adults, the unemployment rate is twice that of whites, and the unemployment rate for Negro teenagers is nearly three times that of white teenagers. A Negro male who completes four years of college can expect a median annual income of merely $110 more than a white male who has only a high school diploma. Although Negroes represent 11.5% of the population, they are only 1.2% of the lawyers and judges, 2% of the physicians, 2.3% of the dentists, 1.1% of the engineers and 2.6% of the college and university professors.

The relationship between those figures and the history of unequal treatment afforded to the Negro cannot be denied. At every point from birth to death the impact of the past is reflected in the still disfavored position of the Negro.

In light of the sorry history of discrimination and its devastating impact on the lives of Negroes, bringing the Negro into the mainstream of American life should be a state interest of the highest order. To fail to do so is to ensure that American (*sic*) will forever remain a divided society.

. . . .

While I applaud the judgment of the Court that a university may consider race in its admissions process, it is more than a little ironic that, after several hundred years of class-based discrimination against Negroes, the Court is unwilling to hold that a class-based remedy for that discrimination is permissible. In declining to so hold, today's judgment ignores the fact that for several hundred years Negroes have been discriminated against, not as individuals, but rather solely because of the color of their skins. It is unnecessary in 20th century America to have individual Negroes demonstrate that they have been victims of racial discrimination; the racism of our society has been so pervasive that none, regardless of wealth or position, has managed to escape its impact. The experience of Negroes in America has been different in kind, not just in degree, from that of other ethnic groups. It is not merely the history of slavery alone but also that a whole people were marked as inferior by the law. And that mark has endured. The dream of America as the great melting pot has not been realized for the Negro; because of his skin color he never even made it into the pot.

. . . .

It is because of a legacy of unequal treatment that we now must permit the institutions of this society to give consideration to race in making decisions about who will hold the positions of influence, affluence, and prestige in America. For far too long, the doors to those positions have been shut to Negroes. If we are ever to become a fully integrated society, one in which the color of a person's skin will not determine the opportunities available to him or her, we must be willing to take steps to open those doors. I do not believe that anyone can truly look into America's past and still find that a remedy for the effects of that past is impermissible.

Justice Blackmun.

I yield to no one in my earnest hope that the time will come when an "affirmative action" program is unnecessary and is, in truth, only a relic of the past. I would hope that we could reach this stage within a decade at the most. But the story of *Brown v. Board of Education,* decided almost a quarter of a century ago, suggests that the hope is a slim one. At some time, however, beyond any period of what some would claim is only transitional inequality, the United States must and will reach a stage of maturity where action along this line is no longer necessary. Then persons will be regarded as persons, and discrimination of the type we address today will be an ugly feature of history that is instructive but that is behind us.

. . . .

I suspect that it would be impossible to arrange an affirmative action program in a racially neutral way and have it be successful. To ask that this be so is to demand the impossible. In order to get beyond racism, we must first take account of race. There is no other way. And in order to treat some persons equally, we must treat them differently. We cannot—we dare not—let the Equal Protection Clause perpetrate racial supremacy.

COMMENTS

1. Note that the Court applied a strict scrutiny standard in examining the special admission program at the medical school. Is it proper to apply the same judicial standard for laws that discriminate *against* blacks as those intended to *favor* blacks?

2. Although it might be argued that in terms of merit Bakke certainly had a strong case, it is as certain that he necessarily was the most "deserving" of admission?

3. One of the arguments made by proponents of affirmative action is that it is unlikely that white males will purposely discriminate against other white males. Do you think this is true? In *Bakke,* if there was discrimination against white males, was it against *all* white males or only against a certain subclass of white males?

Wygant v. Jackson Board of Education, 476 U.S. 267 (1986)

Justice Powell delivered the opinion of the Court.

This case presents the question whether a school board, consistent with the Equal Protection Clause, may extend preferential protection against layoffs to some of its employees because of their race or national origin.

In 1972, the Jackson Board of Education, because of racial tension in the community that extended to its schools, considered adding a layoff provision to the Collective Bargaining Agreement (CBA) between the Board and the Jackson Education Association (the Union) that would protect employees who were members of certain minority groups against layoffs. The Board and the Union eventually approved a new provision, Article XII of the CBA, covering layoffs. It stated:

In the event that it becomes necessary to reduce the number of teachers through layoff from employment by the Board, teachers with the most seniority in the district shall be retained, except that at no time will there be a greater percentage of minority personnel laid off than the current percentage of minority personnel employed at the time of the layoff. In no event will the number given notice of possible layoff be greater than the number of positions to be eliminated. Each teacher so affected will be called back in reverse order for positions for which he is certificated maintaining the above minority balance.

When layoffs became necessary in 1974, it was evident that adherence to the CBA would result in the layoff of tenured nonminority teachers while minority teachers on probationary status were retained. Rather than complying with Article XII, the Board retained the tenured teachers and laid off probationary minority teachers, thus failing to maintain the percentage of minority personnel that existed at the time of the layoff. The Union, together with two minority teachers who had been laid off, brought suit in federal court, claiming that the Board's failure to adhere to the layoff provision violated the Equal Protection Clause of the Fourteenth Amendment and Title VII of the Civil Rights Act of 1964. . . .

. . . .

The Court of Appeals examined the means chosen to accomplish the Board's race-conscious purpose under a test of "reasonableness." That standard has no support in the decisions of this Court. . . . [O]ur decisions always have employed a more stringent standard—however artic-

ulated—to test the validity of the means chosen by a State to accomplish its race-conscious purposes. . . . Under strict scrutiny the means chosen to accomplish the State's asserted purpose must be specifically and narrowly framed to accomplish that purpose. Racial classifications are simply too pernicious to permit any but the most exact connection between justification and classification.

We have recognized, however, that in order to remedy the effects of prior discrimination, it may be necessary to take race into account. As part of this Nation's dedication to eradicating racial discrimination, innocent persons may be called upon to bear some of the burden of the remedy. "When effectuating a limited and properly tailored remedy to cure the effect of prior discrimination, such a 'sharing of the burden' by innocent parties is not impermissible." In *Fullilove v. Klutznick*, 448 U.S. 448 (1980), the challenged statute required at least 10 percent of federal public works funds to be used in contracts with minority-owned business enterprises. This requirement was found to be within the remedial powers of Congress in part because the "actual burden shouldered by nonminority firms is relatively light."

Significantly, none of the cases discussed above involved layoffs. Here, by contrast, the means chosen to achieve the Board's asserted purposes is that of laying off nonminority teachers with the greater seniority in order to retain minority teachers with less seniority. . . . In cases involving valid hiring goals, the burden to be borne by innocent individuals is diffused to a considerable extent among society generally. Though hiring goals may burden some innocent individuals, they simply do not impose the same kind of injury that layoffs impose. Denial of a future employment opportunity is not as intrusive as loss of an existing job.

Many of our cases involve union seniority plans with employees who are typically heavily dependent on wages for their day-to-day living. Even a temporary layoff may have adverse financial as well as psychological effects. A worker may have invested many productive years in one job and one city with the expectation of earning the stability and security of seniority. At that point, the rights and expectations surrounding seniority make up what is probably the most valuable capital asset that the worker "owns," worth even more than the current equity in his home. Layoffs disrupt these settled expectations in a way that general hiring goals do not.

While hiring goals impose a diffuse burden, often foreclosing only one of several opportunities, layoffs impose the entire burden of achieving racial equality on particular individuals, often resulting in serious disruption of their lives. That burden is too intrusive. We therefore hold that, as a means of accomplishing purposes that otherwise may be legitimate, the Board's layoff plan is not sufficiently narrowly tailored. Other, less intrusive means of accomplishing similar purposes—such as the adoption of hiring goals—are available. For these reasons, the Board's selection of layoffs as the means to accomplish even a valid purpose cannot satisfy the demands of the Equal Protection Clause.

Justice Marshall, with whom Justice Brennan and Justice Blackmun join, dissenting.

The sole question posed by this case is whether the Constitution prohibits a union and a local school board from developing a collective-bargaining agreement that apportions layoffs between two racially determined groups as a means of preserving the effects of an affirmative hiring policy, the constitutionality of which is unchallenged.

. . . .

Under Justice Powell's approach, the community of Jackson, having painfully watched the hard-won benefits of its integration efforts vanish as a result of massive layoffs, would be informed today, simply, that preferential layoff protection is

never permissible because hiring policies serve the same purpose at a lesser cost. As a matter of logic as well as fact, a hiring policy achieves no purpose at all if it is eviscerated by layoffs. Justice Powell's position is untenable.

Justice Powell has concluded, by focusing exclusively on the undisputed hardship of losing a job, that the Equal Protection Clause always bars race-conscious layoff plans. This analysis overlooks, however, the important fact that Article XII does not cause the loss of jobs; someone will lose a job under any layoff plan and, whoever it is, that person will not deserve it. Any per se prohibition against layoff protection, therefore, must rest upon a premise that the tradition of basing layoff decisions on seniority is so fundamental that its modification can never be permitted.

. . . .

Article XII is a narrow provision because it allocates the impact of an unavoidable burden proportionately between two racial groups. It places no absolute burden or benefit on one race, and, within the confines of constant minority proportions, it preserves the hierarchy of seniority in the selection of individuals for layoff. Race is a factor, along with seniority, in determining which individuals the school system will lose; it is not alone dispositive of any individual's fate. Moreover, Article XII does not use layoff protection as a tool for increasing minority representation; achievement of that goal is entrusted to the less severe hiring policies. And Article XII is narrow in the temporal sense as well. The very bilateral process that gave rise to Article XII when its adoption was necessary will also occasion its demise when remedial measures are no longer required. Finally, Article XII modifies contractual expectations that do not themselves carry any connotation of merit or achievement; it does not interfere with the "cherished American ethic" of "[f]airness in individual competition," depriving individuals of an opportunity that they could be said to deserve. In all of these important ways, Article XII metes out the hardship of layoffs in a manner that achieves its purpose with the smallest possible deviation from established norms.

Justice Stevens dissenting.

In my opinion, it is not necessary to find that the Board of Education has been guilty of racial discrimination in the past to support the conclusion that it has a legitimate interest in employing more black teachers in the future. Rather than analyzing a case of this kind by asking whether minority teachers have some sort of special entitlement to jobs as a remedy for sins that were committed in the past, I believe that we should first ask whether the Board's action advances the public interest in educating children for the future. If so, I believe we should consider whether that public interest, and the manner in which it is pursued, justifies any adverse effects on the disadvantaged group.

The Equal Protection Clause absolutely prohibits the use of race in many governmental contexts. To cite only a few: the government may not use race to decide who may serve on juries, who may use public services, who may marry, and who may be fit parents. The use of race in these situations is "utterly irrational" because it is completely unrelated to any valid public purpose; moreover, it is particularly pernicious because it constitutes a badge of oppression that is unfaithful to the central promise of the Fourteenth Amendment.

Nevertheless, in our present society, race is not always irrelevant to sound governmental decisionmaking. To take the most obvious example, in law enforcement, if an undercover agent is needed to infiltrate a group suspected of ongoing criminal behavior—and if the members of the group are all of the same race—it would seem perfectly rational to employ an agent of that race rather than a member of a different racial class. Similarly, in a city with a recent history of racial unrest, the su-

perintendent of police might reasonably conclude that an integrated police force could develop a better relationship with the community and thereby do a more effective job of maintaining law and order than a force composed only of white officers.

In the context of public education, it is quite obvious that a school board may reasonably conclude that an integrated faculty will be able to provide benefits to the student body that could not be provided by an all white, or nearly all white, faculty. For one of the most important lessons that the American public schools teach is that the diverse ethnic, cultural, and national backgrounds that have been brought together in our famous "melting pot" do not identify essential differences among the human beings that inhabit our land. It is one thing for a white child to be taught by a white teacher that color, like beauty, is only "skin deep"; it is far more convincing to experience that truth on a day-to-day basis during the routine, ongoing learning process.

In this case, the collective-bargaining agreement between the Union and the Board of Education succinctly stated a valid public purpose—"recognition of the desirability of multi-ethnic representation on the teaching faculty," and thus "a policy of actively seeking minority group personnel." Nothing in the record—not a shred of evidence—contradicts the view that the Board's attempt to employ, and to retain, more minority teachers in the Jackson public school system served this completely sound educational purpose. Thus, there was a rational and unquestionably legitimate basis for the Board's decision to enter into the collective-bargaining agreement that petitioners have challenged, even though the agreement required special efforts to recruit and retain minority teachers.

COMMENTS

1. In his majority opinion Justice Powell differentiates between losing a job and not being hired in the first place. He rationalizes that the

harm to "innocent" whites is much greater in the former situation than in the latter. Is this true?

2. Given the Supreme Court's holding in the present case, white teachers with seniority will really not be a part of the remedy of alleviating racial imbalance or of eradicating racial discrimination. Is this fair? Could there not be some kind of remedy framed so that the burden was more equal?

Johnson v. Transportation Agency, Santa Clara County, 480 U.S. 616 (1987)

Justice Brennan delivered the opinion of the Court.

Respondent, Transportation Agency of Santa Clara County, California, unilaterally promulgated an Affirmative Action Plan applicable to promotions of employees. In selecting applicants for the promotional position of road dispatcher, the Agency, pursuant to the Plan, passed over petitioner Paul Johnson, a male employee, and promoted a female employee applicant, Diane Joyce. The question for decision is whether in making the promotion the Agency impermissibly took into account the sex of the applicants in violation of Title VII of the Civil Rights Act of 1964, 42 U.S.C. Sec. 2000e et seq.[1]. . . .

In December 1978, the Santa Clara County Transit District Board of Supervisors adopted an Affirmative Action Plan

(Plan) for the County Transportation Agency. The Plan implemented a County Affirmative Action Plan, which had been adopted, declared the County, because "mere prohibition of discriminatory practices is not enough to remedy the effects of past practices and to permit attainment of an equitable representation of minorities, women and handicapped persons." Relevant to this case, the Agency Plan provides that, in making promotions to positions within a traditionally segregated job classification in which women have been significantly underrepresented, the Agency is authorized to consider as one factor the sex of a qualified applicant.

In reviewing the composition of its work force, the Agency noted in its Plan that women were represented in numbers far less than their proportion of the county labor force in both the Agency as a whole and in five of seven job categories. Specifically, while women constituted 36.4% of the area labor market, they composed only 22.4% of Agency employees. Furthermore, women working at the Agency were concentrated largely in EEOC job categories traditionally held by women: women made up 76% of Office and Clerical Workers, but only 7.1% of Agency Officials and Administrators, 8.6% of Professionals, 9.7% of Technicians, and 22% of Service and Maintenance workers. As for the job classification relevant to this case, none of the 238 Skilled Craft Worker positions was held by a woman. . . .

---

[1] Section 703(a) of the Act, provides that it shall be an unlawful employment practice for an employer—

(1) to fail or refuse to hire or to discharge any individual, or otherwise to discriminate against any individual with respect to his compensation, terms, conditions, or privileges of employment, because of such individual's race, color, religion, sex, or national origin; or

(2) to limit, segregate, or classify his employees or applicants for employment in any way which would deprive or tend to deprive any individual of employment opportunities or otherwise adversely affect his status as an employee, because of such individual's race, color, religion, sex, or national origin.

The Agency stated that its Plan was intended to achieve "a statistically measurable yearly improvement in hiring, training and promotion of minorities and women throughout the Agency in all major job classifications where they are underrepresented." As a benchmark by which to evaluate progress, the Agency stated that its long-term goal was to attain a work force whose composition reflected the proportion of minorities and women in the area labor force. Thus, for the Skilled Craft category in which the road dispatcher position at issue here was classified, the Agency's aspiration was that eventually about 36% of the jobs would be occupied by women.

The Plan acknowledged that a number of factors might make it unrealistic to rely on the Agency's long-term goals in evaluating the Agency's progress in expanding job opportunities for minorities and women. Among the factors identified were low turnover rates in some classifications, the fact that some jobs involved heavy labor, the small number of positions within some job categories, the limited number of entry positions leading to the Technical and Skilled Craft classifications, and the limited number of minorities and women qualified for positions requiring specialized training and experience. As a result, the Plan counselled that short-range goals be established and annually adjusted to serve as the most realistic guide for actual employment decisions. . . .

The Agency's Plan thus set aside no specific number of positions for minorities or women, but authorized the consideration of ethnicity or sex as a factor when evaluating qualified candidates for jobs in which members of such groups were poorly represented. One such job was the road dispatcher position that is the subject of the dispute in this case.

On December 12, 1979, the Agency announced a vacancy for the promotional position of road dispatcher in the Agency's Roads Division. Dispatchers assign road crews, equipment, and materials, and main-

tain records pertaining to road maintenance jobs. The position requires at minimum four years of dispatch or road maintenance work experience for Santa Clara County. The EEOC job classification scheme designates a road dispatcher as a Skilled Craft Worker.

Twelve County employees applied for the promotion, including Joyce and Johnson. Joyce had worked for the County since 1970, serving as an account clerk until 1975. She had applied for a road dispatcher position in 1974, but was deemed ineligible because she had not served as a road maintenance worker. In 1975, Joyce transferred from a senior account clerk position to a road maintenance worker position, becoming the first woman to fill such a job. During her four years in that position, she occasionally worked out of class as a road dispatcher.

Petitioner Johnson began with the county in 1967 as a road yard clerk, after private employment that included working as a supervisor and dispatcher. He had also unsuccessfully applied for the road dispatcher opening in 1974. In 1977, his clerical position was downgraded, and he sought and received a transfer to the position of road maintenance worker. He also occasionally worked out of class as a dispatcher while performing that job.

Nine of the applicants, including Joyce and Johnson, were deemed qualified for the job, and were interviewed by a two-person board. Seven of the applicants scored above 70 on this interview, which meant that they were certified as eligible for selection by the appointing authority. The scores awarded ranged from 70 to 80. Johnson was tied for second with a score of 75, while Joyce ranked next with a score of 73. A second interview was conducted by three Agency supervisors, who ultimately recommended that Johnson be promoted. Prior to the second interview, Joyce had contacted the County's Affirmative Action Office because she feared that her application might not receive disinterested review. The Office in turn contacted the

Agency's Affirmative Action Coordinator, whom the Agency's Plan makes responsible for, inter alia, keeping the Director informed of opportunities for the Agency to accomplish its objectives under the Plan. At the time, the Agency employed no women in any Skilled Craft position, and had never employed a woman as a road dispatcher. The Coordinator recommended to the Director of the Agency, James Graebner, that Joyce be promoted.

. . . .

The assessment of the legality of the Agency Plan must be guided by our decision in *Weber.* In that case, the Court addressed the question whether the employer violated Title VII by adopting a voluntary affirmative action plan designed to "eliminate manifest racial imbalances in traditionally segregated job categories." The respondent employee in that case challenged the employer's denial of his application for a position in a newly established craft training program, contending that the employer's selection process impermissibly took into account the race of the applicants. The selection process was guided by an affirmative action plan, which provided that 50% of the new trainees were to be black until the percentage of black skilled craft-workers in the employer's plant approximated the percentage of blacks in the local labor force. Adoption of the plan had been prompted by the fact that only 5 of 273, or 1.83%, of skilled craftworkers at the plant were black, even though the work force in the area was approximately 39% black. . . .

We upheld the employer's decision to select less senior black applicants over the white respondent, for we found that taking race into account was consistent with Title VII's objective of "break[ing] down old patterns of racial segregation and hierarchy." As we stated:

It would be ironic indeed if a law triggered by a Nation's concern over centuries of racial injustice and intended to improve the lot of those who had "been excluded from the American

dream for so long" constituted the first legislative prohibition of all voluntary, private, race-conscious efforts to abolish traditional patterns of racial segregation and hierarchy (quoting remarks of Sen. Humphrey, 110 *Cong. Rec.* 6552 [1964]).

We noted that the plan did not "unnecessarily trammel the interests of the white employees," since it did not require "the discharge of white workers and their replacement with new black hirees." Nor did the plan create "an absolute bar to the advancement of white employees," since half of those trained in the new program were to be white. Finally, we observed that the plan was a temporary measure, not designed to maintain racial balance, but to "eliminate a manifest racial imbalance." As Justice Blackmun's concurrence made clear, *Weber* held that an employer seeking to justify the adoption of a plan need not point to its own prior discriminatory practices, nor even to evidence of an "arguable violation" on its part. Rather, it need point only to a "conspicuous . . . imbalance in traditionally segregated job categories." Our decision was grounded in the recognition that voluntary employer action can play a crucial role in furthering Title VII's purpose of eliminating the effects of discrimination in the workplace, and that Title VII should not be read to thwart such efforts.

In reviewing the employment decision at issue in this case, we must first examine whether that decision was made pursuant to a plan prompted by concerns similar to those of the employer in Weber. Next, we must determine whether the effect of the plan on males and non-minorities is comparable to the effect of the plan in that case.

. . . .

It is clear that the decision to hire Joyce was made pursuant to an Agency plan that directed that sex or race be taken into account for the purpose of remedying underrepresentation. The Agency Plan acknowledged the "limited opportunities that have existed in the past," for women to find employment in certain job classifications "where women have not been traditionally employed in significant numbers." . . .

As an initial matter, the Agency adopted as a benchmark for measuring progress in eliminating underrepresentation the long-term goal of a work force that mirrored in its major job classifications the percentage of women in the area labor market. Even as it did so, however, the Agency acknowledged that such a figure could not by itself necessarily justify taking into account the sex of applicants for positions in all job categories. For positions requiring specialized training and experience, the Plan observed that the number of minorities and women "who possess the qualifications required for entry into such job classifications is limited." The Plan therefore directed that annual short-term goals be formulated that would provide a more realistic indication of the degree to which sex should be taken into account in filling particular positions. The Plan stressed that such goals "should not be construed as 'quotas' that must be met," but as reasonable aspirations in correcting the imbalance in the Agency's work force. These goals were to take into account factors such as "turnover, layoffs, lateral transfers, new job openings, retirements and availability of minorities, women and handicapped persons in the area work force who possess the desired qualifications or potential for placement." . . .

. . . .

The Agency's Plan emphatically did not authorize blind hiring. It expressly directed that numerous factors be taken into account in making hiring decisions, including specifically the qualifications of female applicants for particular jobs. . . .

. . . .

We next consider whether the Agency Plan unnecessarily trammeled the rights of male employees or created an absolute bar to their advancement. . . . The Plan ex-

pressly states that "[t]he 'goals' established for each Division should not be construed as 'quotas' that must be met." Rather, the Plan merely authorizes that consideration be given to affirmative action concerns when evaluating qualified applicants. As the Agency Director testified, the sex of Joyce was but one of numerous factors he took into account in arriving at his decision. The Plan thus resembles the "Harvard Plan" approvingly noted by Justice Powell in *University of California Regents v. Bakke,* which considers race along with other criteria in determining admission to the college. . . . Similarly, the Agency Plan requires women to compete with all other qualified applicants. No persons are automatically excluded from consideration; all are able to have their qualifications weighed against those of other applicants.

In addition, petitioner had no absolute entitlement to the road dispatcher position. Seven of the applicants were classified as qualified and eligible, and the Agency Director was authorized to promote any of the seven. Thus, denial of the promotion unsettled no legitimate firmly rooted expectation on the part of the petitioner. Furthermore, while the petitioner in this case was denied a promotion, he retained his employment with the Agency, at the same salary and with the same seniority, and remained eligible for other promotions.

. . . .

Justice Scalia, with whom the Chief Justice joins, and with whom Justice White joins in Parts I and II, dissenting.

With a clarity which, had it not proven so unavailing, one might well recommend as a model of statutory draftsmanship, Title VII of the Civil Rights Act of 1964 declares:

It shall be an unlawful employment practice for an employer—
(1) to fail or refuse to hire or to discharge any individual, or otherwise to discriminate against any individual with respect to his compensation,

terms, conditions, or privileges of employment, because of such individual's race, color, religion, sex, or national origin; or

(2) to limit, segregate, or classify his employees or applicants for employment in any way which would deprive or tend to deprive any individual of employment opportunities or otherwise adversely affect his status as an employee, because of such individual's race, color, religion, sex, or national origin.

The Court today completes the process of converting this from a guarantee that race or sex will not be the basis for employment determinations, to a guarantee that it often will. Ever so subtly, without even alluding to the last obstacles preserved by earlier opinions that we now push out of our path, we effectively replace the goal of a discrimination-free society with the quite incompatible goal of proportionate representation by race and by sex in the workplace. . . .

. . . .

. . . [T]he plan's purpose was assuredly not to remedy prior sex discrimination by the Agency. It could not have been, because there was no prior sex discrimination to remedy. The majority, in cataloguing the Agency's alleged misdeeds, neglects to mention the District Court's finding that the Agency "has not discriminated in the past, and does not discriminate in the present against women in regard to employment opportunities in general and promotions in particular." This finding was not disturbed by the Ninth Circuit.

. . . .

. . . [T]oday's decision goes well beyond merely allowing racial or sexual discrimination in order to eliminate the effects of prior societal discrimination. The majority opinion often uses the phrase "traditionally segregated job category" to describe the evil against which the plan is legitimately (according to the majority) directed. As originally used in *Steelworkers v. Weber*, 443 U.S. 193 (1979), that phrase described skilled jobs from which employers and unions had systematically and intentionally

excluded black workers—traditionally segregated jobs, that is, in the sense of conscious, exclusionary discrimination. But that is assuredly not the sense in which the phrase is used here. It is absurd to think that the nationwide failure of road maintenance crews, for example, to achieve the Agency's ambition of 36.4% female representation is attributable primarily, if even substantially, to systematic exclusion of women eager to shoulder pick and shovel. It is a "traditionally segregated job category" not in the *Weber* sense, but in the sense that, because of long-standing social attitudes, it has not been regarded by women themselves as desirable work. . . . There are, of course, those who believe that the social attitudes which cause women themselves to avoid certain jobs and to favor others are as nefarious as conscious, exclusionary discrimination. Whether or not that is so (and there is assuredly no consensus on the point equivalent to our national consensus against intentional discrimination), the two phenomena are certainly distinct. And it is the alteration of social attitudes, rather than the elimination of discrimination, which today's decision approves as justification for state-enforced discrimination. This is an enormous expansion, undertaken without the slightest justification or analysis.

. . . .

It is unlikely that today's result will be displeasing to politically elected officials, to whom it provides the means of quickly accommodating the demands of organized groups to achieve concrete, numerical improvement in the economic status of particular constituencies. Nor will it displease the world of corporate and governmental employers (many of whom have filed briefs as amici in the present case, all on the side of Santa Clara) for whom the cost of hiring less qualified workers is often substantially less—and infinitely more predictable than the cost of litigating Title VII cases and of seeking to convince federal agencies by nonnumerical means that no discrimination exists. In fact, the only losers in the process are the Johnsons of the country, for whom Title VII has been not merely repealed but actually inverted. The irony is that these individuals—predominantly unknown, unaffluent, unorganized—suffer this injustice at the hands of a Court fond of thinking itself the champion of the politically impotent. I dissent.

COMMENTS

1. Are the rationales for affirmative action for women the same, or different, than for blacks? Consider this situation. There is one tenure slot available at a college at which white males dominate the ranks of the faculty. There are three well-qualified candidates: a white male, a white female, and a black male. Who should get this position?

2. Does racial and sexual discrimination still exist in our society? Will those who discriminate admit to it? How do you prove racial discrimination? In *City of Richmond v. J. A. Croson Co.*, 102 L. Ed. 2d 854 (1989), the Supreme Court struck down a city's affirmative action program setting aside 30 percent of the public works subcontracting jobs for minority-owned businesses on the ground that there had been no proof of actual racial discrimination. In dissent, Justice Marshall pointed out that, while there are equal numbers of minorities and non-minorities in Richmond, minority-owned businesses received *one seventy-fifth* the public contracting funds awarded to other businesses. Marshall concluded that this was very strong evidence of racial discrimination. Do you think he was correct?

9

WORKERS AND THEIR WORTH

It would be difficult to characterize the judiciary's role in the protection of workers in our society, but a strong case could be made that throughout American history, courts have often sided with the employer over the employee, management over labor.[1] The best evidence of this, of course, is the so-called Lochner period, from approximately 1905 to 1938, during which the Supreme Court repeatedly struck down legislative efforts by the states and the federal government that sought to protect workers from harm and oppressive conditions.[2] During this period, for example, the Supreme Court overturned federal legislation seeking to prohibit child labor. The Court employed the rationale that the federal government did not possess the power either under the commerce clause[3] or the taxing power[4] to enact such legislation. The end result of these Supreme Court decisions was the continuation of child labor.

The facts and the Court's reasoning in *Lochner v. New York*,[5] the case that came to symbolize an era, are instructive. The New York state legislature in Albany had enacted legislation that prohibited the employment of bakery employees for more than ten hours a day or sixty hours per week. The aim of this legislation was to protect bakery employees who had been required to work what would be for us (and was for them) exceedingly long hours. The Supreme Court, however, viewed this legislation, and others of its kind, with a jaundiced eye. The Court held that the "statute necessarily interferes with the right to contract between the employer and employees. The general right to make a contract in relation to his business is part of the liberty of the individual protected by the Fourteenth Amendment." In short, the Supreme Court held that such legislation took away from individuals their right to work more than sixty hours per week on a particular job.

   The history of labor unions and of the role played by the judicial
branch in this process also has relevance. During most of the nineteenth
century and well into the twentieth century, business elites were successful
in preventing labor unions from forming. The judicial branch greatly
aided these efforts by interpreting antitrust laws to apply to unions. In
fact, until passage of the Clayton Antitrust Act of 1914, which exempted
unions from antitrust laws, trust busters spent as much time breaking up
labor unions as they did breaking up business trusts and monopolies. Even
after passage of this act, however, striking workers were regularly subjected to court injunctions and criminal prosecutions.

   Labor gained strength during the New Deal of President Roosevelt. In
1935, Congress passed the National Labor Relations Act, also known as
the Wagner Act, which guaranteed workers the right of collective bargaining—that is, the right to have representatives of their labor unions negotiate with management to determine working conditions. The Wagner Act
also established rules to protect unions and organizers. For example, an
employer could not fire a worker who talks about the possibility of union-
izing. The Wagner Act also created the National Labor Relations Board,
which regulated labor-management relations and negotiations. Despite
these gains, the labor movement was not without its obstacles. Witness the
Taft-Hartley Act of 1947, which continued to allow unions the right of
collective bargaining but also permitted states to adopt right to work laws
that forbid mandatory union membership.

   Although the mechanisms for collective bargaining are now in place,
unions are still concerned about the scope of bargainable issues. The first
two cases in this chapter highlight this issue. *Fibreboard Paper Products
Corp. v. NLRB* involved the question whether the Wagner Act mandated
collective bargaining when work originally done by union members was
"contracted out" to a nonunion firm. *First National Maintenance Corporation
v. NLRB* concerned the question whether an employer had a statutory
duty to bargain collectively with a union regarding the termination of a
major contract with a customer that led to large layoffs. Are the decisions
in the two cases consistent? What do these two decisions say about the
power of unions and about efforts by the courts to protect workers?

   Brown v. Ferro Corp. involved a legal challenge to what has been termed
"golden parachutes," provisions designed to protect the top management
of a corporation, usually in the form of salary and stock compensation,
when the managers' jobs are jeopardized by a corporate takeover. The
question initially raised in *Brown*, but ultimately avoided by the court, was
whether such protective measures were in the best interest of the corporation. The trial court dismissed this suit by a shareholder of a corporation,
and the appellate court upheld the decision. According to the courts, although this golden parachute money had been set aside in a special escrow account, because it had not yet been paid to the corporate officers, it
was premature to consider whether shareholders were harmed. (The legal
term used in the case is *ripeness*, which essentially means that adjudication

is not proper at the time because harm has not yet occurred.) The dissent argued instead that shareholders were already being harmed because these corporate funds could not be used for other purposes. The dissent also claimed that after the fact might be too late, as there was no certainty that this shareholder would be able to bring such a lawsuit after a change in corporate identity occurred.

The *Brown* case examined (but really avoided) the issue whether golden parachutes harm corporate shareholders. Another question not addressed by the court, but that deserves to be asked, is whether it is fair or just that golden parachutes have protected only the top management of a corporation, while rank-and-file workers are left on their own. Moreover, the amounts involved can often be staggering. For example, Revlon chairman Michael Bergerac was the beneficiary of a $36 million golden parachute when Revlon was acquired by Pantry Pride.[6] Can we be so sure that heads of corporations will necessarily look out for the best interests of the corporation, the shareholders of the corporation, and rank-and-file workers of the corporation when they can stand to benefit so much from a merger or takeover?

The final two cases in this chapter concern employer-employee relations on a microlevel. *Fullerton Lumber Co. v. Torburg* involved the legality of a particular "restrictive covenant" in a private contract agreement. One of the provisions in this contract was that if the employee, Torburg, left the employ of Fullerton Lumber, he was not to work for a competitor for a period of ten years. To what extent should courts be sensitive to the bargaining power of individuals to a contract? The contract provision was drafted by the employer and was in the corporation's best interest. The provision served to restrict Torburg (or other employees with similar contracts) from leaving and seeking employment with a business in a related field. On the other hand, Torburg did sign this agreement and thus gave his consent to such a provision.

Many employees have no contracts at all. Perhaps many of you have worked in a fast food restaurant, and, I think it is safe to say, most of you did not have a contract with your employer. Can employees with no contracts be fired for no reason? *Guy v. Travenol Laboratories* involved a case in which an employer had a reason to fire an employee: the corporation was upset because Guy, the employee, refused to falsify records. Do individuals have a right to their jobs absent poor work performance? If you maintain this position, must you reach the same conclusion in a case such as *First National Maintenance Corporation*? There was no evidence that the employees at Greenpark were not doing their job. Did they have a right, then, to continued employment?

NOTES

1. An issue that will not be explored, but that deserves some mention, is how little protection courts provided workers harmed in industrial accidents in the latter part of the nineteenth century and the early part of the twentieth century.

Sometimes the privity of contract rule, discussed in Chapter 10, was employed, but employers had a wide range of defenses and seldom had to pay much compensation to the injured worker or the family of a worker who was killed at the worksite. For an excellent discussion of this, see Jethro K. Lieberman, *The Litigious Society* (New York: Basic Books, 1981).

2. The Lochner era demonstrates that so-called judicial activism is not necessarily liberal in its political ideology.

3. *Hammer v. Dagenhart*, 247 U.S. 251 (1918). The vehemence with which the Supreme Court opposed child labor legislation is evidenced in this language from Justice Day's majority opinion in Hammer:

> The far reaching result of upholding the act [prohibiting child labor] cannot be more plainly indicated than by pointing out that if Congress can thus regulate matters entrusted to local authority by prohibition of the movement of commodities in interstate commerce, all freedom of commerce will be at an end, and the power of the States over local matters may be eliminated, and thus our system of government be practically destroyed.

In due time, however, the Supreme Court took a much more expansive view of the powers that Congress possessed under the Commerce Clause. See *Wickard v. Filburn*, 317 U.S. 111 (1942). Congress, in turn, greatly expanded the nature and scope of its legislation without any apparent destruction of our system of government, as Justice Day so fervently believed.

4. *Bailey v. Drexel Furniture Co.*, 259 U.S. 20 (1922).

5. 198 U.S. 45 (1905).

6. Clemens P. Work, "Are Golden Parachutes Turning Platinum?" *U.S. News & World Report*, February 3, 1986, p. 49.

Fibreboard Paper Corp. v. NLRB, 379 U.S. 203 (1964)

Chief Justice Warren delivered the opinion of the Court.

[Based on ostensible financial conditions, management at Fibreboard Paper Corporation decided that it would henceforth "contract out" maintenance work that formerly had been done by its own employees. The union representing Fibreboard employees challenges this unilateral decision, claiming that this constituted an "unfair labor practice" because Fibreboard did not collectively bargain with the union as required under the National Labor Relations Act (NLRA). The National Labor Relations Board (NLRB) held for the union.]

This case involves the obligation of an employer and the representative of his employees under Sec. 8(a)(5), 8(d) and 9(a) of the National Labor Relations Act to "confer in good faith with respect to wages, hours, and other terms and conditions of employment." The primary issue is whether the "contracting out" of work being performed by employees in the bargaining unit is a statutory subject of collective bargaining under those sections.

Section 8(a)(5) of the National Labor Relations Act provides that it shall be an unfair labor practice for an employer "to refuse to bargain collectively with the representatives of his employees." Collective bargaining is defined in Sec. 8(d) as "the performance of the mutual obligation of the employer and the representative of the employees to meet at reasonable times and confer in good faith with respect to wages, hours, and other terms and conditions of employment."

Read together, these provisions establish the obligation of the employer and the representative of its employees to bargain with each other in good faith with respect to wages, hours, and other terms and conditions of employment. . . .

The subject matter of the present dispute is well within the literal meaning of the phrase "terms and conditions of employment." A stipulation with respect to the contracting out of work performed by members of the bargaining unit might appropriately be called a "condition of employment." The words even more plainly cover termination of employment which, as the facts of this case indicate, necessarily results from the contracting out of work performed by members of the established bargaining unit.

The inclusion of "contracting out" within the statutory scope of collective bargaining also seems well designed to effectuate the purposes of the National Labor Relations Act. One of the primary purposes of the Act is to promote the peaceful settlement of industrial disputes by subjecting labor-management controversies to the mediatory influence of negotiation. The Act was framed with an awareness that refusals to confer and negotiate had been one of the most prolific causes of industrial strife. To hold, as the Board has done, that contracting out is a mandatory subject of collective bargaining would promote the fundamental purpose of the Act by bringing a problem of vital concern to labor and management within the framework established by Congress as most conducive to industrial peace.

. . . .

The facts of the present case illustrate the propriety of submitting the dispute to collective negotiation. The Company's decision to contract out the maintenance work did not alter the Company's basic operation. The maintenance work still had to be performed in the plant. No capital investment was contemplated; the Company merely replaced existing employees with those of an independent contractor to do the same work under similar conditions of employment. Therefore, to require the employer to bargain about the matter would not significantly abridge his freedom to manage the business.

The Company was concerned with the high cost of its maintenance operation. It was induced to contract out the work by assurances from independent contractors that economies could be derived by reducing the work force, decreasing fringe benefits, and eliminating overtime payments. These have long been regarded as matters peculiarly suitable for resolution within the collective bargaining framework, and industrial experience demonstrates that collective negotiation has been highly successful in achieving peaceful accommodation of the conflicting interests. Yet, it is contended that when an employer can effect cost savings in these respects by contracting the work out, there is no need to attempt to achieve similar economies through negotiation with existing employees or to provide them with an opportunity to negotiate a mutually acceptable alternative. The short answer is that, although it is not possible to say whether a satisfactory solution could be reached, national labor policy is founded upon the congressional determination that the chances are good enough to warrant subjecting such issues to the process of collective negotiation.

Justice Stewart, with whom Justice Douglas and Justice Harlan join, concurring.

Viewed broadly, the question before us stirs large issues. The Court purports to limit its decision to "the facts of this case." But the Court's opinion radiates implications of such disturbing breadth that I am persuaded to file this separate statement of my own views.

Section 8(a)(5) of the National Labor Relations Act, as amended, makes it an unfair labor practice for an employer to "refuse to bargain collectively with the representatives of his employees." Collective bargaining is defined in Sec. 8(d) as "the performance of the mutual obligation of the employer and the representative of the employees to meet at reasonable times and confer in good faith with respect to wages, hours, and other terms and conditions of employment."

The question posed is whether the particular decision sought to be made unilaterally by the employer in this case is a subject of mandatory collective bargaining within the statutory phrase "terms and conditions of employment." That is all the Court decides. The Court most assuredly does not decide that every managerial decision which necessarily terminates an individual's employment is subject to the duty to bargain. Nor does the Court decide that subcontracting decisions are as a general matter subject to that duty. The Court holds no more than that this employer's decision to subcontract this work, involving "the replacement of employees in the existing bargaining unit with those of an independent contractor to do the same work under similar conditions of employment," is subject to the duty to bargain collectively. Within the narrow limitations implicit in the specific facts of this case, I agree with the Court's decision.

. . . .

It is important to note that the words of the statute are words of limitation. The National Labor Relations Act does not say that the employer and employees are bound to confer upon any subject which interests either of them; the specification of wages, hours, and other terms and conditions of employment defines a limited category of issues subject to compulsory bargaining. The limiting purpose of the statute's language is made clear by the legislative history of the present Act. As originally passed, the Wagner Act contained no definition of the duty to bargain collectively. In the 1947 revision of the Act, the House bill contained a detailed but limited list of subjects of the duty to bargain, excluding all others. In conference the present language was substituted for the House's detailed specification. While the language thus incorporated in the 1947 legislation as enacted is not so stringent as that contained in the House bill, it nonetheless adopts the same basic approach in seeking to define a limited class of bargainable issues.

The phrase "conditions of employment" is no doubt susceptible of diverse interpretations. At the extreme, the phrase could be construed to apply to any subject which is insisted upon as a prerequisite for continued employment. . . .

. . . .

While employment security has . . . properly been recognized in various circumstances as a condition of employment, it surely does not follow that every decision which may affect job security is a subject of compulsory collective bargaining. Many decisions made by management affect the job security of employees. Decisions concerning the volume and kind of advertising expenditures, product design, the manner of financing, and sales, all may bear upon the security of the workers' jobs. Yet it is hardly conceivable that such decisions so involve "conditions of employment" that they must be negotiated with the employees' bargaining representative.

In many of these areas the impact of a particular management decision upon job security may be extremely indirect and uncertain, and this alone may be sufficient reason to conclude that such decisions are not "with respect to . . . conditions of employment." Yet there are other areas where decisions by management may quite clearly imperil job security, or indeed terminate employment entirely. An enterprise may decide to invest in labor-saving machinery. Another may resolve to liquidate its assets and go out of business. Nothing the Court holds today should be understood as imposing a duty to bargain collectively regarding such managerial decisions, which lie at the core of entrepreneurial control. Decisions concerning the commitment of investment capital and the basic scope of the enterprise are not in themselves primarily about conditions of employment, though the effect of the decision may be necessarily to terminate employment. If, as I think clear, the purpose of Sec. 8(d) is to describe a limited area subject to the duty of collective bargaining, those management decisions which are fundamental to the basic direction of a corporate enterprise or which impinge only indirectly upon employment security should be excluded from that area.

. . . .

I am fully aware that in this era of automation and onrushing technological change, no problems in the domestic economy are of greater concern than those involving job security and employment stability. Because of the potentially cruel impact upon the lives and fortunes of the working men and women of the Nation, these problems have understandably engaged the solicitous attention of government, of responsible private business, and particularly of organized labor. It is possible that in meeting these problems Congress may eventually decide to give organized labor or government a far heavier hand in controlling what until now have been considered the prerogatives of private business management. That path would mark a sharp departure from the traditional principles of a free enterprise economy. Whether we should follow it is, within constitutional limitations, for Congress to choose. But it is a path which Congress certainly did not choose when it enacted the Taft-Hartley Act.

First National Maintenance Corp. v. NLRB, 452 U.S. 666 (1981)

Justice Blackmun delivered the opinion of the Court.

[First National Maintenance Corporation (FMN) provides maintenance and housekeeping services. One of its clients is Greenpark Nursing Home. Because management thought it was losing money on the contract, FMN sought an increase in its fees. This proposed increase was rejected by Greenpark, at which point FMN terminated the job. As a result of this termination, some employees at FMN— those working on the Greenpark contract—lost their jobs.]

Must an employer, under its duty to bargain in good faith "with respect to wages, hours, and other terms and conditions of employment," Secs. 8(d) and 8(a)(5) of the National Labor Relations Act (Act), negotiate with the certified representative of its employees over its decision to close a part of its business? In this case, the National Labor Relations Board (Board) imposed such a duty on petitioner with respect to its decision to terminate a contract with a customer, and the United States

Court of Appeals, although differing over the appropriate rationale, enforced its order.

. . . .

A fundamental aim of the National Labor Relations Act is the establishment and maintenance of industrial peace to preserve the flow of interstate commerce. Central to achievement of this purpose is the promotion of collective bargaining as a method of defusing and channeling conflict between labor and management. Congress ensured that collective bargaining would go forward by creating the Board and giving it the power to condemn as unfair labor practices certain conduct by unions and employers that it deemed deleterious to the process, including the refusal "to bargain collectively."

Although parties are free to bargain about any legal subject, Congress has limited the mandate or duty to bargain to matters of "wages, hours, and other terms and conditions of employment." A unilateral change as to a subject within this category violates the statutory duty to bargain and is subject to the Board's remedial order. . . . Congress deliberately left the words "wages, hours, and other terms and conditions of employment" without further definition, for it did not intend to deprive the Board of the power further to define those terms in light of specific industrial practices.

Nonetheless, in establishing what issues must be submitted to the process of bargaining, Congress had no expectation that the elected union representative would become an equal partner in the running of the business enterprise in which the union's members are employed. . . .

Some management decisions, such as choice of advertising and promotion, product type and design, and financing arrangements, have only an indirect and attenuated impact on the employment relationship. See *Fibreboard Corp. v. NLRB*, 379 U.S., at 223 (Stewart, J., concurring). Other management decisions, such as the

order of succession of layoffs and recalls, production quotas, and work rules, are almost exclusively "an aspect of the relationship" between employer and employee. The present case concerns a third type of management decision, one that had a direct impact on employment, since jobs were inexorably eliminated by the termination, but had as its focus only the economic profitability of the contract with Greenpark, a concern under these facts wholly apart from the employment relationship. This decision, involving a change in the scope and direction of the enterprise, is akin to the decision whether to be in business at all, "not in [itself] primarily about conditions of employment, though the effect of the decision may be necessarily to terminate employment." *Fibreboard*, 379 U.S., at 223 (Stewart, J., concurring). At the same time, this decision touches on a matter of central and pressing concern to the union and its member employees: the possibility of continued employment and the retention of the employees' very jobs.

Petitioner contends it had no duty to bargain about its decision to terminate its operations at Greenpark. This contention requires that we determine whether the decision itself should be considered part of petitioner's retained freedom to manage its affairs unrelated to employment. The aim of labeling a matter a mandatory subject of bargaining, rather than simply permitting, but not requiring, bargaining, is to "promote the fundamental purpose of the Act by bringing a problem of vital concern to labor and management within the framework established by Congress as most conducive to industrial peace." The concept of mandatory bargaining is premised on the belief that collective discussions backed by the parties' economic weapons will result in decisions that are better for both management and labor and for society as a whole. This will be true, however, only if the subject proposed for discussion is amenable to resolution through the bargaining process. Management must be free from the constraints of the bargaining process to the extent essential for the running of a profitable business. It also must have some degree of certainty beforehand as to when it may proceed to reach decisions without fear of later evaluations labeling its conduct an unfair labor practice. Congress did not explicitly state what issues of mutual concern to union and management it intended to exclude from mandatory bargaining. Nonetheless, in view of an employer's need for unencumbered decision making, bargaining over management decisions that have a substantial impact on the continued availability of employment should be required only if the benefit, for labor-management relations and the collective-bargaining process, outweighs the burden placed on the conduct of the business.

· ·

Both union and management regard control of the decision to shut down an operation with the utmost seriousness. As has been noted, however, the Act is not intended to serve either party's individual interest, but to foster in a neutral manner a system in which the conflict between these interests may be resolved. It seems particularly important, therefore, to consider whether requiring bargaining over this sort of decision will advance the neutral purposes of the Act.

A union's interest in participating in the decision to close a particular facility or part of an employer's operations springs from its legitimate concern over job security. The union's practical purpose in participating, however, will be largely uniform: it will seek to delay or halt the closing. No doubt it will be impelled, in seeking these ends, to offer concessions, information, and alternatives that might be helpful to management or forestall or prevent the termination of jobs. It is unlikely, however, that requiring bargaining over the decision itself, as well as its effects, will augment this flow of information and suggestions. . . .

· ·

Management's interest in whether it should discuss a decision of this kind is much more complex and varies with the particular circumstances. If labor costs are an important factor in a failing operation and the decision to close, management will have an incentive to confer voluntarily with the union to seek concessions that may make continuing the business profitable. At other times, management may have great need for speed, flexibility, and secrecy in meeting business opportunities and exigencies. It may face significant tax or securities consequences that hinge on confidentiality, the timing of a plant closing, or a reorganization of the corporate structure. The publicity incident to the normal process of bargaining may injure the possibility of a successful transition or increase the economic damage to the business. The employer also may have no feasible alternative to the closing, and even good-faith bargaining over it may both be futile and cause the employer additional loss.

· ·

We conclude that the harm likely to be done to an employer's need to operate freely in deciding whether to shut down part of its business purely for economic reasons outweighs the incremental benefit that might be gained through the union's participation in making the decision, and we hold that the decision itself is not part of Sec. 8(d)'s "terms and conditions," over which Congress has mandated bargaining.

Justice Brennan, with whom Justice Marshall joins, dissenting.

Section 8(d) of the National Labor Relations Act, as amended, requires employers and employee representatives "to meet at reasonable times and confer in good faith with respect to wages, hours, and other terms and conditions of employment." The question in this case is whether First National Maintenance Corporation's decision to terminate its Greenpark Care Center operation and to discharge the workers employed in that operation was a decision with respect to "terms and conditions of employment" within the meaning of the Act, thus rendering its failure to negotiate with the union unlawful.

As this Court has noted, the words "terms and conditions of employment" plainly cover termination of employment resulting from a management decision to close an operation. *Fibreboard Paper Products Corp. v. NLRB,* 379 U.S. 203, 210 (1964). As the Court today admits, the decision to close an operation "touches on a matter of central and pressing concern to the union and its member employees." Moreover, as the Court today further concedes, Congress deliberately left the words "terms and conditions of employment" indefinite, so that the NLRB would be able to give content to those terms in light of changing industrial conditions. In the exercise of its congressionally delegated authority and accumulated expertise, the Board has determined that an employer's decision to close part of its operations affects the "terms and conditions of employment" within the meaning of the Act, and is thus a mandatory subject for collective bargaining. Nonetheless, the Court today declines to defer to the Board's decision on this sensitive question of industrial relations, and on the basis of pure speculation reverses the judgment of the Board and of the Court of Appeals. I respectfully dissent.

The Court bases its decision on a balancing test. It states that "bargaining over management decisions that have a substantial impact on the continued availability of employment should be required only if the benefit, for labor-management relations and the collective-bargaining process, outweighs the burden placed on the conduct of the business." I cannot agree with this test, because it takes into account only the interests of management; it fails to consider the legitimate employment interests of the workers and their union. . . . This one-sided approach hardly serves "to foster in

a neutral manner" a system for resolution of these serious, two-sided controversies.

Even if the Court's statement of the test were accurate, I could not join in its application, which is based solely on speculation. Apparently, the Court concludes that the benefit to labor-management relations and the collective-bargaining process from negotiation over partial closings is minimal, but it provides no evidence to that effect. The Court acknowledges that the union might be able to offer concessions, information, and alternatives that might obviate or forestall the closing, but it then asserts that "[i]t is unlikely, however, that requiring bargaining over the decision . . . will augment this flow of information and suggestions." . . .

The Court further presumes that management's need for "speed, flexibility, and secrecy" in making partial closing decisions would be frustrated by a requirement to bargain. In some cases the Court might be correct. In others, however, the decision will be made openly and deliberately, and considerations of "speed, flexibility, and secrecy" will be inapposite. Indeed, in view of management's admitted duty to bargain over the effects of a closing, it is difficult to understand why additional bargaining over the closing itself would necessarily unduly delay or publicize the decision.

I am not in a position to judge whether mandatory bargaining over partial closings *in all cases* is consistent with our national labor policy, and neither is the Court. The primary responsibility to determine the scope of the statutory duty to bargain has been entrusted to the NLRB, which should not be reversed by the courts merely because they might prefer another view of the statute. I therefore agree with the Court of Appeals that employers presumptively have a duty to bargain over a decision to close an operation, and that this presumption can be rebutted by a showing that bargaining would be futile, that the closing was due to emergency financial circumstances, or that, for some other reason, bargaining would not further the purposes of the National Labor Relations Act.

COMMENTS

1. Have unions won the battle but lost the war?

2. If you disagree with the Court's holding in the *First National Maintenance Corp.* case, what kinds of decisions would you mandate for collective bargaining? The price of the goods and services provided by the company? Plant relocation? Salaries and bonuses for management?

3. One of the more controversial topics in the area of labor-management relations involves plant closing laws. In 1988, Congress passed legislation that mandated that companies provide sixty days notice of plant closings or mass layoffs of longer than six months. Do you agree with such legislation? Should corporations have to give some kind of notice to employees if they are closing down? Are any other restrictions on corporate mobility justified? For example, if a state has given a corporation ten years of tax abatement, free utility hook-ups, and has built schools for the children of employees of the corporation, should the corporation enjoy unfettered mobility when it decides to move to Mexico in year eleven?

Brown v. Ferro Corp., 763 F. 2d 798 (1985)

Judge Gilmore delivered the opinion of the Court.

Plaintiff is the owner of ten shares of common stock of defendant Ferro Corporation. Ferro Corporation is a nominal defendant, and the principal defendants are eleven members of Ferro's Board of Directors. . . .

While plaintiff's original complaint challenged several decisions made by Ferro directors, only one of these decisions, the adoption of a severance agreement program, is the subject of this appeal. The severance agreement program is what is commonly known as a "golden parachute" agreement, that is, an agreement between the officers and the corporation providing that in the event of a take-over and change of leadership, the officers can "bail out" and retain very favorable benefits from the corporation.

The severance agreements were adopted in response to a perceived take-over attempt by Crane Company. . . . Ferro's Compensation and Organization Committee, comprised of five outside directors, recommended the severance agreements for fourteen key executives in July 1981. These were authorized by Ferro's Board of Directors by unanimous vote, with the three inside directors who were covered by the agreement abstaining.

The severance agreements require Ferro to pay severance benefits to certain officers if their employment is terminated for any reason other than death or normal retirement within two years after a "change in control." The benefits include: (1) a lump-sum severance payment equal to three years' pay for three officers/directors and two years' pay for the remaining officers; (2) a lump-sum payment calculated to approximate present value of the additional retirement benefits; (3) continued participation in Ferro's Group Life, Health, and Medical Insurance coverage for at least two years; and (4) a cash payment representing the value of all outstanding stock options held by the officers on the date of termination.

The agreements require Ferro to establish an irrevocable escrow account and to make deposits reflecting a certain percentage of the amounts that would be payable to each officer. Under the provisions of the agreements, as well as the terms of the escrow agreement, the funds on deposit remain Ferro's unless and until a change in control occurs. Under the escrow agreement, Ferro directs the investment of the funds and receives all income derived from these investments.

To date, approximately $1,500,000 has been deposited into an escrow account, and deposits into the account continue. None of the key officers subject to the agreement left Ferro during the turbulent period in which Crane's holdings threatened uncertainty as to the future course of the corporation. No change of control has occurred, no monies have been paid out of the accounts to any officers, and the agreements remain in full force and effect. The funds have been invested in certificates of deposit earning from 8 to 14 percent interest.

In her complaint, plaintiff alleged that the adoption of the severance agreement program served no valid business purpose or interest of Ferro or its stockholders, and was designed solely to serve the pecuniary interest of the directors involved, to preserve the directors' control over Ferro, and to discourage potential acquirers from obtaining a controlling interest in Ferro. Plaintiff claims that the corporation has been damaged as a result of the payment of nearly $1,500,000 into the irrevocable escrow account as it cannot withdraw, lend, borrow upon, or hypothecate these escrowed funds.

. . . .

. . . The Court recognizes that "golden parachute" agreements of the type adopted by Ferro have been the subject of much controversy in recent years and that rec-

ommendation has been made by the SEC to Congress to enact legislation prohibiting their adoption. This Court expresses no opinion upon the validity of such agreements for the reason that the controversy here is not yet ripe for determination and declaration with reference to such agreements. . . .

Article III of the Constitution of the United States requires that parties seeking to invoke the power of federal courts must allege an actual case of controversy.

. . . .

The ripeness doctrine not only depends on the finding of a case and controversy and hence jurisdiction under Article III, but it also requires that the court exercise its discretion to determine if judicial resolution would be desirable under all of the circumstances. As the Court in *Pacific Gas & Electric Co. v. Energy Resources Commission,* 461 U.S. 190 (1983), pointed out:

The basic rationale of the ripeness doctrine "is to prevent the courts, through avoidance of premature adjudication, from entangling themselves in abstract disagreements. . . ." In Abbott Laboratories, which remains our leading discussion of the doctrine, we indicated that the question of ripeness turns on "the fitness of the issues for judicial decision" and "the hardship to the parties of withholding court consideration."

. . . .

In resolving the ripeness issue, we cannot conclude that the lower court abused its discretion in declining to adjudicate the validity of the severance agreement program. Throughout this litigation, the only damages that plaintiff has shown is the unavailability of the escrowed funds for unrestricted corporate use and the possible deterrent effect of the existence of the "golden parachute" agreements on future take-over attempts. The district court correctly concluded that the damage resulting from tying up these funds is nominal at best, as the corporation continues to receive a healthy return on its investment. These funds have not been lost to the corporation, but are actually being put to good use.

The fact that all sides have tended to speculate as to the future course of events also supports the district court's decision to decline jurisdiction at this time. Plaintiff suggests that a fabricated contractual "change in control" might be brought about by the officers themselves solely to collect severance benefits. The district court, on the other hand, suggested that a new board of directors might be inclined to challenge the validity of these payments on their own, or that the directors of Ferro might decide to alter significantly or even eliminate the current severance agreements before any change in control occurs, thus obviating the need for court intervention. All of this speculation serves to highlight the fact that it is still unclear how these events will play out, and that judicial intervention at this time would be premature, as the case is not ripe for decision.

Circuit Judge Merritt dissenting.

The plaintiff stockholder alleges that Ferro Corporation has been injured because $1.5 million has been removed from the Corporation's unrestricted use and placed in an escrow account to assure that funds are available to cover the "golden parachute" severance agreements. The fact that interest is being earned on the funds in the escrow account is beside the point; the foregone opportunity to put the funds to their most profitable use constitutes a tangible, real and continuing injury to the Corporation. . . .

The majority opinion ignores these allegations of immediate injury, and argues that the case is not ripe for adjudication because it is unclear whether a change in control will occur, triggering the golden parachutes, and because a new board may decide to alter or eliminate the golden parachutes at some time in the future. This argument misapplies the ripeness doctrine and has the plain consequence of eliminating any opportunity to challenge the

legality of the severance agreements through a shareholder's derivative action.

. . . .

. . . [V]ery real hardship may be caused by our failure to consider the validity of the golden parachutes at this time. The hardship is the probable loss of any possibility of challenging the severance agreements through a shareholder's derivative action. A shareholder's derivative action is the property right of the corporation on whose behalf it is asserted, and under O.R.C. Sec. 1701.82, all "property of every description" of a merged corporation is possessed by the surviving or new corporation into which it is merged.

Interpreting a very similar Delaware statute, the Delaware Supreme Court has recently held that a target company's former shareholder had no standing after the target had become the wholly owned subsidiary of its acquiror to bring a derivative action challenging golden parachutes because only the parent held stock in its wholly owned subsidiary and hence only the parent could maintain a derivative action against the subsidiary's former officers.

The clear implication of the statutory passage of the derivative action to the acquiring corporation is that Ferro Corporation shareholders will lose their opportunity to challenge the golden parachutes after a merger or change of control, even as that same change of control activates the parachutes and delivers up to $5 million in compensation to the departing officers. Thus, under the majority's decision, the shareholder is barred by the ripeness doctrine from challenging the parachutes before an acquisition or merger, and barred by the statutory passage of corporate property rights from challenging the parachutes after the acquisition or merger. A derivative action challenging the golden parachutes could only be brought by the acquiring corporation, but the practical likelihood of this is slim; the possibility that the acquiror would challenge the golden parachutes would only stiffen target management's opposition and thereby negate a primary reason for creating the golden parachutes.

Consequently, I would hold that ripeness does not bar Brown from bringing the present action, and that the prerequisites for maintaining this derivative action have been met.

COMMENT

1. As noted in the introductory material for this chapter, golden parachutes only cover one class of individuals in a corporation—top management. Is this "just" or "fair"? Or is this simply a case of the rich getting richer and the poor losing their jobs?

Fullerton Lumber Co. v. Torburg, 70 N.W. 2d 585 (1955)

Justice Martin delivered the opinion of the Court.

[Albert Torburg and Fullerton Lumber entered into a contract in 1946. Among the terms of the contract agreement was a restrictive covenant which read in part:

If, I cease to be employed by the company for any reason; I will not, for a period of ten years thereafter, work directly or indirectly for any establishment or on my own account handling lumber, building materials or fuel at retail in any city, village or town, or within a radius of fifteen miles thereof, where I have served as manager for the company within a period of five years preceding the date of termination of my employment, unless first obtaining permission, in writing, from the company.

In November 1953, Torburg voluntarily quit work with Fullerton and attempted to set up his own lumber company in the same town, Clintonville. The present action is brought by Fullerton to prevent this, pursuant to the restrictive covenant.]

. . . .

There is no question that restrictive covenants of the type involved in this contract are lawful and enforceable if they meet the tests of necessity and reasonableness.

As stated in Restatement of the Law, Contracts, sec. 516, p. 995:

The following bargains do not impose unreasonable restraint of trade unless effecting, or forming part of a plan to effect, a monopoly. . . .

(f) A bargain by an assistant, servant, or agent not to compete with his employer, or principal, during the term of the employment or agency, or thereafter, within such territory and during such time as may be reasonably necessary for the protection of the employer or principal, without imposing undue hardship on the employee or agent.

At sec. 515, p. 988, of the same text it is stated:

A restraint of trade is unreasonable, in the absence of statutory authorization or dominant social or economic justification, if it

(a) is greater than is required for the protection of the person for whose benefit the restraint is imposed.

It is established that

the burden rests upon the employer to establish both the necessity for, and the reasonableness of, the restrictive covenant he seeks to enforce by enjoining the employee from violating its terms.

. . . .

We agree with the trial court that the ten-year period of restraint imposed by the instant contract is unreasonably long. There is no case cited where this court has upheld a covenant in an employment contract restricting the employee from engaging in competitive activity for so long a time, and the evidence in this case does not establish that a ten-year restraint is necessary for the protection of plaintiff's business.

It cannot be seriously disputed, however, that defendant was plaintiff's key employee in the Clintonville yard. Being a foreign corporation with all its officers and supervisory employees outside of the state, the plaintiff necessarily depended for the growth and maintenance of good will in the Clintonville area upon the efforts and personal assets of the defendant. In the first three years of his employment as manager there he tripled the business of the yard and thereafter (with the exception of 1952 when the entire country experienced a building "boom") he maintained the sales at a level averaging well over $200,000 per year. He terminated his employment at the end of 1953 and immediately commenced operations in Clintonville in competition with the plaintiff. The sales of plaintiff's yard for 1954, based upon its business for the first five months of that year, were estimated at approximately $60,000, a decline of more than two-thirds of the average annual sales of the previous year (excluding the peak year 1952).

These facts conclusively show not only that the business of plaintiff's Clintonville yard depended largely on the efforts, and customer contacts of the defendant, but that it suffered an irreparable loss when defendant took those efforts and customer contacts, as well as three other employees of plaintiff's yard, into a competitive business immediately after he left its employ.

. . . .

There has been no case in this court where the facts presented such a clear need for the kind of protection plaintiff thought it was bargaining for when this contract was made. The facts show that it had every reason to anticipate its business would suffer if defendant, after developing and establishing personal relations with its customers in Clintonville, chose to leave its employ and enter into competition with it in that vicinity.

. . . .

The judgment is reversed and the cause remanded for a determination by the trial court of the extent of time as to which the restrictive covenant with respect to defendant's operations in Clintonville is reasonable and necessary for plaintiff's protection, and for judgment enjoining defendant from a breach thereof. It appears to us that a minimum period of three years would be supported by the evidence. It was established that after defendant took over the managership of plaintiff's yard in 1945 he built the business to a fairly constant level in that period of time, and it must be assumed that any manager taking his place could accomplish the same thing if the restrictions of the contract were enforced against the defendant during that time. In view of the fact that defendant has engaged in continuous competitive activities since December 1, 1953, employing the advantage gained while he was in the service of the plaintiff, the injunction should run from the date of the judgment rather that the date the employment terminated.

Justice Gehl dissenting.

The majority agree that the ten-year restraint imposed by the contract is unreasonably long. This court has consistently held that an unreasonably long restraint is unenforceable, void and illegal, and that a void contract, one against public policy, cannot be made the foundation of any action, whether in law or equity.

It is true, as the majority say, that there has been a tendency on the part of some courts to ascertain whether a contract in restraint of trade is divisible and, if found to be, to hold it unreasonable only to the extent necessary for the protection of the covenantee. Unless that position is limited, however, as it has been by this court, it gives effect to the court's notion as to what should be included in the contract, rather than to the intent of the parties as expressed in the contract, the parties, who had they desired a narrower or a broader provision, should and could have expressed it in the writing. If the provision is to be treated as being divisible, such purpose must be found in the contract itself; that quality should not be supplied by the court simply because it might be considered that the parties should have made broader or narrower provision against possible competition than they did. That is the rule of this state.

COMMENTS

1. Do you agree with Judge Gehl in dissent that Judge Martin effectively rewrote the contract for the parties?

2. Would you have decided this case the same way depending on whether this kind of restrictive covenant was in all of Fullerton's contracts or just the one with Torburg?

3. In its opinion the court pointed out that Torburg was invaluable to Fullerton Lumber as evidenced by the fact that he maintained sales of more than $200,000 per year and that there had been a noticeable drop in sales after Torburg departed. Of course, one reason why Torburg might have wanted to leave was that he felt he was not getting paid what he was worth (as evidenced by these very same factors). The court, however, never even began to consider *why* he wanted to leave. Should it have? Given that the court thought it had the freedom to renegotiate one provision of the employment contract, could it have renegotiated the salary provision as well?

4. What happens to Torburg now?

Guy v. Travenol Laboratories, 812 F. 2d 911 (1987)

Circuit Judge Wilkinson delivered the opinion of the Court.

Robert Guy brought this wrongful discharge action after being fired from his supervisory position at Travenol's North Carolina drug manufacturing plant, allegedly for refusing to falsify certain production and control records. Travenol denied those allegations in its answer and responded that, under North Carolina's doctrine of employment at will, an employer may fire an employee for virtually any reason. . . .

In his complaint, Guy alleged that Travenol employees were falsifying certain records "pertaining to the quality and quantity" of pharmaceuticals that drug manufacturers are required to keep under the Food and Drug Administration regu-

lations. Falsification of these records may violate the Food, Drug, and Cosmetic Act. When Guy allegedly notified his supervisors that they were violating federal law, he was told to cooperate. When he allegedly refused to falsify the records to exclude wasted and defective drugs, he was fired. Travenol denies these allegations. Because the complaint was dismissed under Fed. R. Civ. P. 12(b)(6) for failure to state a claim, however, these alleged facts must be accepted as true. In his prayer for relief, plaintiff claims compensatory damages of $12,138 and punitive damages of $1,000,000.

Federal courts must consider the availability of any wrongful discharge suit in North Carolina against the backdrop of North Carolina's manifest commitment to the doctrine of employment at will. The North Carolina Supreme Court first recognized the doctrine in the 19th century and has reaffirmed its contemporary vitality. . . .

In its pristine form, the doctrine of employment at will permits an employee to be discharged for almost any reason. As a matter of tort law, the doctrine precludes an action for wrongful discharge. . . .

The doctrine of employment at will apparently began in *Edwards v. Seaboard R. R. Co.*, where the court stated that an employee and employer were free "to sever their relationship at will, for their own convenience." 28 S.E. 137 (N.C. 1897). During the following ninety years, the North Carolina Supreme Court has continuously accorded employers broad freedom in employment decisions. For example, when an employer offered an employee a "regular permanent job," the court found an at will employment relationship. *Malever v. Kay Jewelry Co.*, 25 S.E. 2d 436 (N.C. 1943).

. . . .

The North Carolina Supreme Court has recognized but two exceptions to the doctrine: an employee has a wrongful discharge suit only when he obtains an employment contract of fixed duration or gives some extra consideration, such as a change of residence or the dismissal of a personal injury claim, in return for permanent employment. While Guy alleges not that he was arbitrarily discharged, but that he was discharged for refusal to perform a wrongful act, his lawsuit cannot be viewed apart from a near-century of commitment in the state of North Carolina to the doctrine of employment at will. Indeed, Guy pleads the very tort and contract claims that the doctrine has always been thought to proscribe.

Confronted with this body of precedent, Guy relies upon the recent case of *Sides v. Duke Hospital*, which he believes creates a public policy exception to the at will doctrine. In *Sides*, the North Carolina Court of Appeals held that an employer cannot fire an employee for refusing to commit perjury. 328 S.E. 2d 818 (N.C. App. 1985). As the *Sides* opinion and three subsequent appellate cases recognize, this decision created only a narrow public policy exception to the doctrine of at will employment. Because it is a limited exception, most readily explained as an exercise of the judiciary's supervisory powers over the proper conduct of court proceedings, *Sides* does not provide Guy with a viable cause of action.

In *Sides*, a nurse alleged that she was fired because she refused to perjure herself both as a deponent and a witness in a medical malpractice case. The court's opinion emphasized the need to prevent perjury and preserve judicial integrity. As the court noted, perjury is "an affront to the integrity of our judicial system, an impediment to the constitutional mandate of the courts to administer justice fairly, and a violation of the right that all litigants in this State have to have their cases tried upon honest evidence fully given." *Sides*, at 823–24. To deny a cause of action in that case would have been a "grave disservice to the public and the system of law that we are sworn to administer." *Sides*, at 824. Despite some language dealing with the general need to uphold the law and support public policy, the court's holding was very specific: "No employer in this State, notwithstanding that an employment is at will, has the right to discharge an employee because he refuses to testify untruthfully or incompletely in a court case." *Sides*, at 826. The holding rests on the belief that the need to protect the judicial process from the perjured testimony of an intimidated witness outweighs the employer's right to fire an employee. This limited exception to the doctrine is not surprising. The courts obviously have a special obligation to promote the integrity and truthfulness of the judicial process.

The *Sides* case is limited, however, by more than its holding and its language. Three subsequent appellate cases reaffirm the narrow scope of that decision. In *Walker v. Westinghouse Elec. Co.*, 335 S.E. 2d 79 (N.C. App. 1985), the North Carolina Court of Appeals demonstrated its reluctance to expand the *Sides* exception. In that case, an employee alleged that he was fired in retaliation for raising safety concerns relating to the Westinghouse plant. Although North Carolina has a statute protecting employees who file a complaint with the state OSHA commission, N.C. Gen. Stat. 95–130(b) (1981), the court was unwilling to establish a general cause of action for any employee who raised a safety concern.

. . . .

In *Trought v. Richardson,* 338 S.E. 2d 617 (N.C. App. 1986), a nurse alleged that she was fired for transferring two licensed practical nurses from the emergency room. She claimed that the "at will" doctrine did not apply because in removing the nurses she was following state law, here the state Nursing Practice Act. The court, however, stated that "we do not believe this allegation is sufficient to come within or enlarge the exception created by *Sides.*" *Trought,* at 619. The *Trought* decision, which the district court in this case found dispositive of the motion to dismiss, held that an employee does not come within the *Sides* exception by alleging that she was fired for attempting to comply with state law. The North Carolina Court of Appeals continued to limit the new exception in *Hogan v. Forsyth Country Club Co.,* 340 S.E. 2d 116 (N.C. App. 1986). In *Hogan,* several female employees claimed that they were fired in retaliation for complaining about the sexual advances of a fellow male employee. The employees argued that *Sides* allowed a wrongful discharge suit whenever an employee is terminated in violation of public policy. *Hogan* quickly rejected this interpretation, noting that "though *Sides* spoke in broad terms of 'public policy,' its holding was actually very narrow." *Hogan,* at 125. While noting that the claim appeared cognizable under Title VII of the 1964 Civil Rights Act, the court rejected the employees' request to recognize a new public policy exception to the doctrine of employment at will in North Carolina.

In sum, the *Sides* opinion and the holdings of three subsequent appellate cases reveal that, instead of seriously eroding the at will doctrine, *Sides* was intended to be a limited perjury exception. At this point, the law of North Carolina is well established. An employer may terminate any employee for any reason unless the employee has a specific duration contract, gave some additional consideration for permanent employment, or lost his job for refusing to give perjured testimony. Because his complaint does not come within any of these exceptions, Guy has failed to state a cause of action under state law.

COMMENTS

1. Is the employment-at-will doctrine for the benefit of *both* employee and employer, as the court suggested here?

2. Do businesses ever need to give a reason for firing you? Should you be able to keep your job unless and until you somehow "mess up"? A state following the employment-at-will doctrine, at least as I read it, would not mandate this. Is this fair?

·3. Did the decision in *Travenol Laboratories* take the free-market system to its logical (but unjust?) conclusion?

10

CONSUMERS

The political branches and the courts did not begin to offer certain protections to workers in this country until the 1930s. In many respects, the American consumer had to wait just as long, if not longer, for similar kinds of protection. For much of American history the governing principle for economic transactions was summed up by the Latin phrase *caveat emptor,* "let the buyer beware."

The development of product liability law in this country is instructive in terms of what the law used to be and in terms of *how* the law changed and by what method. The old rule, a very harsh one, developed in the first half of the nineteenth century, was that a manufacturer, seller or furnisher of an article was not liable to outside parties who had no contractual relations with him for negligence in the construction, manufacture, or sale of an article. The courts held that in order to recover for damages incurred, there must be "privity of contract."

Consider the leading case of this era, *Winterbottom v. Wright,* an 1842 English case that through our judge-made, or common law tradition, became the dominant law in the United States as well.[1] Winterbottom was a driver of a mail coach who was injured when the coach he was driving overturned because of defective construction. Winterbottom sued Wright, who was under a contractual relationship with the post office to keep the vehicle in repair. The court denied Winterbottom's recovery on the grounds that there was no privity of contract between Winterbottom and Wright. Lord Abinger writes:

> If the plaintiff [Winterbottom] can sue, every passenger or even any person passing along the road, who was injured by the upsetting of the coach, might bring a similar action. Unless we confine the operation of such contracts as this to the parties who enter into them, the most absurd and outrageous consequences, to which I can see no limit, would ensue.

Although the privity of contract rule prevented most harmed consumers and workers (see Chapter 9) from recovering for damages they suffered from defective work, courts began to carve out certain exceptions to this harsh rule. *Thomas v. Winchester* became the leading exception to the privity of contract requirement.[2] Winchester was a drug manufacturer of sorts who sold vegetable extracts for medicinal purposes. His agent put belladonna, a poison, into a jar, but mislabeled it as an extract of dandelion, a harmless medicine. The jar was then sold to one druggist, Aspinwall, who then sold it to another druggist, Foord. Foord in turn sold the mislabeled belladonna to an unsuspecting customer, Mrs. Thomas, who became gravely ill after taking what she thought was dandelion. Mrs. Thomas then sued Winchester. Although there was no privity of contract between Thomas and Winchester (in fact, they were several transactions removed), the court allowed Mrs. Thomas to recover damages from Winchester.

The court based its opinion on two grounds. The first was that injury from mislabeled poisonous drugs was not likely to fall on the immediate purchaser of the goods. Although this was undoubtedly true, the same argument could have been made for Winterbottom, and individuals like him, as well. The court also held that this case was distinguished from others that required privity of contract in order to recover damages because the poison was "imminently dangerous to the lives of others."

The exception eventually began to swallow the rule.[3] The case of *Torgesen v. Schultz* involved a suit by a domestic servant who lost an eye when a bottle of club soda exploded on a very hot evening in July 1901.[4] A druggist had delivered two bottles of soda water to Torgesen's place of employment. The bottles were initially placed in a room in the third story of the house but later moved into the cellar and placed on blocks of ice. After placing the bottles on ice, the plaintiff was then struck in the eye by glass from the exploding bottle. Torgesen sued the bottler, Schultz. The trial court denied recovery, but this decision was overturned on appeal. Judge Bartlett writes:

> It is manifest that there was no contract relation between the plaintiff and the defendant, but the defendant is sought to be held liable under the doctrine of *Thomas v. Winchester* . . . and similar cases based upon the duty of the vendor of an article dangerous in its nature, or *likely to become so in the course of the ordinary usage to be contemplated by the vendor,* either to exercise due care to warn user of the danger or to take reasonable care to prevent the article sold from proving dangerous when subjected only to customary usage (emphasis supplied).

The court then went on to say that the vendor should have known that it was likely that soda water would be placed on ice, as it was in the case at hand, and that the expert testimony indicated that the vendor had not adequately tested to ensure against explosions that might result when this occurred.

The general rule of privity of contract was fully laid to rest in *Mac-Pherson v. Buick Motor Co.* in an opinion by the great Judge (later Justice) Cardozo.[5] In his inimitable style, Cardozo lays out the facts of the case:

> The defendant is a manufacturer of automobiles. It sold an automobile to a retail dealer. The retail dealer resold to the plaintiff. While the plaintiff was in the car, it suddenly collapsed. He was thrown out and injured. One of the wheels was made of defective wood, and its spokes crumbled into fragments. The wheel was not made by the defendant; it was bought from another manufacturer. There is evidence, however, that its defects could have been discovered by reasonable inspection, and that inspection was omitted. There is no claim that the defendant knew of the defect and wilfully concealed it. . . . The charge is one, not of fraud, but of negligence. The question to be determined is whether the defendant owed a duty of care and vigilance to any one but the immediate purchaser.

After reviewing cases such as *Winchester* and *Torgesen,* Cardozo sets forth a new rule, one that overturns *Winterbottom:*

> We hold, then, that the principle of *Thomas v. Winchester* is not limited to poisons, explosives, and things of like nature, to things which in their normal operation are implements of destruction. If the nature of a thing is such that it is reasonably certain to place life and limb in peril when negligently made, it is then a thing of danger. Its nature gives warning of the consequences to be expected. If to the element of danger there is added knowledge that the thing will be used by persons other than the purchaser, and used without new tests, then irrespective of contract, the manufacturer of this thing of danger is under a duty to make it carefully.

No longer could manufacturers of goods hide behind the doctrine of privity of contract, and *caveat emptor* certainly was weakened. But despite the development of product liability law, we should not conclude that government has necessarily devoted considerable energies to protecting consumers. In fact, most of the myriad consumer legislation that we have at present is of very recent origin. Much of the credit, of course, goes to the pioneering work of Ralph Nader. Nader's 1965 book, *Unsafe at Any Speed,* about the appalling lack of interest in safety shown by the automobile industry, was certainly not an immediate success. It became a bestseller, however, when General Motors attempted to "get back" at Nader by trying to dig up some dirt on him. The short-term result was the sudden flowering of the consumer movement in this country and the remarkable rise to fame of the reclusive Nader. In the long term, we now see the common acceptance of the notion that government has a responsibility to protect consumers.

The two cases in this chapter examine different aspects of consumer protection. The first case, *Williams v. Walker-Thomas Furniture Co.,* was a suit involving the legality of an agreement between buyer and seller in which the contract stipulated that title to all the goods sold to the buyer would remain with the seller until *all* money due on *all* purchased items had been paid. Is this a modern example of *caveat emptor?* On the other hand, should we expect government generally, and courts in particular, to protect individuals from what appears to be poor business judgment? A final point to note is that this contract was actually challenged in court. The vast majority of situations like this will not be. This raises the question of consumer rights when many consumers are completely ignorant of what these rights happen to be.

The second principal case, *Roysdon v. R. J. Reynolds Tobacco Co.,* involved a much different "consumer" issue. It is an example of a growing number of cases by smokers against the tobacco industry for damages caused by smoking. Even if one believes, as I do, that smoking is a vile practice, does it necessarily follow that the tobacco industry should pay damages for injuries that, arguably, an individual has brought upon himself or herself? One of the more interesting questions to pursue here is the government's role. Is it doing enough to protect consumers by putting labels on cigarette packages, and how does that effort square with government price supports for tobacco growers? Should the tobacco industry be able to "use" such warnings for its own purposes, by being able to claim that if smoking cigarettes is dangerous (a position that the industry refuses to admit), these warnings absolve the tobacco industry from liability because smokers have been put on notice of this fact.

Roysdon represents the thinking of the overwhelming majority of cases that have been heard in this area. But there might be a crack in the armor of the tobacco industry. In the summer of 1988, a jury awarded $400,000 to Antonio Cipollone, whose wife died of cancer allegedly caused by her smoking. Whether *Cipollone v. Liggett* will establish a new precedent is problematic. Most noteworthy is the fact that the damages were limited to the Liggett Corporation, whose cigarettes Mrs. Cipollone smoked prior to 1966, when warnings began to be printed on cigarette packages. Lorillard and Phillip Morris, whose brands she smoked after 1966, were found not liable of fraudulently misrepresenting the risks of smoking and conspiring to misrepresent the facts.

NOTES

1. 152 Eng. Rep. 402 (1842).
2. 6 N.Y. 397 (1852).
3. Not all at once, however. For example, in *Loop v. Litchfield,* 42 N.Y. 351 (1870), the court refused to extend the principle of *Thomas v. Winchester,* reasoning that poison and articles like it (such as gunpowder, a spring gun, and a torpedo) are "in their nature calculated to do injury to mankind," whereas a wheel was not, even a defectively constructed wheel.
4. 192 N.Y. 156 (1908).
5. 111 N.E. 1050 (1916).

Williams v. Walker-Thomas Furniture Co., 350 F. 2d 445 (1965)

Circuit Judge Skelly Wright delivered the opinion of the Court.

Appellee, Walker-Thomas Furniture Company, operates a retail furniture store in the District of Columbia. During the period from 1957 to 1962 each appellant in these cases purchased a number of household items from Walker-Thomas, for which payment was to be made in installments. The terms of each purchase were contained in a printed form contract which set forth the value of the purchased item and purported to lease the item to appellant for a stipulated monthly rent payment. The contract then provided, in substance, that title would remain in Walker-Thomas until the total of all the monthly payments made equaled the stated value of the item, at which time appellants could take title. In the event of a default in the payment of any monthly installment, Walker-Thomas could repossess the item.

The contract further provided that "the amount of each periodical installment payment to be made by [purchaser] to the Company under this present lease shall be inclusive of and not in addition to the amount of each installment payment to be made by [purchaser] under such prior leases, bills or accounts; *and all payments now and hereafter made by [purchaser] shall be credited pro rata on all outstanding leases, bills and accounts* due the Company by [purchaser] at the time each such payment is made." (Emphasis added.) The effect of this rather obscure provision was to keep a balance due on every item purchased until the balance due on all items, whenever purchased, was liquidated. As a result, the debt incurred at the time of purchase of each item was secured by the right to repossess all the items previously purchased by the same purchaser, and each new item purchased automatically became subject to a security interest arising out of the previous dealings.

On May 12, 1962, appellant Thorne purchased an item described as a Daveno, three tables, and two lamps, having total stated value of $391.10. Shortly thereafter, he defaulted on his monthly payments and appellee sought to replevy all the items purchased since the first transaction in 1958. Similarly, on April 17, 1962, appellant Williams bought a stereo set of stated value of $514.95. She too defaulted shortly thereafter, and appellee sought to replevy all the items purchased since December, 1957. . . .

Appellants' principal contention, rejected by both the trial and the appellate courts below, is that these contracts, or at least some of them, are unconscionable and, hence, not enforceable. In its opinion in *Williams v. Walker-Thomas Furniture Company,* 198 A. 2d 914, 916 (1964), the District of Columbia Court of Appeals explained its rejection of this contention as follows:

Appellant's second argument presents a more serious question. The record reveals that prior to the last purchase appellant had reduced the balance in her account to $164. The last purchase, a stereo set, raised the balance due to $678. Significantly, at the time of this and the preceding purchases, appellee was aware of appellant's financial position. The reverse side of the stereo contract listed the name of appellant's social worker and her $218 monthly stipend from the government. Nevertheless, with full knowledge that appellant had to feed, clothe and support both herself and seven children on this amount, appellee sold her a $514 stereo set.

We cannot condemn too strongly appellee's conduct. It raises serious questions of sharp practice and irresponsible business dealings. A review of the legislation in the District of Columbia affecting retail sales and the pertinent decisions of the highest court in this jurisdiction disclose, however, no ground upon which this court can declare the contracts in question contrary to public policy. . . . We think Congress should consider corrective legislation to protect the public from such exploitive contracts as were utilized in the case at bar.

We do not agree that the court lacked the power to refuse enforcement to contracts found to be unconscionable. In other jurisdictions, it has been held as a matter of common law that unconscionable contracts are not enforceable. While no decision of this court so holding has been found, the notion that an unconscionable bargain should not be given full enforcement is by no means novel.

. . . .

Unconscionability has generally been recognized to include an absence of meaningful choice on the part of one of the parties together with contract terms which are unreasonably favorable to the other party. Whether a meaningful choice is present in a particular case can only be determined by consideration of all the circumstances surrounding the transaction. In many cases the meaningfulness of the choice is negated by a gross inequality of bargaining power. The manner in which the contract was entered is also relevant to this consideration. Did each party to the contract, considering his obvious education or lack of it, have a reasonable opportunity to understand the terms of the contract, or were the important terms hidden in a maze of fine print and minimized by deceptive sales practices? Ordinarily, one who signs an agreement without full knowledge of its terms might be held to assume the risk that he has entered a one-sided bargain. But when a party of little bargaining power, and hence little real choice, signs a commercially unreasonable contract with little or no knowledge of its terms, it is hardly likely that his consent, or even an objective manifestation of his consent, was

ever given to all the terms. In such a case the usual rule that the terms of the agreement are not to be questioned should be abandoned and the court should consider whether the terms of the contract are so unfair that enforcement should be withheld.

In determining reasonableness or fairness, the primary concern must be with the terms of the contract considered in light of the circumstances existing when the contract was made. The test is not simple, nor can it be mechanically applied. The terms are to be considered "in the light of the general commercial background and the commercial needs of the particular trade or case."

Because the trial court and the appellate court did not feel that enforcement could be refused, no findings were made on the possible unconscionability of the contracts in these cases. Since the record is not sufficient for our deciding the issue as a matter of law, the cases must be remanded to the trial court for further proceedings.

Circuit Judge Danaher dissenting.

The District of Columbia Court of Appeals obviously was as unhappy about the situation here presented as any of us can possibly be. Its opinion in the *Williams* case, quoted in the majority text, concludes: "We think Congress should consider corrective legislation to protect the public from such exploitive contracts as were utilized in the case at bar."

My view is thus summed up by an able court which made no finding that there had actually been sharp practice. Rather the appellant seems to have known precisely where she stood.

There are many aspects of public policy here involved. What is a luxury to some may seem an outright necessity to others. Is public oversight to be required of the expenditures of relief funds? A washing machine, e.g., in the hands of a relief client might become a fruitful source of income. Many relief clients may well need credit, and certain business establishments will take long chances on the sale of items, expecting their pricing policies will afford a degree of protection commensurate with the risk. . . .

I mention such matters only to emphasize the desirability of a cautious approach to any such problem, particularly since the law for so long has allowed parties such great latitude in making their own contracts. I dare say there must annually be thousands upon thousands of installment credit transactions in this jurisdiction, and one can only speculate as to the effect the decision in these cases will have.

I join the District of Columbia Court of Appeals in its disposition of the issues.

COMMENTS

1. Exactly what is an unconscionable contract? If illegal aliens will work in this country for less than minimum wage, is employing them at that amount unconscionable? What if these subminimum wages (in U.S. dollars) would still be far greater than the wages to be made at home?

2. Should the government step in and protect individuals as the court ultimately did in this case?

Roysdon v. R. J. Reynolds Tobacco Co., 623 F. Supp. 1189 (1985)

District Judge Hill.

This products liability action came to trial by jury on December 9, 1985. Plaintiffs, Mr. and Mrs. Floyd R. Roysdon, claimed that Mr. Roysdon suffers severe peripheral vascular disease as a proximate result of many years of smoking cigarettes manufactured by the defendant R. J. Reynolds Tobacco Company [R. J. Reynolds]. The Roysdons made two claims: that the defendant's cigarettes are defective and unreasonably dangerous to the health of users and that the warnings on cigarette packages and in their advertising are inadequate to fully apprise users of the medical risks involved in smoking.

. . . .

THE ADEQUACY OF THE WARNINGS

In this lawsuit, it was undisputed that R. J. Reynolds had at all times pertinent fully complied with the relevant federal Cigarette Labeling and Advertising Act [the

Act]. 15 U.S.C. Sec. 1331–1340. The issue to be resolved was whether, in light of this compliance, plaintiff still could claim that labels were inadequate or whether the labels must be ruled adequate as a matter of law.

R. J. Reynolds took the position that Congress had preempted any claim based on the adequacy of the warning labels. It relied on very specific preemption language contained in 15 U.S.C. Sec. 1334, which reads as follows:

(a) No statement relating to smoking and health, other than the statement required by section 1331 of this title, shall be required on any cigarette package.

(b) No requirement or prohibition based on smoking and health shall be imposed under State law with respect to the advertising or promotion of any cigarettes the packages of which are labeled in conformity with the provisions of this chapter.

It is obvious that this statute prohibits the Tennessee legislature from requiring R. J. Reynolds to use any statement relating to smoking and health other than the one congressionally mandated. The statute does not explicitly prohibit state common law tort actions based on labeling. However, congressional intent need not be expressly stated but may be implied from the structure and purpose of the particular statute, and state law must yield when incompatible with federal legislation.

In order to determine whether common law tort actions based on labeling have been preempted, the Court must determine whether permitting an award of damages on the basis of an inadequate warning label would be incompatible with the intent of the legislation in question. Section 1331 is a declaration of the legislative intent. It reads:

It is the policy of the Congress, and the purpose of this chapter, to establish a comprehensive Federal program to deal with cigarette labeling and advertising with respect to any relationship between smoking and health, whereby—(1) the public may be adequately informed that cigarette smoking may be hazardous to health by inclusion of a warning to that effect on each package of cigarettes; and (2) commerce and the national economy may be (A) protected to the maximum extent consistent with this declared policy and (B) not impeded by diverse, nonuniform, and confusing cigarette labeling and advertising regulations with respect to any relationship between smoking and health.

It is evident from this language that the congressional purpose was twofold—to inform the public of the health hazards related to smoking and to insure uniformity of labeling. While the imposition of tort damages would not be contrary to the first objective, exposing a manufacturer to potential damages in regards to its labeling would be inconsistent with the second. It would permit a state to achieve indirectly, through exposure to tort liability, what it could not achieve directly through legislation. Certainly exposing a manufacturer to potential damages on the basis of its warning label is a way of requiring a more stringent label. And, if the courts were to impose any duty to go beyond the congres-

sionally mandated labeling, this would thwart the stated intent of Congress to have uniformity in the warnings. . . .

THE CONDITION OF THE PRODUCTS

Through the introduction of the Surgeon General's reports and medical expert testimony, the plaintiffs made a prima facie case that the defendant's cigarettes are dangerous to health, and that they have been harmful to Mr. Roysdon. Of course, many dangerous products, from axes to alcohol, are in the stream of commerce and occasionally injure their users. For R. J. Reynolds, or any manufacturer, to be held liable for the harm caused by its products, the products must be found "unreasonably dangerous."

Under Tennessee law, the test of whether or not a product is unreasonably dangerous is defined as follows:

"Unreasonably dangerous" means that a product is dangerous to an extent beyond that which would be contemplated by the ordinary consumer who purchases it, with the ordinary knowledge common to the community as to its characteristics, or that the product because of its dangerous condition would not be put on the market by a reasonably prudent manufacturer or seller assuming that he knew of its dangerous condition.

Tenn. Code Ann. Sec. 29–28–102(8)

The Tennessee Supreme Court has stated that this is determinable from the "knowledge of the ordinary consumers of the product." *Pemberton v. American Distilled Spirits*, 664 S.W. 2d 690, 692 (1984). Tennessee tort law has also been held to incorporate comment i to the Restatement (Second) of Torts. Comment i used "good tobacco" (such as that at issue in this lawsuit) as an illustration of what kind of product would not be considered unreasonably dangerous due to the widespread common knowledge as to its characteristics.

In the *Pemberton* case, supra, which involved "good alcohol" rather than "good tobacco," the court took judicial notice of the widespread public understanding of the dangers inherent in alcohol. It said, "Alcohol has been present and used in society during all recorded history and its characteristics and qualities have been fully explored and developed and are a part of the body of common knowledge."

In the instant action, this Court takes a similar approach. It finds that tobacco has been used for over 400 years and that its characteristics also have been fully explored. Knowledge that cigarette smoking is harmful to health is widespread and can be considered part of the common knowledge of the community. For this reason, as well as because of the language in comment i to section 402A of Restatement (Second) of Torts, this Court finds that the plaintiffs did not make a prima facie case that the defendant's products are "unreasonably dangerous."

Accordingly, judgment will enter on behalf of the defendant R. J. Reynolds and the plaintiffs will take nothing on their claim.

COMMENTS

1. The decision in *Roysdon* has been the rule in the United States. There has, however, been one successful challenge against cigarette manufacturers in *Cipollone v. Liggett*, although damages were limited to the manufacturer of cigarettes smoked by the plaintiff prior to 1966. It might surprise you to know (and contrary to the language in the *Roysdon* case) that cigarette smoking used to be thought of, and advertised as, being beneficial to one's health. Such claims seem to be one of the bases for the $400,000 award in the *Cipollone* case.

2. In terms of the cigarettes produced and smoked after 1966, the jury in *Cipollone* did not award damages against these cigarette manufacturers, presumably on two bases: the fact that the surgeon general's warning about the health risks involved in smoking now put the smoker on notice of such danger, and these cigarettes had not been advertised as safe. Should the cigarette manufacturers be allowed to hide behind this warning?

3. On January 11, 1989—exactly twenty-five years after the first official warnings on the perils of cigarette smoking—the Surgeon General issued a report that attributed 390,000 deaths a year to smoking—more than one out of six deaths in the United States. The U.S. government, nevertheless, continues to *pay* millions of dollars each year in price supports to tobacco growers.

11

THE DEFINITION OF COMMUNITY

Most of the cases and discussion thus far have focused on the concept of rights and there truly have been a litany of them. The cases in Part I examined the notion of a right to privacy. In Part II we looked at other rights or at least the claim that certain rights exist—shelter, education, food, a job, freedom of speech, and so on. In Part III we will look at the flip side of the notion of rights and examine the concept of duties or responsibilities to others.

Individuals in this society are far more willing to proclaim the rights that they purportedly have than to recognize and honor duties to others. Rights affirm our individuality and autonomy. In contrast, duties are infringements on these very same qualities. Duties mean responsibility, and responsibility means not always having things our way.

Much of the blame for this state of affairs is laid at the feet of a lost sense of "community." According to this view, loneliness and despair are the price we have paid for our autonomy and individuality. This theme will be explored later in this chapter, but first we need to come to terms with what we mean by community.

If you listen around, "community" is a commonly used term, but its meaning remains unexplained. If you are at church services, you will invariably hear talk of your church community. There is also talk of local community. In addition, we speak of the United States in communal terms. What do we mean by all this talk of community? What does a community comprise? Does membership in a community mean, almost by definition, some kind of responsibility to others who are also members of this community? If there are duties to others in the same community, does that necessarily mean that there are no duties to those who are outside of this community? Can a person pick and choose which community he wishes to join? Can members of a community exclude nonmembers?

The question raised in the first principal case, *New York State Club Association v. New York City,* was whether a New York City ordinance that forbid discrimination by private clubs violated the "freedom of association" of the members of male-only organizations. Some may phrase the issue in these terms: do we always have a right to decide or determine our own "community" and thereby exclude others?

Let me change the situation around a bit by proposing a not very hypothetical situation I used in class a few years ago. It came to my attention that at the public university at which I teach *none* of the sororities (and very few of the fraternities) had members of the other race. That is, white sororities were all white, and black sororities (there were only a few) were all black. Indiana state law allows certain preferential tax treatment for sororities and fraternities that are "recognized" by the university. All of the fraternities and sororities on campus had been recognized, which also entailed following certain university guidelines and regulations, such as not serving alcohol during rush activities.

The question that I asked the class was whether the state, or the university, could mandate that all sororities and fraternities be racially integrated. This would, of course, entail some involvement or oversight by university officials in terms of the sorority admission process. It could be argued, however, that there is a "compelling" state interest in having integrated housing units in organizations "recognized" by the university. It also could be said that there already is a great deal of university supervision and oversight at the present time. Needless to say, the discussion of this question raised a lot of emotion. The vast majority of students—many of whom were members of the Greek system—emphatically stated that such a mandate would interfere with the members' "freedom of association." In nonlegal terms, it would violate the right of a group to form its own community, which by definition means excluding others. Wrestle with the question, if you would, to what extent the state can or cannot shape or enforce a certain concept of community.

The other cases in this chapter examine the concept of community in a different way, and the questions raised here concern whether we have lost our sense of community. By way of introducing this subject, I relate an incident that occurred about twenty-five years ago but still haunts many. One spring evening, Kitty Genovese was returning to her home on a residential street in New York when she was suddenly and brutally attacked by a knife-wielding assailant. There were actually three separate attacks during a thirty-five minute period. Thirty-eight of Genovese's neighbors witnessed these attacks, but not one of them came to her rescue *or even bothered to phone the police for assistance.* It was only after Genovese had died that someone called the police, who came to the scene within two minutes.

The Genovese case has served as a symbol for a variety of people and purposes. For some, it represents the loss of community values in this country. For others, it has been taken to symbolize the urban jungle. I use it here to raise the question whether there should be a legal duty to assist others in peril when we could do so with little effort or risk to ourselves.

The Queen v. Instan is an old English case involving a niece who lived with her aunt, and through the niece's obvious neglect of the old woman the latter died of gangrene. The niece, Instan, was charged with feloniously killing her aunt, although she took no positive action to bring about this result. In *Yania v. Bigan,* Bigan stood idly and watched as a business associate, Yania, drowned.[1] Yania's widow sued Bigan for her husband's wrongful death. The *Yania* decision is the law in most states in this country. Is it a good rule? If Bigan had shot and killed Yania, there would be no question of legal responsibility for this death. Should it make a difference that rather than committing an *act* of harm, he simply *omitted* doing anything but at the same time allowed the same sort of harm to occur? The act-omission distinction is often made in American law. Is it logical? Why is this distinction made?

Instan and *Yania* also raise questions that have been examined before— namely, the relationship that exists (or should exist) between law and morality. In *Instan,* Lord Coleridge writes, "The prisoner [Instan] was under a moral obligation to the deceased from which arose a legal duty to her." In *Yania,* on the other hand, although the court thought there was a moral obligation present to offer assistance, it was unwilling to premise a legal duty on this moral duty. Which is a better-reasoned view, and why?

Another issue involving the relationship between law and morality is whether the existence of one will *cause* the recognition of the other one. For example, in the Genovese situation those who relate the chilling tale presume that these onlookers *had* a moral obligation and that these individuals *recognized* such an obligation but failed to act on it. But perhaps this presumes too much. Perhaps these onlookers felt no moral obligation toward Kitty Genovese. Moreover, if this is true, could it be that they felt no moral obligation because there was no legal duty to assist? Under this line of reasoning, if individuals in our society are hesitant in accepting duties to others, one reason could be that they do not feel as if they have a moral duty to offer such assistance. One possible means of changing this is to impose legal duties to offer assistance, the thought being that the existence of moral duties is either illusory or simply not strong enough to prompt action on the part of bystanders. The comments following *Instan* and *Yania* explore a few state efforts to do just that. The question that this raises, however, is whether the law can attempt to force us to act as a community, when perhaps no community actually exists.

The final case in this chapter, *Kelly v. Gwinnell,* concerned the question of "social host" liability. Put in other terms, should we be responsible for the foolishness of others? *Kelly* involved a party situation in which one of the guests had too much to drink. Should the hosts of the party have prevented this person from drinking as much as he did? Do you agree with the holding of this case, and if so, how far would you extend its principles? For example, should only the hosts of the party have been held responsible, or do you think other guests bore some responsibility as well (or at least those who knew how much other guests were drinking)?

NOTE

1. Leo Katz reports a number of interesting experiments and findings about when individuals are apt to assist others in peril and when they are not likely to do so. As a general rule, individuals in groups (or those who think they are in groups) are much less apt to assist others in peril than are individuals who are by themselves (or believe they are alone). Katz quotes from Darley and Latane, two researchers in this area:

> If only one bystander is present at an emergency, he carries all of the responsibility for dealing with it; he will feel all of the guilt for not acting; he will bear all of the blame that accrues for nonintervention. If others are present, the onus of responsibility is diffused, and the finger of blame points less directly at any one person. The individual may be more likely to resolve his conflict between intervening and nonintervening in favor of the latter alternative.

In terms of Kitty Genovese, Katz concludes from the empirical findings: "If Kitty Genovese failed to receive help, it was because, being part of a large group, nobody felt responsible. For Kitty Genovese, then, there was no safety in numbers." Leo Katz, *Bad Acts and Guilty Minds: Conundrums of the Criminal Law* (Chicago: University of Chicago Press, 1987), pp. 149–50.

New York State Club Association v. New York City, 101 L. Ed. 2d 1 (1988)

Justice White delivered the opinion of the Court.

In 1965, New York City adopted a Human Rights Law that prohibits discrimination by any "place of public accommodation, resort or amusement." This term is defined broadly in the Law to cover such various places as hotels, restaurants, retail stores, hospitals, laundries, theatres, parks, public conveyances, and public halls, in addition to numerous other places that are specifically listed. Yet the Law also exempted from its coverage various public educational facilities and "any institution, club or place of accommodation which proves that it is in its nature distinctly private."

In 1984, New York City amended its Human Rights Law. The basic purpose of the amendment is to prohibit discrimination in certain private clubs that are determined to be sufficiently "public" in nature that they do not fit properly within the exemption for "any institution, club, or place of accommodation which is in its nature distinctly private." As the City Council stated at greater length:

It is hereby found and declared that the city of New York has a compelling interest in providing its citizens an environment where all persons, regardless of race, creed, color, national origin or sex, have a fair and equal opportunity to participate in the business and professional life of the city, and may be unfettered in availing themselves of employment opportunities. Although city, state and federal laws have been enacted to eliminate discrimination in employment, women and minority group members have not attained equal opportunity in business and the professions. One barrier to the advancement of women and minorities in the business and professional life of the city is the discriminatory practices of certain membership organizations where business deals are often made and personal contacts valuable for business purposes, employment and professional advancement are formed. While such organization may avowedly be organized for social, cultural, civic, or educational purposes, and while many perform valuable services to the community, the commercial nature of some of the activities occurring therein and the prejudicial impact of these activities on business, professional and employment opportunities of minorities and women cannot be ignored. Local Law No. 63 of 1984, Sec. 1, App. 14–15.

For these reasons, the City Council found that "the public interest in equal opportunity" outweighs "the interest in private association asserted by club members." It cautioned, however, that it did not propose "to interfere in club activities or subject club operations to scrutiny beyond what is necessary in good faith to enforce the human rights law," and the amendments were not intended as an attempt "to dictate the manner in which certain private clubs conduct their activities or select their members, except insofar as is necessary to ensure that clubs do not automatically exclude persons from consideration for membership or enjoyment of club accommodations and facilities and the advantages and privileges of membership, on account of invidious discrimination."

The specific change wrought by the amendment is to extend the antidiscrimination provisions of the Human Rights Law

to any "institution, club or place of accommodation [that] has more than four hundred members, provides regular meal service and regularly receives payment for dues, fees, use of space, facilities, services, meals or beverages directly or indirectly from or on behalf of nonmembers for the furtherance of trade or business." Any such club "shall not be considered in its nature distinctly private." . . .

. . . .

. . . Appellant conceded at oral argument, understandably we think, that the antidiscrimination provisions of the Law certainly could be constitutionally applied at least to some of the large clubs, under this Court's decision in Rotary and Roberts [*Rotary International v. Rotary Club of Duarte*, 481 U.S. 537 (1987) and *Roberts v. U.S. Jaycees*, 468 U.S. 609 (1984). In both cases the Court upheld statutes mandating the end to the exclusion of women on the grounds that much of the organization's central activities were carried out in the presence of strangers, and thus not private]. The clubs that are covered under the Law contain at least 400 members. They thus are comparable in size to the local chapters of the Jaycees that we found not to be protected private associations in Roberts, and they are considerably larger than many of the local clubs that were found to be unprotected in Rotary, some which included as few as 20 members. The clubs covered by Local Law 63 also provide "regular meal service" and receive regular payments "directly or indirectly from or on behalf of nonmembers for the furtherance of trade or business." The city found these two characteristics to be significant in pinpointing organizations which are "commercial" in nature, "where business deals are often made and personal contacts valuable for business purposes, employment and professional advancement are formed."

These characteristics are at least significant in defining the nonprivate nature of these associations, because of the kind of role that strangers play in their ordinary existence, as is the regular participation of strangers at meetings, which we emphasized in *Robert* and *Rotary*. It may well be that a considerable amount of private or intimate association occurs in such a setting, as is also true in many restaurants and other places of public accommodation, but that fact alone does not afford the entity as a whole any constitutional immunity to practice discrimination when the Government has barred it from doing so. . . .

The same may be said about the contention that the Law infringes upon every club member's right of expressive association. The ability and the opportunity to combine with others to advance one's views is a powerful practical means of ensuring the perpetuation of the freedoms the First Amendment has guaranteed to individuals as against the Government. Effective advocacy of both public and private points of view, particularly controversial ones, is undeniably enhanced by group association, as this Court has more than once recognized by remarking upon the close nexus between the freedoms of speech and assembly. This is not to say, however, that in every setting in which individuals exercise some discrimination in choosing associates, their selective process of inclusion and exclusion is protected by the Constitution.

On its face, Local Law 63 does not affect "in any significant way" the ability of individuals to form associations that will advocate public or private viewpoints. It does not require the clubs "to abandon or alter" any activities that are protected by the First Amendment. If a club seeks to exclude individuals who do not share the views that the club's members wish to promote, the Law erects no obstacle to this end. Instead, the Law merely prevents an association from using race, sex, and the other specified characteristics as shorthand measures in place of what the city considered to be more legitimate criteria for determining membership. It is conceivable, of course, that an association might be able to show that it is organized for specific expressive purposes and that it will not be able to advocate its desired viewpoints nearly as effectively if it cannot confine its membership to those who share the same sex, for example, or the same religion. In the case before us, however, it seems sensible enough to believe that many of the large clubs covered by the Law are not of this kind. . . .

COMMENTS

1. Return to the "hypothetical" situation discussed in the introductory material to this chapter. Would fraternities and sororities constitute "intimate associations"?

2. Is the Supreme Court unduly interfering in areas in which government intrusion does not belong, namely, in the self-definition of a community or is it proper for the Court to help shape the notion of what constitutes a community?

The Queen v. Instan, 1 Q.B. 450 (1893)

Case stated by Judge Day.

Kate Instan was tried before me at the last assizes for the county of Worcester upon a charge of feloniously killing one Ann Hunt. The prisoner, who is between thirty and forty years of age and unmarried, had no occupation and no means of her own living. She was a niece of the deceased.

At the time of the committal of the alleged offence, and for some time previous thereto, she had been living with and had been maintained by the deceased. Deceased was a woman of some seventy-three years of age, and until a few weeks before her death was healthy and able to take care of herself. She was possessed of a small life income, and had in the house in which she lived some little furniture, and a few other articles of trifling value. The two women lived together in a house taken by the deceased; no one lived with them or in any way attended to them.

The deceased shortly before her death suffered from gangrene in the leg, which rendered her during the last ten days of her life quite unable to attend to herself or to move about or to do anything to procure assistance. No one but the prisoner had previous to the death any knowledge of the condition in which her aunt thus was. The prisoner continued to live in the house at the cost of the deceased, and took in the food supplied by the tradespeople; but does not appear to have given any to the deceased, and she certainly did not give or procure any medical or nursing attendance to or for her, or give notice to any neighbor of her condition or wants, although she had abundant opportunity and occasion to do so.

The body of the deceased was on August 2, while the prisoner was still living in the house, found much decomposed, partially dressed in her day clothes, and lying partly on the ground and partly prone upon the bed. The death probably occurred from four to seven days before August 3, the date of the post-mortem examination of the body. The cause of death was exhaustion caused by the gangrene, but substantially accelerated by neglect, want of food, of nursing, and of medical attendance during several days previous to the death. All these wants could and would have been supplied if any notice of the condition of the deceased had been given by the pris-

oner to any of the neighbors, of whom there were several living in adjoining houses, to the relations of the deceased, who lived within a few miles. It was proved that the prisoner, while the deceased must have been just about dying, had conversations with neighbors about the deceased, but did not avail herself of the opportunities thus afforded of disclosing the condition in which she then was.

[The jury found Instan guilty over the objection made by her solicitor that there was no legal duty for her to provide assistance.]

Chief Justice Lord Coleridge.

We are all of opinion that this conviction must be affirmed. It would not be correct to say that every moral obligation involves a legal duty; but every legal duty is founded on a moral obligation. A legal common law duty is nothing else than the enforcing by law of that which is a moral obligation without legal enforcement. There can be no question in this case that it was the clear duty of the prisoner to impart to the deceased so much as was necessary to sustain life of the food which she from time to time took in, and which was paid for by the deceased's own money for the purpose of the maintenance of herself and the prisoner; it was only through the instrumentality of the prisoner that the deceased could get the food. There was, therefore, a common law duty imposed upon the prisoner which she did not discharge.

Nor can there be any question that the failure of the prisoner to discharge her legal duty at least accelerated the death of the deceased, if it did not actually cause it. There is no case directly in point; but it would be a slur upon and a discredit to the administration of justice in this country if there were any doubt as to the legal principle, or as to the present case being within it. The prisoner was under a moral obligation to the deceased from which arose a legal duty towards her; that legal duty the prisoner has willfully and deliberately left unperformed, with the consequence that there has been an acceleration of the death of the deceased owing to the non-performance of that legal duty. It is un-necessary to say more than that upon the evidence this conviction was most properly arrived at. Conviction affirmed.

Yania v. Bigan, 155 A. 2d 343 (1959)

Justice Benjamin R. Jones delivered the opinion of the Court.

A bizarre and most unusual circumstance provides the background of this appeal.

On September 25, 1957, John E. Bigan was engaged in a coal strip-mining operation in Shade Township, Somerset County. On the property being stripped were large cuts or trenches created by Bigan when he removed the earthen overburden for the purpose of removing the coal underneath. One cut contained water 8 to 10 feet in depth with side walls or embankments 16 to 18 feet in height; at this cut Bigan had installed a pump to remove the water.

At approximately 4 P.M. on that date, Joseph F. Yania, the operator of another coal strip-mining operation, and one Boyd M. Ross went upon Bigan's property for the purpose of discussing a business matter with Bigan, and while there, were asked by Bigan to aid him in starting the pump. Ross and Bigan entered the cut and stood at the point where the pump was located. Yania stood at the top of one of the cut's side walls and then jumped from the side wall—a height of 16 to 18 feet—into the water and was drowned.

Yania's widow, in her own right and on behalf of her three children, instituted wrongful death and survival actions against Bigan contending Bigan was responsible for Yania's death. . . .

. . . .

The following complaint avers negligence in the following manner: . . .

After [Yania] was in the water, a highly dangerous position, having been induced and inveigled therein by [Bigan], [Bigan] failed and neglected to take reasonable steps and action to protect or assist [Yania], or extradite [Yania] from the dangerous position in which [Bigan] had placed him.

. . . The mere fact that Bigan saw Yania in a position of peril in the water imposed upon him no legal, although a moral, obligation or duty to go to his rescue unless Bigan was legally responsible, in whole or in part, for placing Yania in the perilous position.

The complaint does not aver any facts which impose upon Bigan legal responsibility for placing Yania in the dangerous position in the water and, absent such legal responsibility, the law imposes on Bigan no duty of rescue.

COMMENTS

1. In *Instan*, Lord Coleridge holds that the niece has a moral duty to her aunt and that a legal duty is premised on this moral duty. We have already raised the issue of what the relationship between law and morality should be. Do you answer the question here the same way you did previously?

2. *Yania* represents the general law in the United States: that there is no legal duty to aid those in peril or even to notify the authorities. But courts have also fashioned certain exceptions to this general rule, some of which are noted in the decisions you have just read. Moreover, a few states have passed Bad Samaritan statutes. Listed below is Minnesota's Bad Samaritan statute. Does it go far enough, partic-

ularly in terms of punishment? Does it go too far?

Duty to assist. Any person at the scene of an emergency who knows that another person is exposed to or has suffered grave physical harm shall, to the extent that he can do so without danger or peril to himself or others, give reasonable assistance to the exposed person. Reasonable assistance may include obtaining or attempting to obtain aid from law enforcement or medical personnel. Any person who violates this section is guilty of a petty misdemeanor.

3. A gang rape at Big Dan's Tavern in New Bedford, Massachusetts, in 1983 received a great deal of attention. Attackers repeatedly raped a woman on the pool table of the bar while fifteen patrons looked on and in some cases encouraged the rapists. Not one of these witnesses attempted to aid the victim or to call the police. Would you hold the bar owner or bartenders legally responsible for not assisting? What about the cheering patrons?

4. One of the concerns some people have about creating a legal duty is how far it should extend. Philosopher Peter Singer argues that there is a moral obligation to assist a drowning child in a nearby shallow pond when we could do so at little risk to ourselves. Singer then goes on to say that the world's starving population is much like the drowning child because (1) we have a moral obligation to prevent death and (2) we have it within our means (through charity and foreign aid) to save at least some of the lives that are lost. Do you agree? Are those of us in rich countries Bad Samaritans of a different kind? See Peter Singer, "Famine, Affluence, and Morality," *Philosophy and Public Affairs* 1:229–43 (1972).

5. Let us say you are walking home late one night on a very cold and blustery evening and you trip over an old person huddled on an air vent. Do you have a moral obligation to assist this person? A legal obligation? Are you a Bad Samaritan if you do not provide assistance? (Would it do any good to notify the authorities?) What *should* you do? What *would* you do?

6. As a general rule, if an individual does come to the assistance of one in need she must exercise reasonable care or else be held liable

for any harm caused in the attempt to provide assistance. Some states, however, have enacted Good Samaritan statutes. Indiana's statute reads as follows:

Any person, who in good faith gratuitously renders emergency care at the scene of an accident or emergency care to the victim thereof, shall not be liable for any civil damages for any personal injury as a result of any act or omission by such person in rendering the emergency care or as a result of any act or failure to act to provide or arrange for further medical treatment or care for the injured person, except acts or omissions amounting to gross negligence or willful or wanton misconduct.

7. American law often distinguishes between acts of commission and acts of omission. Is there a difference between Bigan not assisting Yania, as he did here, and Bigan shooting and killing Yania?

8. Is the act-omission distinction always so clear? In *DeShaney v. Winnebago County Department of Social Services*, 103 L. Ed. 2d 249 (1989), the Supreme Court decided a case brought by the guardian of a four-year-old child whose father had beaten him into a life-threatening coma. The suit was brought against the state Department of Social Services (DSS) alleging that the state knew of the abuse that Joshua DeShaney was subjected to (he had been treated at the hospital a number of times), but had persisted in returning him to his father. The basis of Joshua's suit was that the state's failure to act to provide protection deprived him of his liberty in violation of the Due Process Clause of the Fourteenth Amendment. The Court rejected this claim, holding that the purpose of the Due Process Clause was to protect individuals from the government, not private individuals. Writing for a majority of the Court, Chief Justice Rehnquist held that:

While the State may have been aware of the dangers that Joshua faced . . . it played no part in their creation, nor did it do anything to render him any more vulnerable to them. That the State once took temporary custody of Joshua does not alter the analysis, for when it returned him to his father's custody, it placed him in no worse position than that in which he would have been had it not acted at all.

In dissent, Justice Brennan argued that once the State was put on notice of Joshua's child abuse *and* began to take measures accordingly, it then became responsible for the young boy's safety because it had effectively and legally displaced private sources of assistance. Who is correct?

9. Do you notice any difference in responses between males and females to these cases and questions? Based on clinical interviews, Carol Gilligan suggests that men and women have different conceptions of justice and morality. "The moral imperative that emerges repeatedly in interviews with women is an injunction to care, a responsibility to discern and alleviate the "real and recognizable trouble" of this world. For men, the moral imperative appears rather as an injunction to respect the rights of others and thus to protect from interference the rights to life and self-fulfillment." Carol Gilligan, *In a Different Voice: Psychological Theory and Women's Development* (Cambridge, Mass.: Harvard University Press, 1982), p. 100.

Kelly v. Gwinnell, 476 A. 2d 1219 (1984)

Chief Justice Wilentz delivered the opinion of the Court.

[Donald Gwinnell spent an hour or two at Joseph Zak's house where he had two or three drinks. Zak accompanied Gwinnell to his car and watched him drive away. Gwinnell was involved in a head-on collision with Marie Kelly. After the accident, Gwinnell was subjected to a blood test which indicated a blood alcohol concentration of 0.286 percent, or the equivalent of 13 drinks. Kelly sued both Gwinnell and Zak. The issue in this case is whether Zak was negligent and can be held liable.]

This case raises the issue of whether a social host who enables an adult guest at his home to become drunk is liable to the victim of an automobile accident caused by the drunken driving of the guest. . . .

. . . .

Under the facts here defendant provided his guest with liquor, knowing that thereafter the guest would have to drive in order to get home. . . . [O]ne could reasonably conclude that the Zaks must have known that their provision of liquor was causing Gwinnell to become drunk, yet they continued to serve him even after he was visibly intoxicated. By the time he left, Gwinnell was in fact severely intoxicated. A reasonable person in Zak's position could foresee quite clearly that this continued provision of alcohol to Gwinnell was making it more and more likely that Gwinnell would not be able to operate his car carefully. Zak could foresee that unless he stopped providing drinks to Gwinnell, Gwinnell was likely to injure someone as a result of the negligent operation of his car. The usual elements of a cause of action for negligence are clearly present: an action by defendant creating an unreasonable risk of harm to plaintiff, a risk that was clearly foreseeable, and a risk that resulted in an injury equally foreseeable. Under those circumstances the only question remaining is whether a duty exists to prevent such risk or, realistically, whether this Court should impose such a duty.

When the court determines that a duty exists and liability will be extended, it draws judicial lines based on fairness and policy. In a society where thousands of deaths are caused each year by drunken drivers, where the damage caused by such deaths is regarded increasingly as intolerable, where liquor licensees are prohibited from serving intoxicated adults, and where long-standing criminal sanctions against drunken driving have recently been significantly strengthened to the point where the Governor notes that they are regarded as the toughest in the nation, the imposition of such a duty by the judiciary seems both fair and fully in accord with the State's policy. Unlike those cases in which the definition of desirable policy is the subject of intense controversy, here the imposition of a duty is both consistent with and supportive of a social goal—the reduction of drunken driving—that is practically unanimously accepted by society.

· ·

We therefore hold that a host who serves liquor to an adult social guest, knowing both that the guest is intoxicated and will thereafter be operating a motor vehicle, is liable for injuries inflicted on a third party as a result of the negligent operation of a motor vehicle by the adult guest when such negligence is caused by the intoxication. We impose this duty on the host to the third party because we believe that the policy considerations served by its imposition far outweigh those asserted in opposition. While we recognize the concern that our ruling will interfere with accepted standards of social behavior; will intrude on and somewhat diminish the enjoyment, relaxation, and camaraderie that accompany social gatherings at which alcohol is served; and that such gatherings and social relationships are not simply tangential benefits of a civilized society but are regarded by many as important, we believe that the added assurance of just compensation to the victims of drunken driving as well as the added deterrent effect of the rule on such driving outweigh the importance of those other values. Indeed, we believe that given society's extreme concern about drunken driving, any change in social be-

havior resulting from the rule will be regarded ultimately as neutral at the very least, and not as a change for the worse; but that in any event if there be a loss, it is well worth the gain.

Justice Garibaldi, dissenting.

Today, this Court holds that a social host who knowingly enables an adult guest to become intoxicated knowing that the guest will operate a motor vehicle is liable for damages to a third party caused by the intoxicated guest. The imposition of this liability on a social host places upon every citizen of New Jersey who pours a drink for a friend a heavy burden to monitor and regulate guests. It subjects the host to substantial potential financial liability that may be far beyond the host's resources.

· ·

The majority holds that a host will be liable only if he serves alcohol to a guest knowing both that the guest is intoxicated and that the guest will drive. Although this standard calls for a subjective determination of the extent of the host's knowledge, a close reading of the opinion makes clear that the majority actually is relying on objective evidence. The majority takes the results of Gwinnell's blood alcohol concentration test and concludes from that test that "the Zaks must have known that their provision of liquor was causing Gwinnell to become drunk." . . .

Whether a guest is or is not intoxicated is not a simple issue. Alcohol affects everyone differently. The precise effects of a particular concentration of alcohol in the blood varies from person to person depending upon a host of other factors. One individual can consume many drinks without exhibiting any signs of intoxication. Alcohol also takes some time to get into the bloodstream and show its outward effects. Experts estimate that it takes alcohol twenty to thirty minutes to reach its highest level in the bloodstream. Thus, a blood alcohol concentration test demonstrating an elevated blood alcohol level after an accident may not mean that the subject was obviously intoxicated when he left the party some time earlier. . . . Accordingly, to impose on average citizens a duty to comprehend a person's level of intoxication and the effect another drink would ultimately have on such person is to place a very heavy burden on them.

The nature of home entertaining compounds the social host's difficulty in determining whether a guest is obviously intoxicated before serving the next drink. In a commercial establishment, there is greater control over the liquor; a bartender or waitress must serve the patron a drink. Not so in a home when entertaining a guest. At a social gathering, for example, guests frequently serve themselves or guests may serve other guests. Normally, the host is so busy entertaining he does not have time to analyze the state of intoxication of the guests. Without constant face-to-face contact it is difficult for a social host to avoid serving alcohol to a person on the brink of intoxication. . . .

. . . .

A more pressing distinction between the social host and commercial licensees is the host's inability to fulfill the duty the majority has imposed even if the host knows that a particular guest is intoxicated. It is easy to say that a social host can just refuse to serve the intoxicated person. However, due to a desire to avoid confrontation in a social environment, this may become a very difficult task. It is much easier in a detached business relationship for a bartender to flag a patron and either refuse to serve him or ask him to leave. We should not ignore the social pressures of requiring a social host to tell a boss, client, friend, neighbor, or family member that he is not going to serve him another drink. Moreover, a social host does not have a bouncer or other enforcer to prevent difficulties that may arise when requesting a drunk to

stop drinking or not to drive home. We have all heard of belligerent drunks.

The most significant difference between a social host and a commercial licensee, however, is the social host's inability to spread the cost of liability. The commercial establishment spreads the cost of insurance against liability among its customers. The social host must bear the entire cost alone. . . .

The majority cites no authority for its belief that actions against social hosts will be covered under homeowner's insurance. This new cause of action will be common and may result in large awards to third parties. Even if it is assumed that homeowner's insurance will cover this cause of action, it is unrealistic to believe that insurance companies will not raise their premiums in response to it.

Furthermore, many homeowners and apartment renters may not even have homeowner's insurance and probably cannot afford it. Other homeowners may not have sufficient insurance to cover the limitless liability that the Court seeks to impose. These people may lose everything they own if they are found liable as negligent social hosts under the Court's scheme. The individual economic cost to every New Jersey citizen should be weighed before today's result is reached.

I do not propose to fashion a legislative solution. That is for the Legislature. I merely wish to point out that the Legislature has a variety of alternatives to this Court's imposition of unlimited liability on every New Jersey adult. Perhaps, after investigating all the options, the Legislature will determine that the most effective course is to impose the same civil liability on social hosts that the majority has imposed today. I would have no qualms about that legislative decision so long as it was reached after a thorough investigation of its impact on average citizens of New Jersey.

COMMENTS

1. Are the Kellys nothing more than Bad Samaritans? Cannot Gwinnell and people like

him make their own decisions about how much to drink? From the facts, it appears that Gwinnell had the equivalent of thirteen scotches. The factual testimony also indicated that at the Zaks' house he had "only" two or three drinks, but the court concluded that given the amount of alcohol in his blood (0.286 percent) Gwinnell "must have been showing unmistakable signs of intoxication." Do you agree? What about others who provided drinks—should they also have borne responsibility?

2. What about situations such as keg parties? If my long-term memory serves me correctly, at most college parties there are kegs of beer (many) and lots of people. Moreover, people usually serve themselves. Should the social-host rule cover these situations? If not, was Zak's downfall the fact that he was serving "real" drinks and following the rules of etiquette, rather than allowing everyone to serve himself or herself?

3. Would the *Gwinnell* case make you think twice about throwing a party?

4. If you agree with the social-host rule, at what point would you invoke it? Four drinks? Six? Eight? What about serving liquor to minors? Should those who serve minors automatically be held responsible for any injury caused by minors? After even one drink?

12

CRIME AND PUNISHMENT

This chapter focuses on duties of a different kind—duties owed society by those who have violated the criminal law. Before addressing the purposes served by criminal sanctions, however, let us take a more general look at crime in this country and at what it may or may not represent.

In regard to levels of crime, the news is bad. In 1965, there were (per 100,000 inhabitants) 5.1 murders, 12.1 forcible rapes, 72 robberies, 111 aggravated assaults, and 663 burglaries.[1] In 1985, murders had increased to 7.9 per 100,000 inhabitants, rapes to 36.6, robberies to 209, aggravated assaults to 303, and burglaries to 1,287.[2]

A cross-national comparison is revealing. In recent years, Americans have faced roughly seven to ten times the risk of death by homicide as the residents of most European countries and Japan. Americans are more than three times as likely to be raped than West Germans, and six times as likely to be robbed. Though their numbers are roughly the same, Californians are murdered almost six times as often as Canadians. Nor is this simply a reflection of the ease with which people in this country can obtain guns: more Californians are killed with knives alone than Canadians are *by all means put together.*[3]

Is the United States soft on crime? At least in terms of prison population, the answer is no. In 1965, there were 210,895 prison inmates. This number increased to 315,994 in 1980, but in five short years there was an increase to 522,744 inmates in federal and state penal institutions, most of which were well beyond intended capacity. A comparison with other countries is again disconcerting. Currie points out that at the beginning of the 1980s, the incarceration rate in the United States was about 217 per 100,000 (note, it is even higher now). Japan's rate was 44 per 100,000, West Germany's 60, France's 67, and Great Britain's 80.[4]

One reason why incarceration rates are higher in the United States is the much greater level of crime in our society. Another reason is that prison terms are considerably longer in the United States. For example, the average prison term in Holland is 1.3 months, versus 5 months in Britain and 16 in the United States. Even average sentences for a given class of offenses differ greatly. The average maximum sentence for robbery was 150 months in U.S. federal prisons and 68 months in the state prisons, compared with 19 months in Dutch prisons.[5]

How does crime affect American society? One of the leading conservative scholars in this area, James Q. Wilson, sees crime eating away at our social fabric:

> Predatory crime does not merely victimize individuals, it impedes and, in the extreme case, prevents the formation and maintenance of community. By disrupting the delicate nexus of ties, formal and informal, by which we are linked with our neighbors, crime atomizes society and makes of its members mere individual calculators estimating their own advantage, especially their chances for survival amidst their fellows.

The most obvious issue to address is why in the severity of crime rates, the United States resembles some of the most volatile countries of the Third World rather than other developed Western countries. Currie argues that instead of simply responding to crime, government policies have actually caused crime.

> Government can fairly be said to have adopted a pro-crime policy for decades in America. It subsidized the mechanization of agriculture that pushed masses of the rural poor into the cities, simultaneously encouraging the flight of urban industry and employment. Similarly, it subsidizes the transfer of capital and jobs overseas, and routinely adopts monetary and fiscal policies, in the name of fighting inflation, that create widespread unemployment and its resulting community and family fragmentation. Government then establishes a minimal and inadequate system of support for those whom it has helped deprive of sustaining work, which dictates that many families will have neither the time nor the resources to ensure the healthy development of their children. Far from being a passive bystander whose social role is purely reactive, confined to the operation of the criminal-justice system, government now invokes the system with its right hand to respond after-the-fact to conditions which it helps to create with its left.[7]

Currie maintains that combatting crime in the United States will mean changing our social relations.

> We must build a society that is less unequal, less depriving, less insecure, less disruptive of family and community ties, less corrosive of cooperative values. In short, we must begin to take on the enormous task of creating the conditions of community life in which individuals can live together in compassionate and cooperative ways.[8]

The focus of this chapter will not be on the causes of crime but instead, on what we hope to achieve when we apply criminal sanctions. Nevertheless, the two questions—causes and sanctions—are related in the sense that our answer to the first will largely determine our answer to the second. In addition, as Currie's analysis indicates, the level of crime that we experience in our country relates to some of the other questions raised throughout this book.

What are we attempting to achieve when we apply criminal sanctions against the lawbreaker? The criminal justice system is unclear in its answer, as there are at least three responses commonly given. One theory maintains that the criminal justice system should attempt to *rehabilitate* the criminal and that criminal sanctions should work toward that end. This theory was ascendant in the 1960s, and although it still has its adherents, it is currently a minority position. A second theory contends that the purpose of criminal sanctions is to *punish* the transgressor (retribution does not necessarily have to take the form of "an eye for an eye," it can exist in modified forms as well). A third theory maintains that the only function of criminal sanctions, particularly prison, is to *incapacitate* the criminal and thereby prevent him from committing more crimes. According to this view, criminal sanctions are not going to change a criminal's behavior, but a long stint in prison will prevent a particular individual from committing any more crimes, at least for the period of incarceration.

We begin with a most difficult and disturbing case, *The Queen v. Dudley and Stephens,* a case involving the murder of a young boy by two starving seamen while stranded on the high seas. Three questions obtain in regard to this old English case. What purpose would be served by punishing these two seamen? Or, should the law simply look the other way at what occurred, albeit in a situation of desperation? Which theory of criminal sanctions, if any, best applies to this kind of situation? (In fact, can there be any *one* theory behind criminal sanctions?)

The second case, *State v. Kroncke,* involved a crime done in the name of civil disobedience. What should the law do to those who violate a criminal statute but do so under the claim of some greater good or for the purported protection of society? (Many students might be familiar with Sophocles's play *Antigone,* the story of a young woman torn between her conscience and the dictates of the law.) Civil disobedience is still very much with us today, as evidenced by the Sanctuary movement in this country. Members of this church-based movement provide a safe haven to Salvadorans and Guatemalans who have fled the widespread violence in their country, but who are unable to obtain refugee status in the United States. Do we treat these "criminals" like all others who have violated the law? Can the law ever allow illegal behavior? At the same time, do we allow the accused to use the trial as a political platform for the expression of their beliefs?

A most emotional topic is capital punishment, which was examined in *Gregg v. Georgia. Gregg* followed *Furman v. Georgia,*[9] in which the Supreme Court invalidated the capital punishment statutes of a number of states because of the "arbitrary" manner in which the death sentence was given. *Gregg* is an example of a reworked capital punishment statute, but the bigger question remains: does society ever have the right to take the life of another human being, no matter how egregious his behavior has been? If yes, under what circumstances? If no, why not? In response to the latter, is it because capital punishment constitutes cruel and unusual punishment? Or is it because you think capital punishment is immoral?

Note that Justices Marshall and Brennan argue that there has been a moral evolution of sorts in this country that now views capital punishment as morally repugnant. How do we recognize society's fundamental values? Do we simply have *USA Today* take another poll to determine this? Remember Michael Perry's comments in the introduction about the courts leading the nation in what he terms "moral evolution." Is capital punishment such an area? Is this what Marshall and Brennan are attempting to do in *Furman?*

Booth v. Maryland examined the role that victims should play in the criminal justice system. Centuries ago crimes were treated as private disputes, with the ruler serving as an overseer of sorts. Eventually this system changed so that now crimes are treated as violations against the state rather than against private individuals. Thus, a criminal action is *People v. Criminal* rather than *Victim v. Criminal.* But many argue that the victim is lost in this system.[10]

To pursue this line of thought, as many of you know, the overwhelming number of cases in the criminal justice system are plea bargained: the accused pleads guilty to a reduced charge.[11] One question this raises, however, is whether those who have been harmed by the criminal act—the rape victim, for example—ought to have a say (and what kind of say) in whether to offer a plea or what its terms should be.[12]

The next two cases in this chapter, *Rummel v. Estelle* and *People v. Harmon*, raised the question of the role prison serves in our criminal justice system. *Rummel* involves a "habitual offender" statute under which a small-town, nickel-and-dime hood faced the prospect of a life behind bars for his repeated offenses. Did Rummel belong behind bars? If not, can you come up with a viable alternative? *People v. Harmon* was a variation on the "necessity" claim that we have seen before in cases such as *State v. Moe* and *The Queen v. Dudley and Stephens.* Here Harmon claimed that his attempted prison escape was precipitated by the repeated homosexual attacks he suffered. If you find Harmon's position sympathetic, where can we possibly draw the line, particularly when homosexual rape is such a commonplace occurrence in prisons in this country?

The last case in this chapter may or may not be a glimpse at the future. In *People v. Gauntlett,* a judge ordered chemical castration as punishment for a rapist. This is just one example of alternative means of sentencing, some of which are further explored in the comments that follow the case. In addition to the question of the propriety of this kind of sentence, another question that *Gauntlett* raised is whether the criminal himself ought to play any kind of role in the sentencing decision. For example, would you have felt differently about chemical castration as a sentence if the judge had made that option (rather than prison) available to the defendant and allowed *him* to choose? The same kind of situation could also arise in the area of capital punishment. Even if you oppose the death sentence, would you prevent a criminal from being executed if he preferred this to life without parole?

NOTES

1. The information on crime rates comes from Harold W. Stanley and Richard G. Niemi, *Vital Statistics on American Politics* (Washington, D.C.: Congressional Quarterly Press, 1988), p. 337.

2. These are *reported* crimes, not actual crimes. Mitchell Klein writes:

> It is difficult to calculate the amount of crime present in society. For a long time sole reliance was placed on the *Uniform Crime Reports* of the FBI. The basic defect with these data is that they represent only those crimes reported to the police. Yet, many crimes go unreported—particularly those that are less serious, those that are not covered by insurance, and those that involve a low-income person as victim. One way to circumvent the crime-reporting problem is to survey citizens to determine how many times they were victimized in the past year. A startling lesson from such studies is that a large number of victimizations occur which are never reported to the police.

Mitchell S. G. Klein, *Law, Courts, and Policy* (Englewood Cliffs, N.J.: Prentice-Hall, 1984), p. 214 (cites omitted).

3. Elliott Currie, *Confronting Crime: An American Challenge* (New York: Pantheon Books, 1985), p. 5.

4. Ibid., pp. 28–29.

5. Ibid., p. 29.

6. James Q. Wilson, *Thinking About Crime* (New York: Vintage Books, 1985), p. 26.

7. Currie, *Confronting Crime*, p. 226.

8. Ibid., pp. 225–26.

9. 408 U.S. 238 (1972).

10. Robert Elias writes:

> Even prosecutors, who might be reluctant to admit the victim's minor role, tell us that they rarely consult victims for plea bargaining. In one study, for example, 59% of the prosecutors claimed they rarely sought victim input, and only 15% said they sometimes talked to victims in very serious cases they sought to negotiate. For those relatively few who do consult victims, only 31% gave their views much weight, and 15% gave them no weight at all.

Robert Elias, *The Politics of Victimization: Victims, Victimology and Human Rights* (New York: Oxford University Press, 1986), p. 152.

Despite the Courts' holding in *Booth v. Maryland*, there appears to be some movement to involve victims. According to figures from the American Bar Association, seven states—New York, Kentucky, Michigan, Montana, South Carolina, South Dakota and West Virginia—have laws requiring consultation with the victim before a plea is presented to the court by the prosecution. In addition, thirty-five states allow a victim to be heard, usually in writing, at the sentencing (although some of these might be on infirm constitutional grounds, given the Supreme Court's holding in *Booth*). See Kirk Johnson, "Crime Victims Getting a Day, and a Say, in Court," *New York Times*, April 1, 1988, p. 23.

11. See, for example, Herbert Jacob, *Justice in America: Courts, Lawyers, and the Judicial Process*, 4th ed. (Boston: Little, Brown, 1984); Milton Heumann, *Plea Bargaining: The Experiences of Prosecutors, Judges and Defense Attorneys* (Chicago: University of Chicago Press, 1978).

12. This is not the only place where the victim could play a role, but given the overwhelming propensity to plea bargain cases, it seems to be the most natural.

The Queen v. Dudley and Stephens, 14 Q.B. 273 (1884)

Chief Justice Lord Coleridge delivered the opinion of the Court.

[Two English seamen, Thomas Dudley and Edward Stephens, were charged with murder based on the following facts:]

[O]n July 5, 1884, the prisoners, Thomas Dudley and Edward Stephens, with one Brooks, all able-bodied English seamen, and the deceased also an English boy, between seventeen and eighteen years of age, the crew of an English yacht, a registered English vessel, were cast away in a storm on the high seas 1600 miles from the Cape of Good Hope, and were compelled to put into an open boat belonging to the said yacht. That in this boat they had no supply of water and no supply of food, except two 1 lb. tins of turnips, and for three days they had nothing else to subsist upon. That on the fourth day they caught a small turtle, upon which they subsisted for a few days, and this was the only food they had up to the twentieth day when the act now in question was committed. That on the twelfth day the remains of the turtle were entirely consumed, and for the next eight days they had nothing to eat. That they had no fresh water, except such rain as they from time to time caught in their oilskin capes. That the boat was drifting on the ocean, and was probably more than 1000 miles away from land. That on the eighteenth day, when they had been seven days without food and five without water, the prisoners spoke to Brooks as to what should be done if no succour came, and suggested that some one should be sacrificed to save the rest, but Brooks dissented, and the boy, to whom they were understood to refer, was not consulted. That on the 24th of July, the day before the act now in question, the prisoner Dudley proposed to Stephens and Brooks that lots should be cast who should be put to death to save the rest, but Brooks refused to consent, and it was not put to the boy, and in point of fact there was no drawing of lots. That on that day the prisoners spoke of their having families, and suggested it would be better to kill the boy that their lives should be saved, and Dudley proposed that if there was no vessel in sight by the morrow morning the boy should be killed. That next day, the 25th of July, no vessel appearing, Dudley told Brooks that he had better go and have a sleep, and made signs to Stephens and Brooks that the boy had better be killed. The prisoner Stephens agreed to the act, but Brooks dissented from it. That the boy was then lying at the bottom of the boat quite helpless, and extremely weakened by famine and by drinking sea water, and unable to make any resistance, nor did he ever assent to his being killed. The prisoner Dudley offered a prayer asking forgiveness for them all if either of them should be tempted to commit a rash act, and that their souls might be saved. That Dudley, with the assent of Stephens, went to the boy, and telling him that his time was come, put a knife into his throat and killed him then and there; that the three men fed upon the body and blood of the boy for four days; that on the fourth day after the act had been committed the boat was picked up by a passing vessel, and the prisoners were rescued, still alive, but in the lowest state of prostration. That they were carried to the port of Falmouth, and committed for trial at Exeter. That if the men had not fed upon the body of the boy they would probably not have survived to be so picked up and rescued, but would within the four days have died of famine. That the boy, being in a much weaker condition, was likely to have died before them. That at the time of the act in question there was no sail in sight, nor any reasonable prospect of relief. That under these circumstances there appeared to the prisoners every probability that unless they then fed or very soon fed upon the boy or one of themselves they would die of starvation. That there was no appreciable chance of saving life except by killing some one for the others to eat. That assuming any necessity to kill anybody, there was no greater necessity for killing the boy than any of the other three men. . . .

Now it is admitted that the deliberate killing of this unoffending and unresisting boy was clearly murder, unless the killing can be justified by some well-recognised excuse admitted by the law. It is further admitted that there was in this case no such excuse, unless the killing was justified by what has been called "necessity." But the temptation to the act which existed here was not what the law has ever called necessity. Nor is this to be regretted.

Though law and morality are not the same, and many things may be immoral which are not necessarily illegal, yet the absolute divorce of law from morality would be of fatal consequence; and such divorce would follow if the temptation to murder in this case were to be held by law an absolute defence of it. It is not so. To preserve one's life is generally speaking a duty, but it may be the plainest and the highest duty to sacrifice it. . . . It is not correct, therefore, to say that there is any absolute or unqualified necessity to reserve one's life. . . . It is not needful to point out the awful danger of admitting the principle which has been contended for. Who is to be the judge of this sort of necessity? By what measure is the comparative value of lives to be measured? Is it to be strength, or intellect, or what? It is plain that the principle leaves to him who is to profit by it to determine the necessity which will justify him in deliberately taking another's life to save his own. In this case the weakest, the youngest, the most unresisting, was chosen. Was it more necessary to kill him than one of the grown men? The answer must be "No." . . .

It must not be supposed that in refusing to admit temptation to be an excuse for crime it is forgotten how terrible the temptation was; how awful the suffering; how hard in such trials to keep the judgment straight and the conduct pure. We are often compelled to set up standards we cannot reach ourselves, and to lay down rules which we could not ourselves satisfy. But a man has no right to declare temptation to be an excuse, though he might himself have yielded to it, nor allow compassion for the criminal to change or weaken in any manner the legal definition of the crime. It is therefore our duty to declare that the prisoners' act in this case was wilful murder, that the facts as stated in the verdict are no legal justification of the homicide; and to say that in our unanimous opinion the prisoners are upon this special verdict guilty of murder. [The Court then proceeded to pass the sentence of death upon the prisoners.]

COMMENTS

1. Were Dudley and Stephens morally blameworthy in taking the life of the young boy? If not, could they—should they—have been held criminally responsible for their actions? If you conclude that they were morally blameworthy, should they have been treated like any other cold-blooded murderers?

2. It might or might not relieve you to know that the Crown ultimately commuted their death sentence to six months in prison. Was this the just thing to do?

3. Consider another case of self-help and executive clemency. Leslie Brown's husband, Clarence, began to beat her shortly after they began living together in 1974. Over the years, he threatened her with a gun and a knife, kicked her when she was pregnant, beat the children, and once set their house on fire. But when she called the police, officers would take Mr. Brown for a ride and then release him. When she asked for a divorce, he held a knife to her throat.

In 1982, a friend offered to kill Mr. Brown; Ms. Brown accepted, paid him, and later pleaded guilty to murder. She had served six years of a twenty-year sentence when the governor commuted her sentence. Susan Diesenhouse, "View of Women Is Changing, Some Say," *New York Times*, January 30, 1989, p. 7. Was justice served?

State v. Kroncke, 459 F. 2d 697 (1972)

Circuit Judge Heaney delivered the opinion of the Court.

[Defendants Francis Kroncke and Michael Therriault were arrested for breaking into a Selective Service office and destroying draft registration material.]

. . . .

The defendants admit that they entered the Little Falls draft board office with the express intent to hinder and interfere with the administration of the Selective Service Act. By way of defense, they claim that their actions were justified.

Kroncke asserted at trial that he was compelled by his religious convictions to perform the act in order to bring the evils of the Vietnam War to the attention of the public and Congress. He stated that this act was necessary because the Vietnamese War is immoral and illegal, and because the political leadership in the United States lacks the moral sensitivity and courage to bring an end to the war. On these bases, and also on the basis that the governmental institutions and political leadership are not responsive to the will of the majority of the people, Kroncke argued that his belief in the necessity of acting as he did was reasonable. He described his act as measured, dramatic, symbolic and religious.

Therriault asserted that he embraced the principles of pacifism and nonviolence, and that, because of this, it was necessary for him to cease cooperating with the Selective Service system and to violate its laws. He stated his belief that the United States' participation in the war in Vietnam is illegal and that, by its participation, the United States is breaking international laws, particularly the 1954 Geneva accords. He testified that he believes that if there is not a legal recourse which can bring the war to an end, then people have to resort to nonviolent extralegal efforts based on morality and reason. He stated that his actions were intended to raise a moral challenge which alone possessed the possibility and potentiality of ending the war.

. . . We turn to their contention that they were legally justified in violating the provisions of the Selective Service Act as a protest to the "immoral" war in Indochina and as a means of bringing that war to an end.

This issue was dealt with in *United States v. Moylan*, 417 F. 2d 1002 (4th Cir. 1969), wherein several defendants, including the Berrigan brothers, were convicted of seizing and mutilating draft records. They had attempted to raise a similar defense which the trial court rejected. The Fourth Circuit, in affirming the convictions, stated:

From the earliest times when man chose to guide his relations with fellow men by allegiance to the rule of law rather than force, he has been faced with the problem how best to deal with the individual in society who through moral conviction concluded that a law with which he was confronted was unjust and therefore must not be followed. Faced with the stark reality of injustice, men of sensitive conscience and great intellect have sometimes found only one morally justified path, and that path led them inevitably into conflict with established authority and its laws. Among philosophers and religionists throughout the ages there has been an incessant stream of discussion as to when, if at all, civil disobedience, whether by passive refusal to obey a law or by its active breach, is morally justified. However, they have been in general agreement that while in restricted circumstances a morally motivated act contrary to law may be ethically justified, the action must be non-violent and the actor must accept the penalty for his action. In other words, it is commonly conceded that the exercise of a moral judgment based upon individual standards does not carry with it legal justification or immunity from punishment for breach of the law.

It follows that the defendants' motivation in this case cannot be accepted as a legal defense or justification. We do not question their sincerity, but we also recognize that society cannot tolerate the means they chose to register their opposition to the war.

We need not decide here in what extreme circumstance, if any, governmental acts may be legally resisted. We confine ourselves to this case and hold only that the law does not permit an attempt to seize and destroy Selective Service records even if this is done as an act of conscience. We make no moral judgment on the defendants' acts. We counsel only that the fabric of our democratic society is fragile, that there are broad opportunities for peaceful and legal dissent, and that the power of the ballot, if used, is great. Peaceful and constant progress under the Constitution remains, in our view, the best hope for a just society.

We come, then, to Kroncke's contention that his acts were religious ones committed in response to the continuation of the "illegal and immoral war in Indochina," that these acts were protected by the First Amendment, and that he was entitled to have the jury so instructed.

We do not engage in argument about the theological soundness of Kroncke's religious beliefs; to do so would violate the Free Exercise Clause of the First Amendment. Furthermore, Kroncke's religious creed and the sincerity of his beliefs are not at issue here. What is involved is Kroncke's right to attempt to destroy Selective Service records. The freedom to act is not absolute. . . .

The convictions are affirmed.

COMMENTS

1. If you were a judge, to what extent would you be influenced by a defendant's claim of some moral/political justification for her illegal actions? Would you ever listen to the person's rationale for why she did what she did, or would you treat the accused just like everyone else accused of this particular crime?

2. Political philosopher Ronald Dworkin suggests that the arguments for prosecuting individuals such as Kroncke and Therriault are not as compelling as they might appear at first glance. Dworkin maintains that in the context of the Vietnam War, many of those committing civil disobedience did so because they considered the war unconstitutional (because there was no declaration of war) but that the Supreme Court studiously avoided making such a judg-

ment. He argues that we ought not punish individuals when the law itself is so hazy (and when the courts make no effort to clear up the confusion). Dworkin also says that the "slippery slope" argument—if you allow these individuals to violate the law without prosecution, then soon everyone will do so—is much too convenient simply because everyone will not begin violating the law just because the government decides not to prosecute in some cases. See Ronald Dworkin, "Civil Disobedience," *Taking Rights Seriously* (Cambridge, Mass.: Harvard University Press, 1978), pp. 206–222.

3. The Sanctuary movement represents another instance of civil disobedience. Since 1980, only 665 Guatemalans and Salvadorans have been granted refugee status in the United States (worldwide, the United States has granted this status to more than 600,000) despite the widespread human rights violations in those countries. Because of these policies of the U.S. government, the Sanctuary movement arose to provide refuge to Guatemalans and Salvadorans who are in this country illegally.

During a trial against Sanctuary leaders for smuggling illegal aliens into the United States, the defendants were not able to testify about their religious, moral, and political beliefs and how these beliefs led them to break the law. The jury found the defendants guilty as charged.

Was this justice? Is there ever any justification for breaking the law?

4. There have been other recent examples of civil disobedience. For example, in 1988 segments of the pro-life movement participated in what they called Operation Rescue. Demonstrators throughout the country blocked entry to abortion clinics and refused to desist when ordered by the police. One of the aims of Operation Rescue was to paralyze the judicial system. Demonstrators refused to cooperate with the police in the hope of overloading local jails. The justification offered by those participating was that they were answering to a higher law. Can conservatives criticize the Sanctuary movement? Can liberals criticize Operation Rescue? Are there any differences between these two examples of civil disobedience?

5. I find that when I have used the *Kroncke* case in class, students usually agree with the holding, mainly on the grounds that the destruction of property—no matter for what reason—must be punished. Consider this hypothetical. It is the year 1943, and Kroncke and Therriault are German citizens who set out one night to destroy Auschwitz, the German concentration camp. After taking a few swings and knocking out some bricks, the two are arrested and they come before you as judge. How do you handle this situation?

Gregg v. Georgia, 428 U.S. 153 (1976)

Judgment of the Court, and opinion of Justice Stewart, Justice Powell, and Justice Stevens, announced by Justice Stewart.

[Defendant Troy Gregg shot and killed Fred Simmons and Bob Moore in the course of attempting to rob them. Gregg challenges the constitutionality of the death sentence he was given at trial.]

The issue in this case is whether the imposition of the sentence of death for the crime of murder under the law of Georgia

violates the Eighth and Fourteenth Amendments.

. . . .

Before considering the issues presented, it is necessary to understand the Georgia statutory scheme for the imposition of the death penalty. The Georgia statute, as amended after our decision in *Furman v. Georgia*, 408 U.S. 238 (1972), retains the death penalty for six categories of crime: murder, kidnapping for ransom or where the victim is harmed, armed robbery, rape, treason, and aircraft hijacking (1972). The capital defendant's guilt or innocence is determined in the traditional manner, either by a trial judge or a jury, in the first stage of a bifurcated trial.

If trial is by jury, the trial judge is required to charge lesser included offenses when they are supported by any view of the evidence. After a verdict, finding, or plea of guilty to a capital crime, a presentence hearing is conducted before whoever made the determination of guilt. The sentencing procedures are essentially the same in both bench and jury trials. At the hearing:

[T]he judge [or jury] shall hear additional evidence in extenuation, mitigation, and aggravation of punishment, including the record of any prior criminal convictions and pleas of guilty or pleas of nolo contendere of the defendant, or the absence of any prior conviction and pleas: Provided, however, that only such evidence in aggravation as the State has made known to the defendant prior to his trial shall be admissible. The judge [or jury] shall also hear argument by the defendant or his counsel and the prosecuting attorney . . . regarding the punishment to be imposed.

The defendant is accorded substantial latitude as to the types of evidence that he may introduce. Evidence considered during the guilt stage may be considered during the sentencing stage without being resubmitted.

In the assessment of the appropriate sentence to be imposed the judge is also required to consider or to include in his instructions to the jury "any mitigating circumstances or aggravating circumstances otherwise authorized by law and any of [10] statutory aggravating circumstances which may be supported by the evidence." Sec. 27–2534.1(b) (Supp 1975). The scope of the nonstatutory aggravating or mitigating circumstances is not delineated in the statute. Before a convicted defendant may be sentenced to death, however, except in cases of treason or aircraft hijacking, the jury, or the trial judge in

cases tried without a jury, must find beyond a reasonable doubt one of the 10 aggravating circumstances specified in the statute. [Discussed below.] The sentence of death may be imposed only if the jury (or judge) finds one of the statutory aggravating circumstances and then elects to impose that sentence. If the verdict is death the jury or judge must specify the aggravating circumstance(s) found. In jury cases, the trial judge is bound by the jury's recommended sentence.

We address initially the basic contention that the punishment of death for the crime of murder is, under all circumstances, "cruel and unusual" in violation of the Eighth and Fourteenth Amendments of the Constitution. . . .

. . . .

The imposition of the death penalty for the crime of murder has a long history of acceptance both in the United States and in England. The common-law rule imposed a mandatory death sentence on all convicted murderers. And the penalty continued to be used into the 20th century by most American States, although the breadth of the common-law rule was diminished, initially by narrowing the class of murders to be punished by death and subsequently by widespread adoption of laws expressly granting juries the discretion to recommend mercy.

It is apparent from the text of the Constitution itself that the existence of capital punishment was accepted by the Framers. At the time the Eighth Amendment was ratified, capital punishment was a common sanction in every State. Indeed, the First Congress of the United States enacted legislation providing death as the penalty for specified crimes. The Fifth Amendment, adopted at the same time as the Eighth, contemplated the continued existence of the capital sanction by imposing certain limits on the prosecution of capital cases. And the Fourteenth Amendment, adopted over three-quarters of a century later, similarly contemplates the existence of the capital sanction in providing that no State shall deprive any person of "life, liberty, or property" without due process of law.

For nearly two centuries, this Court repeatedly and often expressly, has recognized that capital punishment is not invalid per se. . . .

Four years ago, the petitioners in *Furman* and its companion cases predicated their argument primarily upon the asserted proposition that standards of decency had evolved to the point where capital punishment no longer could be tolerated. The petitioners in those cases said, in effect, that the evolutionary process had come to an end, and that standards of decency required that the Eighth Amendment be construed finally as prohibiting capital punishment for any crime regardless of its depravity and impact on society. . . .

The petitioners in the capital cases before the Court today renew the "standards of decency" argument, but developments during the four years since *Furman* have undercut substantially the assumptions upon which their argument rested. Despite the continuing debate, dating back to the 19th century, over the morality and utility of capital punishment, it is now evident that a large proportion of American society continues to regard it as an appropriate and necessary criminal sanction.

The most marked indication of society's endorsement of the death penalty for murder is the legislative response to *Furman*. The legislatures of at least 35 States have enacted new statutes that provide for the death penalty for at least some crimes that result in the death of another person. And the Congress of the United States, in 1974, enacted a statute providing the death penalty for aircraft piracy that results in death. These recently adopted statutes have attempted to address the concerns expressed by the Court in *Furman* primarily (i) by specifying the factors to be weighed and the procedures to be followed in deciding when to impose a capital sentence, or (ii) by making the death penalty mandatory for specified crimes. But all of the post-

Furman statutes make clear that capital punishment itself has not been rejected by the elected representatives of the people.

. . . .

We hold that the death penalty is not a form of punishment that may never be imposed, regardless of the circumstances of the offense, regardless of the character of the offender, and regardless of the procedure followed in reaching the decision to impose it.

We now turn to consideration of the constitutionality of Georgia's capital-sentencing procedures. In the wake of *Furman*, Georgia amended its capital punishment statute, but chose not to narrow the scope of its murder provisions. . . .

Georgia did act, however, to narrow the class of murderers subject to capital punishment by specifying 10 statutory aggravating circumstances, one of which must be found by the jury to exist beyond a reasonable doubt before a death sentence can ever be imposed. In addition, the jury is authorized to consider any other appropriate aggravating or mitigating circumstances. The jury is not required to find any mitigating circumstance in order to make a recommendation of mercy that is binding on the trial court, but it must find a statutory aggravating circumstance before recommending a sentence of death.

These procedures require the jury to consider the circumstances of the crime and the criminal before it recommends sentence. No longer can a Georgia jury do as Furman's jury did: reach a finding of the defendant's guilt and then, without guidance or direction, decide whether he should live or die. Instead, the jury's attention is directed to the specific circumstances of the crime: Was it committed in the course of another capital felony? Was it committed for money? Was it committed upon a peace officer or judicial officer? Was it committed in a particularly heinous way or in a manner that endangered the lives of many persons? In addition, the jury's attention is focused on the characteristics of the person who committed the crime: Does he have a record of prior convictions for capital offenses? Are there any special facts about this defendant that mitigate against imposing capital punishment (e.g., his youth, the extent of his cooperation with the police, his emotional state at the time of the crime). As a result, while some jury discretion still exists, the discretion to be exercised is controlled by clear and objective standards so as to produce nondiscriminatory application.

As an important additional safeguard against arbitrariness and caprice, the Georgia statutory scheme provides for automatic appeal of all death sentences to the State's Supreme Court. That court is required by statute to review each sentence of death and determine whether it was imposed under the influence of passion or prejudice, whether the evidence supports the jury's finding of a statutory aggravating circumstance, and whether the sentence is disproportionate compared to those sentences imposed in similar cases.

In short, Georgia's new sentencing procedure requires as a prerequisite to the imposition of the death penalty, specific jury findings as to the circumstances of the crime or the character of the defendant. Moreover to guard further against a situation comparable to that presented in *Furman,* the Supreme Court of Georgia compares each death sentence with the sentences imposed on similarly situated defendants to ensure that the sentence of death in a particular case is not disproportionate. On their face these procedures seem to satisfy the concerns of *Furman.* . . .

Justice Brennan dissenting.

The Cruel and Unusual Punishment Clause "must draw its meaning from the evolving standards of decency that mark the progress of a maturing society." . . .

In *Furman v. Georgia,* I read "evolving standards of decency" as requiring focus upon the essence of the death penalty itself and not primarily or solely upon the procedures under which the determination to inflict the penalty upon a particular person was made. . . .

This Court inescapably has the duty, as the ultimate arbiter of the meaning of our Constitution, to say whether, when individuals condemned to death, stand before our Bar, "moral concepts" require us to hold that the law has progressed to the point where we should declare that the punishment of death, like punishments on the rack, the screw, and the wheel, is no longer morally tolerable in our civilized society. My opinion in *Furman v. Georgia* concluded that our civilization and the law had progressed to this point and that therefore the punishment of death, for whatever crime and under all circumstances, is "cruel and unusual" in violation of the Eighth and Fourteenth Amendments of the Constitution. I shall not again canvass the reasons that led to that conclusion. I emphasize only that foremost among the "moral concepts" recognized in our cases and inherent in the Clause is the primary moral principle that the State, even as it punishes, must treat its citizens in a manner constituent with their intrinsic worth as human beings—a punishment must not be so severe as to be degrading to human dignity. A judicial determination whether the punishment of death comports with human dignity is therefore not only permitted but compelled by the Clause.

. . . Death for whatever crime and under all circumstances is truly an awesome punishment. The calculated killing of a human being by the State involves, by its very nature, a denial of the executed person's humanity. . . . An executed person has indeed lost the right to have rights. Death is not only an unusually severe punishment, unusual in its pain, in its finality, and in its enormity, but it serves no penal purpose more effectively than a less severe punishment; therefore the principle inherent in the Clause that prohibits pointless infliction of excessive punishment when less severe punishment can adequately achieve the same purposes invalidates the punishment.

The fatal constitutional infirmity in the punishment of death is that it treats members of the human race as nonhumans, as objects to be toyed with and discarded. It is thus inconsistent with the fundamental premise of the Clause that even the vilest criminal remains a human being possessed of common human dignity. As such it is a penalty that subjects the individual to a fate forbidden by the principle of civilized treatment guaranteed by the Clause. I therefore would hold, on that ground alone, that death is today a cruel and unusual punishment prohibited by the Clause. Justice of this kind is obviously no less shocking than the crime itself, and the new official murder, far from offering redress for the offense committed against society, adds instead a second defilement to the first.

Justice Marshall dissenting.

. . . .

In *Furman* I concluded that the death penalty is constitutionally invalid for two reasons. First, the death penalty is excessive. And second, the American people, fully informed as to the purposes of the death penalty and its liabilities, would in my view reject it as morally unacceptable.

Since the decision in *Furman*, the legislatures of 35 States have enacted new statutes authorizing the imposition of the death sentence for certain crimes, and Congress has enacted a law providing the death penalty for air piracy resulting in death. I would be less than candid if I did not acknowledge that these developments have a significant bearing on a realistic assessment of the moral acceptability of the death penalty to the American people. But if the constitutionality of the death penalty turns, as I have urged, on the opinion of an informed citizenry, then even the enactment of new death statutes cannot be viewed as conclusive. In *Furman*, I observed that the American people are largely unaware of the information critical to a judg-

ment on the morality of the death penalty, and concluded that if they were better informed they would consider it shocking, unjust, and unacceptable. . . .

COMMENTS

1. Do you agree with Justices Brennan and Marshall that given the moral evolution of American society, capital punishment now constitutes "cruel and unusual punishment"? How would we, or a court, recognize this?

2. If you disagree with Justices Brennan and Marshall, for what crimes would you, as judge, think that capital punishment was appropriate? Armed robbery? Child pornography? Rape? Kidnapping? Spying? What are you trying to achieve with the use of the death penalty?

3. In *McClesky v. Kemp*, 481 U.S. 279 (1987), the Supreme Court upheld Georgia's capital punishment statute despite strong evidence that racial considerations, particularly in terms of the color of the victim, were influential in capital punishment cases. Does *McClesky* change anyone's mind about the imposition of the death penalty?

4. In *Enmund v. Florida*, 458 U.S. 782 (1982), the U.S. Supreme Court reversed the imposition of the death penalty for an accomplice who aided in the commission of a robbery during which murder was committed but in which the accomplice had not actually killed and had not attempted, intended, or contemplated killing. The Court held that such a penalty was violative of the Eighth Amendment.

5. The Supreme Court has continued to give a narrow reading to the Eighth Amendment. In *Penry v. Lynaugh* (1989 Lexis 3148), the Court held that the death sentence given to a criminal defendant with a mental age of 6 years did not constitute "cruel and unusual" punishment. In *Stanford v. Kentucky* and *Wilkins v. Missouri* (1989 Lexis 3195), the Court refused to overturn the capital punishment sentences given to two defendants who had committed murder while under the age of 18. The Court held that such punishment would not have been considered "cruel and unusual" in the eighteenth century, where the common law set a rebuttable presumption of incapacity to commit felonies at 14. The Court also held that there was no "evolving standard" of liberalization in this area,

given the fact that of the 37 states that permit capital punishment, 15 decline to impose it on 16-year-olds and 12 on 17-year-olds; in the Court's opinion, this did not establish a sufficient degree of national agreement on this issue. Do you agree?

Booth v. Maryland, 482 U.S. 496 (1987)

Justice Powell delivered the opinion of the Court.

The question presented is whether the Constitution prohibits a jury from considering a "victim impact statement" during the sentencing phase of a capital murder trial.

In 1983, Irvin Bronstein, 78, and his wife Rose, 75, were robbed and murdered in their West Baltimore home. The murderers, John Booth and Willie Reid, entered the victims' home for the apparent purpose of stealing money to buy heroin. Booth, a neighbor of the Bronsteins, knew that the elderly couple could identify him. The victims were bound and gagged, and then stabbed repeatedly in the chest with a kitchen knife. The bodies were discovered two days later by the Bronsteins' son.

A jury found Booth guilty of two counts of first-degree murder, two counts of robbery, and conspiracy to commit robbery. The prosecution requested the death penalty, and Booth elected to have his sentence determined by the jury instead of the judge. Before the sentencing phase began, the State Division of Parole and Probation (DPP) compiled a presentence report that described Booth's background, education and employment history, and criminal record. Under a Maryland statute, the presentence report in all felony cases also must include a victim impact statement (VIS) describing the effect of the crime on the victim and his family. . . . Although the VIS is compiled by the DPP, the information is supplied by the victim or the victim's family. The VIS may be read to the jury during the sentencing phase, or the family members may be called to testify as to the information.

The VIS in Booth's case was based on interviews with the Bronsteins' son, daughter, son-in-law, and granddaughter. Many of their comments emphasized the victims' outstanding personal qualities, and noted how deeply the Bronsteins would be missed. Other parts of the VIS described the emotional and personal problems the family members have faced as a result of the crimes. The son, for example, said that he suffers from lack of sleep and depression, and is "fearful for the first time in his life." He said that in his opinion, his parents were "butchered like animals." The daughter said she also suffers from lack of sleep, and that since the murders she has become withdrawn and distrustful. She stated that she can no longer watch violent movies or look at kitchen knives without being reminded of the murders. The daughter concluded that she could not forgive the murderer, and that such a person could "[n]ever be rehabilitated." Finally, the granddaughter described how the deaths had ruined the wedding of another close family member, that took place a few days after the bodies were discovered. Both the ceremony and the reception were sad affairs, and instead of leaving for her honeymoon, the bride attended the victims' funeral. The VIS also noted that the granddaughter had received counseling for several months after the incident, but eventually had stopped because she concluded that "no one could help her."

. . . .

The jury sentenced Booth to death for the murder of Mr. Bronstein and to life imprisonment for the murder of Mrs. Bronstein. . . .

We granted certiorari to decide whether the Eighth Amendment prohibits a capital sentencing jury from considering victim impact evidence. We conclude that it does, and now reverse.

It is well-settled that a jury's discretion to impose the death sentence must be "suitably directed and limited so as to minimize the risk of wholly arbitrary and capricious action." *Gregg v. Georgia,* 428 U.S. 153, 189 (1976) (joint opinion of Stewart, Powell, and Stevens, JJ.). Although this Court normally will defer to a state legislature's determination of what factors are relevant to the sentencing decision, the Constitution places some limits on this discretion. Specifically, we have said that a jury must make an "individualized determination" of whether the defendant in question should be executed, based on "the character of the individual and the circumstances of the crime." And while this Court has never said that the defendant's record, characteristics, and the circumstances of the crime are the only permissible sentencing considerations, a state statute that requires consideration of other factors must be scrutinized to ensure that the evidence has some bearing on the defendant's "personal responsibility and moral guilt." To do otherwise would create the risk that a death sentence will be based on considerations that are "constitutionally impermissible or totally irrelevant to the sentencing process."

. . . .

The greater part of the VIS is devoted to a description of the emotional trauma suffered by the family and the personal characteristics of the victims. The State claims that this evidence should be considered a "circumstance" of the crime because it reveals the full extent of the harm caused by Booth's actions. In the State's view, there is a direct, foreseeable nexus between

the murders and the harm to the family, and thus it is not "arbitrary" for the jury to consider these consequences in deciding whether to impose the death penalty. Although "victim impact" is not an aggravating factor under Maryland law, the State claims that by knowing the extent of the impact upon and the severity of the loss to the family, the jury was better able to assess the "gravity or aggravating quality" of the offense.

While the full range of foreseeable consequences of a defendant's actions may be relevant in other criminal and civil contexts, we cannot agree that it is relevant in the unique circumstance of a capital sentencing hearing. In such a case, it is the function of the sentencing jury to "express the conscience of the community on the ultimate question of life or death." When carrying out this task the jury is required to focus on the defendant as a "uniquely individual human bein[g]." The focus of a VIS, however, is not on the defendant, but on the character and reputation of the victim and the effect on his family. These factors may be wholly unrelated to the blameworthiness of a particular defendant. As our cases have shown, the defendant often will not know the victim, and therefore will have no knowledge about the existence or characteristics of the victim's family. Moreover, defendants rarely select their victims based on whether the murder will have an effect on anyone other than the person murdered. Allowing the jury to rely on a VIS therefore could result in imposing the death sentence because of factors about which the defendant was unaware, and that were irrelevant to the decision to kill. This evidence thus could divert the jury's attention away from the defendant's background and record, and the circumstances of the crime.

. . . .

One can understand the grief and anger of the family caused by the brutal murders in this case, and there is no doubt that jurors generally are aware of these feelings.

But the formal presentation of this information by the State can serve no other purpose than to inflame the jury and divert it from deciding the case on the relevant evidence concerning the crime and the defendant. . . . [A]ny decision to impose the death sentence must be, and appear to be, based on reason rather than caprice or emotion. The admission of these emotionally charged opinions as to what conclusions the jury should draw from the evidence clearly is inconsistent with the reasoned decision making we require in capital cases.

We conclude that the introduction of a VIS at the sentencing phase of a capital murder trial violates the Eighth Amendment, and therefore the Maryland statute is invalid to the extent it requires consideration of this information. . . .

Justice White, with whom the Chief Justice, Justice O'Connor, and Justice Scalia join, dissenting.

"[T]he decision that capital punishment may be the appropriate sanction in extreme cases is an expression of the community's belief that certain crimes are themselves so grievous an affront to humanity that the only adequate response may be the penalty of death." *Gregg v. Georgia*, 428 U.S. 153, 184 (1976) (opinion of Stewart, Powell and Stevens, JJ.). The affront to humanity of a brutal murder such as petitioner committed is not limited to its impact on the victim or victims; a victim's community is also injured, and in particular the victim's family suffers shock and grief of a kind difficult even to imagine for those who have not shared a similar loss. Maryland's legislature has decided that the jury should have the testimony of the victim's family in order to assist it in weighing the degree of harm that the defendant has caused and the corresponding degree of punishment that should be inflicted. This judgment is entitled to particular deference; determinations of appropriate sentencing considerations are peculiarly questions of legislative policy, and the Court should recognize that in a democratic society legislatures, not courts, are constituted to respond to the will and consequently the moral values of the people. I cannot agree that there was anything "cruel or unusual" or otherwise unconstitutional about the legislature's decision to use victim impact statements in capital sentencing hearings.

The Court's judgment is based on the premises that the harm that a murderer causes a victim's family does not in general reflect on his blameworthiness, and that only evidence going to blameworthiness is relevant to the capital sentencing decision. Many if not most jurors, however, will look less favorably on a capital defendant when they appreciate the full extent of the harm he caused, including the harm to the victim's family. . . . If anything, I would think that victim impact statements are particularly appropriate evidence in capital sentencing hearings: the State has a legitimate interest in counteracting the mitigating evidence which the defendant is entitled to put in, by reminding the sentencer that just as the murderer should be considered as an individual, so, too, the victim is an individual whose death represents a unique loss to society and in particular to his family.

. . . .

The Court's concern that the grief and anger of a victim's family will "inflame the jury" is based in large part on its view that the loss which such survivors suffer is irrelevant to the issue of punishment—a view with which I have already expressed my disagreement. To the extent that the Court determines that in this case it was inappropriate to allow the victims' family to express their opinions on, for example, whether petitioner could be rehabilitated, that is obviously not an inherent fault in all victim impact statements and no reason to declare the practice of admitting such statements at capital sentencing hearings per se unconstitutional. I respectfully dissent.

. . . .

Recent years have seen an outpouring of popular concern for what has come to be known as "victims' rights"—a phrase that describes what its proponents feel is the failure of courts of justice to take into account in their sentencing decisions not only the factors mitigating the defendant's moral guilt, but also the amount of harm he has caused to innocent members of society. Many citizens have found one-sided and hence unjust the criminal trial in which a parade of witnesses comes forth to testify to the pressures beyond normal human experience that drove the defendant to commit his crime, with no one to lay before the sentencing authority the full reality of human suffering the defendant has produced—which (and not moral guilt alone) is one of the reasons society deems his act worthy of the prescribed penalty. Perhaps these sentiments do not sufficiently temper justice with mercy, but that is a question to be decided through the democratic processes of a free people, and not by the decrees of this Court. There is nothing in the Constitution that dictates the answer, no more in the field of capital punishment than elsewhere.

COMMENTS

1. The larger question raised in *Booth*, but not directly addressed by the Supreme Court, was what role *should* the victim play in criminal proceedings? Our legal system has evolved to a point at which many think the victim has become almost irrelevant in criminal proceedings. Some think that the *Booth* decision will dampen the move to have the victim play a more central role in criminal dispositions. What do you think? Should victims have a say in terms of whether the prosecutor accepts a plea bargain (if yes, what kind of say?) or in terms of sentencing?

What are the arguments for and against victim involvement?

2. A different kind of "victim" involvement occurred in the Bernhard Goetz subway shootings. To what degree should such self-help measures be protected by the law?

Another example of self-help occurred in Detroit, where some members of a neighborhood burned down a "crack" house after repeated complaints to the police went unanswered. Were they justified in their actions? On what do you base your answer? Would neighbors be justified, for example, in killing two pit bulls whom they thought *might* be a danger to others?

3. A part of the movement for victim's rights is to have a criminal defendant make restitution to the victim of the crime. Several states now mandate victim restitution where feasible. For example, in New York authorities can confiscate any property of a convicted felon equivalent in value to the fruits of a crime as well as the cars, boats, or other instrumentalities used to commit crimes. Proceeds from the sale of forfeited property must be distributed first to the victim as restitution or damages. One of the stumbling blocks to the institutionalization of restitution, however, is the well-entrenched view that crimes occur against the state, rather than against a particular victim.

4. A pilot program at the Deuel Vocational Institute in Tracy, California, has attempted to teach prison inmates about the pain that their victims have suffered from their criminal actions. Some days, inmates listen to personal accounts of crime victims, including those of domestic violence. Other days, they watch television programs like "The Burning Bed," a vivid account of the life of a battered woman. To date, the results of this program appear encouraging. Jane Gross, "Inmates Find Ways to Lock Anger Inside," *New York Times*, January 16, 1989, p. 8

Rummel v. Estelle, 445 U.S. 263 (1980)

Justice Rehnquist delivered the opinion of the Court.

[Defendant Rummel is currently serving a life sentence imposed by the state of Texas under its "recidivist" statute, which provides that "whoever shall have been three times convicted of a felony less than capital shall on such third conviction be imprisoned for life in the penitentiary." In 1964 Rummel pleaded guilty to the fraudulent use of a credit card to obtain $80 worth of goods and services. He was sentenced to 3 years in prison. In 1969 Rummel pleaded guilty to passing a bad check in the amount of $28.86, and he received a term of 4 years. In 1973 he was convicted of obtaining $120.75 by false pretenses. Although punishment for this crime is 2–10 years, the prosecution sought sentencing under the recidivist statute.]

. . . .

This Court has on occasion stated that the Eighth Amendment prohibits imposition of a sentence that is grossly disproportionate to the severity of the crime. . . .

. . . .

In an attempt to provide us with objective criteria against which we might measure the proportionality of his life sentence, Rummel points to certain characteristics of his offenses that allegedly render them "petty." He cites, for example, the absence of violence in his crimes. But the presence or absence of violence does not always affect the strength of society's interest in deterring a particular crime or in punishing a particular criminal. A high official in a large corporation can commit undeniably serious crimes in the area of antitrust, bribery, or clean air or water standards without coming close to engaging in any "violent" or short-term "life threatening" behavior. Additionally, Rummel cites the "small"

amount of money taken in each of his crimes. But to recognize that the State of Texas could have imprisoned Rummel for life if he had stolen $5,000, $50,000, or $500,000, rather than the $120.75 that a jury convicted him of stealing, is virtually to concede that the lines to be drawn are indeed "subjective," and therefore properly within the province of legislatures, not courts. Moreover, if Rummel had attempted to defraud his victim of $50,000, but had failed, no money whatsoever would have changed hands; yet Rummel would be no less blameworthy, only less skillful, than if he had succeeded.

In this case, however, we need not decide whether Texas could impose a life sentence upon Rummel merely for obtaining $120.75 by false pretenses. Had Rummel only committed that crime, under the law enacted by the Texas Legislature he could have been imprisoned for no more than 10 years. In fact, at the time that he obtained the $120.75 by false pretenses, he already had committed and had been imprisoned for two other felonies, crimes that Texas and other States felt were serious enough to warrant significant terms of imprisonment even in the absence of prior offenses. Thus the interest of the State of Texas here is not simply that of making criminal the unlawful acquisition of another person's property; it is in addition the interest, expressed in all recidivist statutes, in dealing in a harsher manner with those who by repeated criminal acts have shown that they are simply incapable of conforming to the norms of society as established by its criminal law. By conceding the validity of recidivist statutes generally, Rummel himself concedes that the State of Texas, or any other State, has a valid interest in so dealing with that class of persons.

. . . .

Undaunted . . . Rummel attempts to ground his proportionality attack on an alleged "nationwide" trend away from mandatory life sentences and toward "lighter, discretionary sentences." According to Rummel, "no jurisdiction in the United States or the Free World punishes habitual offenders as harshly as Texas. . . .

. . . .

. . . Even were we to assume that the statute employed against Rummel was the most stringent found in the 50 States, that severity hardly would render Rummel's punishment "grossly disproportionate" to his offenses or to the punishment he would have received in the other States. . . . In one State theft of $100 will earn the offender a fine or a short term in jail; in another State it could earn him a sentence of 10 years' imprisonment. Absent a constitutionality imposed uniformity inimical to traditional notions of federalism, some State will always bear the distinction of treating particular offenders more severely than any other State.

Perhaps, "time works changes" upon the Eighth Amendment, bringing into existence "new conditions and purposes." We all, of course, would like to think that we are "moving down the road toward human decency." Within the confines of this judicial proceeding, however, we have no way of knowing in which direction that road lies. Penologists themselves have been unable to agree whether sentences should be light or heavy, discretionary or determinate. This uncertainty reinforces our conviction that any "nationwide trend" toward lighter, discretionary sentences must find its source and its sustaining force in the legislatures, not in the federal courts.

Justice Powell, with whom Justice Brennan, Justice Marshall, and Justice Stevens join, dissenting.

The scope of the Cruel and Unusual Punishments Clause extends not only to barbarous methods of punishment, but also to punishments that are grossly disproportionate. Disproportionality analysis measures the relationship between the nature and number of offenses committed and the severity of the punishment inflicted upon the offender. The inquiry focuses on whether a person deserves such punishment, not simply on whether punishment would serve a utilitarian goal. A statute that levied a mandatory life sentence for overtime parking might well deter vehicular lawlessness, but it would offend our felt sense of justice. . . .

. . . .

Each of the crimes that underlies the petitioner's conviction as a habitual offender involves the use of fraud to obtain small sums of money ranging from $28.36 to $120.75. In total, the three crimes involved slightly less than $230. None of the crimes involved injury to one's person, threat of injury to one's person, violence, the threat of violence, or the use of a weapon. Nor does the commission of any such crimes ordinarily involve a threat of violent action against another person or his property. It is difficult to imagine felonies that pose less danger to the peace and good order of a civilized society than the three crimes committed by the petitioner. Indeed, the state legislature's recodification of its criminal law supports this conclusion.

Since the petitioner was convicted as a habitual offender, the State has reclassified his third offense, theft by false pretext, as a misdemeanor.

Apparently, only 12 States have ever enacted habitual offender statutes imposing a mandatory life sentence for the commission of two or three nonviolent felonies and only 3, Texas, Washington, and West Virginia, have retained such a statute. Thus, three-fourths of the States that experimented with the Texas scheme appear to have decided that the imposition of a mandatory life sentence upon some persons who have committed three felonies represents excess punishment. . . .

. . . .

More than three-quarters of American jurisdictions have never adopted a habitual offender statute that would commit the petitioner to mandatory life imprisonment. The jurisdictions that currently employ habitual offender statues either (i) require the commission of more than three offenses, (ii) require the commission of at least one violent crime, (iii) limit a mandatory penalty to less than life, or (iv) grant discretion to the sentencing authority. In none of the jurisdictions could the petitioner have received a mandatory life sentence merely upon the showing that he committed three nonviolent property-related offenses.

. . . .

. . . A comparison of petitioner to other criminals sentenced in Texas shows that he has been punished for three property-related offenses with a harsher sentence than that given first-time offenders or two-time offenders convicted of far more serious offenses. The Texas system assumes that all three-time offenders deserve the same punishment whether they commit three murders or cash three fraudulent checks.

The petitioner has committed criminal acts for which he may be punished. He has been given a sentence that is not inherently barbarous. But the relationship between the criminal acts and the sentence is grossly disproportionate. For having defrauded others of about $230, the State of Texas has deprived petitioner of his freedom for the rest of his life. The State has not attempted to justify the sentence as necessary either to deter other persons or to isolate a potentially violent individual. Nor

has petitioner's status as a habitual offender been shown to justify a mandatory life sentence. My view . . . is that this punishment violates the principle of proportionality contained within the Cruel and Unusual Punishments Clause.

COMMENTS

1. Does the punishment fit the crime in this case? At the present time, prisons in this country are overflowing, as there are now many more prisoners than at any time in our history, both in terms of absolute numbers and prisoners per capita. Does Rummel even belong in jail?

2. Although *Rummel* is ostensibly still good law, the defendant himself has since been freed. After he lost before the Supreme Court, he filed a motion in federal court on the grounds that his court-appointed attorney at his original trial did not defend him properly. The court granted Rummel a new trial. This time, his attorney entered into a plea bargain with the prosecutor, part of which was to drop the habitual offender charge in exchange for a guilty plea. Rummel was sentenced to seven years in prison, but because he had already served seven years, nine months, and fifteen days of his previous life sentence, the judge declared him free.

Contrast *Rummel* with *Solem v. Helm*, 463 U.S. 277 (1983), in which the Court struck down a life-without-parole sentence given to Jerry Helm. In 1964, 1966, and 1969, Helm was convicted of third-degree burglary. In 1972, he was convicted of obtaining money under false pretenses. In 1973, he was convicted of grand larceny, and in 1975 he was convicted of driving while intoxicated for the third time. In 1979, Helm pled guilty to the charge of passing a bad check. South Dakota has a habitual offender statute, and he was given a sentence for his latest criminal offense of life without parole. The Supreme Court held that the penalty was not proportionate to the crime and therefore violative of the Eighth Amendment. The Court noted that none of his offenses was violent, and all were alcohol related. The Court distinguished *Rummel* on the basis that unlike Texas, South Dakota had completely barred the possibility of parole in such cases.

3. If you were a judge, how quick would you be to send people to jail? For what offenses? And for how long? What would you do with a first-time child molester? A rapist? Someone convicted of insider trading?

4. The U.S. Sentencing Commission recently computed estimates for time served for certain crimes and also made recommendations for suggested sentences, some of which are listed below. What do you think?

Crime	Average Time Served Now	Proposed Guidelines
Kidnapping	7.2 to 9 years	4.2 to 5.2 years
First-degree murder	10 to 12.5 years	30 years to life in all cases
Income-tax evasion: $5,000 or less	4 to 10 months; only 30% serve time	Virtually all subject to some confinement for 1 to 7 months
Drug dealing (1 ounce of cocaine)	21 to 27 months; only 33% serve time	Virtually all serve 21 to 27 months

Source: "Doing Hard Time, Fairly." From *Newsweek*, February 16, 1987, p. 79. © 1987, Newsweek, Inc. All rights reserved. Reprinted by permission.

People v. Harmon, 220 N.W. 2d (1974)

Justice Brennan delivered the opinion of the Court.

Defendant, Terry Lee Harmon, appeals from his conviction by a jury in the Ionia County Circuit Court of escaping from prison. . . .

Defendant concedes that he was lawfully committed to the Michigan reformatory at Ionia and that he escaped therefrom on June 29, 1972. Defendant contends, however, as he did in the court below, that his departure from prison was done under duress in order to avoid threatened homosexual attacks by other inmates. Although testimony supportive of such a claim was presented in the court below, the trial judge instructed the jury that, even if they did find that defendant fled to avoid homosexual attacks, such a claim would not serve as a defense to a charge of prison escape. It is defendant's contention that the trial judge erred reversibly in giving such an instruction. We agree. The time has come when we can no longer close our eyes to the growing problem of institutional gang rapes in our prison system. Although a person sentenced to serve a period of time in prison for the commission of a crime gives up certain of his rights, it has never been held that upon entering a prison one is entirely bereft of all of his civil rights and forfeits every protection of the law. Indeed, the State has a duty to assure inmate safety. The persons in charge of our prisons and jails are obliged to take reasonable precautions in order to provide a place of confinement where a prisoner is safe from gang rapes and beatings by fellow inmates, safe from guard ignorance of pleas for help and safe from intentional placement into situations where an assault of one type or another is likely to result. If our prison system fails to live up to its responsibilities in this regard, we should not, indirectly, countenance such a failure by precluding the presentation of a defense based on those facts.

In the case at bar defendant, an 18-year-old male, was sentenced to serve a term of imprisonment in the penal institution at Ionia. He was originally confined within the regular prison facilities but later transferred to the dormitory system from which he later escaped. Defendant testified that during the first two weeks he was at the institution he requested to be transferred to the segregation ward because he was afraid of being pressed for sex. This request was denied, however, and he remained in the main facility until June of 1972, when he was transferred to the dormitory system.

Defendant testified that in a conversation with Mr. Robert Mayer, a prison social worker, he expressed his fear of being sent to the dormitory because of the "things" he heard went on out there. . . .

Defendant further testified that within a few days of his transfer to the dormitory, he was accosted by seven or eight inmates who demanded sex from him. He refused their demands and the group of inmates then began to beat and kick him. This beating continued until another inmate, Carl Shepherd, entered the room. Shepherd testified at the trial and corroborated defendant's story to the extent that a beating occurred and that it ceased upon his entrance to the room.

On June 28, 1972, defendant was again approached by a group of inmates who started hitting him and saying they would continue to do so until he gave them some sex. The group dispersed, however, without achieving their expressed goal. The next night defendant escaped.

At his trial defendant stated that he did not report these episodes or attempt to get back in the main facility because he was afraid of reprisals by his attackers and other prisoners. Deputy Warden Dale Folz testified that defendant's fears in this regard were not unfounded. He stated that any prisoner who reported on another prisoner would certainly have a "problem." He also testified that there definitely was a homosexual problem at the institution and that the person generally pressed for sex was one who had a youthful appearance.

The prosecution argues that the presentation of the above facts at trial did not warrant or require any instruction on duress. We disagree. To establish the defense of duress it is necessary that a defendant show that the violation of law for which he stands charged was necessitated by threatening conduct of another which resulted in defendant harboring a reasonable fear of imminent or immediate death or serious bodily harm. . . . The facts in the instant case were more than sufficient to require the submission of the defense of duress to the jury in the appropriate manner. . . . Under these circumstances, and in light of the fact that a homosexual problem was stated to exist at the institution, we find that the trial judge erred in not submitting the defense of duress to the jury.

. . . .

Accordingly, the defendant's conviction is reversed and the case remanded for a new trial.

COMMENT

1. If you were the judge, would you give Harmon extra time because of his escape attempt? Even if Harmon's duress can be considered as a factor in his escape, he still will be sent back to prison—that much seems certain. Will he not face the same exact problem? Is the court avoiding the larger issue (homosexual rape as a part of everyday life in prisons) by focusing on the smaller, more technical issue?

People v. Gauntlett, 352 N.W. 2d 310 (1984)

Per Curiam.

In the Fall of 1982, a complaint and warrant issued, charging defendant with two counts of criminal sexual conduct in the first degree arising from defendant's acts of sexual intercourse with his 14-year-old stepdaughter in April and October, 1981. The complaint also charged three counts of criminal sexual conduct in the second degree arising from defendant's sexual fondling of his 12-year-old stepson in January, 1982. . . .

Defendant . . . offered to plead nolo contendere to one count of criminal sexual conduct in the first degree with the stepdaughter pursuant to an agreement that the other counts would be dismissed at sentencing. . . .

. . . .

In a preamble to the sentence, Judge Borsos said, in part:

Recently . . . there have been important scientific discoveries and medical studies on what medical people have always known to be true, that some men are truly over-sexed; they have a greater supply of male hormones that causes them to have much stronger sex urges than the normal male and are much less able to resist temptation; like a furnace which overheats a house if the thermostat is set too high.

Judge Borsos said to defendant:

On your behalf, there are many things that you are not. You are not a violent rapist who drags women and girls off the street and into the bushes or into your car from a parking lot; and I have had a lot of these in my courtroom, and I'm sure we have many in our community that I will see in the future, and we probably have some that I won't see. You are not a child chaser, one whose obsession with sex causes him to seek neighborhood children or children in parks or in playgrounds, and we see these people in court. You are a man who has warm personal feelings for your stepchildren, but you let them get out of hand, and we see a number of people like you in our courts.

Judge Borsos sentenced defendant to five years probation, with the first year in the county jail "with no credit for time you have already served." Judge Borsos also ordered defendant to pay "to the County of Kalamazoo as court costs the sum of $25,000 for part of the expense the county has been put to by this case." Finally, Judge Borsos ordered that defendant "within 30 days submit yourself to castration by chemical means patterned after the research and treatment of the Johns Hopkin[s] Hospital in Baltimore, Maryland, and continue same for the five years of your probation under the supervision of this Court." . . .

. . . .

Defendant's primary argument on appeal is a challenge to the condition of probation which requires that he submit to Depo-Provera treatment.

Defendant argues that the condition of probation requiring the taking of Depo-Provera (what the trial court referred to as "castration by chemical means") is unconstitutional and unlawful and, therefore, incapable of acceptance. Defendant argues that chemical castration is a form of sterilization which is unconstitutional as cruel and unusual punishment, a violation of fundamental rights of liberty, privacy, bodily integrity, equal protection and procedural and substantive due process.

It is unnecessary to reach defendant's constitutional arguments because the condition of probation is an unlawful condition. It is elementary that appellate courts will not decide constitutional questions when the issue raised can be decided on alternative, nonconstitutional grounds raised in the appeal.

· ·

The starting point for the analysis is the probation statute. MSA 28.1133(4) begins: "The court may impose other *lawful* conditions of probation as the circumstances of the case may require or warrant, or as in its judgment may be proper." (Emphasis added.)

. . . When administered to males, Depo-Provera lowers the level of testosterone, reduces the sex drive and in most instances causes temporary impotence. "Clinically, it has been reported that subjects receiving the drug experience a lowered sex drive and a decrease in the frequency of erotic imagery." Connecticut Department of Correction, "Report of the Depo-Provera Study Group." However, the drug is not approved by the FDA for suppressing the sex drive in the male, but its experimental use for that purpose is allowed. The drug produces an alphabet of adverse reactions from acne to cancer to weight gain. *Physician's Desk Reference,* pp. 1765, 1766. Long-term toxicology studies in monkeys, dogs and rats disclose that the drug produces cancer in female organs, although the relevancy of any of those findings with respect to humans has not been established.

Some sex offenders in other states have been given the voluntary option of participating in a Depo-Provera program as a condition of probation in very limited instances. However, our research reveals that no appellate court in the United States, either state or federal, has ever passed upon or approved either voluntary or mandatory treatment of sex offenders with medroxyprogesterone acetate or Depo-Provera. . . .

· ·

Furthermore, even in the few studies undertaken to treat sex offenders with medroxyprogesterone acetate, participation was voluntary. In those cases, the chemical treatment was accompanied by psycho-therapy. And, the subjects chosen for the studies were generally chronic, deviant and dangerous sex offenders.

· ·

The Depo-Provera treatment prescribed by the trial judge also fails as a lawful condition of probation because it has not gained acceptance in the medical community as a safe and reliable medical procedure.

. . . As noted, the use of Depo-Provera to reduce the sexual drive in male sex offenders is experimental only. The medical-psychiatric literature on the topic is limited. The practice is apparently limited to a few institutions. In light of that, the questions left unanswered by Judge Borsos's order are, where is defendant to get the treatment (he's in county jail for at least a year)? Who is to administer this treatment? What if, as defendant alleges, the medicine would be detrimental to his alleged heart and psychiatric conditions? Is defendant entitled to psychotherapy along with the drug treatment, as appears to be the practice in the studies referred to by the trial court?

· ·

None of the above considerations touches at all on defendant's constitutional objections to the Depo-Provera treatment. Yet the considerations mentioned demonstrate overwhelmingly that the condition of defendant's probation, that he submit to Depo-Provera treatment, is clearly an unlawful condition of probation and invalid under MSA 28.1133(4).

COMMENTS

1. The *Gauntlett* case is one indication of what I term "new" punishment. Do you think chemical castration is an appropriate punishment in child abuse cases? Rape cases? (Before you answer too quickly, because rape has as much to do with aggression as it does with sex, is it clear that chemical castration would prevent such aggressive behavior in the future?) Should the decision be up to the accused, or could/

should the state be able to pursue this punishment even against the wishes of the accused? For an excellent discussion of these novel issues, see William Green, "Depo-Provera, Castration, and the Probation of Rape Offenders: Statutory and Constitutional Issues," *University of Dayton Law Review* 12:1–26 (1986).

2. Another issue that warrants some thought (and presumably some discussion) is behavior modification. In Anthony Burgess's best selling book, *A Clockwork Orange,* individuals who were convicted of committing violent crimes had their behavior changed by repeatedly showing them violent images, to the point where violence repulsed them. Does this go much too far?

3. Recently a California judge attempted a rather unique form of punishment by sentencing a slumlord to his rat-infested apartment complex for one month. Was this an appropriate punishment? Can we reasonably expect "the ratlord" (as he was called) to now see the light and mend his ways?

4. Would it be fair to say that the criminal justice system oftentimes lacks imagination? Our choices often seem to be jail or no jail, and neither option seems appealing. Think of crimes, and think of punishments for these crimes that get us out of this rut. Let us return to *Rummel* once again. Can we think of a better resolution of his propensity to bounce checks than life imprisonment?

5. Some courts have shown a lot of imagination, perhaps too much imagination. In some cases, drunk drivers have been made to hang a bumper sticker announcing this fact, and in one case a pickpocket was forced to wear taps on his shoes so that he could not sneak up on people. Are these just punishments? Some of these punishments make one think of Hester Prynne in *The Scarlet Letter,* forced to wear an "A" on her clothing for the act of adultery. Were the Pilgrims really ahead of their time?

13

JUSTICE AND LAWYERS

Thus far in Part III we have looked at two different kinds of duties. In Chapter 11 we examined whether there is a moral or legal duty (or both) to offer assistance to those who are in need. In Chapter 12 we examined the duties the criminal owes to society and how sanctions compel the criminal to these duties; whether these were owed to the society as a whole, to the smaller community, or to the victim. In this chapter we raise the question of what duties lawyers have and to whom they owe those duties.

A question that seems to intrigue undergraduate students and nonlawyers generally far more than it does lawyers is whether they ever could represent someone who was guilty or had transgressed legal boundaries. Consider this situation. You are fresh out of law school, and you have decided to hang up your own shingle. You wait several weeks, and finally your first would-be client walks through your doorway. This person announces to you that he has just brutally raped and killed a thirteen-year-old mentally retarded girl. He believes he will be arrested for these crimes and asks if you would represent him. Would you?

I know very few lawyers who would not offer representation to this person. They would answer that the lawyer's job is not to find guilt or innocence (that role belongs to the judicial system); rather, the lawyer's job is to ensure that his or her client gets a fair hearing. Lawyers will also tell you that the system of justice that we have in our society, both criminal and civil, is based on the adversarial system, in which "the truth" will emerge in a court of law from the contest between the two competing sides. (Forget that the vast majority of civil and criminal cases are settled out of court. Presumably the two sides have come to a common agreement on what is just.)

Although most lawyers pretend not to like the description, they are sometimes referred to as "hired guns," willing to represent anyone for anything to ensure this vigorous representation, for a small fee of course. An interesting point, and one that seems to sharply differentiate the lawyer from the nonlawyer, is the fact that many lawyers are not interested in knowing if their clients are guilty of crimes. That is, many times lawyers will tell you that they have never asked their clients if they actually did what they are accused of doing, whereas most nonlawyers I have discussed this with say this is the first question they would ask. (They really *do* want to know the answer.)

In contrast to the rather set answers that lawyers give to the question of representing a guilty person, undergraduates and nonlawyers generally seem to feel much less at ease with this proposition. Some self-righteous students announce in class that they would never represent a guilty person, but certainly the accused jay-walker does not present the same moral qualms as our killer-rapist might. It is unclear why nonlawyers seem to be so different from lawyers on this question. Perhaps nonlawyers (and students in particular) are naive, whereas lawyers are not. Perhaps undergraduates see the world in black-white, good guys–bad guys terms, whereas lawyers have seen a lot of gray. Perhaps nonlawyers are capable of having a conscience, whereas lawyers are not. Or perhaps lawyers understand that it is one thing to have a conscience in theory and another in practice.[1]

In any case, lawyers and nonlawyers have different views about responsibility. For the lawyer, although she is an officer of the court and a member of the community, her overriding concern—perhaps her *only* concern—is with the client. Nonlawyers, on the other hand, think lawyers should play myriad roles and have a host of duties—to the society at large, to the victim, and to some abstract notion of justice.

To draw out some of these distinctions and then to critically appraise the questions raised, consider a few factual situations. What should a lawyer do with the client who is going to commit perjury on the stand? Let us say the would-be client referred to earlier tells you about the rape and murder but wants to get on the stand and manufacture an alibi that will have him far away from the scene of the crime.

> Would you withdraw from the case (assuming you took it in the first place)? Would you not allow the person on the stand (presumably he will fire you, although it is unclear what would happen if you were a court-appointed attorney)?
> Would you allow this person on the stand and ask him the questions he wants to be asked, not indicating that you know these answers to be complete fabrications?

The first case in this chapter *Whiteside v. Scurr,* involved a lawyer's duty in the case of a perjurious client. We will discuss shortly some of the duties that lawyers have under the Model Rules of Professional Conduct. Do the Model Rules sufficiently address situations such as this one? The other case in this chapter, *People v. Belge,* raised some interesting questions about a lawyer's duties. In *Belge,* a lawyer was told by his client about a number of unsolved murders that he had committed and the whereabouts of these corpses. As you will see, the lawyer did not divulge this information immediately to the police; in fact, the whereabouts of these victims did not become public knowledge until there was an insanity hearing some time later. Should lawyers have some duty to law enforcement officials, or to society, or to the victims? If you say yes, will such duties interfere with the "vigorous representation" that the Model Rules of Professional Conduct places on the lawyer in our society?

Consider also a situation in which a lawyer thinks his client might be dangerous to society and might commit a crime. Let us return to the rapist-murderer whom you did represent, and who was acquitted, largely because you allowed him to take the stand and commit perjury (you rationalized that it was the court's role to determine guilt or innocence). He thanks you, pays you (not necessarily in that order), and then announces his intention to commit the same sorts of brutal acts. What duties does a lawyer have here? It might or might not surprise you to learn that the Model Rules of Professional Conduct are quite equivocal here. Rule 1.6 reads:

a. A lawyer shall not reveal information relating to representation of a client unless the client consents after consultation, except for disclosures that are impliedly authorized in order to carry out the representation, and except as stated in paragraph (b).
b. A lawyer may reveal such information to the extent the lawyer reasonably believes necessary:
   1. to prevent the client from committing a criminal act that the lawyer believes is likely to result in imminent death or substantial bodily harm; or
   2. to establish a claim or defense on behalf of the lawyer in a controversy between the lawyer and the client, to establish a defense to a criminal charge or civil claim against the lawyer based upon conduct in which the client was involved, or to respond to allegations in any proceeding concerning the lawyer's representation of the client.

The "comment" corresponding to this rule states:

The lawyer may learn that a client intends prospective conduct that is criminal and likely to result in imminent death or substantial bodily harm. As stated in paragraph (b)(1), the lawyer has professional discretion to reveal information in order to prevent such consequences. The lawyer may make a disclosure in order to prevent homicide or serious bodily injury which the lawyer reasonably believes is intended by a client. It is very difficult for a lawyer to "know" when such a heinous purpose will actually be carried out, for the client may have a change of mind.

Note how often the word "may" is used in this rule. Should the word "shall" be used instead?

NOTE

1. Milt Heumann describes the socialization process that young defense attorneys go through in his book *Plea Bargaining.* Most defense attorneys come out of law school expecting to do what they had been taught in law school—filing Bills of Particular and Motions for Discovery, trying cases in court, and representing innocent clients. They soon find out that they are not able to do any of those things. In terms of the latter, Heumann writes:

> Newcomers have difficulty coming to grips with the factual culpability of most defendants. They begin their jobs with a vague notion that "many" defendants are innocent. After several months in the system, they offer estimates that about 50 percent are guilty. The figure contrasts with the 90 percent estimate given by almost all experienced defense attorneys. It takes time for the newcomers to learn about, to accept, and to be comfortable with the factual guilt of their clients.

Milton Heumann, *Plea Bargaining: The Experiences of Prosecutors, Judges, and Defense Attorneys* (Chicago: University of Chicago Press, 1977), p. 58.

Whiteside v. Scurr, 794 F. 2d 1323 (1984)

Circuit Judge McMillan delivered the opinion of the Court.

A state court jury convicted appellant of second degree murder for the stabbing death of Calvin Love in 1977. Appellant was sentenced to forty years imprisonment. Appellant and two companions had gone to Love's apartment to get some marijuana. During an argument about the marijuana, appellant stabbed Love as Love was moving toward him. Appellant's theory of defense was self-defense. According to appellant, Love had been reaching for a gun beneath a pillow when appellant stabbed him. When questioned by defense counsel in preparation for trial, appellant stated that he had not actually seen the gun, but that he thought that he had seen a gun and was convinced that Love had one because Love had a reputation for carrying a gun. Counsel questioned appellant's two companions and Love's girlfriend about the gun. They denied actually seeing a gun, although appellant's companions believed that Love probably did have a gun. Counsel also learned that the police had found no gun during a quick search of the room where the stabbing occurred. Nor had the apartment manager found a gun. Counsel personally searched the room for the gun without success. During the course of his investigation, however, counsel discovered that several hours after the stabbing, Love's girlfriend and his family had forced the police padlock on the apartment and had removed everything from the apartment.

Appellant was anxious about the success of his theory of self-defense if the gun was not found. Counsel had earlier advised appellant that the gun itself was not essential to his theory of self-defense and that the defense would be successful if the jury was convinced that appellant reasonably believed that Love had had a gun. Shortly before trial, appellant told counsel that he had seen something "metallic" in Love's hand just before the stabbing. This discrepancy precipitated the disagreement between appellant and counsel that underlies this appeal. Counsel told appellant that if he insisted upon testifying that he saw a gun, then he (counsel) would move to withdraw, advise the state trial judge that the testimony was perjurious and testify against him.

At trial appellant testified only that he thought Love had a gun and that he had acted to protect himself from an assault by Love with the gun. Appellant was found guilty of second degree murder. . . .

In 1981 appellant filed a petition for writ of habeas corpus alleging that counsel's threats to withdraw, advise the state trial judge and testify against him denied him the right to effective assistance of counsel, the right to present a defense and due process in violation of the Fifth, Sixth and Fourteenth Amendments. . . . The district court noted the constitutional right to testify did not include perjury and concluded that appellant was not denied due process or effective assistance of counsel because counsel prevented him from testifying falsely. The district court denied the petition and this appeal followed.

. . . .

The problem presented on the merits in this case is what kind of action defense counsel, representing a defendant in a criminal case, may constitutionally pursue when counsel believes that the client intends to testify falsely. . . .

. . . .

Our discussion begins with the following observation: our analysis does not deal with the ethical problem inherent in appellant's claim. We are concerned only with the constitutional requirements of due process and effective assistance of counsel. . . . [T]he Constitution prevails over rules of professional ethics, and a lawyer who does what the Sixth and Fourteenth Amendments command cannot be charged with violating any precepts of professional ethics. . . .

. . . .

In the present case defense counsel was confronted shortly before trial with appellant's intention to testify in his own defense in a manner that defense counsel had a firm factual basis for believing would be false. Counsel threatened appellant that he would withdraw from the case, advise the state court trial judge of appellant's intention, and testify against him as a rebuttal witness for the prosecution. Counsel's actions prevented appellant from testifying falsely. We hold that counsel's action deprived appellant of due process and effective assistance of counsel. . . .

As recently noted by the Supreme Court in *Strickland v. Washington,*

The Constitution guarantees a fair trial through the Due Process Clauses, but it defines the basic elements of a fair trial largely through the several provisions of the Sixth Amendment, including the Counsel Clause. . . . Thus, a fair trial is one in which evidence subject to adversarial testing is presented to an impartial tribunal for resolution of issues defined in advance of the proceeding. The right to counsel plays a crucial role in the adversarial system embodied in the Sixth Amendment, since access to counsel's skill and knowledge is necessary to accord defendants the "ample opportunity to meet the case of the prosecution" to which they are entitled.

. . . The Sixth Amendment recognizes the right to the assistance of counsel because it envisions counsel's playing a role that is critical to the ability of the adversarial system to produce just results. An accused is entitled to be assisted by an attorney, whether retained or appointed, who plays the role necessary to ensure that the trial is fair.

. . . Representation of a criminal defendant entails certain basic duties. *Counsel's function is to assist the defendant, and hence counsel owes the client a duty of loyalty, a duty to avoid conflicts of interest.* From counsel's function as assistant to the defendant derive the overarching duty to advocate the defendant's cause and the more particular duties to consult with the defendant on important decisions and to keep the defendant informed of important developments in the course of the prosecution. Counsel also has a duty to bring to bear such skill and knowledge as will render the trial a reliable adversarial testing process.

Thus, the fair and effective operation of the adversary system depends upon the attorney who must zealously advocate the defendant's cause to judge and jury for determination. Counsel's ability to serve as an effective advocate, in turn, depends upon the defendant's ability to disclose information fully and in confidence to counsel. When an attorney unnecessarily discloses the confidences of the client, the attorney creates a chilling effect which inhibits the mutual trust and independence necessary to effective representation.

In the present case counsel's actions in threatening to withdraw, advise the state trial judge and testify against appellant if appellant testified falsely, impermissibly compromised appellant's right to effective assistance of counsel. Despite counsel's legitimate ethical concerns, counsel's actions were inconsistent with the obligations of confidentiality and zealous advocacy. Counsel's actions, in particular the threat to testify against appellant, indicate that a conflict of interest had developed between counsel and appellant, even though this conflict was admittedly precipitated by appellant's intention to testify falsely. At this point counsel had become a potential adversary and ceased to serve as a zealous advocate of appellant's interests. . . .

Counsel's actions also impermissibly compromised appellant's right to testify in his own defense by conditioning continued representation by counsel and confidentiality upon appellant's restricted testimony. We hold that criminal defendants have the constitutional right to testify which, although not specifically expressed in the Constitution or the Bill of Rights, is implicit in the Fifth and Fourteenth Amendments' due process guarantee of a fair adversarial process and in the Sixth Amendment's guarantee of the right to meet and confront accusations, to be present and to present evidence and witnesses on one's behalf, including the right to present oneself as a witness. Counsel's actions improperly forced appellant in effect to choose between two constitutional rights, the right to testify in one's own defense and the right to effective assistance of counsel, and infringed both.

COMMENTS

1. This decision was overturned by the U.S. Supreme Court in *Nix v. Whiteside*, 475 U.S. 157 (1986). The majority opinion written by Chief Justice Burger views this case as one involving the ethical obligations of an attorney. The opinion downplays the constitutional rights of the accused. At one point Burger writes, "[W]e can discern no breach of professional conduct in Robinson's admonition to [respondent] that he would disclose respondent's perjury to the court. The crime of perjury in this setting is indistinguishable in substance from the crime of threatening or tampering with a witness or a juror. . . . An attorney's duty of confidentiality, which totally covers the client's admission of guilt, does not extend to a client's announced plans to engage in future criminal conduct."

2. Do you think you could represent a guilty person? Would it matter what the crime was? Why?

3. If you were a lawyer representing a person accused of dealing in cocaine, would it bother you that the money you were paid for your services came from the drug trade?

People v. Belge, 372 N.Y.S. 2d 798 (1975)

Judge Gale.

In the summer of 1973 Robert F. Garrow, Jr., stood charged in Hamilton County with the crime of murder. The defendant was assigned two attorneys, Frank H. Armani and Francis R. Belge. A defense of insanity had been interposed by counsel for Mr. Garrow. During the course of the discussions between Garrow and his two counsel, three other murders were admitted by Garrow, one being in Onondaga County. On or about September of 1973 Mr. Belge conducted his own investigation based upon what his client had told him and with the assistance of a friend the location of the body of Alicia Hauck was found in Oakwood Cemetery in Syracuse. Mr. Belge personally inspected the body and was satisfied, presumably, that this was the Alicia Hauck that his client had told him that he murdered.

The discovery was not disclosed to the authorities, but became public during the trial of Mr. Garrow in June of 1974, when to affirmatively establish the defense of insanity, these three other murders were brought before the jury by the defense in the Hamilton County trial. [Criminal charges were then brought against attorney Belge for violating a Public Health Law requiring anyone knowing of the death of a person to notify the proper authorities.]

. . . .

Our system of criminal justice is an adversary system and the interests of the State are not absolute, or even paramount. The dignity of the individual is respected to the point that even when the citizen is known by the State to have committed a heinous offense, the individual is nevertheless accorded such rights as counsel, trial by jury, due process, and the privilege against self-incrimination.

A trial is in part a search for truth, but it is only partly a search for truth. The mantle of innocence is flung over the defendant to such an extent that he is safeguarded by rules of evidence which frequently keep out absolute truth, much to the chagrin of juries. Nevertheless, this has been a part of our system since our laws were taken from the laws of England and over these many years has been found to best protect a balance between the rights of the individual and the rights of society.

. . . .

The effectiveness of counsel is only as great as the confidentiality of its client-attorney relationship. If the lawyer cannot get all the facts about the case, he can only give his client half of a defense. This, of necessity, involves the client telling his attorney everything remotely connected with the crime.

Apparently, in the instant case, after analyzing all the evidence, and after hearing of the bizarre episodes in the life of their client, they decided that the only possibility of salvation was in a defense of insanity. For the client to disclose not only everything about this particular crime but also everything about other crimes which might have a bearing upon his defense, requires the strictest confidence in, and on the part of, the attorney.

When the facts of the other homicides became public, as a result of the defendant's testimony to substantiate his claim of insanity, members of the public were shocked at the apparent callousness of these lawyers, whose conduct was seen as typifying the unhealthy lack of concern of most lawyers with the public interest and with simple decency. A hue and cry went up from the press and other news media suggesting that the attorneys should be found guilty of such crimes as obstruction of justice or becoming an accomplice after the fact. From a layman's standpoint, this certainly was a logical conclusion. However, the Constitution of the United States of America attempts to preserve the dignity of the individual and to do that guarantees him the services of an attorney who will bring to the bar and to the bench every conceivable protection from the inroads of the State against such rights as are vested in the Constitution for one accused of crime. Among those substantial constitutional rights is that a defendant does not have to incriminate himself. His attorneys were bound to uphold that concept and maintain what has been called a sacred trust of confidentiality.

. . . .

In the case at bar we must weigh the importance of the general privilege of confidentiality in the performance of the defendant's duties as an attorney, against the inroads of such a privilege on the fair administration of criminal justice as well as the heart tearing that went on in the victim's family by reason of their uncertainty as to the whereabouts of Alicia Hauck. In this type situation the court must balance the rights of the individual against the rights of society as a whole. There is no question but Attorney Belge's failure to bring to the attention of the authorities the whereabouts of Alicia Hauck when he first verified it, prevented bringing Garrow to the immediate bar of justice for this particular murder. This was in a sense, obstruction of justice. This duty, I am sure, loomed large in the mind of Attorney Belge. However, against this was the Fifth Amendment right of his client, Garrow, not to incriminate himself.

It is the decision of this court that Francis R. Belge conducted himself as an officer of the court with all the zeal at his command to protect the constitutional rights of his client. Both on the grounds of a privileged communication and in the interests of justice the indictment is dismissed.

COMMENTS

1. How would you characterize the role that lawyers play in our legal system? Do they have duties to society, or would a duty to society interfere with their duty to their clients?

2. If the three other murders were not discovered at trial as part of an insanity defense, presumably Belge would never be under any legal (moral?) obligation to disclose this information. Is this right?

3. According to the Model Rules for Professional Conduct, a lawyer *may* reveal to law enforcement authorities the fact that she believes her client is about to commit a crime. Should "may" be changed to "shall," or would this violate (and possibly destroy) the relationship between attorney and client?

4. Consider a question in civil law. How would you feel about representing a wealthy individual/corporation against a party with considerably smaller resources when you know the law goes against your position but you might well win because the opposing party does not have the resources to pursue its claim to the fullest? Could you rationalize your answer by recognizing that this is the way the system might, at times, work and that you are not responsible for the system of justice we have in our society?

5. Consider the following civil suit in Florida. Mark Baltes was killed by a hit-and-run driver. More than a day later an unidentified person went to see lawyer Barry Krischer and said that he might have been involved in a hit-and-run accident and asked Krischer to negotiate a plea bargain with law enforcement agents without disclosing his name. Law enforcement officials refused to negotiate. Subsequently, no headway was made in the criminal investigation. The parents of Mr. Baltes then filed a $6 million damage suit against an unidentified defendant, Doe I, and sought to compel Krischer to disclose the name of his client. Krischer refused, and this action was upheld in court, Judge Poulton reasoning that this would violate lawyer-client confidentiality.

14

JUSTICE BETWEEN GENERATIONS AND AMONG POLITICAL SUBDIVISIONS

Thus far our discussion of the various concepts of justice has been confined to the domestic sphere. Some would argue that this is as far as our notions of justice can be extended because they are premised on some notion of a shared community and the shared values that serve as a basis of that community. Others would claim that if our notions of justice cannot carry beyond our own national borders, then they are not true reflections of justice. The last two chapters of this book will examine how community specific our notions of justice are. Recall Peter Singer's hypothetical case of the drowning child. Singer claims that individuals in other countries who are on the edge of subsistence are very much like a child drowning nearby in the sense that we *can* offer assistance, but, more importantly, that we are *morally obligated* to offer assistance. Under this view, family ties and community boundaries, although important, should not serve as a demarcation of where our moral obligations begin and end.

Singer is not the only political philosopher to address the question of our duties to others. In his seminal book *Basic Rights: Subsistence, Affluence, and U.S. Foreign Policy,* Henry Shue takes the position that every individual possesses certain "basic rights," which "are a restraint upon economic and political forces that would otherwise be too strong to be resisted. They are social guarantees against actual and threatened deprivations of at least some basic needs. Basic rights are an attempt to give the powerless a veto over some of the forces that would otherwise harm them the most. . . . Basic rights are the morality of the depths. They specify the line beneath which no one is to be allowed to sink."[1]

Shue sets forth three basic rights: the right to security, the right to subsistence, and the right to liberty (which, as Shue describes it, turns into a right to participate in the process of governing in order to protect the other two basic rights). Shue also describes the duties that Western societies have: the duty not to deprive, the duty to protect, and the duty to give aid. These duties do not fall on everyone equally. For example, those who are responsible for the destitution that others face—Shue uses the example of the Dutch agricultural export policies in Java, which have had disastrous consequences for the people of Java—have a much stronger duty to provide assistance than do those who bear no responsibility. Ultimately, however, Shue recognizes that there is a moral duty that all of us, the so-called affluent, have to those who do not have their right to subsistence met.

In addition to examining justice across political boundaries, the cases in this chapter will ask the student to examine justice as an intergenerational phenomenon. Simply stated, does one generation have any duties and responsibilities to subsequent generations? And if so, what are they?

If you have trouble thinking in terms of international and intergenerational justice (and going beyond the issue of foreign assistance), a few examples should serve to sharpen your thinking. Consider the recent furor concerning the rapid depletion of ozone in the atmosphere.[2] Scientists now almost universally claim that the ozone layer has dramatically eroded because of the amount of carbon dioxide spewed into the atmosphere. As a result, we will be witnessing a "greenhouse effect" that will raise average world temperatures between three and nine degrees by as early as the year 2030. The effects of this global warming could be disastrous: fertile agricultural land turned into dustbowls, the melting of ice caps, and with that the rise of the oceans.

The loss of ozone can be viewed as an issue of justice among political subdivisions because ozone loss has been caused largely by industrialized nations and by some industrialized nations more than others. For example, in 1985 the United States emitted 1,186 million tons of carbon dioxide, compared with 780 million tons emitted by Western Europe, 244 by Japan, 958 by the Soviet Union, 508 by China, and 819 by the developing nations.[3] Although the industrialized nations are certainly more responsible for the production and emission of carbon dioxide in the atmosphere, many developing nations have pursued policies that have only exacerbated the problem, particularly through deforestation.

It is also possible to see the ozone situation as involving a matter of justice between generations. Efforts are now under way to arrest this erosion, but do we do so only to save our own skins (literally)? Or do we do so because we also recognize some as-yet-undefined duty to those who will live after us? This latter answer certainly sounds good, but just what kind of duty is it, and what will it entail? But if we were to demand that each generation leave the world in as good a shape as that generation found it (if this were somehow possible to determine), would not this eliminate many of the so-called advances that Western societies now enjoy?

Similar topics that raise issues of justice from both an intergenerational and international perspective are nuclear power, nuclear waste and hazardous chemical wastes. The first case, *Duke Power Co. v. Carolina Environmental Study Group,* involved a challenge to the Price-Anderson Act, which established a liability limit of $560 million in the event of a nuclear accident. Again, the Supreme Court did not fully address the larger issues of justice involved in the question of nuclear power, but remember that the Court's confident tone here preceded Three Mile Island and Chernobyl.

The second case, *Washington State Bldg. & Const. Trades v. Spellman,* involved a state initiative to keep radioactive waste produced outside the state of Washington from entering the state. Although the court in *Spellman* was certainly correct that Washington's efforts violated the supremacy and the commerce clauses of the Constitution by going against federal action and federal interests, should the residents of Washington have to be a repository for the radioactive waste produced elsewhere? What if the residents of that state wanted to eliminate *all* nuclear waste—could it do so? Should it be able to do so?

Consider a related question involving the export of hazardous chemical wastes across national boundaries. Is it just that Western societies have begun to dump hazardous wastes in some of the poorest countries in Africa?[4] Does it matter that these African nations have apparently agreed to this practice? Does it matter if the money earned from this practice will bring in much needed foreign currency to these African nations? Does it matter if these backward nations do not have the technological capabilities to properly handle highly toxic material?[5]

Chemical and nuclear waste also raises the question of intergenerational justice. There is a great deal of concern that the storage of nuclear waste, to choose that example, has been very poorly performed. The media frequently report that some of the barrels housing nuclear waste have been leaking, with very real fears that this residue will ultimately harm human and animal life, perhaps on a widespread basis.[6] Given that radioactive substances have a half-life of thousands of years, much of the burden for storing nuclear waste created by *us* will fall on subsequent generations.[7] Is this fair?

The last two cases in this chapter involved more traditional forms of pollution. In *Georgia v. Tennessee Copper Co.,* the Supreme Court allowed the state of Georgia to halt the production of noxious fumes by a corporation in another state because of the fumes' harmful effects on the residents of Georgia. In *Ohio v. Wyandotte Chemicals Corp.,* the Supreme Court held in a similar suit that the resolution of such matters was best left to the political branches. What rule emerges from the juxtaposition of these two cases? Is judicial deference in such a situation the better policy, notwithstanding the desire we all share to have a clean environment? If so, why? On the other hand, can we be assured that the political branches will arrive at a just and expedient result? After all, the political branches (but really the world community) did very little to prevent the ozone destruction discussed earlier. Is there any reason to believe that they can work to halt pollution in general?

NOTES

1. Henry Shue, *Basic Rights: Subsistence, Affluence, and U.S. Foreign Policy* (Princeton, N.J.: Princeton University Press, 1980), p. 18.

2. James Gleick, "Even With Action Today, Ozone Loss Will Increase," *New York Times*, March 20, 1988, p. 1; Robert C. Cowen, "Ozone Study Prompts a Double Take," *Christian Science Monitor*, March 17, 1988, p. 3.

3. Philip Shabecoff, "Major 'Greenhouse' Impact is Unavoidable, Experts Say," *New York Times*, July 19, 1988, p. 19.

4. See Kristin Helmore, "Dumping on Africa: West Exports Its Industrial Wastes," *Christian Science Monitor*, July 1, 1988, p. 1.

5. For an excellent discussion of these and related issues, see Henry Shue, "Exporting Hazards," *Ethics* 91:579–606 (1981). Shue succinctly sums his concern with the dumping of wastes in other lands this way: "Why should I defend defenseless human beings? Because they are human beings and they are defenseless."

6. Keith Schneider, "Leaky Mine Threatens Waste Storage Plan," *New York Times*, February 1, 1988, p. 10 (plant in New Mexico); Keith Schneider, "Plutonium Leak in Idaho Symptom of Atomic Ills," *New York Times*, April 17, 1988, p. 24.

7. Schneider, Ibid., writes, "The leaks at the 36-year-old waste site, part of the Government's Idaho National Engineering Laboratory, were first identified in June 1987. It is a problem that has arisen in 12 other states at the national laboratories and industrial plants that spent almost five decades making nuclear weapons for the military, leaving behind radioactivity waste that could take until the 22nd century to clean up."

Duke Power Co. v. Carolina Environmental Study Group, 438 U.S. 59 (1978)

Chief Justice Burger delivered the opinion of the Court.

These appeals present the question of whether Congress may, consistent with the Constitution, impose a limitation on liability for nuclear accidents resulting from the operation of private nuclear power plants licensed by the Federal Government.

When Congress passed the Atomic Energy Act of 1946, it contemplated that the development of nuclear power would be a Government monopoly. Within a decade, however, Congress concluded that the national interest would be best served if the Government encouraged the private sector to become involved in the development of atomic energy for peaceful purposes under a program of federal regulation and licensing. The Atomic Energy Act of 1954 implemented this policy decision, providing for licensing of private construction, ownership, and operation of commercial nuclear power reactors for energy production under strict supervision by the Atomic Energy Commission (AEC).

Private industry responded to the Atomic Energy Act of 1954 with the development of an experimental power plant constructed under the auspices of a consortium of interested companies. It soon became apparent that profits from the private exploitation of atomic energy were uncertain and the accompanying risks substantial. Although the AEC offered incentives to encourage investment, there remained in the path of the private nuclear power industry various problems—the risk of potentially vast liability in the event of a nuclear accident of a sizable magnitude being the major obstacle. Notwithstanding comprehensive testing and study, the uniqueness of this form of energy production made it impossible totally to rule out the risk of a major nuclear accident resulting in extensive damage. Private industry and the AEC were confident that such a disaster would not occur, but the very uniqueness of nuclear power meant that the possibility remained, and the potential liability dwarfed the ability of the industry and private insurance companies to absorb the risk. Thus, while repeatedly stressing that the risk of a major nuclear accident was extremely remote, spokesmen for the private sector informed Congress that they would be forced to withdraw from the field if their liability were not limited by appropriate legislation.

Congress responded in 1957 by passing the Price-Anderson Act. The Act had the dual purpose of "[protecting] the public and . . . [encouraging] the development of the atomic energy industry." . . . The Act limited the aggregate liability for a single nuclear incident to $500 million plus the amount of liability insurance available on the private market—some $60 million in 1957. . . .

. . . .

Appellant Duke Power Co., is an investor-owned public utility which is construct-

ing one nuclear power plant in North Carolina and one in South Carolina. Duke Power, along with the NRC, was sued by appellees, two organizations—Carolina Environmental Study Group and the Catawba Central Labor Union—and 40 individuals who live within close proximity to the planned facilities. The action was commenced in 1973, and sought, among other relief, a declaration that the Price-Anderson Act is unconstitutional.

. . . .

The District Court held that the Price-Anderson Act contravened the Due Process Clause because "[the] amount of recovery is not rationally related to the potential losses." . . .

Our due process analysis properly begins with a discussion of the appropriate standard of review. Appellants, portraying the liability-limitation provision as a legislative balancing of economic interests, urge that the Price-Anderson Act be accorded the traditional presumption of constitutionality generally accorded economic regulations and that it be upheld absent proof of arbitrariness or irrationality on the part of Congress. Appellees, however, urge a more elevated standard of review on the ground that the interests jeopardized by the Price-Anderson Act are far more important than those in the economic due process and business-oriented cases where the traditional rationality standard has been invoked. . . .

As we read the Act and its legislative history, it is clear that Congress' purpose was to remove the economic impediments in order to stimulate the private development of electric energy by nuclear power while simultaneously providing the public compensation in the event of a catastrophic nuclear incident. The liability-limitation provision thus emerges as a classic example of an economic regulation—a legislative effort to structure and accommodate the burdens and benefits of economic life. It is by now well established that [such] legislative Acts . . . come to the Court with a presumption of constitutionality, and that the burden is on one complaining of a due process violation to establish that the legislature has acted in an arbitrary and irrational way. That the accommodation struck may have profound and far-reaching consequences, contrary to appellees' suggestion, provides all the more reason for this Court to defer to the congressional judgment unless it is demonstrably arbitrary or irrational.

When examined in light of this standard of review, the Price-Anderson Act, in our view, passes constitutional muster. The record before us fully supports the need for the imposition of a statutory limit on liability to encourage private industry participation and hence bears a rational relationship to Congress' concern for stimulating the involvement of private enterprise in the production of electric energy through the use of atomic power; nor do we understand appellees or the District Court to be of a different view. Rather their challenge is to the alleged arbitrariness of the particular figure of $560 million, which is the statutory ceiling on liability. The District Court aptly summarized its position:

The amount of recovery is not rationally related to the potential losses. Abundant evidence in the record shows that although major catastrophe in any particular place is not certain and may not be extremely likely, nevertheless, in the territory where these plants are located, damage to life and property for this and future generations could well be many, many times the limit which the law places on liability.

. . . .

Given our conclusion that, in general, limiting liability is an acceptable method for Congress to utilize in encouraging the private development of electric energy by atomic power, candor requires acknowledgment that whatever ceiling figure is selected will, of necessity, be arbitrary in the sense that any choice of a figure based on imponderables like those at issue here can always be so characterized. This is not, however, the kind of arbitrariness which flaws otherwise constitutional action. When appraised in terms of both the extremely remote possibility of an accident where liability would exceed the limitation and Congress' now statutory commitment to "take whatever action is deemed necessary and appropriate to protect the public from the consequences of" any such disaster, we hold the congressional decision to fix a $560 million ceiling, at this stage in the private development and production of electric energy by nuclear power, to be within permissible limits and not violative of due process.

COMMENTS

1. Note the very deferential stance toward the legislative body taken by the Supreme Court here. On one level, nuclear power (its production and storage) is a very technical issue, one that most judges presumably are ill-equipped to handle. On another level, however, are there not some larger issues of justice involved here that may or may not get a hearing in the legislative setting? To date, efforts at nuclear waste storage have been very poorly performed. In addition, because radioactivity remains for thousands of years, subsequent generations are going to have to care for nuclear waste that *we* produce. Is this a part of the "social contract" between generations, or have the rules of the game been drastically altered?

2. Nuclear power is only one of several issues that have an intergenerational effect. Another is the depletion of the ozone layer, apparently brought on by world industrialization (but mainly industrialization in Western societies). What does justice dictate in terms of how we leave the world to subsequent generations? Do we have any duties to those who follow us? Did previous generations have a duty to us, and if so, did they fulfill those duties?

Washington State Bldg. & Const. Trades v. Spellman, 684 F. 2d 627 (1982)

Circuit Judge Goodwin delivered the opinion of the court.

For more than fifteen years, the State of Washington has leased from the United States 1,000 acres in an area known as the Hanford Reservation. During this time, the State has sub-leased part of the land for use as a commercial low-level radioactive waste dump. By arrangement with the United States under Sec. 274 of the Atomic Energy Act, Washington monitors the dumping site (Richland) and inspects shipments of waste to determine their compliance with state and federal regulations concerning radioactive material. The State also licenses users and collects a fee from them.

Richland is one of three low-level radioactive dump sites in operation nationwide and receives about 40 percent of the country's low-level radioactive waste. It is also the only currently operating site accepting absorbed-liquid low-level radioactive waste. Approximately 95 percent of the waste received by Richland originates outside the State of Washington.

In November 1980, the voters of the State of Washington enacted Initiative Measure No. 383 ("383") prohibiting the transportation and storage within Washington of radioactive waste produced outside the state. . . .

[The present suit is a challenge to 383. The court's Supremacy Clause analysis is omitted.]

. . . .

Initiative 383 . . . violates the Commerce Clause. The initiative is based upon an impermissible exercise of the State of Washington's police powers. Congress has established in the Atomic Energy Act a

pervasive statutory scheme to regulate nuclear activity. . . . Through Sec. 274 of the Act and through the Low-Level Waste Act, Congress has also ceded some regulatory authority to the states. But Congress stopped short of granting the states power to ban wastes transported from outside their borders.

Even in the absence of pervasive federal legislation, the Commerce Clause prevents the States from erecting barriers to the free flow of interstate commerce. A state statute may affect commerce without violating the Commerce Clause, however, if the statute serves a legitimate state interest and if it is applied in a nondiscriminatory manner.

The criteria for determining whether the Commerce Clause has been violated are articulated in *Pike v. Bruce Church, Inc.*, 397 U.S. 137, 142 (1970). The *Pike* test asks whether the state law (1) regulates evenhandedly; (2) accomplishes a legitimate local public purpose; and (3) has only an incidental effect on interstate commerce.

Low-level waste from within Washington and that traveling through the state are exempted from the initiative. Only out-of-state waste bound for disposal within Washington is banned. Such uneven treatment of in-state and out-of-state parties fails the first part of the *Pike* test.

. . . .

A challenge to bona fide safety regulations must overcome a strong presumption of validity. However, the Supreme Court has recently held that "the incantation of a purpose to promote the public health or safety does not insulate a state law from Commerce Clause attack." *Kassel v. Consolidated Freightways Corp.*, 450 U.S. 662, 670 (1981).

The state relies upon the proposition that "releases of radioactive materials and emissions to the environment are inimical to the health and welfare of the people of Washington." . . . Initiative 383, Sec. 1. Undoubtedly, the release of radioactive materials and emissions is inimical to the safety of the people of any state. The State of Washington neglects to address, however, the manner in which local waste, transported and stored within Washington has superior safety and environmental virtues over waste produced elsewhere and similarly controlled by state regulatory measures. Initiative 383, therefore, also fails the second part of the *Pike* test.

Finally, Initiative 383 has more than an incidental effect on interstate commerce. Washington receives two-fifths of the country's low-level radioactive waste and has the only site currently available to receive absorbed-liquid low-level waste. Closing Washington's borders would significantly aggravate the national problem of low-level waste disposal. Thus, 383 fails to meet the last part of the *Pike* test and violates the Commerce Clause.

COMMENTS

1. In terms of its legal analysis involving the supremacy clause and the commerce clause, the court was correct. But are there not larger issues of justice that also need to be addressed? For example, should the citizens of Washington (or the citizens of any other state, for that matter) have to shoulder the burden of caring for most of the nation's nuclear waste? Although this is apparently good public policy, is it necessarily a just result? Does it allow those of us not living in such areas to effectively pass off our problems to others and at the same time miss some of the serious shortcomings and problems inherent in nuclear waste disposal?

2. If the argument in question #1 seems compelling enough, consider the alternative argument: whether "good" or "bad," nuclear power has become an essential part of our daily energy supply (and might become ever more important because it does not produce carbon dioxide, as do other energy sources). As such, nuclear waste has to be disposed *somewhere*, and we might as well store it where those in the "know" (legislators) think will ensure the safety for the greatest numbers.

3. Western nations have begun to buy dumping rights for chemical wastes in Third World countries. Is this justice free-market style, or is this unjust by any measure or standard?

4. A final issue involves the decommissioning of nuclear power plants and nuclear weapons factories. Because the costs of tearing down these structures are apparently prohibitive, the federal government is now making plans to simply fence off these structures. The *New York Times* reports that "the government, say some lawmakers, may have no option other than erecting fences, posting guards and warning people to stay away from the most dangerous plants. Engineers at the Energy Department have privately begun calling such contaminated sites 'national sacrifice zones.' They grimly joke that some of the zones could turn out to be larger than many of the 39 national parks." Keith Schneider, "Nuclear Plants' Deaths: The Birth of New Problems," *New York Times*, October 31, 1988, p. 1.

Georgia v. Tennessee Copper Company, 206 U.S. 230 (1907)

Justice Holmes delivered the opinion of the Court.

This is a bill in equity filed in this court by the State of Georgia, in pursuance of a resolution of the legislature and by direction of the Governor of the State, to enjoin the defendant Copper Companies from discharging noxious gas from their works in Tennessee over the plaintiff's territory. It alleges that in consequence of such a discharge a wholesale destruction of forests, orchards and crops is going on, and other injuries are done and threatened in five counties of the State. It alleges also a vain application to the State of Tennessee for relief. . . .

The case has been argued largely as if it were one between two private parties; but it is not. The very elements that would be relied upon in a suit between fellow-citizens as a ground for equitable relief are wanting here. The State owns very little of the territory alleged to be affected, and the damage to it capable of estimate in money, possibly, at least, is small. This is a suit by a State for an injury to it in its capacity of quasi-sovereign. In that capacity the State has an interest independent of and behind the titles of its citizens, in all the earth and air within its domain.

. . . .

It is a fair and reasonable demand on the part of a sovereign that the air over its territory should not be polluted on a great scale by sulphurous acid gas, that the forests on its mountains, be they better or worse, and whatever domestic destruction they have suffered, should not be further destroyed or threatened by the act of persons beyond its control, that the crops and orchards on its hills should not be endangered from the same source. If any such demand is to be enforced this must be, notwithstanding the hesitation that we might feel if the suit were between private parties, and the doubt whether for the injuries which they might be suffering to their property they should not be left to an action at law.

The proof requires but a few words. It is not denied that the defendants generate in their works near the Georgia line large quantities of sulphur dioxide which becomes sulphurous acid by its mixture with the air. It hardly is denied and cannot be denied with success that this gas often is carried by the wind great distances and over great tracts of Georgia land. On the evidence the pollution of the air and the magnitude of that pollution are not open to dispute. Without any attempt to go into details immaterial to the suit, it is proper to add that we are satisfied by a preponderance of evidence that the sulphurous fumes cause and threaten damage on so considerable a scale to the forests and vegetable life, if not to health, within the plaintiff state. . . . Whether Georgia by insisting upon this claim is doing more harm than good to her own citizens is for her to determine. The possible disaster to those outside the State must be accepted as a consequence of her standing upon her extreme rights.

Justice Harlan concurring.

The State of Georgia is, in my opinion, entitled to the general relief sought by its bill, and, therefore, I concur in the result. With some things, however, contained in the opinion, or to be implied from its language, I do not concur. When the Constitution gave this court original jurisdiction in cases "in which a State shall be a party," it was not intended, I think, to authorize the court to apply in its behalf, any principle or rule of equity that would not be applied, under the same facts, in suits wholly between private parties. If this was a suit between private parties, and if under the evidence, a court of equity would not give the plaintiff an injunction, then it ought not to grant relief, under like circumstances, to the plaintiff, because it happens to be a State possessing some powers of sovereignty. Georgia is entitled to the relief sought, not because it is a State, but because it is a party which has established its right to such relief by proof. The opinion, if I do not mistake its scope, proceeds largely upon the ground that this court, sitting in this case as a court of equity, owes some special duty to Georgia as a State, although it is a party, while under the same facts, it would not owe any such duty to the plaintiff, if an individual.

Ohio v. Wyandotte Chemicals Corp., 401 U.S. 493 (1971)

Justice Harlan delivered the opinion of the Court.

By motion for leave to file a bill of complaint, Ohio seeks to invoke this Court's original jurisdiction. . . . For reasons that follow we deny the motion for leave to file.

The action, for abatement of a nuisance, is brought on behalf of the State and its citizens, and names as defendants Wyandotte Chemicals Corp. (Wyandotte), Dow Chemical Co. (Dow America), and Dow Chemical Company of Canada, Ltd. (Dow Canada). . . .

The complaint alleges that Dow Canada and Wyandotte have each dumped mercury into streams whose courses ultimately reach Lake Erie, thus contaminating and polluting that lake's waters, vegetation, fish, and wildlife, and that Dow America is jointly responsible for the acts of its foreign subsidiary. Assuming the State's ability to prove these assertions, Ohio seeks a decree: (1) declaring the introduction of mercury into Lake Erie's tributaries a public nuisance; (2) perpetually enjoining these defendants from introducing mercury into Lake Erie or its tributaries; (3) requiring defendants either to remove the mercury from Lake Erie or to pay the costs of its removal into a fund to be administered by Ohio and used only for that purpose; (4) directing defendants to pay Ohio monetary damages for the harm done to Lake Erie, its fish, wildlife, and vegetation, and the citizens and inhabitants of Ohio.

Original jurisdiction is said to be conferred on this Court by Art. III of the Federal Constitution. Section 2, cl. 1, of that Article, provides: "The judicial Power shall extend . . . to Controversies . . . between a State and Citizens of another State . . . and between a State . . . and foreign . . . Citizens or Subjects." Section 2, cl. 2, provides: "In all cases . . . in which a State shall be Party, the Supreme Court shall have original Jurisdiction." Finally, 28 U.S.C. Sec. 1251 (b) provides: "The Supreme Court shall have original but not exclusive jurisdiction of . . . (3) [a]ll actions or proceedings by a State against the citizens of another State or against aliens."

While we consider that Ohio's complaint does state a cause of action that falls within the compass of our original jurisdiction, we have concluded that this Court should nevertheless decline to exercise that jurisdiction.

That we have jurisdiction seems clear enough. Beyond doubt, the complaint on its face reveals the existence of a genuine "case or controversy" between one State and citizens of another, as well as a foreign subject. . . . This Court has often adjudicated controversies between States and between a State and citizens of another State seeking to abate a nuisance that exists in one State yet produces noxious consequences in another. In short, precedent leads almost ineluctably to the conclusion that we are empowered to resolve this dispute in the first instance.

Ordinarily, the foregoing would suffice to settle the issue presently under consideration: whether Ohio should be granted leave to file its complaint. For it is a time-honored maxim of the Anglo-American common-law tradition that a court possessed of jurisdiction generally must exercise it. Nevertheless, although it may initially have been contemplated that this Court would always exercise its original jurisdiction when properly called upon to do so, it seems evident to us that changes in the American legal system and the development of American society have rendered untenable, as a practical matter, the view that this Court must stand willing to adjudicate all or most legal disputes that may arise between one State and a citizen or citizens of another, even though the dispute may be one over which this Court does have original jurisdiction.

. . . .

This Court is . . . structured to perform as an appellate tribunal, ill-equipped for the task of factfinding and so forced, in original cases, awkwardly to play the role of factfinder without actually presiding over the introduction of evidence. . . .

. . . .

. . . It can fairly be said that what is in dispute is not so much the law as the facts. And the factfinding process we are asked to undertake is, to say the least, formidable. We already know, just from what has been placed before us on this motion, that Lake Erie suffers from several sources of pollution other than mercury; that the scientific conclusion that mercury is a serious water pollutant is a novel one; that whether and to what extent the existence of mercury in natural waters can safely or reasonably be tolerated is a question for which there is presently no firm answer; and that virtually no published research is available describing how one might extract mercury that is in fact contaminating water. Indeed, Ohio is raising factual questions that are essentially ones of first impression to the scientists. The notion that appellate judges, even with the assistance of a most competent Special Master, might appropriately undertake at this time to unravel these complexities is, to say the least, unrealistic. . . .

. . . .

To sum up, this Court has found even the simplest sort of interstate pollution case an extremely awkward vehicle to manage. And this case is an extraordinarily complex one both because of the novel scientific issues of fact inherent in it and the multiplicity of governmental agencies already involved. Its successful resolution would require primarily skills of factfinding, conciliation, detailed coordination with—and perhaps not infrequent deference to—other adjudicatory bodies, and close supervision of the technical performance of local industries. We have no claim to such expertise or reason to believe that, were we to adjudicate this case, and others like it, we would not have to reduce drastically our attention to those controversies for which this Court is a proper and necessary forum. Such a serious intrusion on society's interest in our most deliberate and considerate performance of our paramount role as the supreme federal appellate court could, in our view, be justified only by the strictest necessity, an element which is evidently totally lacking in this instance.

. . . .

Ohio's motion for leave to file its complaint is denied without prejudice to its right to commence other appropriate judicial proceedings.

Justice Douglas dissenting.

The complaint in this case presents basically a classic type of case congenial to our original jurisdiction. It is to abate a public nuisance. Such was the claim of Georgia against a Tennessee company which was discharging noxious gas across the border into Georgia. *Georgia v. Tennessee Copper Co.*, 206 U.S. 230. The Court said:

It is a fair and reasonable demand on the part of a sovereign that the air over its territory should not be polluted on a great scale by sulphurous acid gas, that the forests on its mountains, be they better or worse, and whatever domestic destruction they have suffered, should not be further destroyed or threatened by the act of persons beyond its control, that the crops and orchards on its hills should not be endangered from the same source.

Dumping of sewage in an interstate stream, *Missouri v. Illinois*, 200 U.S. 496, or towing garbage to sea only to have the tides carry it to a State's beaches, *New Jersey v. New York City*, 283 U.S. 473, have presented analogous situations which the Court has entertained in suits invoking our original jurisdiction. The pollution of Lake Erie or its tributaries by the discharge of mercury or compounds thereof, if proved, certainly creates a public nuisance of a seriousness and magnitude which a State by our historic standards may prosecute or pursue as parens patriae [state as sovereign].

. . . .

Much is made of the burdens and perplexities of these original actions. . . .

. . . .

. . . But the practice has been to appoint a Special Master, which we certainly would do in this case. We could also appoint—or authorize the Special Master to retain—a panel of scientific advisers. The problems in this case are simple compared with those in the water cases discussed above. It is now known that metallic mercury deposited in water is often transformed into a dangerous chemical. This lawsuit would determine primarily the extent, if any, to which the defendants are contributing to that contamination at the present time. It would determine, secondarily, the remedies within reach—the importance of mercury in the particular manufacturing processes, the alternative processes available, the need for a remedy against a specified polluter as contrasted to a basin-wide regulation, and the like.

The problem, though clothed in chemical secrecies, can be exposed by the experts. It would indeed be one of the simplest problems yet posed in the category of cases under the head of our original jurisdiction.

The Department of Justice in a detailed brief tells us there are no barriers in federal law to our assumption of jurisdiction. I can think of no case of more transcending public importance than this one.

COMMENTS

1. Do you agree with Justice Douglas in *Wyandotte* that the Court's prior decision in *Tennessee Copper* should be controlling?

2. Is the Supreme Court showing undue deference to the political branches through its decision in *Wyandotte*? Might the decision give the wrong signal to those who are polluting?

3. Could the differences in results between these two cases be the result of political power wielded by a multinational corporation (Dow)?

15

JUSTICE BEYOND NATIONAL BORDERS

This final chapter examines the question of international justice by generally focusing on how courts in this country have treated the claims of foreigners. The most logical place to begin is with U.S. immigration and refugee policy, an absolutely fascinating area of study. The tie-in with notions of community are quite direct here. As I have written elsewhere:

> It has been in the context of alien admissions that the concept of an autonomous American political community has often been expressed, for better or for worse. Even if most matters of the day are not explicitly premised on this idea of community, the area of alien admissions seems driven by it. On a very basic level, the various grounds for exclusion and deportation are a clear indication that we only wish to admit certain kinds of people for membership in this community.[1]

Michael Walzer similarly suggests that a nation's alien admission policy essentially defines that political community: "Admission and exclusion are at the core of communal independence. They suggest the deepest meaning of self-determination. Without them, there could not be *communities of character,* historically stable, ongoing associations of men and women with some special commitment to one another and some special sense of their common life."[2]

We return again to the question raised in Chapter 11—namely, whether the notion of a community, in this instance the national community, entails control over who is or is not a member or who is or is not admitted to membership. It might come as no surprise to you that nations have long asserted absolute control over their own borders in terms of alien admissions. Such control has often been said to lie at the very root of sovereign independence.[3]

As in many other areas of international politics and relations, however, political philosophers have begun to question the moral basis for the assertion that nations have an absolute right to determine alien admission questions. One of the most radical arguments has been presented by Bruce Ackerman, who maintains that this long-established right really rests on the rather flimsy ground that those who arrive first can, if they so choose, exclude all of those who arrive later.[4] In order to show the absurdity of this reasoning, Ackerman uses an example of two spaceships that arrive at an unclaimed planet, one a split second ahead of the other. Ackerman claims that the early arrival does not give the inhabitants of that spaceship the right to own and control everything on this planet. He further maintains that the same thing can be said (and should be said) for a nation's immigration practices. In Ackerman's view, the *only* rationale that can be employed by a Liberal democracy in excluding foreigners is that the influx of these outsiders threatens the very existence of the Liberal democracy.

Another noteworthy position on this issue has been given by Michael Walzer. In Walzer's view, national communities ought to be free to admit those of its choosing because in doing so the community takes on its own form of identification. Walzer also recognizes, however, that all the claims of those seeking admission do not carry the same moral weight. "The victims of political and religious persecution . . . make the most forceful claim for admission. 'If you don't take me in,' they say, 'I shall be killed, persecuted, brutally oppressed by the rulers of my own country.' What can we reply?"[5]

Beyond this, Walzer also recognizes that of the 13 million or so refugees in the world, we might have a stronger duty to some than to others.[6] "Toward some refugees, we may well have obligations of the same sort that we have toward fellow nationals. This is obviously the case with regard to any group whom we have helped turn into refugees. The injury we have done makes for an affinity between us; thus Vietnamese refugees had, in a moral sense, been effectively Americanized even before they arrived on these shores."[7]

Historically, U.S. immigration policy has been premised on two related bases. One is that a nation has absolute control over its own borders. The second is that notwithstanding the image of the United States as the great "melting pot," the presence of certain foreigners is anathema to the American community.

The first case in this chapter, *Fong Yue Ting v. United States,* was an example of continuing efforts in the latter part of the nineteenth century to exclude Chinese laborers from our midst as well as remove those who were lawfully here. In order to fully grasp this, it is necessary to put U.S. immigration policy with regard to Chinese laborers into some kind of perspective. In 1868, the United States and China entered into the Burlingame Treaty, which provided for unlimited migration between the two nations. Some time after this—perhaps because the intercontinental railroad had been completed, largely with Chinese labor—the attitude and policies of the U.S. government began to change. Chinese laborers were viewed as threats to "American" workers, and a number of brutal race riots erupted on the West Coast. As a result, in 1882, Congress passed legislation that suspended the flow of Chinese nationals to this country.

What about those who had already been admitted to the United States? Both the 1882 act and the 1884 supplement to this legislation allowed Chinese laborers who had lawfully been admitted to leave and come back to the United States as long as they had obtained a certificate of residence before departing and had this proper documentation at the time of reentry. In 1887, Chae Chan Ping, a lawfully admitted Chinese laborer, departed from the United States. Before leaving he obtained the necessary certificate of residence. On October 1, 1888, Congress passed a law that provided, in pertinent part, "that from and after the passage of this Act, it shall be unlawful for any Chinese laborer who shall at any time heretofore have been, or who may now or hereafter be, a resident within the United States, and who shall have departed, or shall depart therefrom, and shall not have returned before the passage of this Act to return to, or remain in, the United States."

On October 8, 1888, Chae Chan Ping sailed into San Francisco harbor, where he was excluded based on the act of October 1, 1888. His challenge to this law was denied by the Supreme Court.[8] Ignoring the obvious inequities in such legislation, the Court instead focused on the apparent need for such restrictive measures.

> Notwithstanding the favorable provisions of the new articles of the Treaty of 1868, by which all the privileges, immunities, and exemptions were extended to subjects of China in the United States which were accorded to citizens or subjects of the most favored nation, they remained strangers in the land, residing apart by themselves, and adhering to the customs and usages of their own country. It seems impossible for them to assimilate with our people or to make any change in their habits or modes of living. As they grew in numbers each year the people of the coast saw, or believed they saw, in the facility of immigration, and in the crowded millions of China, where population presses upon the means of subsistence, great danger that at no distant day that portion of our country would be overrun by them unless prompt action was taken to restrict their immigration. The people there accordingly petitioned earnestly for protective legislation.

Congress did not stop its efforts here. The challenged statute in *Fong Yue Ting,* entitled "An Act to Prohibit the Coming of Chinese People into the United States," not only continued to extend the suspension of Chinese nationals into the United States but also provided that within one year after passage of the statute all lawfully admitted Chinese laborers were to apply to the collection of internal revenue for a certificate of residence. If found without this certificate, the alien was to be taken before any judge in the United States and deported unless she could prove that this fact was due to accident, sickness, or another unavoidable cause. If this was not proved, deportation was to be ordered. The petitioners in this case had applied for such a certificate, but they had been unable to produce corroboration of their lawful status by one white witness, as required by the act.

The Chinese were not the only ethnic group to be excluded. The "Gentleman's Agreement" of 1907 placed severe restrictions on Japanese immigration to the United States. In addition, the national origins quota system established in the 1920s was purposely designed to limit immigration from the "inferior" races of Southern and Eastern Europe.[9] This "racist" legislation, to use President Harry Truman's language, was essentially preserved in the McCarran-Walter Act of 1952 (over a presidential veto) and only abandoned in 1965. Since that time no nation or ethnic group is favored in our immigration system.

The reader will note that the cases in this chapter are generally marked by judicial deference to the political branches. Nowhere is this more evident than in the area of alien admissions.[10] The principal issue raised in the second case, *Shaughnessy v. Mezei*, was whether the Constitution protects those seeking admission to the United States, and the answer provided by the Court was that in many instances it does not.[11] Mezei was a resident alien who had lived a life of "unrelieved·insignificance"[12] for twenty-five years in Buffalo, New York. His troubles began when he attempted to visit his dying mother in Rumania. Denied entry there, Mezei went to Hungary, where he stayed for nineteen months because he had "difficulty in securing an exit permit." When he tried to return to the United States, the attorney general denied him reentry, claiming Mezei was a risk to the national security. Moreover, the attorney general took the position that he did not have to divulge the evidence against Mezei to him or to any court, including the highest court in the land. The Supreme Court agreed: "Whatever the procedure authorized by Congress is, it is due process as far as an alien denied entry is concerned."[13]

Two points need to be made here. The first is that although both *Fong Yue Ting* and *Mezei* are old cases, they are still "good law." The second point is that although we often speak in terms of the "American community," and Mezei certainly seemed to be a part of this community (he lived here for twenty-five years and raised a family) in terms of his efforts to *reenter* the United States his membership in this community meant absolutely nothing. Under U.S. law, an alien who seeks to reenter is treated like a first-time entrant.[14]

As mentioned earlier, the judicial deference exhibited in the *Fong Yue Ting* and in *Mezei* is the norm. The third principal case, *Haitian Refugee Center v. Civiletti*, was a rare exception in which a court in this country, in this case a federal district court, closely examined the alien admission policy of the political branches. In 1980, the United States greeted "with open arms"[15] more than 125,000 Cubans in what was called the Freedom

Flotillas. Seemingly as a result of this action, boatloads of Haitians began to arrive on the shores of Florida. U.S. refugee policy has long been dominated by ideological concerns,[16] and although the Cubans could be portrayed as fleeing from a totalitarian regime, the same claim could not be made for the Haitians. All that they could claim was that they were fleeing from the most oppressive regime in the Western Hemisphere. What ensued was the Haitian Program, which is described in Judge King's opinion as a systematic effort to remove all Haitians from the United States as quickly as possible, with little concern for whether these individuals would face persecution back in Haiti. This particular judicial opinion contained page after page of the testimony from the Haitian asylum seekers, only a small part of which can be reproduced here, but which should give a flavor for the kinds of claims made by many of these people.

Some judicial commentators have maintained that *Korematsu v. United States* represents a nadir in American civil liberties. The case was an unsuccessful challenge to the internment of Japanese-Americans during World War II. As a result, more than 112,000 individuals—70,000 of them U.S. citizens—were confined to a concentration camp for the duration of the war. Of course, it is quite easy to second-guess the motives and the actions of the executive branch here, but is there not some truth to Justice Jackson's assertion that what makes this decision that much worse is that the internment now has the imprimatur of the highest court in the land? Although the internment being challenged occurred almost fifty years ago, certain aspects of this policy are still with us today. For example, in 1988 Congress passed into law a bill that will pay $20,000 to the 60,000 interned Japanese-Americans who are still alive. Has justice finally been achieved?

In re: Yamashita raised the question of the responsibility for war crimes, only here the question was whether a military general—the commander of Japanese forces in the Philippine Islands during World War II—could be held responsible for the war crimes of soldiers under his authority. The converse situation is also interesting to explore: whether military orders from superiors should absolve rank-and-file soldiers from responsibility for the war crimes that they might commit.

The *Filartiga* case was a landmark decision in the area of international human rights law, although it did not open the floodgates to human rights cases in American courts as many thought it would immediately after it was decided. Although the political torture and murder charges of *Filartiga v. Pena-Irala* were, sadly enough, not novel in the world, what was unique about the case was that it was heard in a U.S. court, although both the plaintiff and the defendant were from Paraguay and the activities upon which the suit was based also occurred in Paraguay.

Contrast the decision by a U.S. court to hear this case with the dismissal of the suit in *Sanchez-Espinoza v. Reagan,* challenging U.S. activities in Nicaragua. The most interesting and noteworthy part of the suit is that brought by a group of Nicaraguan citizens against officials of the U.S.

government based on the U.S. support of the contras. *Sanchez-Espinoza* raised a very fascinating question: to what extent can citizens of one country sue officials in another country for harm caused by the latter in the pursuit of foreign policy goals?[17] The decision in *Sanchez-Espinoza* may or may not be satisfactory to you, but there is more than a little irony involved when a U.S. court will hear a suit involving alleged human rights violations committed by another country *(Filartiga)*, but it refuses to hear such a case when the U.S. government allegedly bears some responsibility for similar acts.

The final case in this book, *United States v. Stanley*, involved a suit by a former serviceman alleging that the U.S. government essentially used him as a human guinea pig. The case raised several important questions, most notably, should our military personnel have any constitutional rights? If so, should military personnel have the same rights as civilians?

NOTES

1. Mark Gibney, *Strangers or Friends: Principles for a New Alien Admission Policy* (Westport, Conn.: Greenwood Press, 1986), p. 55.

2. Michael Walzer, *Spheres of Justice: A Defense of Pluralism and Equality* (New York: Basic Books, 1983), p. 62.

3. Some nations have not only asserted absolute control over who is admitted, but also over who leaves. For an excellent discussion of this twentieth century phenomenon, see Alan Dowty, *Closed Borders: The Contemporary Assault on Freedom of Movement* (New Haven, Conn.: Yale University Press, 1987).

4. Bruce Ackerman, *Social Justice in the Liberal State* (New Haven, Conn.: Yale University Press, 1980).

5. Walzer, *Spheres of Justice*, p. 49.

6. I have also addressed this issue in some great detail. In capsule I maintain that based on moral considerations, a country such as the United States should admit far larger numbers of refugees than those admitted for family reunification purposes or to meet certain national labor goals. At the present time the United States does the converse. That is, it admits far larger numbers of "normal flow" immigrants than refugees. In addition, among the refugee populations of the world, I maintain, like Walzer, that our strongest moral obligations go to those we have helped turn into refugees—Salvadorans, for example—and that our obligations here are very far ranging (and certainly more far ranging than under Walzer's scheme). Gibney, *Strangers or Friends*.

7. Walzer, *Spheres of Justice*, p. 49.

8. *Chae Chan Ping v. United States* [The Chinese Exclusion Case] 130 U.S. 581 (1889).

9. What makes this policy even more chilling is that it was purportedly based on scientific evidence. Jews were described as "the polar opposite of our pioneer breed. Undersized and weak muscled, they shun bodily activity and are exceedingly sensitive to pain." Italians possessed "a distressing frequency of low foreheads, open mouths, weak chins, poor features, skewed faces, small or knobby crania and backless heads." Quoted from T. Alexander Aleinikoff and David Martin, *Immigration Process and Policy* (St. Paul: West Publishing, 1985), p. 44.

10. For an extended discussion of this point, see Mark Gibney, "The role of the Judiciary in Alien Admissions," *Boston College International and Comparative Law Review* 8:341–76 (1985).

11. The Supreme Court distinguishes between exclusion and deportation hearings. The former applies to the initial entrant or the resident alien who leaves the United States and then attempts to come back. Deportation hearings are granted to individuals who are in the United States. The Constitution has been interpreted to protect those in deportation hearings but not those in exclusionary hearings. (But these constitutional protections have, at times, been illusory. For example, in *Yamataya v. Fisher*, 189 U.S. 86 [1903], the Supreme Court held that "due process" required a hearing for one in a deportation hearing, although the Court had no objection to the fact that the hearing in this case was conducted in English, a language that was completely foreign to the deportee). If the exclusion-deportation distinction seems to make sense, consider this description given by Aleinikoff and Martin:

> You should now be quite familiar with the curious results occasioned by a constitutional test that turns on the location of the alien. For example, an alien who arrives at the border with an immigrant visa and a job or family awaiting him in the United States is essentially unprotected by the Constitution's due process clause. However, an alien who is apprehended a few hours after making a surreptitious entry is afforded, as a matter of constitutional right, a hearing, an opportunity to present evidence and cross-examine witnesses, an unbiased decision-maker and, sometimes, counsel.

Aleinikoff and Martin, *Immigration Process and Policy*, p. 453.

12. This is the description provided in Justice Jackson's powerful dissent in this case.

13. Mezei's situation gets even more complicated. After he was denied reentry into the United States, he applied for admission to other countries, but his attempts were systematically denied. As a result, Ignatz Mezei spent nearly four years in detention on Ellis Island before his relief by special clemency.

14. Some of the harshness of the "reentry" doctrine is apparently being removed by the Supreme Court, although the Court is still unwilling to overturn *Mezei*. In *Landon v. Plasencia*, 459 U.S. 21 (1982), a resident alien of the United States since 1970 was arrested in 1975 for smuggling illegal aliens into this country. The evidence showed that Plasencia's stay in Mexico had been "brief." She claimed that she should be afforded a deportation hearing rather than an exclusionary hearing, but the Court disagreed. What is significant about the decision, however, is that the Supreme Court held that the reentering resident alien is not without any constitutional rights: "Once an alien gains admission to our country and begins to develop the ties that go with permanent residence, his constitutional status changes accordingly."

15. I put this phrase in quotes because although President Carter initially made this statement, he later had to retract it, as well as U.S. policy, when there appeared to be no end in sight to Cuban migration and when the reaction of the American public was decidedly cooler than he had anticipated.

16. For example, until 1980 the definition of "refugee" in U.S. law included only those who were from Communist countries or those from the Middle East. Moreover, the vast number of those admitted as refugees, both before and after the 1980 Refugee Act, have been from Communist countries. Consider 1985 as an

example of this. That year the United States admitted 2,234 refugees from Afghanistan, 11,380 from Cambodia, 984 from Czechoslovakia, 534 from Hungary, 4,305 from Laos, 3,001 from Poland, 4,650 from Rumania, 23,799 from Vietnam, and 639 from the Soviet Union. Contrast these numbers with the following admissions from non-Communist countries: 10 refugees from the Philippines, 31 from South Africa, 0 from South Korea, 0 from Haiti, 0 from Guatemala, and 0 from El Salvador. See, generally, Mark Gibney, "A 'Well-Founded Fear' of Persecution," *Human Rights Quarterly* 10:109–21 (1988).

17. For an extended discussion of this case, see Mark Gibney, "Human Rights and Human Consequences: A Critical Examination of *Sanchez-Espinoza*," *Loyola of Los Angeles International and Comparative Law Review* 10:299–320 (1988).

Fong Yue Ting v. United States, 149 U.S. 698 (1893)

Justice Gray delivered the opinion of the Court.

The general principles of public law which lie at the foundation of these cases are clearly established by previous judgments of this court, and by the authorities therein referred to.

In the recent case of *Ekiu v. United States*, 142 U.S. 651, 659 (1892) the court, in sustaining the action of the executive department, putting in force an Act of Congress for the exclusion of aliens, said: "It is an accepted maxim of international law, that every sovereign nation has the power, as inherent in sovereignty, and essential to self-preservation, to forbid the entrance of foreigners within its dominions, or to admit them only in such cases and upon such conditions as it may see fit to prescribe. In the United States, this power is vested in the national government, to which the Constitution has committed the entire control of international relations, in peace as well as in war. It belongs to the political department of the government, and may be exercised either through treaties made by the President and Senate, or through statutes enacted by Congress."

. . . .

The right of a nation to expel or deport foreigners, who have not been naturalized or taken any steps towards becoming citizens of the country, rests upon the same grounds, and is as absolute and unqualified as the right to prohibit and prevent their entrance into the country.

Chinese laborers . . . like all other aliens residing in the United States for a shorter or longer time, are entitled, so long as they are permitted by the government of the United States to remain in the Country, to the safeguards of the Constitution, and to the protection of the laws, in regard to their rights of person and of property, and to their civil and criminal responsibility. But they continue to be aliens, having taken no steps towards becoming citizens, and incapable of becoming such under the naturalization laws; and therefore remain subject to the power of Congress to expel them, or to order them to be removed and deported from the country, whenever in its judgment their removal is necessary or expedient for the public interest.

The question whether, and upon what conditions, these aliens shall be permitted to remain within the United States being one to be determined by the political departments of the government, the judicial department cannot properly express an opinion upon the wisdom, the policy or the justice of the measure enacted by Congress in the exercise of the powers confided to it by the Constitution over this subject.

Justice Brewer dissenting.

. . . .

. . . We must take judicial notice of that which is disclosed by the census, and which is also a matter of common knowledge. There are 100,000 and more of these persons [Chinese] living in this country, making their homes here, and striving by their labor to earn a livelihood. They are not travelers, but resident aliens.

But, further, this section six recognizes the fact of a lawful residence, and only applies to those who have such; for the parties named in the section, and to be reached by its provisions are "Chinese laborers within the limits of the United States at the time of the passage of this Act, and who are entitled to remain in the United States." These appellants, therefore, are lawfully within the United States, and here as residents, and not as travelers. They have lived in this country, respectively, since 1879, 1877, and 1874—almost as long a time as some of those who were members of the Congress that passed this Act of punishment and expulsion.

. . . .

Whatever rights a resident alien might have in any other nation, here he is within the express protection of the Constitution especially in respect to those guaranties which are declared in the original amendments. It has been repeated so often as to become axiomatic, that this government is one of enumerated and delegated powers, and, as declared in Article 10 of the amendments, "The powers not delegated to the United States by the Constitution, nor prohibited by it to the states, are re-

served to the states respectively, or to the people."

It is said that the power here asserted is inherent in sovereignty. This doctrine of powers inherent in sovereignty is one both indefinite and dangerous. Where are the limits to such powers to be found, and by whom are they to be pronounced? . . . The governments of other nations have elastic powers—ours is fixed and bounded by a written constitution. The expulsion of a race may be within the inherent powers of a despotism. History, before the adoption of this Constitution, was not destitute of examples of the exercise of such a power; and its framers were familiar with history, and wisely, as it seems to me, they gave to this government no general power to banish. Banishment may be resorted to as punishment for crime; but among the powers reserved to the people and not delegated to the government is that of determining whether whole classes in our midst shall, for no crime but that of their race and birthplace, be driven from our territory.

Whatever may be true as to exclusion . . . I deny that there is any arbitrary and unrestrained power to banish residents, even resident aliens. What, it may be asked, is the reason for any difference? The answer is obvious. The Constitution has no extraterritorial effect, and those who have not come lawfully within our territory cannot claim any protection from its provisions. And it may be that the national government, having full control of all matters relating to other nations, has the power to build, as it were, a Chinese wall around our borders and absolutely forbid aliens to enter. But the Constitution has potency everywhere within the limits of our territory, and the powers which the national government may exercise within such limits are those, and only those, given to it by that instrument. . . .

. . . .

It is true this statute is directed only against the obnoxious Chinese; but if the power exists, who shall say it will not be exercised tomorrow against other classes and other people? If the guaranties of these amendments can be thus ignored, in order to get rid of this distasteful class, what security have others that a like disregard of its provisions may not be resorted to? . . .

In view of this enactment of the highest legislative body of the foremost Christian nation, may not the thoughtful Chinese disciple of Confucius fairly ask. Why do they send missionaries here?

Justice Field dissenting.

I utterly dissent from and reject the doctrine expressed in the opinion of the majority, that "Congress, under the power to exclude or expel aliens, might have directed any Chinese laborer found in the United States without a certificate of residence to be removed out of the country by executive officers, without judicial trial or examination, just as it might have authorized such officers absolutely to prevent his entrance into the country." An arrest in that way for that purpose would not be a reasonable seizure of the person within the meaning of the Fourth Articles of the Amendments to the Constitution. It would be brutal and oppressive. The existence of the power thus stated is only consistent with the admission that the government is one of unlimited and despotic power so far as aliens domiciled in the country are concerned. According to its theory, Congress might have ordered executive officers to take the Chinese laborers to the ocean and put them into a boat and set them adrift, or to take them to the borders of Mexico and turn them loose there, and in both cases without any means of support; indeed, it might have sanctioned towards these laborers the most shocking brutality conceivable. I utterly repudiate all such notions, and reply that brutality, inhumanity, and cruelty cannot be made elements in any procedure for the enforcement of the laws of the United States.

. . . .

It will be seen by its provisions that the sixth section recognizes the right of certain Chinese laborers to remain in the United States, but to render null that right it declares that if within one year after the passage of the Act any Chinese laborer shall have neglected, failed, or refused to comply with the provisions of the act to obtain a certificate of residence, or shall be found within the jurisdiction of the United States without a certificate of residence, he shall be deemed and adjudged to be unlawfully within the United States, and may be arrested by any United States customs official, collector of internal revenue or his deputies, United States marshal or his deputies, and taken before a United States judge, whose duty it shall be to order that he be deported from the United States, unless he shall establish clearly to the satisfaction of the judge that by reason of accident, sickness, or other unavoidable cause he has been unable to secure his certificate, and to the satisfaction of the judge by at least one credible white witness that he was a resident of the United States at the time of the passage of the Act. His deportation is thus imposed for neglect to obtain a certificate of residence, from which he can only escape by showing his inability to secure it from one of the causes named. That is the punishment for his neglect, and that being of an infamous character can only be imposed after indictment, trial and conviction. If applied to a citizen, none of the justices of this court would hesitate a moment to pronounce it illegal. Had the punishment been a fine, or anything else than of an infamous character, it might have been imposed without indictment; but not so now, unless we hold that a foreigner from a country at peace with us, though domiciled by the consent of our government, is withdrawn from all the guaranties of due process of law prescribed by the Constitution, when charged with an offense to which the grave punishment designated is affixed.

The punishment is beyond all reason in its severity. It is out of all proportion to the alleged offense. It is cruel and unusual. As to its cruelty, nothing can exceed a forcile deportation from a country of one's residence, and the breaking up of all the relation of friendship, family and business there contracted. . . .

. . . .

I will not pursue the subject further. The decision of the court and the sanction it would give to legislation depriving resident aliens of the guaranties of the Constitution fills me with apprehensions. Those guarantees are of priceless value to every one resident in the country, whether citizen or alien. I cannot but regard the decision as a blow against constitutional liberty, when it declares that Congress has the right to disregard the guaranties of the Constitution intended for the protection of all men, domiciled in the country with the consent of the government, in their rights of person and property. How far will its legislation go? The unnaturalized resident feels it today, but if Congress can disregard the guaranties with respect to any one domiciled in the country with its consent, it may disregard the guaranties with respect to naturalized citizens. What assurance have we that it may not declare that naturalized citizens of a particular country cannot remain in the United States after a certain day, unless they have in their possession a certificate that they are of good moral character and attached to the principles of our Constitution, which certificate they must obtain from a collector of internal revenue upon the testimony of at least one competent witness of a class or nationality to be designated by the government?

What answer could the naturalized citizens in that case make to his arrest for deportation, which cannot be urged in behalf of the Chinese laborers of today.

I am of the opinion that the orders of the court below should be reversed, and the petitioners should be discharged.

Shaughnessy v. Mezei, 345 U.S. 206 (1953)

Justice Clark delivered the opinion of the Court.

This case concerns an alien immigrant permanently excluded from the United States on security grounds but stranded in his temporary haven on Ellis Island because other countries will not take him back. The issue is whether the Attorney General's continued exclusion of respondent without a hearing amounts to an unlawful detention, so that courts may admit him temporarily to the United States on bond until arrangements are made for his departure abroad. . . .

Respondent's present dilemma springs from these circumstances: Though, as the District Court observed, "[there] is a certain vagueness about [his] history," respondent seemingly was born in Gibraltar of Hungarian or Rumanian parents and lived in the United States from 1923 to 1948. In May of that year he sailed for Europe, apparently to visit his dying mother in Rumania. Denied entry there, he remained in Hungary for some 19 months, due to "difficulty in securing an exit permit." Finally, armed with a quota immigration visa issued by the American Consul in Budapest, he proceeded to France and boarded the *Ile de France* in Le Havre bound for New York. Upon arrival on February 9, 1950, he was temporarily excluded from the United States by an immigration inspector acting pursuant to the Passport Act as amended and regulations thereunder. Pending disposition of his case he was received at Ellis Island. After reviewing the evidence, the Attorney General on May 10, 1950, ordered the temporary exclusion to be made permanent without a hearing before a board of special inquiry, on the "basis of information of a confidential nature, the disclosure of which would be prejudicial to the public interest." That determination rested on a finding that respondent's entry would be prejudicial to the public interest for security reasons. But thus far all attempts to effect respondent's departure have failed: Twice he shipped out to return whence he came; France and Great Britain refused him permission to land. The State Department has unsuccessfully negotiated with Hungary for his readmission. Respondent personally applied for entry to about a dozen Latin-American countries but all turned him down. So in June 1951 respondent advised the Immigration and Naturalization Service that he would exert no further efforts to depart. In short, respondent sat on Ellis Island because this country shut him out and others were unwilling to take him in.

. . . .

Courts have long recognized the power to expel or exclude aliens as a fundamental sovereign attribute exercised by the Government's political departments largely immune from judicial control. *Fong Yue Ting v. United States*, 149 U.S. 698 (1893). In the exercise of these powers, Congress expressly authorized the President to impose additional restrictions on aliens entering or leaving the United States during periods of international tension and strife. . . . Under it, the Attorney General, acting for the President, may shut out aliens whose "entry would be prejudicial to the interests of the United States." And he may exclude without a hearing when the exclusion is based on confidential information the disclosure of which may be prejudicial to the public interest. The Attorney General in

this case proceeded in accord with these provisions; he made the necessary determinations and barred the alien from entering the United States.

It is true that aliens who have once passed through our gates, even illegally, may be expelled only after proceedings conforming to traditional standards of fairness encompassed in due process of law. But an alien on the threshold of initial entry stands on a different footing: Whatever the procedure authorized by Congress is, it is due process as far as an alien denied entry is concerned. And because the action of the executive officer under such authority is final and conclusive, the Attorney General cannot be compelled to disclose the evidence underlying his determinations in an exclusion case; it is not within the province of any court, unless expressly authorized by law, to review the determination of the political branch of the Government. In a case such as this, courts cannot retry the determination of the Attorney General.

Neither respondent's harborage on Ellis Island nor his prior residence here transforms this into something other than an exclusion proceeding. . . . For purposes of the immigration laws, moreover, the legal incidents of an alien's entry remain unaltered whether he has been here once before or not. He is an entering alien just the same, and may be excluded if unqualified for admission under existing immigration laws. . . .

Justice Jackson, whom Justice Frankfurter joins, dissenting.

What is our case? In contemplation of law, I agree, it is that of an alien who asks admission to the country. Concretely, however, it is that of a lawful and law-abiding inhabitant of our country for a quarter of a century, long ago admitted for permanent residence, who seeks to return home. After a foreign visit to his aged and ailing mother that was prolonged by disturbed conditions of Eastern Europe, he obtained a visa for admission issued by our consul and returned to New York. There the Attorney General refused to honor his documents and turned him back as a menace to this Nation's security. This man, who seems to have led a life of unrelieved insignificance, must have been astonished to find himself suddenly putting the Government of the United States in such fear that it was afraid to tell him why it was afraid of him. He was shipped and reshipped to France, which twice refused him landing. Great Britain declined, and no other European country has been found willing to open its doors to him. Twelve countries of the American Hemisphere refused his applications. Since we proclaimed him a Samson who might pull down the pillars of our temple, we should not be surprised if peoples less prosperous, less strongly established and less stable feared to take him off our timorous hands. With something of a record as an unwanted man, neither his efforts nor those of the United States Government any longer promise to find him an abiding place. For nearly two years he was held in custody of the immigration authorities of the United States at Ellis Island, and if the Government has its way he seems likely to be detained indefinitely, perhaps for life, for a cause known only to the Attorney General.

Is respondent deprived of liberty? The Government answers that he was "transferred to Ellis Island on August 1, 1950, for safekeeping," and "is not being detained in the usual sense but is in custody solely to prevent him from gaining entry to the United States in violation of law. He is free to depart from the United States to any country of his own choice." Government counsel ingeniously argued that Ellis Island is his "refuge" whence he is free to take leave in any direction except west. That might mean freedom, if only he were an amphibian! Realistically, this man is incarcerated by a combination of forces which keep him as effectually as a prison, the dominant and proximate of these forces being the United States im-

migration authority. It overworks legal fiction to say that one is free in law when by the commonest of common sense he is bound. Despite the impeccable legal logic of the Government's argument on this point, it leads to an artificial and unreal conclusion. We must regard this alien as deprived of liberty, and the question is whether the deprivation is a denial of due process of law.

The Government on this point argues that "no alien has any constitutional right to entry into the United States"; that "the alien has only such rights as Congress sees fit to grant in exclusion proceedings." . . .

. . . .

Because the respondent has no right of entry, does it follow that he has no rights at all? Does the power to exclude mean that exclusion may be continued or effectuated by any means which happen to seem appropriate to the authorities? It would effectuate his exclusion to eject him bodily into the sea or to set him adrift in a rowboat. Would not such measures be condemned judicially as a deprivation of life without due process of law? Suppose the authorities decide to disable an alien from entry by confiscating his valuables and money. Would we not hold this a taking of property without due process of law? Here we have a case that lies between the taking of life and the taking of property; it is the taking of liberty. It seems to me that this, occurring within the United States or its territorial waters, may be done only by proceedings which meet the test of due process of law.

Exclusion of an alien without judicial hearing, of course, does not deny due process when it can be accomplished merely by turning him back on land or returning him by sea. But when indefinite confinement becomes the means of enforcing exclusion, it seems to me that due process requires that the alien be informed of its grounds and have a fair chance to overcome them. This is the more due him when he is entrapped into leaving the other shore by reliance on a visa which the Attorney General refuses to honor.

It is evident that confinement of respondent no longer can be justified as a step in the process of turning him back to the country whence he came. Confinement is no longer ancillary to exclusion; it can now be justified only as the alternative to normal exclusion. It is an end, in itself.

The Communist conspiratorial technique of infiltration poses a problem which sorely tempts the Government to resort to confinement of suspects on secret information secretly judged. I have not been one to discount the Communist evil. But my apprehensions about the security of our form of government are about equally aroused by those who refuse to recognize the dangers of Communism and those who will not see danger in anything else.

Congress has ample power to determine whom we will admit to our shores and by what means it will effectuate its exclusion policy. The only limitation is that it may not do so by authorizing United States officers to take without due process of law the life, the liberty or the property of an alien who has come within our jurisdiction; and that means he must meet a fair hearing with fair notice of the charges.

It is inconceivable to me that this measure of simple justice and fair dealing would menace the security of this country. No one can make me believe that we are that far gone.

COMMENT

1. *Fong* and *Mezei* are examples of the kind of judicial deference to the political branches in the immigration area that essentially continues to the present day. Is there any role that courts can play in the area of "foreign affairs" or "international relations"? What causes this deference?

Haitian Refugee Center v. Civiletti, 503 F. Supp. 442 (1980)

Judge King.

This case involves thousands of black Haitian nationals, the brutality of their government, and the prejudice of ours. Perhaps thirty thousand Haitians have flocked to the shores of South Florida over the past twenty years, fleeing the most repressive government in the Americas. From among that group come the plaintiffs: five thousand persons who have sought political asylum in the United States. They claim that if they are returned to Haiti they will face persecution, imprisonment and death. All of their asylum claims were denied by the Immigration and Naturalization Service.

. . . .

The Haitians allege that the actions of INS constitute impermissible discrimination on the basis of national origin. They have proven their claim. This court cannot close its eyes, however, to a possible underlying reason why these plaintiffs have been subjected to intentional "national origin" discrimination. The plaintiffs are part of the first substantial flight of black refugees from a repressive regime to this country. All of the plaintiffs are black. In contrast, for example, only a relatively small percent of the Cuban refugees who have fled to this country are black. Prior to the most recent Cuban exodus, all of the Cubans who sought political asylum in individual hearings were granted asylum routinely. None of the over 4,000 Haitians processed during the INS "program" at issue in this lawsuit were granted asylum. No greater disparity can be imagined.

. . . .

In reaching its conclusion the court has listened to a wealth of in-court testimony, examined numerous depositions, and read hundreds of documents submitted by the parties. Much of the evidence is both shocking and brutal, populated by the ghosts of individual Haitians—including those who have been returned from the United States—who have been beaten, tortured and left to die in Haitian prisons. Much of the evidence is not brutal but simply callous—evidence that INS officials decided to ship all Haitians back to Haiti simply because their continued presence in the United States had become a problem. The manner in which INS treated the more than 4,000 Haitian plaintiffs violated the Constitution, the immigration statutes, international agreements, INS regulations and INS operating procedures. It must stop.

FINDINGS OF FACT: CONDITIONS IN HAITI

No asylum claim can be examined without an understanding of the conditions in the applicant's homeland. Similarly, the uniform rejection of the claims of the present 5,000 member class cannot be reviewed, regardless how lenient the standard of review, without inquiring into the conditions in Haiti. The evidence on that topic has been stark, brutal and bloody.

The central question can be rather specifically drawn: How would these plaintiffs be treated if returned to Haiti? But that question cannot be fully answered without a more searching inquiry. The treatment of returnees in Haiti is part of a systematic and pervasive oppression of political opposition which uses prisons as its torture chambers and "Tontons Macoutes" as its enforcers. The extent of that political oppression must be established in order to review the INS's uniform conclusion that the plaintiffs are economic refugees.

Haiti has been accurately described as "the most oppressive regime in the hemisphere." (Quoting Jerry DeSantillana, State Department Country Officer for Haiti); accord (International Commission of Jurists, *The Review* 3, 4 (Dec. 1977) ("the most ruthless and oppressive regime in the world").

(My husband) was working at Customs in Port-au-Prince. . . . He kept telling me that they were talking to him about politics, that he should join the Ton Tons Macoutes. . . . In '75 at midnight he left work. . . . Night had come and it was time to go to bed. They came and got him, the Ton Tons Macoutes came and took him away. . . . They left with him. They took him on Wednesday night. Thursday at 1 o'clock I went to Fort Dimanche. I went to the police station. . . . They told me they knew of no such person.

I knew that if he was not released, he would be killed. So I didn't go anymore. I never saw him. . . . My son (was) in school. He was finishing up. He was complaining while he was in school. He kept complaining that if his father was still alive, his mother would not suffer so much and go through such misery. . . . He was complaining that his father was there, and that the Ton Tons Macoutes took his father away.

They took him. His schoolmates came and told me that they had picked him up at school. I started screaming, saying that the child's father had died. They took my child away from me. I have no more hope.

The next day three Macoutes came and arrested me. They started knocking on the door. . . . They didn't allow me to speak. They took me and stuck me in a dungeon. . . . They took me before the Chief of the Ton Tons Macoutes. . . . When I got there, he asked me what was wrong with me, what was my problem that I was screaming at the top of my lungs like that. . . . He said okay, and then he would send me home if I would shut my mouth and never wanted to hear anything out of me. . . . Well, if I did not shut my mouth, I would have gone the same way my child went.

I could not go selling anymore because I was scared. I did not have a husband or child. I was scared. I stayed there and spent a month.

After a month, I saw I could no longer live.

Augusta Germain, Tr. at 1219–27.

Substantial evidence was presented at trial concerning treatment of returnees in Haiti. A largely uncontradicted pattern emerged. Upon return to Haiti, persons whom the Haitian government views as political opponents will be mistreated. Persons who have fled Haiti and sought asylum elsewhere are seen as opponents of the Duvalier regime. They are taken to Cassernes Dessalines for questioning. Many are further imprisoned and persecuted. Of those allowed to return home, many more are later imprisoned or persecuted.

One piece of evidence stands in stark contrast to this pattern. The State Department sent a Study Team to Haiti to interview returnees in 1979. The team concluded there was no pattern of abuse. This Court, however, has concluded that the Study Team report is unworthy of belief.

[The court rejected the findings of the State Department Study Team which attempted to investigate whether Haitians returned to the United States faced persecution or not. Judge King held that the low sample size—9.3%—was too small. In addition, no attempt was made to locate returnees in prison. The sample was also non-selective because it was dependent upon those who were allegedly persecuted coming forward with those allegations, although there were no guarantees of the safety of those who would testify.]

HAITIAN PRISONS: PERSECUTION EXEMPLIFIED

To be marked as a political opponent in Haiti is to be sentenced, in most cases, to prison. In each of the stories told to this Court, the conclusion was death, flight, or imprisonment. The full consequences of opposition, therefore, are only revealed by examining the treatment of prisoners in Haitian jails. These are the conditions to which returnees are exposed when deemed part of the political opposition.

. . . .

The conditions in Haitian jails are inhuman. There is almost never sufficient room for the persons in a cell. Single persons are placed in individual cells so small as two feet by three feet, and ones in which they can neither sit nor lie down. Larger cells are overcrowded. Marc Romulus was held in a ten foot by ten foot cell containing between 22 and 33 persons, so crowded that they had to sleep in rotation. One witness lived for two years in a twelve foot by twelve foot cell with as many as 40 persons. The testimony of all the witnesses was substantially the same. Aside from the absence of space, the cells also lacked sanitary facilities. Prisoners were provided with metal cans for toilets, or else they were provided with nothing at all. The food was inadequate; most of the witnesses described having one meal a day of watered-down corn meal (practically no food at Fort Dimanche) (two meals: biscuit in the morning and corn meal in the afternoon) (watery corn meal once a day). One former prisoner testified that when he was given water it "had little things in it, little toads." The prisoners were kept in the nude. When asked if he ever had any visitors while at Fort Dimanche, Jocelyn Marcelus states, "For me, it was rats, all kinds of insects, mice, roaches, vermin, all kinds of bugs." . . . The effect, and perhaps intent, of this treatment is undeniable.

. . . .

The mistreatment of prisoners includes torture and beatings. Four witnesses testified at trial concerning the beatings they received, three plaintiffs included stories of beatings in the sworn statements they gave INS, and several witnesses reported observing beatings or their effects, or hearing reports of beatings. The details of a number of the cruelties were described to the Court. Merilien Mezius told how he was beaten twice a day during a five-day stay at Fort Dimanche. Some aspect of this beating so damaged Solives Romet that to this day he is able to speak with only the greatest effort, and then with a pronounced stutter. . . .

CONCLUSION

The case is now well documented that the Haitians in this class deserved something more than they received from INS. Clearly their claims were more political than recognized, and the uniform rejection of their claims demonstrates a profound ignorance, if not an international disregard, of the conditions in Haiti. It is beyond dispute that some Haitians will be subjected to the brutal treatment and bloody prisons of Francois Duvalier upon their deportation. Until INS can definitely state which Haitians will be so treated and which will not, the brutality and bloodletting is its responsibility.

FINDINGS OF FACT: INS TREATMENT OF HAITIAN ASYLUM CLAIMS

The INS established a Haitian Program during the Spring and Summer of 1978 for the purpose of disposing of a backlog of asylum claims filed by Haitian immigrants. The existence of the program and its impact are uncontroverted. All of the asylum claims were denied.

. . . .

. . . The Haitian asylum claims were prejudged as lacking any merit. Accordingly, they were reviewed with dispatch. An expedited process was set up for the sole purpose of expediting review of Haitian asylum applications, and expelling Haitians from the United States. By its very nature and intent, that process was prejudicial and discriminatory. In its particulars, the process violated the Haitians' due process rights.

[Among the due process violations catalogued by Judge King were the following:

1. The failure to suspend deportation proceedings when an asylum claim was filed by a Haitian, contrary to INS Operational Instructions and the treatment afforded all other nationalities;

2. Denial of a Haitian applicant's right to silence, as the INS inferred the admission of deportability from such silence;

3. The establishment of a 10 day limit for the filing of asylum applications, contrary to INS practice and the treatment afforded other nationalities;

4. The mass scheduling of asylum claims so that Immigration Judges were hearing upwards of 80 cases a day rather than 1–10. In addition, although there were only a handful of attorneys to represent thousands of Haitians, no special allowances were made for this fact.]

CONCLUSION

Those Haitians who came to the United States seeking freedom and justice did not find it. Instead, they were confronted with an Immigration and Naturalization Service determined to deport them. The decision was made among INS officials to expel Haitians, despite whatever claims to asylum individual Haitians might have. A Program was set up to accomplish this goal. The Program resulted in wholesale violations of due process, and only Haitians were affected.

This Program, in its planning and executing, is offensive to every notion of constitutional due process and equal protection. The Haitians whose claims for asylum were rejected during the Program shall not be deported until they are given a fair chance to present their claims for political asylum.

COMMENT

1. One of the hallmarks of immigration (and refugee) cases is judicial deference. We do not find such deference in Judge King's opinion. Has he gone too far in his findings of persecution in Haiti? Are such findings better left to the political branches (such as the State Department)? Apparently the Court of Appeals thought so, criticizing Judge King's findings of fact this way:

The evidence concerning conditions in Haiti was relevant and admissible only for a limited purpose of showing the scope of evidence available to the plaintiffs to support their asylum claims and thus of corroborating the plaintiff's due process contention that the accelerated program [for asylum hearings] made it impossible for them to submit and substantiate their applications. We agree with the government, however, that the district judge exceeded his authority to the extent he implied by his findings a conclusion that the plaintiff's claims of fear of persecution merited the granting of asylum.

Haitian Refugee Center v. Smith, 676 F. 2d 1023, 1042 (5th Cir. 1982).

Korematsu v. United States, 323 U.S. 214 (1944)

Justice Black delivered the opinion of the Court.

The petitioner, an American citizen of Japanese descent, was convicted in a federal district court for remaining in San Leandro, California, a "Military Area," contrary to Civilian Exclusion Order No. 34 of the Commanding General of the Western Command, U.S. Army, which directed that after May 9, 1942, all persons of Japanese ancestry should be excluded from that area. . . .

It should be noted, to begin with, that all legal restrictions which curtail the civil rights of a single racial group are immediately suspect. That is not to say that all such restrictions are unconstitutional. It is to say that courts must subject them to the most rigid scrutiny. Pressing public necessity may sometimes justify the existence of such restrictions; racial antagonism never can.

. . . .

Exclusion Order No. 34, which the petitioner knowingly and admittedly violated, was one of a number of military orders and proclamations, all of which were substantially based upon Executive Order No. 9066, 7 Fed. Reg. 1407. That order, issued after we were at war with Japan, declared that "the successful prosecution of the war requires every possible protection against

espionage and against sabotage to national-defense material, national-defense premises, and national-defense utilities."

. . . .

. . . [W]e cannot reject as unfounded the judgment of the military authorities and of Congress that there were disloyal members of that population, whose number and strength could not be precisely and quickly ascertained. We cannot say that the war-making branches of the Government did not have ground for believing that in a critical hour such persons could not readily be isolated and separately dealt with, and constituted a menace to the national defense and safety, which demanded that prompt and adequate measures be taken to guard against it.

. . . [E]xclusion of those of Japanese origin was deemed necessary because of the presence of an unascertained number of disloyal members of the group, most of whom we have no doubt were loyal to this country. . . . That there were members of the group who retained loyalties to Japan has been confirmed by investigations made subsequent to the exclusion. Approximately five thousand American citizens of Japanese ancestry refused to swear unqualified allegiance to the United States and to renounce allegiance to the Japanese Emperor, and several thousand evacuees requested repatriation to Japan.

We uphold the exclusion order as of the time it was made and when the petitioner violated it. In doing so, we are not unmindful of the hardships imposed by it upon a large group of American citizens. But hardships are part of war, and war is an aggregation of hardships. All citizens alike, both in and out of uniform, feel the impact of war in greater or lesser measure. Citizenship has its responsibilities as well as its privileges, and in time of war the burden is always heavier. Compulsory exclusion of large groups of citizens from their homes, except under circumstances of direst emergency and peril, is inconsistent with our basic governmental institutions. But when under conditions of modern warfare our shores are threatened by hostile forces, the power to protect must be commensurate with the threatened danger.

. . . .

It is said that we are dealing here with the case of imprisonment of a citizen in a concentration camp solely because of his ancestry, without evidence or inquiry concerning his loyalty and good disposition towards the United States. Our task would be simple, our duty clear, were this a case involving the imprisonment of a loyal citizen in a concentration camp because of racial prejudice. Regardless of the true nature of the assembly and relocation centers—and we deem it unjustifiable to call them concentration camps with all the ugly connotations that term implies—we are dealing specifically with nothing but an exclusion order. To cast this case into outlines of racial prejudice, without reference to the real military dangers which were presented, merely confuses the issue. Korematsu was not excluded from the Military Area because of hostility to him or his race. He was excluded because we were at war with the Japanese Empire, because the properly constituted military authorities feared an invasion of our West Coast and felt constrained to take proper security measures, because they decided that the

military urgency of the situation demanded that all citizens of Japanese ancestry be segregated from the West Coast temporarily, and finally, because Congress, reposing its confidence in this time of war in our military leaders—as inevitably it must—determined that they should have the power to do just this. There was evidence of disloyalty on the part of some, the military authorities considered that the need for action was great, and time was short. We cannot—by availing ourselves of the calm perspective of hindsight—now say that at that time these actions were unjustified.

Justice Murphy dissenting.

This exclusion of "all persons of Japanese ancestry, both alien and non-alien," from the Pacific Coast area on a plea of military necessity in the absence of martial law ought not to be approved. Such exclusion goes over "the very brink of constitutional power" and falls into the ugly abyss of racism.

In dealing with matters relating to the prosecution and progress of a war, we must accord great respect and consideration to the judgments of the military authorities who are on the scene and who have full knowledge of the military facts. The scope of their discretion must, as a matter of necessity and common sense, be wide. And their judgments ought not to be overruled lightly by those whose training and duties ill-equip them to deal intelligently with matters so vital to the physical security of the nation.

At the same time, however, it is essential that there be definite limits to military discretion, especially where martial law has not been declared. Individuals must not be left impoverished of their constitutional rights on a plea of military necessity that has neither substance nor support. Thus, like other claims conflicting with the asserted constitutional rights of the individual, the military claim must subject itself to the judicial process of having its reasonableness determined and its conflicts with other interests reconciled. . . .

The judicial test of whether the Government, on a plea of military necessity, can validly deprive an individual of any of his constitutional rights is whether the deprivation is reasonably related to a public danger that is so "immediate, imminent, and impending" as not to admit of delay and not to permit the intervention of ordinary constitutional processes to alleviate the danger. Civilian Exclusion Order No. 34, banishing from a prescribed area of the Pacific Coast "all persons of Japanese ancestry, both alien and non-alien," clearly does not meet that test. Being an obvious racial discrimination, the order deprives all those within its scope of the equal protection of the laws as guaranteed by the Fifth Amendment. It further deprives these individuals of their constitutional rights to live and work where they will, to establish a home where they choose and to move about freely. In excommunicating them without benefit of hearings, this order also deprives them of all their constitutional rights to procedural due process. Yet no reasonable relation to an "immediate, imminent, and impending" public danger is evident to support this racial restriction which is one of the most sweeping and complete deprivations of constitutional rights in the history of this nation in the absence of martial law.

It must be conceded that the military and naval situation in the spring of 1942 was such as to generate a very real fear of invasion of the Pacific Coast, accompanied by fears of sabotage and espionage in that area. The military command was therefore justified in adopting all reasonable means necessary to combat these dangers. In adjudging the military action taken in light of the then apparent dangers, we must not erect too high or too meticulous standards; it is necessary only that the action have some reasonable relation to the removal of the dangers of invasion, sabotage and espionage. But the exclusion, either temporarily or permanently, of all persons with Japanese blood in their veins has no such reasonable relation. And that relation is lacking because the exclusion order necessarily must rely for its reasonableness upon the assumption that all persons of Japanese ancestry may have a dangerous tendency to commit sabotage and espionage and to aid our Japanese enemy in other ways. It is difficult to believe that reason, logic or experience could be marshalled in support of such an assumption.

That this forced exclusion was the result in good measure of this erroneous assumption of racial guilt rather than bona fide military necessity is evidenced by the Commanding General's Final Report [DeWitt] on the evacuation from the Pacific Coast area. In it he refers to all individuals of Japanese descent as "subversive," as belonging to "an enemy race" whose "racial strains are undiluted," and as constituting "over 112,000 potential enemies . . . at large today" along the Pacific Coast. In support of this blanket condemnation of all persons of Japanese descent, however, no reliable evidence is cited to show that such individuals were generally disloyal, or had generally so conducted themselves in this area as to constitute a special menace to defense installations or war industries, or had otherwise by their behavior furnished reasonable ground for their exclusion as a group.

. . . .

The military necessity which is essential to the validity of the evacuation order . . . resolves itself into a few intimations that certain individuals actively aided the enemy, from which it is inferred that the entire group of Japanese Americans could not be trusted to be or remain loyal to the United States. No one denies, of course, that there were some disloyal persons of Japanese descent on the Pacific Coast who did all in their power to aid their ancestral land. Similar disloyal activities have been engaged in by many persons of German, Italian and even more pioneer stock in our country. But to infer that examples of individual disloyalty prove group disloyalty and justify discriminatory action against the entire group is to deny that under our system of law individual guilt is the sole basis for deprivation of rights. Moreover, this inference, which is at the very heart of the evacuation orders, has been used in support of the abhorrent and despicable treatment of minority groups by the dictatorial tyrannies which this nation is now pledged to destroy. To give constitutional sanction to that inference in this case, however well-intentioned may have been the military command on the Pacific Coast, is to adopt one of the cruelest of the rationales used by our enemies to destroy the dignity of the individual and to encourage and open the door to discriminatory actions against other minority groups in the passions of tomorrow.

Justice Jackson dissenting.

The limitation under which courts always will labor in examining the necessity for a military order are illustrated by this case. How does the Court know that these orders have a reasonable basis in necessity? No evidence whatever on that subject has been taken by this or any other court. There is sharp controversy as to the credibility of the DeWitt report. So the Court, having no real evidence before it, has no choice but to accept General DeWitt's own unsworn, self-serving statement, untested by any cross-examination, that what he did was reasonable. And thus it will always be when courts try to look into the reasonableness of a military order.

In the very nature of things, military decisions are not susceptible of intelligent judicial appraisal. They do not pretend to rest on evidence, but are made on information that often would not be admissible and on assumptions that could not be proved. Information in support of an order could not be disclosed to courts without danger that it would reach the enemy. Neither can courts act on communications made in confidence. Hence courts can never

have any real alternative to accepting the mere declaration of the authority that issued the order that it was reasonably necessary from a military viewpoint.

Much is said of the danger to liberty from the Army program for deporting and detaining these citizens of Japanese extraction. But a judicial construction of the due process clause that will sustain this order is a far more subtle blow to liberty than the promulgation of the order itself. A military order, however unconstitutional, is not apt to last longer than the military emergency. Even during that period a succeeding commander may revoke it all. But once a judicial opinion rationalizes such an order to show that it conforms to the Constitution, or rather rationalizes the Constitution to show that the Constitution sanctions such an order, the Court for all time has validated the principle of racial discrimination in criminal procedure and of transplanting American citizens. The principle then lies about like a loaded weapon ready for the hand of any authority that can bring forward a plausible claim of an urgent need. . . .

. . . .

My duties as a justice as I see them do not require me to make a military judgment as to whether General DeWitt's evacuation and detention program was a reasonable military necessity. I do not suggest that the courts should have attempted to interfere with the Army in carrying out its task. But I do not think they may be asked to execute a military expedient that has no place in law under the Constitution. I would reverse the judgment and discharge the prisoner.

COMMENTS

1. Hindsight always is 20/20 but many still consider the present case as one of the nadirs in the protection of civil liberties in this country. Note Justice Jackson's remarks that the Supreme Court's imprimatur adds a legitimacy to these military actions that extends the significance of these actions. But, was the Court in a

position to overrule the military commander? Would a "better" result have been not to decide at all? Could this kind of policy (or something like it) ever happen again? If so, what should be the response by the judiciary?

2. Do you consider the internment of the Japanese—most of them U.S. citizens—justified by military necessity? No aliens or citizens of German or Italian ancestry were interned. Why did military necessity not apply to them?

In re: Yamashita, 327 U.S. 1 (1946)

Chief Justice Stone delivered the opinion of the Court.

The charge, so far as now relevant, is that petitioner, between October 9, 1944, and September 2, 1945, in the Philippine Islands, "while commander of armed forces of Japan at war with the United States of America and its allies, unlawfully disregarded and failed to discharge his duty as commander to control the operations of the members of his command, permitting them to commit brutal atrocities and other high crimes against people of the United States and of its allies and dependencies, particularly the Philippines; and he . . . thereby violated the laws of war."

Bills of particulars, filed by the prosecution by order of the commission, allege a series of acts, one hundred and twenty-three in number, committed by members of the forces under petitioner's command during the period mentioned. The first item specifies the execution of "a deliberate plan and purpose to massacre and exterminate a large part of the civilian population of Batangas Province, and to devastate and destroy public, private and religious property therein, as a result of which more than 25,000 men, women and children, all unarmed noncombatant civilians, were brutally mistreated and killed, without cause or trial, and entire settlements were devastated and destroyed wantonly and without military necessity." Other items specify acts of violence, cruelty and homicide inflicted upon the civilian pop-

ulation and prisoners of war, acts of wholesale pillage and the wanton destruction of religious monuments.

It is not denied that such acts directed against the civilian population of an occupied country and against prisoners of war are recognized in international law as violations of the law of war. But it is urged that the charge does not allege that petitioner has either committed or directed the commission of such acts, and consequently that no violation is charged as against him. But this overlooks the fact that the gist of the charge is an unlawful breach of duty by petitioner as an army commander to control the operations of the members of his command by "permitting them to commit" the extensive and widespread atrocities specified. The question then is whether the law of war imposes on an army commander a duty to take such appropriate measures as are within his power to control the troops under his command for the prevention of the specified acts which are violations of the law of war and which are likely to attend the occupation of hostile territory by an uncontrolled soldiery, and whether he may be charged with personal responsibility for his failure to take such measures when violations result.

It is evident that the conduct of military operations by troops whose excesses are unrestrained by the orders or efforts of their commander would almost certainly result in violations which it is the purpose of the law of war to prevent. Its purpose to protect civilian populations and prisoners of war from brutality would largely be defeated if the commander of an invading army could with impunity neglect to take reasonable measures for their protection. Hence the law of war presupposes that its violation is to be avoided through the control of the operations of war by commanders who are to some extent responsible for their subordinates.

. . . .

We do not make the laws of war, but we respect them so far as they do not conflict with the commands of Congress or the Constitution. There is no contention that the present charge, thus read, is without the support of evidence, or that the commission held petitioner responsible for failing to take measures which were beyond his control or inappropriate for a commanding officer to take in the circumstances. We do not here appraise the evidence on which petitioner was convicted. We do not consider what measures, if any, petitioner took to prevent the commission, by the troops under his command, of the plain violations of the law of war detailed in the bill of particulars, or whether such measures as he may have taken were appropriate and sufficient to discharge the duty imposed upon him. These are questions within the peculiar competence of the military officers composing the commission and were for it to decide. It is plain that the charge on which petitioner was tried charged him with a breach of his duty to control the operations of the members of his command, by permitting them to commit the specified atrocities. This was enough to require the commission to hear evidence tending to establish the culpable failure of petitioner to perform the duty imposed on him by the law of war and to pass upon its sufficiency to establish guilt.

Justice Murphy dissenting.

The significance of the issue facing the Court today cannot be overemphasized. An American military commission has been established to try a fallen military commander of a conquered nation for an alleged war crime. . . . The grave issue raised by this case is whether a military commission so established and so authorized may disregard the procedural rights of an accused person as guaranteed by the Constitution, especially by the due process clause of the Fifth Amendment.

The answer is plain. The Fifth Amendment guarantee of due process of law applies to "any person" who is accused of a crime by the Federal Government or any of its agencies. No exception is made as to those who are accused of war crimes or as to those who possess the status of an enemy belligerent. Indeed, such an exception would be contrary to the whole philosophy of human rights which makes the Constitution the great living document that it is. The immutable rights of the individual, including those secured by the due process clause of the Fifth Amendment, belong not alone to the members of those nations that excel on the battlefield or that subscribe to the democratic ideology. They belong to every person in the world, victor or vanquished, whatever may be his race, color or beliefs. They rise above any status of belligerency or outlawry. They survive any popular passion or frenzy of the moment. No court or legislature or executive, not even the mightiest army in the world, can ever destroy them. Such is the universal and indestructible nature of the rights which the due process clause of the Fifth Amendment recognizes and protects when life or liberty is threatened by virtue of the authority of the United States.

The existence of these rights, unfortunately, is not always respected. They are often trampled under by those who are motivated by hatred, aggression or fear. But in this nation individual rights are recognized and protected, at least in regard to governmental action. They cannot be ignored by any branch of the Government, even the military, except under the most extreme and urgent circumstances.

The failure of the military commission to obey the dictates of the due process requirements of the Fifth Amendment is apparent in this case. The petitioner was the commander of an army totally destroyed by the superior power of this nation. While under heavy and destructive attack by our forces, his troops committed many brutal atrocities and other high crimes. Hostilities ceased and he voluntarily surrendered. At that point he was entitled, as an individual protected by the due process clause of the Fifth Amendment, to be treated fairly and justly according to the accepted rules of law and procedure. He was also entitled to a fair trial as to any alleged crimes and to be free from charges of legally unrecognized crimes that would serve only to permit his accusers to satisfy their desires for revenge.

A military commission was appointed to try the petitioner for an alleged war crime. The trial was ordered to be held in territory over which the United States has complete sovereignty. No military necessity or other emergency demanded the suspension of the safeguards of due process. Yet petitioner was rushed to trial under an improper charge, given insufficient time to prepare an adequate defense, deprived of the benefits of some of the most elementary rules of evidence and summarily sentenced to be hanged. In all this needless and unseemly haste there was no serious attempt to charge or to prove that he committed a recognized violation of the laws of war. He was not charged with personally participating in the acts of atrocity or with ordering or condoning their commission. Not even knowledge of these crimes was attributed to him. It was simply alleged that he unlawfully disregarded and failed to discharge his duty as commander to control the operations of the members of his command, permitting them to commit the acts of atrocity. The recorded annals of warfare and the established principles of international law afford not the slightest precedent for such a charge. This indictment in effect permitted the military com-

mission to make the crime whatever it willed, dependent upon its biased view as to petitioner's duties and his disregard thereof, a practice reminiscent of that pursued in certain less respected nations in recent years.

In my opinion, such a procedure is unworthy of the traditions of our people or of the immense sacrifices that they have made to advance the common ideals of mankind. The high feelings of the moment doubtless will be satisfied. But in the sober afterglow will come the realization of the boundless and dangerous implications of the procedure sanctioned today. No one in a position of commanding an army, from sergeant to general, can escape those implications. Indeed, the fate of some future President of the United States and his chiefs of staff and military advisers may well have been sealed by this decision. But even more significant will be the hatred and ill-will growing out of the application of this unprecedented procedure. That has been the inevitable effect of every method of punishment disregarding the element of personal culpability. The effect in this instance, unfortunately, will be magnified infinitely, for here we are dealing with the rights of man on an international level. To subject an enemy belligerent to an unfair trial, to charge him with an unrecognized crime, or to vent on him our retributive emotions only antagonizes the enemy nation and hinders the reconciliation necessary to a peaceful world.

That there were brutal atrocities inflicted upon the helpless Filipino people, to whom tyranny is no stranger, by Japanese armed forces under the petitioner's command is undeniable. Starvation, execution or massacre without trial, torture, rape, murder and wanton destruction of property were foremost among the outright violations of the laws of war and of the conscience of a civilized world. That just punishment should be meted out to all those responsible for criminal acts of this nature is also beyond dispute. But these factors do not answer the problem in this case. They do not justify the abandonment of our devotion to justice in dealing with a fallen enemy commander. To conclude otherwise is to admit that the enemy has lost the battle but has destroyed our ideals.

War breeds atrocities. From the earliest conflicts of recorded history to the global struggles of modern times inhumanities, lust and pillage have been the inevitable by-products of man's resort to force and arms. Unfortunately, such despicable acts have a dangerous tendency to call forth primitive impulses of vengeance and retaliation among the victimized peoples. The satisfaction of such impulses in turn breeds resentment and fresh tension. Thus does the spiral of cruelty and hatred grow.

If we are ever to develop an orderly international community based upon a recognition of human dignity it is of the utmost importance that the necessary punishment of those guilty of atrocities be as free as possible from the ugly stigma of revenge and vindictiveness. Justice must be tempered by compassion rather than by vengeance. In this, the first case involving this momentous problem ever to reach this Court, our responsibility is both lofty and difficult. We must insist, within the confines of our proper jurisdiction, that the high-est standards of justice be applied in this trial of an enemy commander conducted under the authority of the United States. Otherwise stark retribution will be free to masquerade in a cloak of false legalism. And the hatred and cynicism engendered by that retribution will supplant the great ideals to which this nation is dedicated.

COMMENTS

1. Note that this case involved the question of holding a superior officer responsible for the crimes of his subordinates. There is also a flip side to this: Can subordinate officers be convicted of war crimes when acting under the orders of their superiors? The issue has most recently been raised in Argentina, where the Alfonsin government is wrestling with the enormous problem of whether to prosecute soldiers who carried out torture and murder under orders from their superiors during the time the military was in power.

2. Recently, several Nazis, including Klaus Barbie, were tried for war crimes. Inevitably the key question in such cases involves identity. Do you think there should be something akin to a statute of limitations in terms of bringing such actions? Will memories become too clouded and hazy?

Filartiga v. Pena-Irala, 630 F. 2d 876 (1980)

Circuit Judge Kaufman delivered the opinion of the Court.

The appellants, plaintiffs below, are citizens of the Republic of Paraguay. Dr. Joel Filartiga, a physician, describes himself as a longstanding opponent of the government of President Alfredo Stroessner, which has held power in Paraguay since 1954. His daughter, Dolly Filartiga, arrived in the United States in 1978 under a vis-itor's visa, and has since applied for permanent political asylum. The Filartigas brought this action in the Eastern District of New York against Americo Norberto Pena-Irala (Pena), also a citizen of Paraguay, for wrongfully causing the death of Dr. Filartiga's seventeen-year-old son, Joelito. Because the district court dismissed the action for want of subject matter jurisdiction, we must accept as true the allegations contained in the Filartigas' complaint and affidavits for purposes of this appeal.

The appellants contend that on March 29, 1976, Joelito Filartiga was kidnapped and tortured to death by Pena, who was then Inspector General of Police in Asuncion, Paraguay. Later that day, the police brought Dolly Filartiga to Pena's home where she was confronted with the body of her brother, which evidenced marks of severe torture. As she fled, horrified, from the house, Pena followed after her shouting, "Here you have what you have been looking for for so long and what you deserve. Now shut up." The Filartigas claim that Joelito was tortured and killed in retaliation for his father's political activities and beliefs.

Shortly thereafter, Dr. Filartiga commenced a criminal action in the Paraguayan courts against Pena and the police for the murder of his son. As a result, Dr. Filartiga's attorney was arrested and brought to police headquarters where, shackled to a wall, Pena threatened him with death. This attorney, it is alleged, has since been disbarred without just cause.

During the course of the Paraguayan criminal proceeding, which is apparently still pending after four years, another man, Hugo Duarte, confessed to the murder. Duarte, who was a member of the Pena household, claimed that he had discovered his wife and Joelito in flagrante delicto, and that the crime was one of passion. The Filartigas have submitted a photograph of Joelito's corpse showing injuries they believe refute this claim. Dolly Filartiga, moreover, has stated that she will offer evidence of three independent autopsies demonstrating that her brother's death "was the result of professional methods of torture." Despite his confession, Duarte, we are told, has never been convicted or sentenced in connection with the crime.

In July of 1978, Pena sold his house in Paraguay and entered the United States under a visitor's visa. . . .

Almost immediately, Dolly caused Pena to be served with a summons and civil complaint. . . . The complaint alleged that Pena had wrongfully caused Joelito's death by torture and sought compensatory and punitive damages of $10,000,000. . . .

. . . .

Appellants rest their principal argument in support of federal jurisdiction upon the Alien Tort Statute, 28 U.S.C. Sec. 1350, which provides: "The district courts shall have original jurisdiction of any civil action by an alien for a tort only, committed in violation of the law of nations or a treaty of the United States." Since appellants do not contend that their action arises directly under a treaty of the United States, a threshold question on the jurisdictional issue is whether the conduct alleged violates the law of nations. In light of the universal condemnation of torture in numerous international agreements, and the renunciation of torture as an instrument of official policy by virtually all of the nations of the world (in principle if not in practice), we find that an act of torture committed by a state official against one held in detention violates established norms of the international law of human rights, and hence the law of nations.

. . . .

The United Nations Charter (a treaty of the United States), makes it clear that in this modern age a state's treatment of its own citizens is a matter of international concern. It provides:

With a view to the creation of conditions of stability and well-being which are necessary for peaceful and friendly relations among nations . . . the United Nations shall promote . . . universal respect for, and observance of, human rights and fundamental freedoms for all without distinctions as to race, sex, language or religion.

. . . [A]lthough there is no universal agreement as to the precise extent of the "human rights and fundamental freedoms" guaranteed to all by the Charter, there is at present no dissent from the view that the guaranties include, at a bare minimum, the right to be free from torture. This prohibition has become part of customary international law, as evidenced and defined by the Universal Declaration of Human Rights, General Assembly Resolution which states, in the plainest of terms, "no one shall be subjected to torture." The General Assembly has declared that the Charter precepts embodied in this Universal Declaration "constitute basic principles of international law."

Particularly relevant is the Declaration on the Protection of All Persons from Being Subjected to Torture, General Assembly Resolution 3452 (1975). The Declaration expressly prohibits any state from permitting the dastardly and totally inhuman act of torture.

. . . .

. . . The international consensus surrounding torture has found expression in numerous international treaties and accords. The substance of these international agreements is reflected in modern municipal—i.e., national—law as well. Although torture was once a routine concomitant of criminal interrogations in many nations, during the modern and hopefully more enlightened era it has been universally renounced. According to one survey, torture is prohibited, expressly or implicitly, by the constitutions of over fifty-five nations, including both the United States and Paraguay. Our State Department reports a general recognition of this principle:

There now exists an international consensus that recognizes basic human rights and obligations owed by all governments to their citizens. . . . There is no doubt that these rights are often violated; but virtually all governments acknowledge their validity.

Department of State, *Country Reports on Human Rights for 1979.* . . .

Having examined the sources from which customary international law is derived—the usage of nations, judicial opinions and the works of jurists—we conclude that official torture is now prohibited by the law of nations. The prohibition is clear and unambiguous, and admits of no distinction between treatment of aliens and citizens. . . . The treaties and accords cited above, as well as the express foreign policy of our own government, all make it clear that international law confers fundamental rights upon all people vis-a-vis their own governments. While the ultimate scope of those rights will be a subject for continuing refinement and elaboration, we hold that the right to be free from torture is now among them. . . .

. . . .

In the twentieth century the international community has come to recognize the common danger posed by the flagrant disregard of basic human rights and particularly the right to be free of torture. Spurred first by the Great War, and then the Second, civilized nations have banded together to prescribe acceptable norms of international behavior. From the ashes of the Second World War arose the United Nations Organization, amid hopes that an era of peace and cooperation had at last begun. Though many of these aspirations have remained elusive goals, that circumstance cannot diminish the true progress that has been made. In the modern age, humanitarian and practical considerations have combined to lead the nations of the world to recognize that respect for fundamental human rights is in their individual and collective interest. Among the rights universally proclaimed by all nations, as we have noted, is the right to be free of physical torture. Indeed, for purposes of civil liability, the torturer has become—like the pirate and slave trader before him—hostis humani generis, an enemy of all mankind. Our holding today, giving effect to a jurisdictional provision enacted by our First Congress, is a small but important step in the fulfillment of the ageless dream to free all people from brutal violence.

COMMENTS

1. *Filartiga* is a unique case, particularly given the great reluctance by most courts to enter into anything remotely resembling foreign af-

fairs. If the principle in *Filartiga* is extended to its logical conclusion, it would have a far-ranging impact on the way nations carry out their policies.

2. For a depiction of human rights conditions in other countries, see the *Country Reports on Human Rights* published by the State Department or the *Amnesty International Reports*. A quick glimpse at either of these yearly publications would show that the events depicted in *Filartiga* are, unfortunately, rather standard practice in many parts of the world. Should this fact matter to a U.S. court hearing a similar claim?

Sanchez-Espinoza v. Reagan, 770 F. 2d 202 (1985)

Circuit Judge Scalia delivered the opinion of the Court.

[Suit was brought by a group of Nicaraguan citizens suing President Reagan and various other U.S. government officials alleging, among other things, that the United States authorized, financed, trained and supported the Nicaraguan "contra" forces which terrorized and injured the civilian population of Nicaragua. In particular, the complaint alleged that the U.S. government had already provided at least $19 million to these forces, had trained contra leaders in the U.S. and in Honduras, and provided other forms of assistance. As a result of this assistance, the contras carried out "scores of attacks upon innocent Nicaraguan civilians" which have resulted in "summary execution, murder, abduction, torture, rape, wounding, and the destruction of private property and public facilities."]

. . . .

The Alien Tort Statute provides that "[t]he district courts shall have original jurisdiction of any civil action by an alien for a tort only, committed in violation of the law of nations or a treaty of the United States." This obscure section of the Judiciary Act of 1789, may conceivably have been meant to cover only private, non-governmental acts that are contrary to treaty of the law of nations—the most prominent examples being piracy and assaults upon ambassadors. See *Tel-Oren v. Libyan Arab Republic*, 726 F. 2d 774, 813–15 (D.C. Cir. 1984) (Bork, J., concurring). We are aware of no treaty that purports to make the activities at issue here unlawful when conducted by private individuals. As for the law of nations—so-called "customary international law," arising from "the customs and usages of civilized nations"—we conclude that this also does not reach private, non-state conduct of this sort. Assuming, however, that the Alien Tort Statute covers state acts as well, then it embraces this suit only insofar as the federal appellees are sued in their official, as opposed to their personal, capacities—i.e., to the extent that appellants are seeking to hold them to account for, or to prevent them from implementing in the future, *actions of the United States*. It would make a mockery of the doctrine of sovereign immunity if federal courts were authorized to sanction or enjoin, by judgments nominally against present or former Executive officers, actions that are, *concededly and as a jurisdictional necessity*, official actions of the United States. Such judgments would necessarily "interfere with the public administration," or "restrain the government from acting, or . . . compel it to act." These consequences are tolerated when the officer's action is unauthorized because contrary to statutory or constitutional prescription, but we think that exception can have no application when the basis for jurisdiction requires action authorized by the sovereign as opposed to private wrongdoing.[1] A waiver of sovereign immunity must therefore be found. Insofar as the claim for money damages is concerned, there is none. The Alien Tort Statute itself is not a waiver of sovereign immunity.

· ·

. . . Whether or not the present litigation is motivated by considerations of geopolitics rather than personal harm, we think that as a general matter the danger of foreign citizens' using the courts in situations such as this to obstruct the foreign policy of our government is sufficiently acute that we must leave to Congress the judgment whether a damage remedy should exist.

COMMENTS

1. One of the most unusual aspects of the *Sanchez-Espinoza* case was that citizens of another country sued members of the executive branch of the United States government by alleging that they had been harmed by the pursuit of U.S. foreign policy objectives. As you know, the court, in an opinion by Judge (now Justice) Scalia, holds that the sovereign immunity doctrine protects against such a suit. Do you agree with this? Consider this hypothetical. CIA operatives assassinate the wrong person, killing

---

[1] Since the doctrine of foreign sovereign immunity is quite distinct from the doctrine of domestic sovereign immunity that we apply here, being based upon considerations of international comity, rather than separation of powers, it does not necessarily follow that an Alien Tort Statute suit filed against the officer of a foreign sovereign would have to be dismissed. Thus, nothing in today's decision necessarily conflicts with the decision of the Second Circuit in *Filartiga v. Pena-Irala.*

your Uncle Juan, a citizen of Argentina. Under the holding of *Sanchez-Espinoza,* your aunt would not be able to sue the U.S. government (at least not in a U.S. court) for the death of your uncle. Has justice been served?

2. Some of you might have heard of the suit brought by a group of Vietnam Veterans alleging harm done to them (and, in some cases, their offspring) by the defoliant Agent Orange. The doctrine of sovereign immunity barred suit against the U.S. government itself, but an out-of-court settlement of $180 million was reached in the suit against manufacturers of Agent Orange. An intriguing question that I have not seen raised is whether Vietnam citizens and soldiers should similarly have a cause of action. In many respects, we could easily imagine that both groups have suffered at least as much by the use of Agent Orange as U.S. servicemen have.

3. One of the ironies in the *Sanchez-Espinoza* case is that it treated *Filartiga* as good law. Thus, a Paraguayan citizen can sue in a U.S. court a member of the security forces in Paraguay for personal harm done in Paraguay, but Nicaraguan citizens cannot sue officials of the U.S. government for harm allegedly caused by the United States. Is there not something contradictory about these results?

4. In 1988 the U.S. government provided compensation to the families of victims of an Iranian airliner mistakenly shot down by the battleship *Vincennes.* If the executive branch had not agreed to this compensation, and if these families had filed suit in a U.S. court, the great likelihood is that a judge would have thrown the case out, as in *Sanchez-Espinoza.* Why the difference? Should decisions on compensation be made exclusively by the political branches and not by the judiciary?

5. The federal district court that first heard this case dismissed it on the basis of the "political question" doctrine. This self-imposed judicial constraint allows courts not to entertain cases they deem to be "political" in nature. Although Judge Scalia's opinion does not rest on the political question doctrine, his reasoning comes quite close to it.

United States v. Stanley, 483 U.S. 669 (1987)

Justice Scalia delivered the opinion of the Court.

In February 1958, James B. Stanley, a master sergeant in the Army stationed at Fort Knox, Kentucky, volunteered to participate in a program ostensibly designed to test the effectiveness of protected clothing and equipment as defenses against chemical warfare. He was released from his then-current duties and went to the Army's Chemical Warfare Laboratories at the Aberdeen Proving Grounds in Maryland. Four times that month, Stanley was secretly administered doses of lysergic acid diethylamide (LSD), pursuant to an Army plan to study the effects of the drug on human subjects. According to his Second Amended Complaint (the allegations of which we accept for purposes of this decision), as a result of the LSD exposure, Stanley has suffered from hallucinations and periods of incoherence and memory loss, was impaired in his military performance, and would on occasion "awake from sleep at night and, without reason, violently beat his wife and children, later being unable to recall the entire incident." He was discharged from the Army in 1969. One year later, his marriage dissolved because of the personality changes wrought by the LSD.

On December 10, 1975, the Army sent Stanley a letter soliciting his cooperation in a study of the long-term effect of LSD on "volunteers who participated" in the 1958 tests. This was the Government's first notification to Stanley that he had been given LSD during his time in Maryland. After an administrative claim for compensation was denied by the Army, Stanley filed suit under the Federal Tort Claims Act (FTCA), alleging negligence in the administration, supervision, and subsequent monitoring of the drug testing program.

. . . .

In *Bivens* [403 U.S. 388 (1971)], we held that a search and seizure that violates the Fourth Amendment can give rise to an action for damages against the offending federal officials even in the absence of a statute authorizing such relief. We suggested in dictum that inferring such an action directly from the Constitution might not be appropriate when there are "special factors counselling hesitation in the absence of affirmative action by Congress," or where there is an "explicit congressional declaration that persons injured by a federal officer's violation of the Fourth Amendment may not recover money damages from the agents, but must instead be remitted to another remedy, equally effective in the view of Congress." . . . In *Chappell*, 462 U.S. 367 (1983) . . . that dictum became holding. *Chappell* reversed a determination that no "special factors" barred a constitutional damages remedy on behalf of minority servicemen who alleged that because of their race their superior officer "failed to assign them desirable duties, threatened them, gave them low performance evaluations, and imposed penalties of unusual severity." We found "factors counselling hesitation" in "[t]he need for special regulations in relation to military discipline, and the consequent need and justification for a special and exclusive system of military justice." . . . We observed that the Constitution explicitly conferred upon Congress the power, inter alia, "To make Rules for the Government and Regulation of the land and naval Forces," U.S. Const. Art. I, Sec. 8, cl. 14, thus showing that "the Constitution contemplated that the Legislative Branch have plenary control over rights, duties, and responsibilities in the framework of the Military Establishment." 462 U.S., at 301. Congress, we noted, had exercised that authority to "establish a comprehensive internal system of justice to regulate military life, taking into account the special patterns that define the military structure." We concluded that "[t]aken together, the unique disciplinary structure of the Military Establishment and Congress' activity in the field constitute 'special factors' which dictate that it would be inappropriate to provide enlisted military personnel a *Bivens*-type remedy against their superior officers."

Stanley seeks to distance himself from this holding in several ways. First, he argues that the defendants in this case were not Stanley's superior military officers, and indeed may well have been civilian personnel, and that the chain-of-command concerns at the heart of *Chappell* . . . are thus not implicated. Second, Stanley argues that there is no evidence that this injury was "incident to service," because we do not know the precise character of the drug testing program, the titles and roles of the various individual defendants, or Stanley's duty status when he was at the Maryland testing grounds.

. . . .

. . . Stanley underestimates the degree of disruption that would be caused by the rule he proposes. A test for liability that depends on the extent to which particular suits would call into question military discipline and decision-making would itself require judicial inquiry into, and hence intrusion upon, military matters. Whether a case implicates those concerns would often be problematic, raising the prospect of compelled depositions and trial testimony by military officers concerning the details of their military commands. Even putting aside the risk of erroneous judicial conclusions (which would becloud military deci-

sion-making), the mere process of arriving at correct conclusion would disrupt the military regime. The "incident to service" test, by contrast, provides a line that is relatively clear and that can be discerned with less extensive inquiry into military matters.

. . . .

We therefore reaffirm the reasoning of *Chappell*. . . . We hold that no *Bivens* remedy is available for injuries that arise out of or are in the course of activity incident to service.

Justice Brennan, with whom Justice Marshall joins, and with whom Justice Stevens joins as to Part III, dissenting.

In experiments designed to test the effects of lysergic acid diethylamide (LSD), the Government of the United States treated thousands of its citizens as though they were laboratory animals, dosing them with this dangerous drug without their consent. One of the victims, James B. Stanley, seeks compensation from the Government officials who injured him. The Court holds that the Constitution provides him with no remedy, solely because his injuries were inflicted while he performed his duties in the Nation's Armed Forces. If our Constitution requires this result, the Court's decision, though legally necessary, would expose a tragic flaw in that document. But in reality, the Court disregards the commands of our Constitution, and bows instead to the purported requirements of a different master, "Military Discipline," declining to provide Stanley with a remedy because it finds "special factors counselling hesitation." This is abdication, not hesitation. I dissent.

Before addressing the legal questions presented, it is important to place the Government's conduct in historical context. The medical trials at Nuremberg in 1947 deeply impressed upon the world that experimentation with unknowing human subjects is morally and legally unacceptable.

The United States Military Tribunal established the Nuremberg Code as a standard against which to judge German scientists who experimented with human subjects. Its first principle was:

1. The voluntary consent of the human subject is absolutely essential. The duty and responsibility for ascertaining the quality of the consent rests upon each individual who initiates, directs or engages in the experiment. It is a personal duty and responsibility which may not be delegated to another with impunity.

The United States military developed the Code, which applies to all citizens—soldiers as well as civilians.

In the 1950's, in defiance of this principle, military intelligence agencies and the Central Intelligence Agency (CIA) began surreptitiously testing chemical and biological materials, including LSD. These programs, which were designed to determine the potential effects of chemical or biological agents when used operationally against individuals unaware that they had received a drug, included drug testing on unwitting, nonvolunteer Americans. James B. Stanley, a master sergeant in the Army, alleges that he was one of 1,000 soldiers covertly administered LSD by Army intelligence between 1955 and 1958.[1]

. . . .

The Court historically has conferred absolute immunity on officials who intentionally violate the constitutional rights of citizens only in extraordinary circumstances. Qualified immunity (that is, immunity for acts that an official did not know, or could not have known, violated clearly established constitutional law) "represents the norm."

---

[1] The intelligence community believed that it was necessary "to conceal these activities from the American public in general," because public knowledge of the "unethical and illicit activities would have serious repercussions in political and diplomatic circles and would be detrimental to the accomplishment of its mission." (CIA Inspector General's Survey of the Technical Services Division, p. 217 [1957]).

In *Butz v. Economou*, 438 U.S. 478 (1978), we balanced "the need to protect officials who are required to exercise their discretion and the related public interest in encouraging the vigorous exercise of official authority," against the crucial importance of a damages remedy in deterring federal officials from committing constitutional wrongs and vindicating the rights of citizens. After full consideration of potential adverse consequences, we decided that the extension of absolute immunity to federal officials would "seriously erode the protection provided by basic constitutional guarantees," and undermine the basic assumption of our jurisprudence: "that all individuals, *whatever their position in government*, are subject to federal law." (Emphasis added.) Thus, we concluded that it is "not unfair to hold liable the official who knows or should know he is acting outside the law," and that "insisting on awareness of clearly established constitutional limits will not unduly interfere with the exercise of official judgment."

In *Butz* we acknowledged that federal officials may receive absolute immunity in the exercise of certain functions, but emphasized that the burden is on the official to demonstrate an "exceptional situation" exists, in which "absolute immunity is essential for the conduct of the public business." The official seeking immunity "first must show that the responsibilities of his office embraced a function so sensitive as to require a total shield from liability," and "then must demonstrate that he was discharging the protected function when performing the act for which liability is asserted."

Even when, as here, national security is invoked, federal officials bear the burden of demonstrating that the usual rule of qualified immunity should be abrogated. In *Mitchell v. Forsyth*, 472 U.S. 511 (1985), the Court found "no . . . historical or common-law basis for an absolute immunity for officers carrying out tasks essential to national security." In language applicable here, the Court pointed out that "[n]ational security tasks . . . are carried out in secret. . . . Under such circumstances, it is far more likely that actual abuses will go uncovered than that fancied abuses will give rise to unfounded and burdensome litigation." The Court highlighted the "danger that high federal officials will disregard constitutional rights in their zeal to protect the national security," and deemed it "sufficiently real to counsel against affording such officials an absolute immunity."

Whoever the officials in this case are (and we do not know), and whatever their functions, it is likely that under the Court's usual analysis, they, like most government officials, are not entitled to absolute immunity. The record does not reveal what offices the individual respondents held, let alone what functions they normally performed, or what functions they were performing at the time they (somehow) participated in the decision to administer LSD to Stanley (and 1,000 other soldiers). The Court has no idea whether those officials can carry "the burden of showing that public policy requires [absolute immunity]" for effective performance of those functions. Yet the Court grants them absolute immunity, so long as they intentionally inflict only service-connected injuries, doing violence to the principle that "extension of absolute immunity from damages liability to all federal executive officials would seriously erode the protection provided by basic constitutional guarantees." The case should be remanded and respondents required to demonstrate that absolute immunity was necessary to the effective performance of their functions.

. . . .

In *Chappell* the Court created a narrow exception to the usual rule of qualified immunity for federal officials. Repeatedly referring to the "peculiar and special relationship of the soldier to his superiors," and to the need for "immediate compliance with military procedures and others," the Court held that "enlisted military personnel may not maintain a suit to recover damages from a superior officer for alleged constitutional violations." 462 U.S., at 300, 305. Although the Court concedes this central focus on *Chappell*, it gives short shrift to the obvious and important distinction between *Chappell* and the present case, namely, that the defendants are not alleged to be Stanley's superior officers. . . .

. . . .

. . . The subject of experimentation who has not volunteered is treated as an object, a sample. James Stanley will receive no compensation for this indignity. A test providing absolute immunity for intentional constitutional torts only when such immunity was essential to maintenance of military discipline would take into account the special importance of defending our Nation without completely abandoning the freedoms that make it worth defending. But absent a showing that military discipline is concretely (not abstractly) implicated by Stanley's action, its talismanic invocation does not counsel hesitation in the face of an intentional constitutional tort, such as the Government's experimentation on an unknowing human subject. Soldiers ought not be asked to defend a Constitution indifferent to their essential human dignity. I dissent.

COMMENTS

1. Has not the U.S. government committed a human rights violation against Stanley? Would a damages remedy really be so devastating to military discipline?

2. In *Boyle v. United Technologies*, 101 L. Ed. 2d 442 (1988), the Supreme Court refused to allow the heirs of a U.S. Marine helicopter co-pilot, drowned when his helicopter crashed off the Virginia coast, to sue the manufacturers of the craft for an alleged defect in the emergency escape-hatch system. Although no federal statute barred such a suit, the Court held that because the military contractor would usually be able to pass on the costs of such litigation to the government, for all intents and purposes this would be a suit against the U.S. government (which would be barred by the doctrine of sovereign immunity). Do servicemen have *any* rights?

TABLE OF CASES